Nine Lives to Eternity

ALSO BY SCOTT D. GOTTSCHALK

The Folk and Their Fauna
(The Story of One Man's Love Affair with Animals)

All the animals we cherish and love,
God made the folk and their fauna from high up above.
He bade we should share with each other united,
to keep a world that will remain undivided.
Man and beast working side by side,
'Til the end of all time we shall always abide.

—Scott D. Gottschalk (1982)

Nine Lives to Eternity

A True Story of Repeatedly Cheating Death An Inspirational and Faith-driven Human Triumph

Scott D. Gottschalk

To order additional copies of this book, contact:
Xlibris Corporation
1-888-795-4274
www.Xlibris.com
Orders@Xlibris.com
89855

CONTENTS

With love to my wife, Astrid, along with my devoted sons, Trevor and Travis, you have each blessed my life in so many ways with countless joys and memories throughout all the years.

All praise and honor to our God in his glory,
for His will shall be done thus never to worry.
You can make the world a better place for all,
so simply stop taking up space before the fall.
Express life with a bountiful joy and a zest;
nine lives to eternity reflects our Lord is best.

—Scott D. Gottschalk (2010)

I'm fascinated at how God has miraculously intervened in your life so many times. It causes me to wonder; has God been uniquely intervening in your life over all of your years, or does God work similarly in many of our lives, but we simply fail to recognize his holy presence? Either way, you tell of some fascinating experiences in which God has intervened to save you from the throes of death. You've done an excellent job of capturing your story, especially some parts that appear to be quite emotional for you to describe. Experiences like that are often difficult to put into words. God is definitely at work in your life, Scott, and I hope you are as excited as me to discover what he has in store for you next.

—**Pastor Michael Nelson,** *minister of author*

"Thumbs up! Let me start out by saying that your book has brought a smile to my face. I think it is fabulous, and I love it. As always, you have expressed a sense of your humor in this writing and a bit of suspense. You have a neat perspective to observe life from. The subject matter is great and the lessons inspiring. The point of LIVING life rather than just existing and going through the motions is great. Anything worth having or experiencing usually comes with a little extra effort and is always worth the pain or work. Those are the moments in life that are the most memorable and gratifying!"

—**Sally Vacura,** *sister of author*

It is absolutely marvelous where you derived your thoughts to write this book. Most people do not think about how God has been such an inspiration to them and how he has many times saved us from tragic things by having us in just the right place at the right time. I have always believed that there is a reason for things happening, so your reasoning of God sparing your life so many times and writing a Christian book about it may be just the answer God was hoping you would see. Our God loves to be praised, and all he has ever asked of us is to have FAITH in him.

—**Audrey Folkert,** *godmother and aunt of author*

PROLOGUE

Ever wonder where the phrase "nine lives of a cat" is derived from? Is it a myth, or is there some logic behind the statement?

Anyone with experience with cats will impose that the idea is anything but a myth. Cats can fall from high places yet land on their feet and scamper away when most any other creature would surely perish. Cats have been known to fall asleep under the hood of a car, which then in turn drives off with the cat, yet somehow the cat shows up one day alive.

Perhaps a reason some people believe in the superstition that cats have nine lives is because over the course of history, cats have been known to get run over, shot at, poisoned, thrown off buildings, drowned, or starved; only to appear unharmed at some later point in time. This gives the appearance that cats can return to life after facing fatal circumstances.

A fact is that cats are natural born survivors, capable of escaping situations that most other creatures can't. Their uncanny instincts and physical ability to survive is a reason why they were often worshipped and revered by several ancient cultures, believing that cats could live eternally.

An English/American proverb states, "A cat has nine lives. For three he plays, for three he strays, and for the last three he stays."

According to ancient Greek mythology, nine refers to trinity of all trinities. Nine is a mystic number that invokes tradition and religion.

My own religion and faith have blessed me with an uncanny ability to survive as well. I've often wondered why it appears that some people may die from a mere common cold, while others seem virtually indestructible to anything they confront.

INTRODUCTION

And what do you benefit if you gain the whole world but lose your own soul?

—MATTHEW 16:26

Growing up as a child on a labor-intensive livestock and grain farm in southeastern Minnesota gave me the essence and direction to set the course for my entire life. It was on that farm with my strong Christian upbringing where my parents, my siblings, and I toiled endless hours each day trying to scratch out the barest of an existence from the land. That was not only our farm family's mission in life but was the mission in life of countless other farm families in their inspirational effort to feed the masses of humankind on our increasingly populated planet.

As a direct result of my rural upbringing, what became instilled in my makeup was a strong work ethic, a dedication, and a commitment to succeed that has remained with me my entire life.

It was during my high school days that I once set a lofty goal to one day write a book. The impetus behind this dream of writing a book came as a result of the several hours each week that I spent reading nearly every book that I could lay my hands upon.

My favorite book topics at the time revolved around stories about animals. The endless hours that I spent reading these kinds of books one day eventually helped lead to my lifelong career path in animal agriculture. Just as importantly, reading so many books in those youthful days eventually drove my dream and desire to write my first book, which was filled with animal stories based upon my own personal experiences while growing up on the farm.

Back then, to prepare for that task of becoming an author and to hone my book-writing skills, I began taking extra writing elective courses while still in high school. This brought on a lot of questionable comments from my friends and teachers, but I'd made the decision to secretly keep my objective that I would one day publish a book.

Following my high school graduation, I enrolled in college at the University of Minnesota where I eventually obtained my double bachelor of science degree in both agriculture education and animal science. During those busy college years, I kept my secret book-writing dream alive, yet I received many challenges from my agriculture classmates when they discovered that I was taking so many college elective courses in English and writing courses.

At the time, whenever I was asked why I was taking so many nonagriculture major courses by my classmates, I simply replied, "I really like English and writing-related topics." This was not exactly giving them the entire story, but I simply didn't want to claim that I aspired to write a book one day, only to then have to spend the rest of my life answering the question, "When do you think you will complete the book?"

Through a lot of diligence and perseverance, I was able to complete nearly one-half of my first attempt at writing a book by the time of my graduation from college. Following my graduation, I was hit with the "speed of life," and my dream of writing a book was shelved while I began my career, began my marriage to my wife, Astrid, and started our family.

Somehow, in all the rush of those early days of my young adulthood, I found the fortitude to finish my first book-writing project, and *The Folk and Their Fauna* was published in 1982. Suddenly, at a mere twenty-six years of age, I was in the whirlwind of the experiences resulting from becoming a first-time published author. While writing my first book was a tremendous experience, I pledged at that time that writing one book was more than enough authoring experience in my lifetime.

Fast-forward nearly thirty years, and once again I've pounded out a second book on my keyboard. In the couple of years preceding the development of this story and in conversation, I'd often mentioned some of the amazing events that have occurred in my life where somehow I believe my faith and God has helped me cheat death repeatedly.

As I've shared some of my examples with various acquaintances, their response has nearly always been the same, "Scott, you need to write a book that provides your witness to the miracles that the Lord has blessed upon your life." Since so much time has passed since I wrote my first book many years ago, those same people directing me to write a book have gasped in wide-eyed surprise when I shared with them that I already had in fact written one book.

From my perspective, I personally feel that within each and every human lies an amazing story or tale of some kind. I believe that most everyone could write a book of some consequence from within their own unique set of circumstances and life experiences. The real challenge, however, is that no matter how many individuals dream of writing their own book one day, and many do dream this dream, the basic truth is that a minuscule few will ever actually reach such an objective.

Few people could ever imagine the discipline and commitment it actually takes to compile a story into a book format. Even fewer wishful authors can even comprehend the challenges it takes to get one's story published. Finally, after one invests endless hours preparing, note taking, writing, rewriting, editing, and finally publishing a potential book, then ultimately someone out there must want to buy it in order to read it.

The title I chose for this my second book is *Nine Lives to Eternity*. I've often tried to give witness to the strength of my Christian faith and personal exposure to the wonders of divine spiritual intervention. I've been blessed to experience several instances where I've not only had God by my side, but also actually felt his influence to literally and miraculously save my life.

No doubt that others have had similar experiences, I'm sure, yet perhaps others who may have wondered if it was the Lord working in their lives or simply pure chance that something wonderful or phenomenal had occurred that was left unexplainable.

Following my most recent near-death experience from a motorcycle and deer collision, I was sharing my implausible experience and astounding medical recovery with someone when they indicated, as so many others have, that I should write a book someday about my strong message of faith and the fact that it appears that I have been blessed with either the "nine lives" of a cat, or else, I've been blessed with a guardian angel to watch over me.

After thinking about that statement, which I often hear to describe my life, I strongly contemplated how many times in my life that my number should have been called and where my time clock for life should have been cancelled. I started adding the times in my life where I've cheated death, with a real apprehension that I was perhaps nearing my ninth death-cheating situation and potentially near the statistical end of my existence.

I was especially concerned about this fact since I'm somewhat superstitious about certain matters. I nearly dropped my jaw in surprise when I discovered that I had not only surpassed a possible "nine lives" scenario, but that I had also in fact encountered and survived an almost unbelievable "twenty-seven lives" instead! I was amazed to discover that I was not on my first "nine lives" scenario, but rather I had actually amassed enough near misses with death in my life to tally three complete "nine lives" scenarios!

From the very day of my most recent encounter with death, I've concluded that God's plan for me is somehow not yet finished. I passionately believe that the Lord has a mission for me, and until my job on this earth is finished, I will not be called to my heavenly Creator no matter how dangerous my situation or how severe my injuries may be. For this reason, I'm completely convinced that my Lord and Savior has blessed me with a message that needs to be shared through the words of this book.

Hopefully, the messages about my own personal witness to our Lord may in fact make an impact in your own life. I've not only been given this opportunity through the pages of this book to share these miraculous wonders with you, but I've also been blessed with whatever stubbornness, perseverance, and commitment that it might take to get this message out to you.

I pray that your faith and your beliefs be forevermore strengthened and that God lends his mercies, grace, and love unto you as he miraculously has with me.

BORN TO TAKE CHANCES—0 MONTHS

CHAPTER ONE

Don't be afraid, for I am with you. Do not be dismayed, for I am
your God. I will uphold you with my victorious right hand.
—ISAIAH 41:10

AND SO IT BEGINS

At precisely 7:40 a.m. on the morning of September 16, 1955, following my birth and my entry into this world, I took my first gasping breaths and then filled the hospital delivery room with the echoes of my first audible cries. My mother, Rose Gottschalk, had just given birth to her six-pound, fourteen-ounce firstborn baby boy who was the eldest of what was to become her family of five total offspring.

I was born in southeastern Minnesota in the city of Rochester; and my father, David Gottschalk, along with my mother, Rose, proudly christened their new pride and joy with the name of Scott David Gottschalk. As with most new parents, they could only fantasize of what wonderful possibilities lay ahead for their new child as they were about to help guide him along in his journey through life.

My dear and loving parents were soon to learn, though, that not all children are cut from the same mold in life. They soon discovered that some children like their firstborn could cause higher peaks of joy and lower valleys of sadness and stress to a parent than the other children within the same family. Most parents share the dreams and wishes of success, along with the hope for greatness for their children. Parents the world over do the best that they can to create an environment whereby their children may hopefully succeed and to ultimately develop into well-rounded individuals.

I'm very thankful that my parents provided me with a Christian upbringing. Throughout my life, I've been guided and strengthened by my faith and spirituality. The pages and chapters of my dangerous and life-threatening experiences are filled with countless times where I've been touched by what I'm convinced has been spiritual divine intervention. Without my strong faith and belief in an all-loving and gracious God, I'm convinced that my life would have been cut short on many an occasion as I experienced the close calls and near misses with death time and time again. The world is full of people who have cheated death sometime during their life. My story tells of cheating death twenty-seven times, and yet I'm still alive to tell my story!

Over the years, my parents have stated to me on many occasions, "Scott, why do you have such a death wish in life? Your antics have turned both of us prematurely gray haired, and we are endlessly stressed and worried for your safety." They have further stated, "You keep us continually on a roller coaster of fear and emotions." For the record, I don't know if I'm the total blame for both of my parent's premature graying or not, but I do know that both my mother and father had mostly white hair by the time they were in their thirties. No doubt, I had something to do with their hair color I'm sure.

As my story unfolds, one will quickly recognize how the many chances and risks that I've taken have transposed into life-threatening and life-altering events throughout my lifetime. Many of these events have allowed me to miraculously walk away from death, yet often these same events have left me severely injured and close to death time and again. Traumatic as they may be, these events have also shaped me and blessed me in so many ways that it is beyond description.

It could be argued that over my lifetime, I've attempted activities that were inherently illogical acts, yet I've been continually driven by a triumph of aspiration over sensibility. Most would agree that being driven toward such actions is by classification beyond the influence of reasoned dispute. From a very young age, it became clear to my parents that within our family of five siblings, consisting of my one brother, Jerry, and my three sisters—Julie, Sally, and Marcia—that I was the extreme risk taker who had to do everything on the very edge of life and reality. It became painfully obvious that I was an adrenaline junkie from an early age, compounded by a compulsive and strongly driven personality to succeed in anything that I desired to accomplish.

For my entire life, I've not only been described as a person who continually dreams big of what may come, but I'm also equally described as the type of person who in fact seems to make their dreams become a reality. With all this being said, these combined traits can make for a possible lethal cocktail of danger and risk throughout the course of life.

For most of my existence and from an early age in my life, I've had a personal motto of "Live life like you may die tomorrow." Putting it another way, I've always looked at our short time and existence on this planet with this sentiment, "Live hard, and expect to perhaps die at a young age." I've often been heard during my lifetime stating, "Don't just dream your dreams, but fulfill those dreams no matter the cost or the consequences because there may not be another opportunity within your lifetime." I've often challenged others with comments such as, "What are you waiting for? Just do it." Throughout the years I've often remarked, "I'm going to live life to the very fullest because no matter how young I am when I die, I want to have lived at least three lifetimes worth of experiences."

I simply refuse to let anyone ever claim that I hadn't accomplished everything in my life that I set out to do and then some. My sincerest wish is that while at my eventual funeral and the ultimate celebration of my life, all my family and friends will simply smile in amazement and joy at how much life I was able to fit into one lifetime. I will not go to my grave as so many others often do with the spoken or unspoken words upon my lips of "Someday I'm going to do this when I get enough money or when the kids grow up or when I retire" or any other list of endless excuses for what one aspires to accomplish, yet never will.

A few examples of my thrill-seeking efforts and zest to attack life may help demonstrate how I chose to experience some of my time on this earth. Over the years, I've piloted airplanes, skydived out of airplanes, white-water rafted, bungee jumped from a 150-foot tower, rode bulls and steer-wrestled in rodeos, hunted game in mountain wildernesses, globe-trotted across six continents while completing international consulting assignments in several dangerous third world countries, canoed the Boundary Waters Canoe Wilderness, completed long-distance endurance motorcycle journeys, and mountain-climbed in some extreme scenarios to name a few activities worth noting.

Within each chapter of this book, I'll describe the events that led up to my many extreme accidents and near misses with death and the resulting consequences. Although I've cheated death many times over, I haven't been so lucky when it comes to injuries and the acute pain that follows as a result of such massive wounds and fractures.

People are often fascinated when a discussion turns toward asking me how many bones that I've broken during my lifetime. The fact is that most individuals go throughout their entire lives without breaking a bone, or perhaps breaking one or two bones at most. Due to my many painful accidents and experiences, I've fractured a total of twenty-six bones overall. This painful list of bone fractures is made up of broken foot (one time), broken ankles (two times), broken legs (three times), broken nose (one time), broken fingers (two times), broken toes (two times), broken ribs (eleven times), broken collarbone (one time), and broken back vertebrae (three times).

Several of my bone fractures have required extensive surgical repairs over the years, resulting in enough metal plates and metal screws in my skeleton to prevent me from passing through most airport security systems. I literally have so many surgical scars covering my body that I'm often the brunt of jokes about being some kind of a modern-day Frankenstein. In addition to all my bone fractures, I've also encountered severe dislocations of both of my shoulders, which have required major shoulder reconstructive surgeries. Also as a part of my past, I've suffered several brain concussions from being rendered unconscious no fewer than five times.

Due to all my medical challenges over the years, it should come as no surprise that I've been the recipient of several CAT scans, multiple MRIs, numerous x-rays, and endured multiple surgeries to mend me and to keep me going. Today, I'm exceptionally blessed and fortunate to be able to say that I'm still living a healthy and productive life. Do I have some aches and pains one might ask? Sure, but who doesn't as we all age? I can attest to the statements made by most elderly folks who mention that they can feel a weather pattern change coming from within their joints or within their bones. For me, whenever the atmospheric pressure drops or perhaps a weather front begins moving in, I suddenly have skeletal, joint, or muscle aches and pains beyond description.

What always has kept me happily grounded and continually moving forward through everything that I've been faced with is the tremendous support from my beloved family. For most of my entire adult existence, and for more than three decades, I've been privileged to be married to my best friend who is also my wife, Astrid. As a result of our union, we were blessed with two wonderful sons. Our eldest son, Trevor, is married to Theresa; and our youngest son, Travis, is married to RaeLynn, and they are the parents to granddaughter, Hiltina.

As each chapter of my story unfolded upon these pages, I became more and more confident that I was able to reach my current stage in life simply because of a few important and basic premises.

Number one, I firmly believe in the power of prayer and a strong commitment unto one's faith. In our hurried and rushed society and world, it seems that too many people ignore, suppress, or shy away from their faith and their belief in God.

Number two, so many people these days seem to hide behind their faith by stating that they are spiritual, yet many of these people never seem to find the time to formally practice their faith through personal prayer or celebrating their faith in a place of worship. Are we really so busy anymore that we can't quietly speak to God through prayer at least daily or possibly at least a few times each week? Are we really so busy anymore that we can't make time for the simple and small sacrifice of investing a short period of time on a regular basis to worship within a house of God and to share in our faith and Christian fellowship? I do know that attending *church is habit forming,* in that one can *get in the habit of attending church* or one can *get in the habit of not attending church* on a regular basis.

Number three, do well by others and leave everyone and everything just a little better off because of your influence and the time you invested to make some good happen within this world. I can honestly express that I'm alarmed by how our modern society seems to be mired in the muck of selfishness and egotistical behavior. We have become so driven by our lust of money and for our ultimate desire for materialistic possessions that many completely miss what may be the real mission and calling in life. In my sincerest opinion, I believe that the truest gift one can share with others may be the simple gift of expressing love, or perhaps passing along the gift of compassion, or perhaps volunteering one's gift of mentoring someone to help make their existence better.

Ask yourself, when was the last time that you volunteered for a worthy cause? When was the last time that you made a positive impact on someone's life other than for the benefit of yourself or for the benefit of your immediate family members? I truly believe that perhaps the greatest gift and legacy each of us can have once we leave this earth is to be remembered for what we unselfishly gave of ourselves and how we were able to make other's lives better for having interacted with us.

Thoughts such as these remind me of a fabled story of a little boy standing all alone along the sandy beach by the vast ocean. This little boy was very perplexed because he had witnessed that as the ocean's tide had pulled its waters back, it had left thousands of starfish stranded and slowly dying upon the sandy beach. The concerned little boy felt that his only option was to grab a starfish and then as quickly as possible throw it back into the ocean. Again and again the little boy repeated his process to save as many starfish as he possibly could. Some distance away was an elderly man sitting on the porch of his beach house. He had watched the little boy repeat his starfish process until the little boy was nearly exhausted. Finally, the elderly man could take it no longer and he walked out to the fatigued little boy and said, "Young man, why on earth are you putting so much effort into trying to save these starfish? Surely you must realize that you simply can't make any difference to the thousands of them that are stranded?" Without even slowing down, the little boy grabbed another starfish, and before flinging it into the ocean, he replied with a smile, "I'll bet it will make a difference to at least this one!"

Moving forward now with the theme of my story, *Nine Lives to Eternity*, my wish is that as you read these many pages, you will envision for yourself the wonders and the workings of faith, spirituality, and that you will hold a belief in a god who ceaselessly nurtures us throughout our lives. We are so blessed to have a god who unconditionally loves us all, even though we often fail to reciprocate that love.

INFANT POISONING CALAMITY— 9 MONTHS

CHAPTER TWO

Even when I walk through the dark valley of death,
I will not be afraid, for you are close beside me.
Your rod and your staff protect and comfort me.

—PSALM 23:4

When human beings are birthed into this world, as infants, we generally have very little if any recall of our earliest minutes, hours, days, weeks, or months. We are born into our existence with the most basic of primal necessities, which consist mostly of nourishment, sleep, and protection from the environment. Even though we most often are heavily nurtured by our parents or at the very least by someone who cares deeply for us, the simple relative fact is that we could not survive long at all without such extreme care on our behalf. Isn't it strange then that we mysteriously have little memory of our infant stages of life prior to about one year or more of age?

By the time that I had reached nine months of age, I'm extremely confident that my mother and my father had done nearly everything within their power to love me, care for me, and nourish me through the earliest stages of my infancy. Being a firstborn baby can obviously create its own very unique set of circumstances since new parents are suddenly entering into a strange new world of the unknown.

Thankfully, children are most usually born while their parents are in their more youthful and energetic stages of life. When one considers the amount of time, energy, and commitment it takes to bring a baby into the world and then raise that child, it is simply a wonder how any parent survives such a massive test without succumbing to total exhaustion.

Anyone with experience with neonatal infants can attest to the strains it puts on the parents raising that baby. In the earliest stages of life, we human beings are simply incapable of doing anything for ourselves. Therefore, our caregivers must feed us every few hours, thereby adjusting their own adult sleeping patterns over toward the sleeping patterns of an infant who is in constant need of care. As a result of requirements for repetitive feedings, the diapers then need to be changed on a very regular basis. It can be particularly difficult for the parents to know exactly what to do at times when as infants, our only modes of earliest communications are merely to cry when expressing feelings of distress and to smile or to make cooing sounds when expressing feelings of contentment.

Simply put, raising an infant is hard, it is tiring, and it can be awfully stressful. To make matters all the worse, new parents can read and study all the books on infant care to be found on the bookshelf, yet nothing can replicate the actual trials and errors of having and raising one's own first child.

In the first year following my birth, I resided with my loving mother and father in their rented upstairs apartment home in Rochester, Minnesota. I have absolutely no recall of that dwelling and I have no recall of the devoted parental care provided to me either. My folks have indicated, though, that their first residence was the type of older, slightly dilapidated kind of first rental unit that many young newlyweds and new parents with diminutive finances often dwelled within. Small to be sure, old yes, but the upstairs apartment of this older house was cozy and provided a secure environment for starting a new family.

Ours was a very traditional family for the era. My parents married right out of high school, and my father Dave worked long, grueling hours employed at two different jobs in his effort to try to make financial ends meet for his young family. My mother, Rose, like so many mothers was a homemaker caring for and raising her family on a 24-7 basis. Each day, day after day, my father left for work and endured the long, arduous hours to keep our family unit sustained. Each day my mother facilitated all the essentials that were demanded for caring for her young infant and her new family.

It seems hard to fathom, but back in those days, my father was logging over eighty hours per week working to support our family. Not only was my father putting in long weeks of work, but my mother was logging in excess of one hundred hours per week with the duties and responsibilities of being a young mother and homemaker. Both of my parents served an essential role in my upbringing and both of my parents sacrificed everything within their means to see that their children could reach the fullest potential in life.

This then brings me to the circumstances of my initial near-death event that was to set a precedent and defined my future existence in so many ways. By this time of my life, I had reached the age of nine months; and as a toddler, I was just beginning to explore the world all around me.

As a young and growing baby boy, my mother had ceased nursing me about two months prior, thus skipping the baby bottle stage with me and moving me directly to drinking liquids from a cup. Now at this mark of my life, I'd developed a scant few of my first teeth, although when expressing happiness, I still had mostly a toothless grin. This was the age that I was strong enough to sit up and even began the initial stages of crawling around to see what I might discover.

The upstairs rental apartment within the older home where we lived at that time was relatively small to be sure, but it was perhaps deemed the most capacious environment around through the eyes of a nine-month-old infant determined to be on the move to discover new worlds.

The day of the week was Saturday, and it began like so many of the previous days, except this was an extra-special day. On this very day, my father was going to have the honor of being the best man for his only sibling, his sister and my aunt Audrey, who was getting married. The excitement level within our humble abode must have been at a peak level for sure. My folks scurried around our home that morning in preparation for the big wedding event planned for that afternoon. On that morning, my mother completed all of her tasks involving my care and preparation for our large family gathering yet to come. She worked diligently as she woke me, changed my diapers, bathed me, dressed me, and combed my hair, fed me, and so on.

There was so much to do on that day, and once my mother had met all of her infant son's requirements, she then focused her thoughts toward the rest of her and my father's tasks at hand by readying themselves for the wedding. At that point, I was placed on the floor of our living room in close proximity to the closed door of our enclosed porch. Mother had set out some toys for me to play with and keep me occupied while she then went about her other duties in preparation for my aunt's wedding. I might add that my aunt Audrey and uncle Bud were in fact my godparents, so I've often wondered if I somehow mustered up a kind of devious plan in an infant-sort-of-way to make their wedding day memorable in more ways than one.

As I sat alone on the floor of our living room that morning playing with the same old toys, I'm sure that it became obvious to me even as a nine-month-old infant that my parents were absorbed in a flurry of other activities. Seldom was I ever out of the watchful eye of one or both of my parents, yet on this day and on that morning, I must have detected that I might have had some latitudes and freedoms for some adventuresome discovery that were not often allowed me.

As a matter of record, I left my toys that were scattered upon the floor and began slowly and methodically crawling toward the closed door of our enclosed balcony porch. Upon reaching this door, my tiny head bumped into it as I crawled forward. The door, which was normally carefully closed and latched to prevent my entry, made a subtle creaking sound and opened ever so slowly as my head bumped into it. Somehow the door had not latched the last time it had been closed, so much to my delight; I crawled through the narrow opening of the door and into a wondrous new undiscovered world that I'd never been allowed entry before.

From inside the off-limits domain of that enclosed porch, my mother had been waging a war against an invasion of ants that were continually trying to enter our home. Since our home housed an infant, my mother was not going to have filthy insects crawling all over our living quarters. Therefore, several months earlier, my parents had determined that these persistent insect's entry point into our home was in fact by means of entering through the porch and then on into the inside of our home. For this specific purpose, my parents had purchased a bottle of liquid ant poison in an effort to rid the pests for good. This bottle of poison as per the instructions was opened and laid upon its side on the floor of the porch. The unsuspecting, yet troublesome ants would then migrate to the overturned bottle of sweet yet toxic elixir where they would then meet their death. As anyone who had dealt with the invasion of ants within their home knows, once a group of ants discover that what they and their fellow ants have been ingesting can or will actually harm them, shortly thereafter the ant colony will usually vacate the immediate premises.

Imagine my excitement at my mere nine months of age to somehow have been able to meander my way into the forbidden zone of the porch without my parent's slightest knowledge. One can only speculate how much my pulse sped up and my breath intake quickened as I spotted the open bottle of tasty treat lying on the floor. I'm sure the pupils of my eyes perhaps even narrowed with anticipation as I increased the momentum of my crawl toward this bottle. The only possible thought that now comes to my mind of what I might have been thinking at the time was that since my parents had invested so much time in the past couple of months training me to drink from a cup, then it was now time for me to impress upon them what a "big boy" I was and drink solely on my own merits without their prodding. Without hesitation, I grasped the bottle of poison within my pudgy little fists, and then with a short burst of sucking action, "down the hatch," as they say, went the poison!

I was just gleefully licking my lips in a moment of pure fulfillment when my mother burst through the partially opened porch door and screeched, "Oh my god, Dave, little Scotty is in the porch and he has just drank the entire bottle of ant poison!"

It is hard to imagine any more horrifying nightmare for two young parents to come to the harsh realization that their adventurous nine-month-old firstborn son was now suddenly in the process of dying and could soon be in the grips of death!

My father scooped me up off the ground, ran through the house, sped down the stairwell, and then placed me in the car, while my mother hurriedly gathered my baby belongings, following closely behind. As luck would have it or perhaps God's plan, we amazingly lived in Rochester where we resided only a few blocks from the world renowned Mayo Clinic with all the abundant supporting network of numerous emergency rooms, clinics, and hospitals.

Within mere moments from my ingestion of the poison, I was laying upon the cold, sterile, stainless steel medical table in the hospital emergency room. Thankfully, I have absolutely no memory that day and no recollection of what it must feel like to have one's stomach pumped out, but my guess is that from the perspective of a nine-month-old infant, stomach pumping wasn't nearly so pleasant as was the experience of swallowing the sweet yet deadly nectar from that bottle on that day.

How did it all turn out in the end one might ask? Well, my folks have indicated that following that experience, I was extremely upset with the entire world in general, and that I was mad as only a baby can be when truly angry, but I had survived to live yet another day.

Sure, I spent the next several weeks with a lot of stomachaches, stomach cramps, and digestive upsets. I'm told that I screamed in anguish while I became a master at filling my diapers with explosive diarrhea as a consequence of ingesting poison into my digestive track. My folks became adept at caring for a child that had become more prone to temperament swings and had more susceptibility for ailments since my immune system had been somewhat compromised. They knew each member of our family had been very lucky that day so very long ago, and based on the experiences they had gained, they fully vowed to never let such a potentially dangerous situation arise again.

After returning home from the hospital on the day of my poisoning, my mother went about either locking up or ridding our residence of anything that an adventurous toddler could potentially ingest or get into and then cause them harm.

To follow up on the actual wedding event for my aunt and uncle so long ago and since this was in a pre-cell phone era, they became ever concerned as to why my father who was their best man failed to show up at the church in time for the wedding. There was much concern as the wedding was delayed in hopes that some information would surface as to why my parents and I were absent from such an important occasion. Though late and flustered following my hospital intervention, we finally arrived; and with no further drama, the wedding went off without any further distractions. With a little luck and with the helping hand of God, my parents and I were able to witness Aunt Audrey and Uncle Bud's glorious day of matrimony.

As perhaps an ironic tribute to that day, every year of my life since that fabled day, my aunt and uncle have sent me one of my most cherished birthday cards. I've always been keenly astute that every card that I've ever received from my godparents has come directly from the endearing emotions within their hearts. On each one of those cards that has arrived to me now for over fifty years has been a handwritten note, which affectionately states, "Dearest Scott, you are our most special nephew and godchild. We have always loved you so dearly, and we will always love you."

In the end, I was so blessed to have survived such a close call with my first near-miss death experience and all with only the slightest level of short-term problems. In the long run, I was astonishingly none the worse for having come so close to death at such an early infant stage of life.

Not surprising though, it was at that very moment in their lives that both my parents came face-to-face with the stark realization that perhaps their firstborn son was going to develop into a lifetime of challenges and worries for them. My parents were but mere teenagers, yet already their hair color was starting to gray!

CONFLICTING CONFESSIONS—4 YEARS

CHAPTER THREE

They answered, believe in the Lord Jesus, and you will be saved, you and your household. They spoke the word of the Lord to him and to all who were in his house.

—ACTS 16:31-32

In a previous chapter, I had highlighted the fact that as human beings, we literally have no recall of what transpired in our lives during the earliest stages of life. In nearly all cases, we must rely on others to inform us of how our first experiences in life actually happened. Along those same lines remains the simple fact that most people rarely have little if any memory of events that happened prior to about the age of approximately four or five years. Sure, it's possible as a youth or as a teen or even as a young adult to perhaps remember back to a really memorable activity or possibly retain information about a favorite animal pet during the ages of three or four years, but for the most part, any detailed recall from our earliest years of existence are tiny if not faded memories from long, long ago.

It was the year that I'd reached my fourth birthday. Amazingly, I'd survived up until that point without any further life-threatening incidences since making my self-inflicted poisoning attempt as an infant. Try as I might, though, I have virtually no memory of the events that occurred with my family and me on that fateful fourth year of my life. Extensive changes and difficult times developed on that year that could have or should have left an impact on me for life. Still though, I can't remember even the faintest hint of any of it.

It was not until I was well into my adulthood, married, and had children of my own before I learned of the vast array of conflicting confessions and details from my distant past, which could have catapulted into what might well have been the end of much of my family and me.

The interviews and research I've completed as I delved into this story has left me forever perplexed. This traumatic story is about subject matter so taboo that family secrets and hidden skeletons such as these seldom surface. Within the next few pages, I'll try to outline the two distinctly different versions of what knowledge I've discovered about a family incident from a time long ago.

Conflicting Confession 1: This is an account of my uncle Glen's recall as he shared it with me. My uncle was married to my mother's identical twin sister, my aunt Mary.

The sensitive subject matter of this chapter has never been broached or mentioned by my own immediate family or has it ever been hinted at by my parents during my lifetime. This is one of those deep, dark family secrets, one in which the guarded family skeletons are kept deeply locked within the closet of obscurity; the kind of secrets that are so often taken to the grave with sealed lips. Had my uncle never shared his version, I would never have known, and as I've indicated already, I do not remember much of anything or any details up through my fourth year of life.

Looking back, my family and others have often reflected back on what a tumultuous year it had been for our family. This was a year of massive changes and activities that happened and even the strongest of family units would have weakened under the pressures and circumstances we faced as a family. My family's numbers were rapidly growing by my fourth birthday. No longer was I simply a firstborn and an only child within our family, but I had become a big brother twice over with two more siblings. My sister, Julie, was born about one year after my birth. Shortly prior to my fourth birthday, my mother had given birth to her third child, my new baby brother, Jerry.

Not only were my parents dealing with their rapidly expanding family by giving life to three babies within less than four years, but the winds of change were about to blow in a storm cloud for our family that was to be unprecedented in the course of our history.

My father, Dave, grew up on a farm and throughout most of his entire youth he dreamed of one day entering into that same noble profession of farming. He always knew that choosing a farming career was going to be a challenging and a difficult choice to be sure. It is a given that farmers often endure long, endless days and weeks of work trying to feed the peoples of our world. The dream of farming was not a conviction that my father was willing to compromise. From the moment of his high school graduation, through his marriage to my mother Rose at eighteen years of age, through the birth of his first two children, my father continually dreamed of becoming a farmer.

Finally after paying his dues by living in the city and working two jobs for the first five years of my parent's marriage, my father and family were suddenly packing our belongings and relocating our worldly possessions out to the location of our first farm. Over the years, my father has shared just how much he detested living in the city. After spending so much of his life in the country and growing up with life on a farm, he simply couldn't accept the restrictions that he felt urban dwelling put upon him and his family.

My father never stopped working toward his objective that one day, his children would in fact be raised out in the countryside, alongside farm animals and all of the wonders that nature can bring.

Few people can imagine or identify with the kind of effort it would have required for my folks to locate and then buy a farm, which was located in the sparsely populated countryside several miles to the north of the city of Rochester. Farms and land were extremely expensive to purchase back then even as they are costly yet today. My young parents with their young family did not have a lot of money saved up, yet they leveraged everything they had and borrowed enough money to purchase their farm and enter our family into the occupation of farming.

Imagine if you will, my parents packing all of their worldly belongings and then moving out of the big city, only to relocate themselves and their two children who were under the age of four at the time. To put insult on injury, my mother was also pregnant during that time with her third child. Try as I may, none of the memories of this family transition moving out to the farm lies within my accessible memory. Over the years, however, I've collected many of the specific details in an effort to connect some of the dots from my past.

Near to the time of our family's entry into the realm of farming, my father had taken on his new higher-paying job by working nights for the Mayo Clinic. This was a job that he was to hold for over twenty-five years and throughout much of his farming years. Simply stated, without the income from working his outside job, my father and our family would never have been able to enter into the farming occupation.

It seems tragic to me that farmers all across our nation have always sacrificed so much to feed and nourish the planet, yet not only must farmers endure the most difficult toil and labor requirements in their resolve to produce food, but many of them are forced into having outside job income in order to be able to continue on with their chosen profession of farming.

I dare say that the long hours of back-breaking labor along with inconsistent income would not sit well with the 98 percent majority of United States population by which farmers thankfully sacrifice of themselves in order to feed that segment. I wonder at times how that majority of the population themselves would actually handle being forced to hold another job in order to support their primary occupation.

Envision the stresses and strains on two young parents and their family as their entire world was suddenly turned upside down overnight. Every moment of every day was constantly surrounded by uncertainty. Specifically from my mother's perspective, no longer did she have the ease of simply walking down the street to buy groceries. She questioned where her family would attend church in the isolated rural area we now dwelled. Her mind raced and wondered if she even wanted her children to get their education by having to walk to the one-room schoolhouse which was over one mile away. Fear griped her on the thought of how she'd deal with a medical emergency since each day my father took their only vehicle to work his job, thus leaving my mother alone and to fret about what to do in the event of an emergency. It was soon obvious and no secret for many of my mother's closest family and friends that she was suffering more and more from ever-increasing feelings of despair, loneliness, exhaustion, confusion, and fear.

Needless to say, from my father's perspective, the view of everything was much different. My father was and has always been an eternal optimist. He envisions the positive possibilities in nearly every scenario he faces. In his mind, there was no need to sweat the little details. Surely he felt it would all work out soon. He'd finally been able to transition his family back to the farm and to try to fulfill what he strongly believed was his life's destiny. In the workings of my father's mind, none of the hardships that we were forced to endure at that time of our lives could possibly be permanent, thus in his mind it would all be worth it in the end. OR WOULD IT?

How much stress can a young couple endure and at what point does the breaking point come? From the details I've tried to piece together over the years and from my uncle's assertions to me, I'm deeply conflicted over what may or may not have transpired one fateful evening.

My mother tried her very best to put on a face of joy and contentment for her current situation in life. Each day, though, she became ever more exhausted from not only her role of mothering my younger sister and me, but she had recently given birth to our brother, Jerry.

Somehow between the difficulty of that birth and the strain of all that she was trying to endure, life became nearly unbearable for her. Any mother could attest that the work of caring for three infants and toddlers that are under the age of four would at times seem insurmountable.

To make this challenge even more difficult to bear was the fact that my mother suddenly had her daily farm chores and duties to contend with while living far from the comforts and safety of the big city. This fact was complicated further as each evening she struggled with loneliness as she watched my exhausted father leave for his full-time night-shift work at the Mayo Clinic, following his countless hours of laboring to make our new farm successful by daylight.

With all that she had to contend with, my mother simply did not feel right shortly following her recent birthing of my baby brother. As a result of the information that my uncle divulged to me on what happened so long ago, I've tried to educate myself on what the probable cause was that had occurred. The medical facts are that a certain percentage of new mothers go through various levels of sadness and depression following the birth of a child.

Today, this condition has been termed as postpartum depression, but in the 1950s and at the time of our family's excessive life-changing events, little was known or understood about this potentially dangerous set of symptoms. The consequences of postpartum depression are that it can wreak havoc on the mental state of a new mother. She can become unsteady with a dangerous combination of hormonal imbalances within her body, which can be brought about by pregnancy and, subsequently, by giving birth. Everything can become further convoluted by certain outside influences that a new mother may be facing shortly following the birth of her child.

It was on a day many years ago that my uncle Glen and I were traveling on a long road trip together when he suddenly remarked, "Scott, I want to share some information that happened with you, Jerry, Julie, and your mother a long time ago. I feel the time has come for me to share the details with you."

I listened ever so intently with bated breath as he expressed his compelling version about an event from my family's safeguarded past.

My mother's identical twin sister, my aunt Mary, had become ever more concerned by the frightening and severe mood swings coming from my mother. Since identical twins are in fact genetic equals who share the same exact DNA codes with each other, what was occurring with my mother became very unsettling to say the least for my aunt Mary.

Identical twins have often made claims for years about their unique closeness with each other since they were conceived from the same singular fertilized egg. After spending nine months in gestation developing by each other's side and following their birth, twins often act or feel as if they are one inseparable person. Adult identical twins will make claims of knowing what the other may be feeling or claim to share the same physical pain that only one of them may actually have acquired. Identical twins are often heard completing each other's sentences. There can be little doubt for anyone directly associated with identical twins that they share a most unique and at times secretive relationship with each other.

Since my aunt and my mother as identical twin sisters were so inherently linked, they could feel each other's pain and emotions like few others. Aunt Mary had been investing exorbitant amounts of time counseling her beloved twin sister and my mother but with little avail. Mary made countless visits to our farm during those scary moments, followed by numerous and lengthy phone calls to my mother in hopes of bringing her out of her ever-increasing state of sadness and depression. One must remember just how little was understood about this condition during this era in history.

My uncle Glen shared with me that between my father, my aunt Mary, and himself, they had tried everything within their power to lift my mother's spirits up. Unfortunately, each day my mother seemed to fall into greater despair and hopelessness. She made continual statements about how everything would be better if she were free of this life.

Glen shared with me that my mother was under the constant watchful eyes of her entire extended family. Everyone seemed to know that something was dreadfully wrong with her yet were helpless to assist in the battle with her demons. One can only imagine how difficult it must have been to deal with something such as postpartum depression prior to when modern medicine developed methods of diagnosis followed with safe and effective treatments. Imagine how traumatic it must have been for a young family to deal with a situation such as this so many years ago when very little was understood about the diagnosis and treatment of what is now a relatively common disorder.

The darkest day of all began much like all the previous ones on our lonely and isolated farmstead. My mother was beyond the breaking point as she was flushed with anxiety and emotions. On this day, she was filled with more sadness and greater hopelessness than ever before. This was the day that for her it had now simply become too hard to continue on with life. Her will to live had ebbed, and she was left with only the bad thoughts that surfaced.

On that fateful day according to my uncle's version, my mother finally snapped in the most frightening of ways. She had fully convinced herself that the world would be far better off without her in it. She could not endure the pain any longer as her tormented mind hatched a plan of escape. Most certainly my mother was in a chemically imbalanced state of mind and therein lays the ultimate danger for my brother, my sister, and me. You see few mothers in such a depressed frame of mind could ever envision ending their own existence, only to leave their helpless babies to fend for themselves.

Perhaps my mother had worked out her exit strategy over the period of days, or possibly over several weeks, or just maybe it was so bad for her on that day that she wanted to put an end to it all instantaneously.

As my uncle continued to share his version of a very dark secret, I faced the stark reality of an impending near-death experience that will forever remain with me.

Once my father had left that evening for his night job, my mother set her plan into action. Knowing my mother as I have come to know and love her, I can only speculate that she likely continued on with her loving caregiving by feeding her three children first that evening in our small farmhouse kitchen. Based on my uncle's unsettling testimony, it then appears that following our supper, my mother sealed off the kitchen and then blew out all the pilot flames on our gas kitchen stove while turning each burner valve on high. Next she opened the oven compartment of her gas stove and repeated the same process. In her mind, she might have felt that it would all soon be over as the small kitchen filled with the toxic gases and our lungs struggled for oxygen.

Suddenly, the phone in the kitchen rang. At first, our mother let it ring again and again and again. At last, she pulled herself up to answer the phone.

I was spellbound as my uncle Glen continued on with his version of a conflicting story.

On the other end of the phone was my aunt Mary who was in a very worried frame of mind. Mary in the deepest trenches of her being knew that all was not well with her twin sister and was wrought with emotions about what was happening with my mother. My mother tearfully cried into the phone, "Mary, I love you dear sister, but I can't endure any longer!" With that, my mother supposedly hung up the phone and returned to her kitchen table to be alongside her three babies.

Uncle Glen said that he and my aunt Mary in a panic got into their car that night following such a haunting phone conversation, then broke every speed barrier along the way while driving the many miles to our darkened farm. I listened in disbelief as Glen said they pulled into our farmyard with gravel and dust flying in every direction. My aunt Mary was the first to make her way into our toxic kitchen, followed closely by my uncle Glen. Without hesitation, they scooped us up and thrust us into the pure, crisp, and clean outside air. Lastly, he stated that he made his way back into the kitchen to close all the valves on the stove and to open the windows and the doors to our home for ventilation.

In the many days which followed our near tragic demise, my little brother, little sister, and I were taken care of by my aunt Mary and uncle Glen. We found great enjoyment as we were able to experience what we were told to us at the time was a special vacation time with our cousins. We would not have viewed this as anything suspicious since we were continually spending time with our cousins as a direct result of the ultra closeness that our identical twin mothers held with each other. We simply detected no reason for anything to be out of the ordinary.

We were so young, however, that we failed to realize that over the course of the many days that we spent with our cousins, for some odd reason only our father would stop by each and every day for a visit, but never our mother. The only response we received when we asked where our mother was came back the answer that she was not feeling very well and would visit us real soon when she felt better.

Conflicting Confession 2: This is an account of my mother and father's recall of that day. According to my mother, at that time in her life, admittedly her health and well-being were failing. She confesses that she dealt with ever-increasing symptoms of anxiety as she was unable to sleep, was continually nauseas, and rapidly losing weight. Each day she suffered from a roller coaster of emotions that brought her to the brink of a nervous breakdown. My mother has confirmed that, yes, my aunt Mary and uncle Glen came to her troubled aid one day, but that at no time did she ever think about or attempt harming herself or her beloved children. She is insistent that such a claim is simply untrue.

My mother went on to claim that my father transported her to the hospital where she was admitted for a one-week period. The doctors treated my mother with bed rest and physician-prescribed tranquilizers. Upon her release from the hospital, my parents were given instructions to take a vacation with our family and to try to get away from our family's struggles for a while. The prognosis was that my mother simply needed some rest.

This conflicting version of a hidden family secret is also completely confirmed by my father. He has questioned me as to why my uncle Glen would ever have embellished in such a far-fetched story. My father indicated that he had no awareness of anything that extreme happening when he admitted my mother to the hospital for her care.

Today as I reflect back on those events, I continue to struggle with what did or did not happen with my mother and our family. I question which version of whose story to actually believe. I find it difficult to believe that my uncle would burden me with his spin on such a dark tale if his version was not plausible, yet my parents are insistent that nothing so outlandish ever occurred.

I've questioned my parents on whether it could be remotely possible that my mother was so depressed at that time, that she literally has zero recall from that day long ago. I've further speculated with my father questioning whether there is even a remote possibility that aunt Mary and uncle Glen conspired together so that they personally protected my mother and her family by hiding the facts from him and burying what would have become an incredibly scandalous incident.

As of now, I truly feel that my mother doesn't believe such a horrible event could have happened. Now, I truly believe that my father has never had knowledge of anything so dramatic happening to his wife and children. Presently, based on modern scientific research, it has been determined that severe depression afflicts at least one in fifteen adults nationwide. Furthermore, a report published by the American Academy of Pediatrics cites research showing that every year more than four hundred thousand babies are born to depressed mothers. Estimates indicate that somewhere between 5 to 25 percent of women develop postpartum depression.

It has been several decades since that night where we all possibly cheated death, or did it even occur? I'll forever struggle with which version of the two conflicting stories to rely upon since my aunt Mary and uncle Glen have since taken their secrets to the grave. Although I'll probably never know for sure what transpired long ago, I'm forever thankful that the good Lord provided a path of happiness and redemption for all of us.

Since gaining such privileged information from two conflicting stories, I've resolved to love, honor, and respect my parents more than ever before.

CARBON MONOXIDE DEMISE—8 YEARS

CHAPTER FOUR

And we can be confident that he will listen to us whenever we ask him for anything in line with his will. And if we know he is listening when we make our requests, we can be sure that he will give us what we ask for.

—ACTS 16:31-32

In the previous chapters, I indicated that as humans we have little to no recall of our earliest childhood memories before the ages of four or five years. For that reason, I relied totally upon the recall and inputs from others who were witness to the events that led up to my first two cheating death encounters.

It was then no surprise that during my eighth year of life, I finally had nearly a total recollection of the events that led up to my third near-fatal ending. At that age, I was only in the second grade of elementary school, but my memory is sharp with the events leading up to another near-catastrophic ending for several of my family members and me.

By this point in my life, our family had moved away from our first farm and moved onto the second and final farmstead that my parents would own and dwell on for the rest of their lives. The difficult challenges and struggles we had encountered on our first farm had simply become too harsh to bear. It was within only a short couple of years spent on that first farm that my parents felt it best to relocate to more suitable surroundings. A major underlying concern was that by the time that I had reached the age of five, my mother was not accepting that her firstborn would be attending a one-room schoolhouse. She did not appreciate the educational environment of teaching several neighboring farm children from first grade through the eighth grade all within the confines of the same small one-room schoolhouse.

Today, I carry a certain amount of pride that I'm one of the few rare individuals who have had the experience of walking in excess of one mile to attend one of our nation's historic one-room schoolhouses. Although I only had the special opportunity for a small portion of my first year of education, I have delightful memories nonetheless as I recall hearing the school bell ring for the start of classes each day. I remember asking permission from the teacher to go outside and use the old wooden outhouse bathroom facilities. Young as I was at that age, I don't remember many of my schooling lessons, but I remember how much fun it was to play around outside during our recess playtime.

Following our time outside, my friends and I would get extremely dirty just as most young boys will do. Once we were summoned back into the schoolhouse and before being allowed into the classroom, we had to draw water into a washbasin by pumping the handle of a small hand pump. The icy water would sting our hands and faces as we tried to wash off the playtime grime from ourselves.

Ultimately, however, my mother enforced her decision that such an antiquated educational system was not going to be allowable for her growing brood of youngsters. Shortly thereafter, following relocation, my parents were once again engaged in farming at the site of our second farm located just west of Rochester, Minnesota, near the small community of Byron.

Just after reaching my sixth birthday, my parents had purchased a dilapidated old farmstead with some hilly rough pastureland and with a set of pathetically run-down buildings, which left nothing to be desired. I remember how at that time our family lived for a few short months in a small apartment in Byron while my parents set about renovating the house and buildings of their new farm. As I entered into my first classroom at the Byron Elementary School, I was amazed how many children my same age were all in the same large classroom. My memories of attending a one-room schoolhouse with about a dozen farm kids' grades first through eighth were fading fast.

Once again in our new community, my mother fulfilled the demands of being a homemaker while my father readied our new farm for our permanent residence. He not only made preparations on our farm, but he also set about tilling the land and caring for his livestock animals. By night, my father would head off to work nights at his Mayo Clinic job to supplement our family income.

I'll never forget the memories of my first visit to our new farm at age six. Being an adventurous young boy, I nearly quivered with joy when I spotted the meandering creek that lazily flowed through the partially wooded pastureland of our farm. Even at such a young age, my mind raced at the visions of finding frogs and snakes to play with along the creek bed. The sights and the organic, earthy smells of our new farm are still embedded deep within my fondest childhood memories.

Another shocking memory that was blazed into my mind was what an inhospitable place the building site appeared to be. Several of the outbuildings had collapsed during the course of time and the one-hundred-year-old brick house, if one could even call it a house, didn't appear to have any hope of being a true home one day. I remember asking my parents just how they determined that our family could possibly live in such a horrible place. Inside what seemed to be nothing more than an old wood shack was a most disgusting dwelling with absolutely no modern amenities. There was no running water, no electricity, and there were no bathroom facilities. The scant small inside quarters space were more than half used up with the piles of chopped wood being used in the fireplace to heat the inside. It was painfully obvious at the time that our so-called new home was also being overrun by a hoard of rats and mice.

My father took great delight that day in sharing his vision of our new farm and what he felt it would become one day with a lot of love and effort. He shared how he had hired carpenters, electricians, and plumbers to transform our home into one that we would be more than happy to live in. Little did my father or our family realize at the time about the sheer irony of his statement, "happy to live in," because he might also have added, "or possibly to die in" as a prophetic sentiment!

On a daily basis that fall while we continued to live in the apartment, I spent my daytime hours in school. Once I was off to school each day, my mother would then bring my sister Julie and my brother Jerry out to our new farm. There, while keeping a watchful eye on her toddlers, she would work alongside our father on the massive task of turning our farm into something presentable and livable before the extremes of our Minnesota winter were upon them. They worked tirelessly alongside the carpenters, electricians, and plumbers to finally ready our new home for our family's arrival.

At last, the time had arrived when we made the short one mile move south with our family from our temporary apartment abode in the village of Byron out to our new farm with all of its remodeled outbuildings and our renovated house.

Our newly renovated farmhouse looked absolutely nothing like it had on the first time my parents showed it to me. On the exterior of the house, they'd covered the ancient red bricks with new white shiny insulated steel siding. The roof of the house was topped off with a set of beautiful new water-tight shingles.

As we entered into our revamped residence for the first time, it was shocking to see how the original woodshed portion of the house had been transformed into a small, yet cozy kitchen. In time and for much of my childhood, my mother would spend so many hours of her time cooking and feeding her family inside that tiny kitchen. Although the quarters were quite tight, we next observed for the first time how our parents had directed the installation of a small single bathroom inside our home with all the modern facilities, including running water, a toilet, and a bathtub for bathing. Alongside our tiny newly constructed bathroom was a miniature room hardly larger than a closet, which housed our washing machine and dryer.

The remainder of first floor of our two-story farm house consisted of a small living room adjoining my parent's tiny bedroom. My siblings and I were soon thrilled to discover the steeply inclined stairway leading to the two children's bedrooms located on the second story of the house. From that day forward, my brother, Jerry, and me slept alongside each other in two small beds in the first bedroom while my sister Julie slept on a third bed in the second bedroom in the upstairs of our house.

What a massive reconstruction effort it must have taken not only to create new insulated walls and floors for what was once an old farm shack, but then to have to wire all the rooms for modern-day electricity as well. One can only imagine the work it must have taken at that time to also bring in modern-day plumbing into a building that held absolutely no running water source at all. In fact, my parents had sealed up and abandoned the old hand pump water well out in the yard and opted to drill a new modern and safer well as the source of water for our family and livestock water requirements.

Perhaps the most impressive and possibly best appreciated addition to our modernized home was the installation of a new propane-gas-burning forced-air furnace system intended to heat our home during the frigid

Minnesota winters. My parents had authorized the removal of the original wood burning fireplace and chimney during the remodeling efforts. In place of that sooty, smoky, labor-intensive method of heating was placed a clean, safe mode of heating every room inside our home complete with a thermostat in which one could regulate the temperature of the home. How different the experience must have been switching from a dwelling with the more traditional wood burning heat, which was either too hot or too cold, but seldom ever just right, to a method of pure ease and comfort. Would it be possible for something deemed so safe to actually become deadly?

Fast forward two years, when as an eight years old boy, our family was in the throes of experiencing the harshness of another winter during the cold month of January in Minnesota. It seemed but only a faded memory of the date two years earlier when our family moved onto our new farm to begin living inside our then recently remodeled farm home. Small though it was, we still found it hard to imagine that we were still living in the same run-down shack that our parents initially purchased.

As I left my second-grade classroom on that day, my teacher indicated that we children might be enjoying a snow-day vacation away from school the next day since the weather forecasters were predicting a large blizzard to move into our area throughout the night. The weather was predicted to have massively subzero temperatures compounded with a heavy snowfall, complicated by high winds.

Times such as these are when youngsters and adults are not on the same way of thinking. The threat of such a dangerous weather event during our harsh Minnesota winters will often bring a strong sense of fear and tension to most any adult. Oddly, however, the excitement level for my fellow students and me during the school bus ride home to our farm that afternoon was at a peak level of happiness and joy.

My thoughts soared by envisioning how much fun my seven-year-old sister Julie who was at this time in first grade in school, along with my four-year-old brother, Jerry, and I were going to have the following day. If school was going to truly be called off due to inclement weather, then the winter activities we could complete were nearly limitless. Every cold-climate kid knows that there is no end to one's energy levels when building an army fortress made out of snow, then attacking each other with snowball bombs. Once tired of those games, we could then move on to building snowmen or even sledding down the steep hill in our snow-covered cattle pasture. It never entered our young minds back then just how dangerous and treacherous a storm such as the one coming our way could be.

My sister Julie and I scurried off the school bus and clambered our way up to the house that late afternoon. Following our supper on that evening, my parents expressed their concern with each other about the impending snowstorm. As the evening hours progressed, from time to time, each of us would look out of our frosty windows only to see the snow falling harder and harder. It made all of us shudder as the howl of the wind intensified with every waning hour.

That evening, we went through the normal chain of nightly household activities. My siblings and I went about brushing our teeth, changing into our nighttime pajamas, saying our bedtime prayers as we knelt alongside our beds, then at last we were tucked in for our night of slumber by our loving parents. Before I drifted off to sleep that fateful night, I can remember listening to the muffled discussions of my parents down in our living room immediately beneath the bedroom floor. It was not difficult to make out my father's concerned pitch of voice about having to depart shortly for his nighttime job at the Mayo Clinic. He questioned how he would be able to make it through such harsh weather to his job that evening, but he was even more perplexed about how he would make it back home to his family and for the needs of his livestock the following morning if the snowstorm continued at its current pace. Just before I fell into a deep slumber, I heard my mother's words of encouragement, "We'll be just fine. Once the snowdrifts on the roads are plowed tomorrow morning, you should make it back to our family without any problems."

*　　*　　*

I weakly opened my eyes trying to make out the time on the illuminated hands of the clock sitting on the nightstand between my bed and my brother Jerry's bed. The clock showed 1:30 a.m., and my disorientated mind tried to determine what was happening around me. I slowly dragged my hand forward along the sheets of my bed wondering why there was so much dampness. Was it perspiration, was it vomit, or was it both? Nothing made any sense, and I couldn't reason why my mind was so numb and unresponsive. I had a severe pounding deep in my brain that was not a common condition for an eight-year-old child.

With every bit of strength that I could muster, I pulled myself out of my bed, only to nearly faint from light-headedness. I nearly stumbled and fell as I made my way to the light switch of our upstairs bedroom. As the light filled the bedroom, I hunched over in pain as I witnessed that I had been sleeping in my bed in a large pool of my own vomit. Why had I not awakened as I always had in the past when overtaken by nausea?

I was so weak, that it was difficult to remain standing. With extreme effort, I was able to make my way to my four-year-old brother's bed. Shock set in as I viewed that he was oddly also sleeping in a large pool of his vomit as well. I kept shaking him while calling his name, yet for some reason, he would not respond from his state of unconsciousness. Fear overtook me as I screamed, "Mom, come quick, we are all very sick," as I stumbled next into my sister Julie's bedroom.

The remaining color drained from my face as I switched on my sister's bedroom light only to find her unconscious as well lying in her own large pool of vomit. Once again, I tried to arouse her just as I had with my brother with no success. Although I was extremely ill myself and in a severely weakened state, I screeched over and over, "Mom, come up here right away, we all have the flu really bad, and Jerry and Julie won't wake up."

With no response whatsoever coming from my mother, I began to panic. I made my way toward the steep stairway leading from our upstairs bedrooms down to my parent's bedroom. Knowing that I was bizarrely faint and weakened, I crept backward down the staircase in fear of passing out, then falling down the steep incline of the steps. In what seemed an eternity, I reached my mother's bedroom, which was on the first floor of our old home and directly underneath the upstairs bedrooms of her children. I switched on my mother's bedroom light to once again find the same results that I'd discovered upstairs. I cried and panicked further still as I tried to get my unconscious mother to awaken. Her room just as the other bedrooms of our home was filled with the acrid smell of vomit.

After shaking her and screaming as loudly as possible, she was able to only briefly open her eyes and utter a few words to me. She weakly whispered, "Scott, I need you to go out to the phone in our living room and call your father at his job." My mother further instructed, "Ask your father if he is sick and nauseous like all of us because we must have all gotten food poisoning from something we ate at suppertime."

Before I made the phone call to my father, I distinctly remember bringing my mother a wet, cold washcloth to put on her forehead, along with one of her kitchen pots so that she would have something other than her bed to vomit into.

Somehow, even as the rest of my family lay helpless in their beds, I was blessed with the energy to dial my father's work number on our rotary phone. Fortunately, my father answered immediately, and I asked him the questions as had been instructed by my mother. In response to my questions, he stated, "Scott, I have no possible idea why you are all so sick because I have felt perfectly fine all night long. We all ate the same food for supper, so it can't be food poisoning or I would be sick also." I responded back, "Yes, but Jerry, Julie, and mother have all fainted, and I wasn't able to even get Jerry or Julie to wake up." With that, my father said, "I'm sure you all have a bad case of the stomach flu. For whatever reasons, Scott, you are stronger than the rest of the family, so I need you to find a way to get your little brother and sister downstairs and into bed with your mother." My father went on to remark, "Scott, the weather reports of this severe snowstorm tonight don't sound good. They say the roads are all heavily drifted shut out in the countryside, so rather than making it home by about 7:00 a.m. like I normally do, I may not be able to make it home tomorrow before about noon." My father finished by mentioning, "Scott, you are the man in charge tonight. Everything will be fine and whatever is wrong with all of you may already be over with by the time I get home tomorrow." How could he possibly have imagined that what may already be over by the time he arrived home was that his beloved family's lives might be terminated?

As I said good-bye and hung up the phone, fear gripped me once more as the house hauntingly shuttered in the howling wind. Could it be death just outside our walls seeking a way to claim my family and me?

What I didn't know then as merely an eight-year-old child, but what I've since come to realize as an adult, was that on that frightening night, in that old house in the lonely countryside of our farm, my God directly intervened to save the life of my family and me. In my heart and in my mind, there can be no denying that glorious and miraculous fact as I replay the ensuing events of that near-death experience.

Here is how the rest of the plot unfolded in this amazing gift of life and renewal from my Lord and Savior.

What was happening to all of us inside our home one might ask? Was it food poisoning, or was it some form of stomach ailment? Were we perhaps all experiencing the same symptoms from a possible illness that one of us children possibly contracted and brought home with us from school? Was my father correct when he said, "Whatever it is that is wrong with all of you, most likely you will all probably be better by the time I make it home following the snowstorm tomorrow"? The answer is NO; we would have all been DEAD without the helping hand of God to show me the way.

So what was happening to us that night? It all began a short two years earlier when our new propane gas furnace was installed within our home. Unfortunately, as the exhaust pipe for the furnace was mounted at that time onto the roof of our home, it was done incorrectly. The high roof peak of our house had a steep incline. For proper installation, the furnace exhaust pipe should have been extended above and beyond the peak of the roof. Tragically, the furnace exhaust pipe was improperly installed so that it was a few feet below the peak of the roof.

On the evening of our near-death tragedy, the harsh winds and heavy snowfall created a large snowdrift over the top of our roof, which in turn nearly sealed up the exhaust pipe nearly ceasing the ventilation for our home. While we slept that night, our home was slowly depleted of its life-sustaining oxygen, and our breathable air was replaced with the toxic, odorless, tasteless, yet deadly fumes from carbon monoxide. So many deaths have been caused by this deadly killer over the course of time. My family and I were moments away from dying in our sleep, only to become another carbon-monoxide statistic.

The time was now nearly 2:00 a.m., and I was close to losing consciousness once more. In the thirty minutes that I'd tried in vain to awaken my siblings and mother and then question my father by phone, my lungs and my body were rapidly suffocating from a lack of oxygen. I had no idea that I was dying and would soon succumb to the ravages done to my body. Weak though I was, I tried once again to no avail to bring my mother out of her unconsciousness in an effort to inform her of my father's phone commentary. We were all but mere moments away from our final moments to live in this world.

It was at that very moment that I sensed an unimaginable calmness as the will of God went coursing through my lungs, through my heart, and through my mind. No, I didn't understand it then, but you can judge for yourself based on what happened next.

With absolutely no understanding of why I felt compelled to do so, I began opening each and every window in the downstairs portion of our home. Why would that be such a miracle one may ask? Well I was only a small eight-year-old child who did not have the strength or the ability even under the best of circumstances to open the old warped windows of our home. Somehow, though on that very night, I was somehow able to crack open all of the belligerent windows. Remember also that for some miraculously strange reason, I was opening all of these windows during a raging snowstorm with extreme subzero temperatures. What young child would even think to do something such as that without some form of divine guidance?

As I continued forward on that night, I wondered to myself at what could be guiding me as I clambered up the steps to our upstairs bedrooms. I suddenly was somehow given the strength to pull my unconscious brother from his bed as I literally dragged him along the floor and as carefully as possible lowered him step by step down the treacherous stairway. It seemed to take forever, but somehow, I was able to get my brother into my mother's bed.

Moments later, I repeated the same process by making my way back to my sister's upstairs bedroom. With nearly all the energy left in my small body, I pulled Julie out of her bed and dragged her along the floor to the stairway. Before long, I had Julie lying alongside my brother on my mother's bed.

Outside the strong blustery winds from the snowstorm and literally the breath of God were helping to push the frigid, yet fresh air into our home. Hope started to swell in my heart as first my mother, then my siblings started to regain semiconsciousness. I vividly recall my mother whispering, "Scott, for God's sake, why on earth do you have all the windows opened up in the house? Can't you tell that it is freezing in here?" I suddenly was aware that all of our teeth were chattering.

I went on to inform my mother of exactly what the phone conversation with my father was about. Then I confessed to her that I didn't know why we were all so sick, but it simply seemed reasonable to me that we all needed some fresh air! As the toxins from the deadly air within our lungs retracted, we snuggled down ever deeper under the covers of our mother's bed and relished in the loving body heat we all shared with each other in order to stay warm.

As the horrors of that night elapsed into the quiet calm of a sunny, yet snowy new day, we all waited patiently for the arrival of my father's return from his job. A couple of times throughout the night, he had called to find out how his family was doing. Although neither he nor any of us at the time knew anything about what had caused our near-death experience, we were simply happy to inform him that with some fresh air in the house we all felt much better.

Just as my father had suspected, the storm had created havoc on the rural roads near our farmstead and throughout the area. The snowdrifts on the road were so high in fact that the traditional snowplow trucks were unable to clear a path to our farm. My father had to endure still more delays as the county highway department next had to commission a large dozer to be hauled out and then used to at last clear the mountain of snow from our impassible roadway.

It is as though it were yesterday as we watched my father park his pickup truck at the far end of our snow-plugged driveway, then trudge his way up our driveway to our house. What a glorious moment when he burst through the door and shouted, "I'm finally home, but why in heaven's name is it so cold inside this house? Is the furnace not working and why are all the windows open?" At the time, none of us had many answers for his questions.

Before the hours of darkness fell again that evening, a heating and ventilation expert had been summoned to our home, and they determined the cause of our near demise along with correcting the improperly installed furnace exhaust pipe on the top of our home. As he was about to depart, he explained to my father, "With the back draft created from that exhaust pipe and from the lethal levels of carbon monoxide in your house last night, your family should have died. For whatever reasons they didn't, at least you don't have to prepare funerals for four loved ones."

On the day following one of the worst winter storms anyone could remember, my sister and I really got our wish to have a day off from school, but we were in such a weakened state of health following the carbon monoxide incident that we never actually stepped a foot outside.

Within days, most everything seemed to return back to normal in our lives. That is until one day my parents began thinking more about what had driven me to react in the way I did on that night. I can remember many days later when my father asked me to go around the downstairs of our home and open each of the windows just as I had done on the night that we nearly died. Try as I might, I was unable to open any of those same windows even by the slightest crack! Not only could I not open any of those old and warped windows, but it was not until I was many years older before I was finally able to open them without struggle.

So again I ask you to consider, just as I have so often throughout my life. How exactly does an eight-year-old child deep within the grasp of death suddenly have the strength to open a realm of nearly unmovable windows, and why would he attempt to open them anyway? How does that same young boy, so sickened, find a way to bring his little brother and sister into the life-sustaining air? Why has that young boy experienced three near-death experiences by his eighth birthday, yet he lives on?

When I reflect back on those memories, I have little doubt that my God was standing alongside me and guiding me.

Praise God for he shall not forsake you in your time of need.

MACHINERY MISHAP—10 YEARS

CHAPTER FIVE

And we know that God causes everything to work together for the good of those who love God and are called accordingly to his purpose for them.

—ROMANS 8:28

By the time I'd reached the age of ten, our family was well into our chosen farming lifestyle and occupation of animal agriculture and cropping production. Within the first few short years on our new farm, my folks had invested in some new barns and buildings to accommodate our vast array of livestock. I must share that the privilege of personally growing up on a farm with animals has been one of the highlights of my entire existence.

Our animal menagerie included the standard pet critters consisting of a couple of loving dogs and a host of independent cats to keep the rodent population at bay. Some of the other animals that also took up residence at our farm were ponies, horses, beef cows and calves, dairy cows, pigs, and chickens. It was an occurrence working one day with our chickens that provided the impetus for my next tale.

Along with any livestock and grain farm comes the necessity for the required tractors and the machinery equipment to care for and to feed the animals. Much of this same equipment was also needed to produce and harvest the feed for our animals.

An often unspoken fact that goes along with the responsibilities of feeding and caring for animals is the requirements for removal of their excrement. Anyone who has shared the friendship of a dog or a cat understands that what goes in an animal's mouth must at some point come out the other end. Urban folks have cute little pooper scoopers for their dogs or kitty litter boxes for their cats in their efforts to manage their animal waste products. Farmers also must manage their animal waste as well only in a much greater fashion. It would make only sense that the more massive an animal or the bigger the group of animals, then the larger the effort needed to recycle their organic waste materials. Farmers don't term this animal waste material as "poop" or "litter," but rather, it is considered organic fertilizer or often termed simply as manure. On the farm, manure is an odiferous, unsightly product that truly has high levels of nutrient value when spread upon the farmer's fields. Since manure is naturally organic, it easily breaks down, and it's nutrients absorbed by grain plant roots as a form of plant food fertilizer. This method of manure waste recycling has been occurring since the beginning of human history in our efforts to grow edible foods from the soil.

The most significant difference between the waste disposal for an urban dweller with, let's say, a very large dog and a farmer with various forms of animal livestock lies in the vast quantities of animal "poop"! Now anyone would agree that a person sharing the companionship of a large dog must surely deal with that dog's large appetite for dog food and must then also deal with some seriously large droppings as an aftermath. Those canine droppings require attention and removal to avoid an irritation with other folks who might not be too thrilled to step in someone else's "doggy-doo-doo."

On the farm, all of these same factors are in place, except animal size and animal numbers must be factored in for removal of their bodily waste materials. Size is certainly an issue to be considered. For instance, consider that in order for someone to buy their gallon jug of milk from the grocery store, it takes a one-thousand-five-hundred-pound dairy cow going through several physiological processes in order to manufacture this wholesome dairy product for our human consumption. First, this large cow must eat about fifty to seventy-five pounds of food per day along with drinking between twenty-five and forty gallons of water per day. As a result, this one dairy cow produces a much greater mass of "poop" or manure than the large dog from my previous example.

For those reasons and because farmers have far more than just a couple of companion animals in their care, a livestock farmer will nearly always have a chore tractor attached to a specialized waste handling machine called a manure spreader. This equipment is then used to assist with the disposal of the large quantities of animal manure out to the fields for organic recycling to occur.

Most manure spreaders are hooked to a powerful tractor. This unique piece of farm equipment is often a large rectangular metal or wooden box and is most often purchased in various size capacities ranging from one hundred to five hundred bushels of volume. This specific model of manure spreader will then have a moving conveyor apron chain mounted onto the floor inside of the spreader. Once the manure spreader was loaded with animal waste and driven out to the field, the farmer would then engage the manure spreader gears from the tractor, which then in turn ratcheted the manure on the apron chain to the back of the spreader for removal. At the very back of the manure spreader was a set of large metal beaters or fanlike blades that spun around at a very high velocity. The role of these beaters was to break up the animal waste into a fine film and ultimately spread the organic fertilizer evenly across a wide swath of tillable soil.

By the time I was ten years old, a definitive pattern had been established for me being the eldest son of a farmer. Each and every day it seemed that I was given more chores and greater responsibilities on our farm. All throughout the school week, we got up early as a family to do our early morning farm chores. Then by 7:00 a.m., we'd had breakfast, cleaned up, and changed into our school clothing by the time we were picked up by the school bus at the end of our driveway. Every afternoon following a long day attending school, that same bus would always bring us back to the farm by 4:00 p.m. My siblings and I would then quickly change into our farm clothing and scurry outside to do our designated farm chores. Each evening by suppertime we were summoned back to the house. Supper was never determined by a set time on most farms, but rather families would eat early or late depending on what extra chores or troubles might be encountered on the farm on any given day.

Following supper, we would usually do our homework until it was time to head off to bed. A little thought-about fact is how great the differences are between bedtime for a farm kid and bedtime for an urban kid. Parents often struggle to get their urban children off to bed each night. Their kids want to watch one more show on the television, or they want to play an electronic game for a few more minutes for example. Farm-raised children on the other hand often have a vastly different attitude regarding bedtime. Speaking from experience, my siblings and I heartily welcomed bed rest every evening, knowing that the next morning would only bring about another long, arduous day with the rising of the early morning sun.

As children, we were usually thrilled to not have to go to school on our cherished weekends, but we knew that most of our urban-raised friends were lazily sleeping in on their days away from school. Farm kids on the other hand were getting up at the crack of dawn doing their share of the required work that it takes to feed the people of the world.

By ten years of age, I'd become accustomed to the demands and expectations that my parents placed on their firstborn son. Since I was the oldest child, it was most often me and my father working side by side outside on the farm chores while my younger siblings were left inside our home to be tended by our mother. My father had invested much of his time in teaching me how to safely drive and operate our tractors and farm machinery. Thinking back and knowing the dangers of such equipment makes it seem surreal that at such a young age I was carrying so much responsibility. There is little doubt, though, that those years shaped my being, developed my strong work ethic, and helped set my course in life.

*   *   *

Waking up early on that cold Saturday day in December was like so many other weekend days while growing up on a farm. I'd already been instructed by my father the evening before to get myself off to bed early because we were rising very early the next morning to clean the manure from our large chicken building. I knew from prior experience that this was a monumental task requiring hard, physical labor for the better part of the entire day to complete the task. I was all too familiar with this process because we had to hand scoop the manure from our several thousand chickens each and every weekend.

Ours was not the modern-day mechanized livestock operations so often the case today, but rather one requiring a long, backbreaking effort from my father and me every weekend in order to complete our task. We would first hook up the big manure spreader to the tractor, and then park it outside the door of our egg-laying chicken building. Next, my father and I would each take our wheelbarrows and shovels to begin our tedious task. Obviously, my father had a larger wheelbarrow with a bigger shovel, and due to my young age and small size, I had proportionately smaller sized waste-removal equipment.

None the same, we toiled hour after hour filling our wheelbarrows, and then pushing them through the door of the building and up to the manure spreader. From there we would scoop out the manure from our wheelbarrows with our shovels and throw the waste up over the top and into the manure spreader. Although it was subzero temperatures outside on that frigid December morning, we still unbundled and removed much of our winter clothing as we perspired heavily through all of our work.

After several monotonous trips back and forth to empty the contents of our wheelbarrows into the waiting manure spreader, the machine would eventually fill to capacity. Previously, up until that day, my father would always hop up in the tractor and drive off to spread the manure in the fields while I would run back to our house for a much-needed breather and perhaps ingest a freshly baked cookie. It was on that cold December weekend day that my father looked at me and said, "Scott, you're old enough now that I think the time has come for you to learn to spread the manure on the fields by yourself. That will then free up some of my time to complete a few of the other farm chores while you are out in the field."

This may appear to be a shocking level of responsibility to put on such a young ten-year-old farm boy, but I assure you that every youngster who grows up on a farm ultimately wants and desires the day when they can graduate up to the next level of responsibility by operating a different piece of farm equipment. For the first load of manure that day, my father went with me as I drove the tractor and manure spreader out to the field. He talked me through the entire process of where to drive the tractor, which gear to have the tractor in, how fast to set the engine throttle speed at, how to engage the manure spreader gears in order to empty the spreader, and so on. I remember thinking how easy it seemed when watching my father do all these complex tasks, but suddenly, it all became almost too overwhelming for me to absorb.

Nonetheless, following my lesson, my father was satisfied that I knew what to do, and he was very complimentary of how well I'd done as I drove the two of us with the emptied spreader back down the road and into our farmyard.

Following another arduous session with our wheelbarrows and shovels inside the chicken building, the manure spreader was once again filled to the brim. It was finally time for my initial solo attempt at spreading manure. Although hot and sweaty, I put first put on my thickly quilted sweatshirt, followed by my extra thick winter coat. With the below zero outside temperatures, all of these clothes were essential when preparing to drive a tractor in the open wintery air. Some tractors have heated cabs, but our tractor at the time did not; so although I felt warm enough from my many layers of clothing, it made for some challenges when trying to get up on the big tractor and to move freely enough to operate the equipment.

My father smiled and waved at me as I cautiously put the tractor in gear and started toward the field to empty the contents of the manure spreader. There was little else on my mind other than to try to make my father proud of his son. I was a bit apprehensive as I tried to envision all the many processes that I soon had to do in an effort to safely and successfully operate this large new piece of farm equipment.

Everything was working fine and moving along like clockwork that morning. I'd driven the tractor and the fully loaded manure spreader down the road and into the field adjoining our farmstead. Once in the field, I placed the tractor into the proper gear. Next, I activated the spreader gears, set the engine throttle to the proper speed, while slowly letting the clutch out. I swelled with pride as the tractor moved forward, and I looked back to see the fertile organic material being spread so nicely and evenly across the field. I took a quick peek back to our farmyard and noticed my father waving his approval at me as he ducked into one of our barns to do some chores. Everything was working fine and moving along like clockwork until . . .

Suddenly, to my rear, I heard a very loud crack that rifled through the blustery December air. I immediately looked back toward where the sound had emitted, but everything was still working fine as the tractor pulled the spreader along. I took another quick glance toward our farmyard to see if my father was watching. Since I could not see him and just to be sure, I briefly stopped the tractor and disengaged the spreader gears so that I could take a quick walk around the equipment. Surely whatever made such a loud snap would show up as a broken part on the spreader. Look as I could, there was nothing out of the ordinary, so I mounted the tractor once more and continued on with my manure spreading task at hand.

Within a few more short moments after getting back on the tractor, I nearly lost my life.

Although there had been no outward signs of equipment breakage on the spreader, something had broken and was destined to permanently end my life. As mentioned earlier, one of the main functions of a manure spreader is how it utilizes a conveyer apron chain, which then moves the heavy load of manure back toward the rapidly spinning metal beater blades in the back end of the machine. Since everything was still working okay following the loud snap that had occurred, I drove unsuspectingly onward with the tractor. Unknown to me was that the loud snap was in fact the result of one of the apron chain's steel connecting links completely fracturing. There was no way to know this detail since the spreader was still nearly full of manure and because there was no way to view the equipment failure that had just happened to the one side of the apron.

A lethal set of events began unfolding as the spreader gears kept ratcheting but were only moving the unbroken portion of apron chain toward the speeding metal beater blades. All seemed normal as the manure kept unloading, but underneath all the manure on the inside of the spreader, the broken apron chain started to pile up in a mass of twisted metal parts.

What happened next left me with an indelible impression that there can be no doubt that God's helping hand can be a saving grace.

For no known reasons and which still intrigues my family and me yet to this day, I suddenly did something one would not expect. For starters, one should always sit upon the tractor seat while operating such a large and dangerous piece of equipment. This would be especially true for a small young boy perhaps trying to handle such machinery before he might even be completely physically capable of doing so. For reasons only my Lord understands, I suddenly stood up while operating the moving tractor and manure spreader. At that precise moment, the broken apron chain had finally piled up inside the spreader at the back end by the flailing large metal beater blades. With a tremendous amount of torque, one of the beater blades struck the disabled heap of apron chain, and then broke off, hurling it toward me at a deadly speed.

For no explainable reason and just an instant before the impact I had stood up, just as I was hit in my back by such a damaging force that I was thrown clean over the top of the moving tractor's steering wheel. I landed on top of the tractor's hood precariously dangling above the treacherously rotating wheels and screeching engine. The impact was as though I'd been smashed in my back with the deadly blow from an axe and was so harsh that it knocked the breath out of me, leaving me dazed to say the least. Somehow in terror and while gasping for breath, I found enough inner strength to clasp onto the hood of the moving tractor in a valiant effort to keep from falling under the wheels of the tractor or having my hands and arms pulled into the various belts on the engine.

How I accomplished this, I'll never fully understand, but somehow on that moving operatorless tractor, I dragged myself back along the top of the tractor, pulled myself over the steering wheel, and fell back onto the seat that I'd been sitting on only moments earlier. Although at the time I still had no idea what had actually happened to me, I had the fortitude to immediately disengage the severely damaged manure spreader and then to finally bring the tractor to a complete stop.

It was nearly impossible to climb down from the tractor seat because of the pain emanating from deep within my back and shoulders. Upon reaching the ground, I gritted my teeth as I agonizingly walked around the equipment once again seeking an answer to what had just happened. This time I surveyed the damage to the metal beaters and found the gap where the broken beater blade had been. A moment later, I discovered the broken blade that had nearly killed me lying in the snow on the field alongside the tractor. I gathered the broken section and then gingerly crawled back onto the tractor seat.

As I departed the field and pulled into the farmyard with the remaining load of manure in tow, my father viewed me with a questionable expression on his face. Within moments, he soon understood what had happened to the manure spreader and to me. I had tears streaming from my eyes as I proclaimed how much my back was hurt. My father quickly brought me into our house so he and my mother could survey the wrath that my body had incurred. With careful assistance from both of my parents, my bulky winter coat was carefully removed. Next, since I was having difficulty raising my arms, they aided me out of my thick sweatshirt. Finally, with their help, they removed my flannel shirt and disrobed me of my long winter underwear top.

My parents gasped simultaneously as they saw for the first time the telltale marks that had been so mercilessly inflicted upon my shoulder blades and along my back. The jagged metal manure spreader beater blade had hit me with such blunt force that by the following day the entire top half of my back massively bruised with a grotesque black-and-blue hue.

It was shortly after my parents first viewed my injured back that I was hustled into their car and transported to the hospital emergency room to receive the first x-rays in my life along with a complete doctor's examination. Thankfully, through all of trauma that my body just endured, I somehow hadn't broken any bones or caused any severe internal damage to my heart or lungs. As we departed the examining room, the doctor exclaimed to me, "Son, you must have a guardian angel watching over you!"

With that thought in mind, my folks started adding up all of the pieces from that nearly fatal day once they'd come to the realization that their eldest child by the mere age of ten had already somehow miraculously cheated death for a fourth time.

It is as though yesterday when I first heard my father proclaim a statement that penetrated my ears for the very first time, "Scott, you must have the nine lives of a cat." Over and over again in my lifetime this phrase has been uttered to me, but it was at that moment where I heard it for the first time from my father's reflective words. It was my mother's words that followed as she breathed a massive sigh of relief, "Scott, you must be a specially blessed child of God because few children could have as many encounters with death as what you've had by such a young age, yet still survive."

Our family has always shared a strong faith and a deep reverence for God. Following this incident that nearly took my life, once again, we surmised that God truly had watched over me that day. Imagine if you will the unbelievable circumstances that had to be reconciled in order for that farming accident to not have claimed my life.

Shortly following that accident, many questions arose, which I've spent my entire lifetime reflecting over. Why for some unknown reason did I stand up while driving the tractor, standing up only a split second before being hit with an unseen and deadly force from behind? Had I remained sitting, as I'd always been instructed to do by my father's orders, the speeding metal projectile would have then most assuredly struck me directly in the back of my head with enough blunt force trauma to instantly kill me for sure. Why was I lucky enough on that day for it to be so cold that I had to wear massive amounts of winter clothing which in the end absorbed much of the force of the impact? Had I worn any less clothing, my spine would surely have been severed, leaving me dead or at the very least in a paralyzed state. Upon impact and although injured, why was I thrown forward onto the hood of a moving tractor and not thrown off the tractor and under the massive revolving wheels?

Some would say I had a case of simple luck while others might assume fate took hold of my life that day. For my family and me, we believe with all of our souls that there can be simply little doubt about the helping hand of God blessing our lives that day.

HORSE KICKED DEBACLE—15 YEARS

CHAPTER SIX

We are pressed on every side by trouble, but we are not crushed.
We are perplexed, but not driven to despair. We are hunted down,
but never abandoned by God. We get knocked down, but we are
not destroyed.

—2 CORINTHIANS 4:8-9

Amazing as it may seem, by the time I had reached only my fifteenth year of life, I would soon be staring in the face of death for an implausible fifth time, yet live on to tell about that harrowing experience. With the encounter from my fifth near-death peril, I fractured my first skeletal bone as a result. At the time, my father was forever teasing me by claiming, "We are sure lucky that I have my job working for the Mayo Clinic with my free medical care benefit so that our family won't go broke paying for all of Scott's medical bills."

Following my fifth death-evading experience, it was surprising that I hadn't fractured more bones up until that point, even though I had required hospital emergency room visits for three out of the total five incidents. The first visit had necessitated stomach pumping at the emergency room for poisoning. The second visit had required x-rays for a possible broken back. My third urgent hospital emergency room visit had demanded more x-rays to determine my possible skull fractures, discover my broken nose, and determine brain-concussion damage.

Growing up on the farm provided my family and me with a lot of different animals to love and care for. My siblings and I were continually enjoying our special moments playing with and enjoying the pleasures that animals and humans so often share together.

By the time I had reached the age of fifteen, our family had expanded to its final scope of five children. My little sisters, Sally and Marcia, became instant favorites of their older brothers and sister. With their addition to our family, I was a big brother to three sisters and one brother. Except for me, all my siblings were satisfied with traditional animal relationships while growing up on the farm. They gave and received a lot of love and affections for our dogs and cats but enjoyed their interactions with the cattle, pigs, and chicken farm animals as well. I, on the other hand, migrated toward a more noble specie of animal that is historically exalted for its speed, its endurance, and its fire. I was the sole member of my entire family that desired to have a relationship with a horse.

Within our family, everyone seemed to have a negative opinion about me owning a horse. My father would say, "They are nothing but hay burners and on our farm if they can't pay for their way, then they shouldn't be around the place." My mother never failed to remark, "Horses are so dangerous and unpredictable, Scott. You don't need another reason to find a way to kill yourself." (She wasn't kidding when she said that!) All my siblings were in agreement with comments such as, "We agree with Mom and Dad. Horses scare us."

Undeterred and still on my mission to enjoy the pleasures of an equine, my folks had finally allowed me to initially have and care for two ponies a couple of years earlier. By my teen years, I'd quickly outgrown those ponies; and through constant pleading, I'd finally worn my folks down enough that they allowed me to move up from my two ponies to owning a full-sized horse.

I remember it as though yesterday when I saddled Dixie for the first time. As I eased myself into the saddle and grasped the bridle reins to guide her, I lightly nudged her with my knees. We immediately went effortlessly down our driveway. I steered Dixie down the road at a trot and then reined her into one of our open fields. This time I nudged her a little more firmly, and suddenly, she opened up into a high-speed gallop, which was an exhilarating experience like none other I'd ever felt before. We covered the entire distance of the field in a flash.

Although I'd loved and enjoyed the company of my much smaller ponies, it was beyond description how a full-sized horse could send adrenaline coursing through my veins. In the days and weeks to come, Dixie and I became inseparable as we explored every field, every forest, and every river for many miles around. With every free moment that my parents would allow me to be away from our farm chores, I would be off riding my beloved horse, Dixie.

She was so much a part of my being that a simple whistle from me would bring her running in from the rolling green pasture as she pranced with excitement in hopes of going out on another adventure with me. Feeding all of our other animals on the farm was called doing chores for a reason since it was monotonous and difficult work each and every day. Feeding and taking care of Dixie was just the very opposite in my frame of mind. Here was a beautiful steed that was willing to give her every effort to please me. She seldom tired as we journeyed for miles and never balked at my wishes to cross a deep river or climb a rocky incline. Taking care of Dixie was certainly no chore as with our other animals because even though in my father's eyes she was a hay burner, none of our other animals that were paying for their keep could compare to the pure pleasures shared by my best animal friend, Dixie.

Over the course of time, Dixie and I became almost as one. She knew me and I knew her better than I'd ever known another human being or even anyone else within my family for that matter. For that reason and as the best animal friend that I'd ever encountered, I was nearly devastated one day when I discovered that my dear Dixie had injured herself. She somehow acquired a deep, open wound just above the hoof on her right rear leg.

In no time, I pleaded with my father to summon the veterinarian to our farm to examine the damage Dixie had inflicted upon herself. While waiting for the veterinarian to arrive, I placed a halter and lead rope on Dixie and then tied her up to a post. It brought tears to my eyes to watch my animal friend standing on only three legs and simply unable to put any weight on her injured back leg. Before long, I could detect the dust coming from behind the veterinarian's truck as he raced down the rural gravel road leading to our farm.

Fear gripped my heart as he slowly walked toward Dixie, shaking his head from side to side. Doc calmly stated, "Well, from here it doesn't look too good. Anytime a horse cuts that part of their leg, at the best we have to deal with infection and at the worst she may have torn her Achilles tendon, in which case she will have to be put down."

"Put down!" I shouted back, "You mean we might have to kill her!"

My father caught up to me and caringly squeezed the top of my shoulder, saying, "Scott, a horse with an injured leg will usually only further injure themselves, and if the tendon in her leg is severed, it would be cruel to try to keep her alive."

Never in my life had I felt so ill in my stomach. I began silently praying to God asking to spare Dixie's life.

As my father held tightly to Dixie's halter and rope, I stationed myself as close to our veterinarian as possible. He cautiously reached out for the injured leg of my horse. As a bolt of pain shot through her leg, she forcefully pulled back. Having experience in such matters, however, Doc held on until she steadied herself. Suddenly as though Dixie became aware of his healing powers, she relaxed and allowed him to completely examine her injury. Doc used a bucket with some disinfectant to first cleanse the deep gash above her hoof, then he probed inside the wound with his fingers. I looked toward Dixie's head and noticed that she was wide-eyed with her nostrils flared, yet she remained relatively calm to handle.

At last Doc proclaimed, "This is hard to believe, but she missed cutting her tendon by only a fraction of an inch." Then turning to me, he directed, "Scott, we won't have to put her down, but you will need to work very hard for next several days to stop her wound from getting infected." He went on to instruct me on how much antibiotic injection that I needed to administer as well as how to clean and disinfect the wound each day. Finally, Doc said, "The worst problem is that this is now fly season, so every day you will have to spray some fly deterrent on her wound or else she will get maggots crawling around inside that gash and that won't be a good situation."

I was so relieved by the doc's good news and hearing that I wouldn't have to endure the agony of watching Dixie be put to death. Going forward with the plan, my father and I already had a complete understanding when it came to any kind of care demanded from a horse. Since my father did not particularly appreciate any kind of horse, and since no one else in my family did either, it was simply implied that it would only be me providing the care that Dixie would require.

Each day, I would repeat the same process in my care for Dixie's wound. I would tie her halter and lead rope to a post, and then go about lifting her injured rear leg. I would first scrub the wound with disinfectant, and then place some antibiotic wound dressing on the cut, followed by a spray of fly deterrent. Lastly, I would give Dixie her antibiotic injection with a needle and syringe into the muscle of her rump. Each day was repeated just as the day before. It was simply amazing how fast my horse was healing, and I knew that before long she would be completely healed. Soon we would be able to venture out on our joyous rides together again.

About two weeks following her initial leg injury, I summoned my father to assist me with a portion of her treatment. My father remarked, "Scott, we agreed that you were responsible for Dixie's care, so why are you asking for my help all of a sudden?" I replied back, "Dad, I already did everything with her today, but I forgot to spray on the fly deterrent. I don't want to tie her up again, so could you simply hold her halter for a few seconds and then we will be done?"

My father grudgingly followed my lead while insisting, "This had better not take too long because I have a lot of farm work that needs attending!"

After making our way into the horse pen, just as we had agreed, my father held tightly to Dixie's halter as I walked around to the back of her legs, preparing to spray the fly deterrent on her rapidly healing wound.

What I did next can only be explained as sheer stupidity. First, though one must understand that I spent so much time caring and loving my horse that I considered her almost a part of me. She was my best friend and in my heart I felt there was nothing either of us wouldn't do for the other. In my mind, it was unfathomable that my horse could in any way harm me. For those reasons, I failed to remember one critical danger factor regarding a horse. They can strike with deadly force when kicking with their rear legs.

Although it may be too hard to comprehend, what I did next was beyond redemption. As my father watched, I kneeled down immediately behind Dixie's rear legs. While on my hands and knees merely a couple of feet away from her potentially lethal rear hooves, I reached forward with my spray can of fly deterrent and sprayed her wound.

I remember little else from that day, but this is the rest of the story as described by my father to me.

In a split instant just as the stinging fly spray hit her wound, Dixie reacted out of pure instinct just as any horse might have done. My father watched in shocked disbelief as she kicked straight back with her powerfully and deadly hoof, striking me squarely in the middle of my face. The impact was so great that I was thrown backward several feet through the air.

My father immediately let go of the horse's halter and terror gripped him as he witnessed the aftermath of my poor judgment. Not only was I lying unconscious in a crumpled heap, but blood was spurting from my badly injured nose. The eyeglasses that I'd been wearing were split in half and laying on either side of me with broken lenses.

The critical detail my father remembers most was that although he was originally convinced that I was dead; he reacted quickly once he could feel my pulse. In a flash, he picked up my limp body as he made his way toward a vehicle. Before long, both my parents with me in tow were in the vehicle flying toward the hospital emergency room in fright as they observed my struggle to breath from all the blood gushing from my face.

By the time we reached the emergency room, I had regained some level of consciousness; however, I had received such a severe concussion that even as of this day I still have no recall of being kicked in the face by my horse or even being taken to the hospital.

X-rays later determined just how lucky I had been. As I lay on the examining table in a complete stupor that day, my parents were given the doctor's diagnosis. He shared that it was beyond reason that I hadn't simply been killed. He likened the impact of the horse kick to my face as being the equivalent of a person being hit in the face with the powerful swing of a sledge hammer. He further indicated that nearly everyone would die instantly from such a blow. My parents were then informed about how the doctor had reset my severely fractured nose. They were surprised to learn that I'd somehow escaped fracturing my skull, although it was unclear as to what the overall effects of my concussion would bring in the future.

The following day, as my mind began clearing, I began to realize what a frightening sight I'd become when I looked into the mirror. I joked that it was too bad the kick in my face had not occurred closer to Halloween time because within a couple of days following my injury, my swollen, bruised, and bandaged face was demonstrably more horrifying than any Halloween mask could ever have been.

My poor parents were really starting to wonder about me. They had five total children, but only their eldest child seemed to be destined to kill himself. They wondered how it was possible to have five offspring, yet only one faced death and severe injury on an all too regular basis.

What directly impacted me as a result of that horrible day is that I learned to think and think hard before acting. I learned that not everything may be as it appears to be. I learned that no matter how gentle and loving an animal may be, they are still powerful enough to kill a person in an instant. I learned that for whatever reasons the good Lord puts me through such painful tests, he grants me the will and strength to live on.

The final sentence of the 2 Corinthians scripture, which I selected for the beginning of this chapter, describes it best. *We get knocked down, but we are not destroyed.*

CRUSHING LOAD DISASTER—16 YEARS

CHAPTER SEVEN

Commit your actions to the Lord, and your plans will succeed.
—PROVERBS 16:3

For whatever reasons my Lord decided that I was someone with a need to be tested, as the challenges I faced began escalating over the next few years of my life. During my first fifteen years of existence, I'd cheated death a total of five times. Certainly more than any average person might encounter within an entire lifetime, yet during the subsequent short span of time from my sixteenth until my twenty-first birthdays, I remarkably looked into the face of death an additional four more times. If I really was blessed with nine lives, then I was surely burning through them at an ever-quickening pace.

Did my faith ever falter because of all of those harrowing circumstances one might ask? Was I becoming a pest unto my Lord by continually asking my Creator through prayer, why me? Did I think for even a moment about giving up on my spiritual beliefs because of the sheer amount of challenges I continually encountered?

My honest and most sincere answer to all those questions is resoundingly NO! Throughout the entire span of my lifetime, I've simply continued on with the same zest that I've always held for life. I accepted long ago that with my ambition toward the less-safe havens of life would at times place me in harm's way. I have always sensed that my God was with me at all times and never once have I felt that I was being forsaken or left on my own to deal with my ensuing struggles or suffering from injury and pain.

In analyzing the root cause and scope of my lifetime total of twenty-seven exposures with cheating death, specifically ten of those occurrences happened as a direct result of my lifetime affiliation with the occupation of farming. A documented fact is that farming is the number one most hazardous occupation in America. All the other top-ranked dangerous occupations such as firefighting, mining, and law enforcement fall below farming for death exposure and infliction of tragic injuries.

It was early spring during my sixteenth year when my father requested the help of his firstborn son to complete a must-needed task on our farm. What a glorious, sunny, and bright springtime day it was as the wintery white snows had finally succumbed to the bursting new springtime on our farm. We took great pleasure in viewing the demise of our harsh Minnesota winter as everything around us evolved into sweet-smelling flower blossoms, luscious green shoots of grass, and singing birds fluttering among the budding trees.

One of our main livestock farming enterprises was caring for our Hereford beef cow and calf operation. The same process occurred each year with our herd of white-faced beef cattle. Our cow herd would spend their winter huddled within the confines of the beef cow yard. Within the limitations of this fenced in lot, they had shelter along with abundant food and water. Each pregnant and gestating beef cow would then provide the miracle of birth to the most adorable calves just prior to springtime every year. It would bring smiles of joy to my family's faces to watch the happy little calves scamper around the cow yard while being chased after by their concerned mother cows.

With winter at last turning into spring, the lush green grasses of our fertile pastures would begin to turn the mundane and lackluster grassland into a beautiful Eden. Each spring about this time our cow herd would look forlornly at their pasture as if to wonder if they would ever be released to the superb greenery of the rolling pasture.

Spectacular as it was, our cattle pasture held one major concern for my father. Splitting the pasture was a meandering creek that by late summer was only a mere trickle. The problem that developed in the springtime, however, was that with all the rainfall, our creek constantly became more of an outright river with fast-moving, swirling waters. Each spring as we released the cows and their calves into the pasture for the duration of the spring, summer, and fall, the swollen creek annually became a hazard to our cows and their baby calves. It was not uncommon to view some of the cows being able to cross over to the other side of the pasture while a several other cows and all of the calves remained on the near side of the watery barrier. More than once, we had cows or calves get mired into the thick mud of the creek trying to find a path to cross. It was never a good result when a mother cow ended up on one side of the water while her baby calf remained on the other side bawling at the top of its lungs.

After much time in thought, my father had finally determined that we would install a cement cattle-crossing bridge over the creek so at last our cattle would be able to safely cross over.

We woke early that Saturday morning as always and had our hearty country breakfast while my father planned the entire day of farm chores and livestock-related activities for our family. It was determined that immediately following the animal feeding chores that morning, my father and I would finally fix the cattle crossing dilemma at the treacherous creek in the pasture.

A few weeks earlier, my father and I had disassembled a dilapidated cattle feed bunk, which had a concrete base. We had removed all the old twisted and rusty nails from the ancient lumber, which would in turn be recycled to make something else from wood one day on the farm. My father had remarked at that time that it would be a massive task to break up the large concrete slab of the old feed bunk with sledgehammers in order to dispose of the pieces. With further consideration, though, he surmised a solution to remedy our creek crossing dilemma for our cattle. My father determined that perhaps this cement slab would be just the correct size to be used as a creek-crossing bridge. What better use could this old chuck of useless concrete possibly hold since there was an obvious need? I remember how proud my father was as he proclaimed to my mother, "Now we won't even have to spend any money to construct a crossing bridge for the cattle."

Following our morning chores, my father fired up his tractor with the front-end loader bucket attached as he shouted to me, "Bring along two of our largest log chains to drag the concrete slab with." Doing as instructed, I made my way to the soon-to-be bridge with two heavy-duty chains in tow.

Our first task was to lift the large concrete slab high enough to wrap a chain around it. My father eased his tractor and loader up to the massive slab, and then hooked his tractor loader bucket underneath the slab as he attempted to raise the one end of the concrete piece. Unfortunately, the only item that moved, however, was the back wheels of my father's tractor being lifted completely off the ground much to his surprise.

With frustration in his voice, my father said, "This chuck of concrete must weigh over five tons if the tractor loader can't even budge it in the least!"

Not to be deterred, my father sent me after one of our large lift jacks. Once I'd returned, my father dug a hole just beneath the front end of the slab and then proceeded to hook the corner of the concrete slab with the lift jack and began pumping the handle. The sheer weight strained the heavy-duty lift jack with everything it could handle, but slowly a small portion of daylight developed underneath the concrete.

Next we quickly wrapped the heavy chain around it, removed the lift jack, and then hooked the chain to the hitch on the back of the tractor. I backed off a safe distance as my father engaged the tractor clutch only to have the tractor wheels spin a deep hole into the ground. The seemingly immovable object had in fact moved, but only a fraction. Unwilling to yield defeat, my father backed his tractor up ever so slightly, revved the engine speed ever higher, and then he lurched the tractor forward once again. This time the procrastinate object slid free, only to dig deeply into the ground and halting us once again as my father attempted to pull it forward with the tractor and chain.

Still unwilling to be outdone by such an abstinent object, my father further instructed me to round up several round wooden fence posts to be used as rollers for underneath the concrete slab. Once I'd returned with the posts, I was directed to carefully place one of them in front of the concrete slab whereby my father would then slowly drag the problematic slab forward and hopefully up over the top of the post. This actually worked perfectly, so after a couple of feet with the first post underneath the slab and finally finding a method for lifting it somewhat above the ground, I placed a second post. As my father pulled the giant concrete slab slowly forward, I placed yet another post, then another and so on as we slowly dragged the soon-to-be cattle bridge out of the farmyard, into the cattle pasture, and down to the creek.

In total, the weight of the five-ton concrete slab was evenly distributed underneath its mass by the four or five round wooden posts, which I kept revolving. As the slab moved forward enough, and a post that had rolled all the way from the front to the back, it allowed me to then pick it up and replace it back to the front of the concrete slab as we continued moving forward with our cattle-crossing bridge project.

Everything was going so well, but then again, I've indicated that same thought many times previously with not such positive outcomes.

My father was keeping a watchful eye toward me while maneuvering the tractor and concrete slab toward its final creek destination. I was completing my task with precisionlike timing as I revolved each wooden post coming out the back of the heavy slab and moving the post back up to the front. We had somehow managed to drag this massive object several hundred yards from its origin near the barnyard all the way to within just a few feet away from its final resting place when all at once I was in the wrong place at the wrong time once again!

In a blink of an eye, the corner of my shoe worn on my left foot suddenly somehow got caught underneath the round wooden post that I'd just placed underneath the front of the heavy slab. Instinctively, I tried jerking my shoe and foot free, but the massive weight per square inch of pressure that the five tons of concrete placed upon that round post was unyielding to any attempt at freeing me. Since we were so close to the creek at that moment, my father had been concentrating his vision in a forward direction and not back in my direction.

It happened so fast. As though entering the sequences of a bad nightmare, I tried to jerk my shoe free while screaming at my father to stop the tractor yet watching in horror as the indescribable crushing weight of that round post rolled over my leg and crashed me face first into the ground. Quicker than a heartbeat, my father heard my scream, stopped the tractor, and then turned around to see what all the commotion was about. In only a fraction of a second, the wooden post had rolled over the top of my foot, pancaked over my ankle, and then came to rest with intense downward force on the middle of my lower left leg. It was as though I'd been run over by one of those large highway steamroller machines used to flatten repaired road surfaces.

I simply cannot describe my feelings of despair as all the condensed weight pressing down upon that wooden post was suddenly crushing the life out of my leg, but even worse, I was gripped with fear trying to envision how we could possibly remove it from me at all. Not only had I fractured bones from this accident, but I'd also severely damaged all of my ligaments, my tendons, and my nerves in my lower leg. Time became of the essence as we faced the possible loss of my left leg since for whatever duration of time it took to remove the destructive object from my leg, was how much time would elapse with zero blood circulating through my leg!

My father literally flew off the tractor once he'd stopped its forward movement and knelt beside me. He looked at me in alarm as I lay underneath the crushing force of the concrete slab. There was little doubt in my mind or his that I was severely injured. I howled with the most bloodcurdling screams as I tried to endure more pain than I'd ever experienced before. In terror, I pleaded with my father to lift it off me. In his panic, he actually tried to lift on the wooden post in hopes that the adrenaline coursing through his veins would grant him the superhuman strength required to move it just far enough for me to slip out my injured leg. Obviously, since our large tractor loader hadn't been able to lift the massive weight, neither could my father, albeit he made a valiant effort trying.

As I lay there in excruciating pain, I was keenly aware that I was severely wounded, but the unyielding pressure from the condensed weight being placed on my leg was nearly unbearable to endure.

My father ran off screaming back at me, "I'm running over to Dick's farm across the road to see if he can help us get it off you." I could only pray that my father could quickly locate him and return before I lost consciousness.

During the time my father was tracking down our neighbor and locating a heavy lift jack, I lay alone and ensnared underneath a wretched unyielding object. All the while my father was absent, I grew evermore light-headed as I struggled to remain conscious. In my mind, I convinced myself that I had to do everything within my power to remain awake because I truly felt if I lost consciousness, my father and Dick would possibly pull my shattered leg clean off my body! The fear of that drove my mental state as I clawed away at the soil beneath me out of sheer agony. I waited to be rescued for ten minutes or more, yet it felt like hours to me. By the time my out-of-breath father and our neighbor arrived carrying a heavy-duty lift jack, I'd dug a sizable hole in the earth out of desperation and was in so much agony that I didn't even notice the bleeding from my fingertips where I'd ripped my finger nails to shreds clawing at the dirt.

The lift jack was placed under the wooden post near my crushed leg, but unbelievably the load was so heavy and the ground just soft enough, the jack would only sink into the ground rather than lift upward. My hopes were fading, and my will weakening as everything seemed to darken. I inched ever closer to passing out. Suddenly, my father ran over to near the creek and gathered a very large, flat rock which he then placed underneath the base of the lift jack. Even this large rock sank into the earth somewhat, but the lift jack was finally able to lift the post high enough above my leg for my father and Dick to pull me out from under the weight.

Oh what a tremendous relief it was when the massive pressure on my leg was at last released. I remember my father and Dick standing me up and hoisting me between their two strong shoulders to help support me as we journeyed out of the cattle pasture and toward a vehicle for another one of my all-too-often habit of requiring the services of a hospital emergency room.

I still chuckle when I remember back to my father asking, "Scott, try putting some weight on your left leg, perhaps you didn't break any bones?"

The fact is that my left ankle and leg was flopping around like a limp piece of overcooked spaghetti noodle, so I informed my overly optimistic father that it was most definitely broken and to please get me to the emergency room with no further delay.

I'm surprised that with all the times that my parents have sped on their way to transport me to various hospital emergency rooms over the years, that for some odd reason they have never received a speeding ticket from a law officer. Lord knows, they've had enough opportunities within their lifetimes, but perhaps God felt they had endured enough anguish and punishment from simply being my caregiving parents.

On the hurried route to the hospital that morning, although I was dealing with a great level of pain, I somehow found a way to remove the shoe from my shattered limb. Being the frugal farm kid that I was, I surmised that I didn't want the medical staff to cut my shoe off once we'd arrive at the hospital and thus destroy a perfectly good shoe. As I carefully tried to remove my own shoe, I instantly discovered what a mistake I was making and just how badly I'd injured my ankle as my ankle dislocated from out its ankle socket, sending a new bolt of pain surging through my body!

Once we arrived at the hospital emergency room, being an "old pro," I was all too familiar with the medical emergency room processes. First I was placed upon a hospital gurney so that I could easily be pushed from room to room. I was then injected with a sedative and some painkilling medication. Before long, my left leg had been x-rayed in every imaginable position. Finally, after the doctor set my fractured bones and checked my leg for deep tissue damage, I'd been admitted into a hospital room for what would become an indeterminate period of time.

The Mayo Clinic doctor assigned to my care was fortunately one of the leading orthopedic specialists and surgeons in the nation at the time. He leaned over me and counseled me on just how severely I'd injured my ankle and leg. He held up my x-rays for me to view as he outlined how I had completely shattered the ball and socket joint of my ankle joint as well as had fractured various bones within my lower left leg. He further described how he had reset my ankle and fractured bones, but he was not too optimistic that I would have a very good overall recovery to my traumatized limb.

As I lay in my hospital bed on that Saturday morning, I began to wonder how much school I would miss as a result of such a harsh injury. Being sixteen, I was also concerned about the effect on my abilities to participate in high school sports activities in the future.

I spent the remainder of that weekend in a hospital room alongside another patient who was in his eighties and was being treated for congestive heart failure. I tried to carry on a civil conversation with him, but our vast age difference left us with little to talk about. By my first full night in our room, I soon discovered just how nearly impossible it was to sleep during the night as well since the elderly gentleman emitted continual nocturnal sounds with his loud snoring and passing vast amounts of gas all throughout the night.

The doctor had left me on Saturday stating that he would stop by once again on Monday to further diagnose my condition and determine any further course of action. On his early morning rounds that Monday, true to his word, he stood by my bedside. Once again he was holding up x-rays of my leg injury with before x-rays and x-rays taken after he had set my fractured bones. He reflected that he was very concerned about allowing me to take a course of action to try to mend my injuries on my own merits without some form of surgical intervention. He went on to mention that without being able to surgically view and repair my injury; he simply had no way of knowing if my bones would ever heal properly or not.

After further consultation with my parents and me, we all agreed with the doctor that invasive surgery would most likely provide me the best opportunity to lead a normal life in the future. With no further delay, I was prepped for surgery that same afternoon. After gaining some alertness following my surgery, the doctor reviewed with my parents and I how absolutely correct the choice had been to go the surgical route. He indicated that once the incision was made and it was discovered just how rare my injury was, the Mayo Clinic medical staff had opted to film my procedure for future medical doctor training.

What he discovered was quite profound as his surgical incision exposed the inside of my damaged leg. When he had attempted to realign and set my broken bones and put my displaced ankle back into the joint only days earlier, a portion of my leg muscle had fallen between the fractures without showing up on the x-rays. The doctor shared that I would have been disabled for several months trying to recover from my injury, only to eventually discover that my bones would have been unable to heal with the misplaced leg muscle tissue blocking the skeletal healing process. He said that by electing to go immediately to the surgical process, he was able to make that fortunate discovery and was able to repair my fractures through the insertion of several stainless steel screws to reform my shattered ankle joint. The doctor was jubilant that I would now heal quickly and likely suffer few negative effects in the future.

In all I spent ten days recovering in the hospital following my major injury and surgery. Time flew by rapidly as I had countless friends and family visit me nearly every day. Even some of my high school teachers stopped by bringing my schoolbooks and assigned homework so that I wouldn't fall behind my classmates once I returned back to school. It was during my two-week stay at the hospital, however, which created one the funniest incidences to ever develop between my beloved father and me.

Remember that although my father was a farmer, he also had been working for many years on his secondary nighttime job with the Mayo Clinic as a urology technician. My father was very proud of the medical services that his skilled and specialized position provided to patients. A urology technician in a high-profile medical institution such as the Mayo Clinic holds an extremely important role. For instance, during the long night schedule that my father was working, he always remained on call to the hospital emergency room. Anytime during the night, he could be beckoned whenever an ambulance would bring in vehicular crash victims. Upon arrival, a highly specialized team of emergency medical experts, including my father, would work within their specific areas of expertise to save the life of any crash victim.

In order for the medical doctors to proceed with further diagnosis of injuries, as a urology technician, my father would be required to insert a urinary catheter into the crash victim in order to determine if there was any blood in their urine, thus possibly exposing potential kidney damage as a result of their accident. Over the years, my father was summoned to the emergency hospital room countless times to provide his services for all kinds of emergency urinary crisis, even with medical emergencies that were other than the result of a vehicle crash.

The typical role that my father provided each night on his rounds throughout the more than one thousand bed hospital was to complete the doctor-required catheterizations for patients. The primary reason why one might need the assistance of a urinary catheterization comes most often as a direct aftermath from one's surgery. Sharing from personal experience, I know that prior to surgery, one is restricted from food and fluid intake to clean the digestive tract. Often times, just prior to a major surgery, one is also given a rectal enema to clean out the lower intestinal tract. Then in the surgery room, the patient is anesthetized into a deep, comatose state to eliminate feeling any pain from the surgical procedure. During and following one's surgery, various medications and painkillers are administered intravenously. The next step in the process is one slowly and groggily wakes up in a surgical recovery room. For the next day or two after being transferred to ones' hospital room, only a small portion of liquid and solid food is consumed. One's system can be so ravaged from it all that, oftentimes, vomiting occurs as one tries to get their rebelling body back to some level of normalcy.

The final insult from the aftermath of surgery is that one's body needs to expel the IV fluids acquired throughout the process, but it is often times physiologically impossible to pass one's urine for a day or two following a major surgery. The doctor and nurses will literally tabulate the volume of liquids that went into a one's body through their IV, and if unable to pass a proportionate volume of urine, then a urology technician like my father makes his rounds during his work shift, completing patient catheterization to remedy the problem.

What creates such a humorous outcome to my story is a result of some of the tall tales that my father would share with me following some of his nights at work as we worked alongside each other on our farm. Although for confidential purposes he never shared any names, one can only imagine the famous movie stars, entertainers, professional boxers, and politicians to mention a few that my father had the privilege to serve and, yes, to physically handle their most private parts. It was and always has been against Mayo Clinic policy to discuss the names of the some of the world's most famous people who come to Rochester for their medical procedures.

What do I remember most about some of my father's recollections was saying something such as, "Men will often boast to other guys about how well endowed they are, but every time a urology technician is preparing a catheter tube for insertion, men then are crying to please use the smallest tube you have now as they claim to be rather petite in their endowment."

It is the evening following my afternoon leg surgery. I'm confined to my bed with my damaged leg heavily bandaged and elevated on some form of mechanical contraption. With an IV still attached to my vein, I tried to nibble on some solid food at suppertime, only to vomit it back up. I couldn't believe just how miserable my entire body felt and how much pain was emanating from my severely damaged appendage. The nurse had showed me how to reach over for the stainless steel bedpan if I had to vomit again since I'd made a mess all over myself during my earlier nausea. She also shared that based on the fluids that I'd received from my IVs, it was becoming dire for my need to pass some urine.

She pointed to the plastic urinal on the stand next to me and replied, "I know you've been trying to go, but it is often very difficult for the first couple of days."

She then said something that struck morbid terror into me as she mentioned, "I can feel that your bladder is much distended, and if you don't urinate by 10:30 p.m., then I'll have to request that you be catheterized."

As my eyes widened, she chuckled slightly when she commented, "Oh, I forgot, that would be your father, Dave, who will have to catheterize you, won't it?"

For the next couple of hours, I had a newfound urgency as I held my plastic urinal in place and worked harder at going pee than at any other time of my life. In my mind it was simply unacceptable to have my own father or any other urology technician for that matter catheterize me. I'd grown up hearing too many war stories from my father to become just another notch in his belt of urology achievements. I silently asked myself, "Why won't it come out as badly as my bladder hurts?"

Just like a fine-tuned precision clock, at exactly 10:30 p.m., my father pushed his urology medical cart into my room. He sauntered up alongside my bed and explained that the time had come for me to get catheterized.

In no uncertain terms, I responded back, "You will not touch me down there. I'd rather die first."

Suddenly, my father understood that what he had thought might simply result in a light-hearted moment was in fact cataclysmic to my way of thinking.

My father said, "Scott, there isn't anything to fear, and trust me, your bladder is so engorged right now that you could get very sick or even die if it ruptures from the pressure inside you."

I pleaded with my father to give me one more chance as I claimed that I could will my rebelling body into a response.

My father leaned over my bed and whispered in my ear so no one else could hear him say, "I'll make you this one-time deal. You keep trying to pass your urine while I make my first hospital rounds, but I'll be back in about forty-five minutes, and then I will be required to perform the procedure. If necessary, I'll have the nurse sedate you, and I'll be forced to catheterize you while you sleep, so I don't want any more foolishness when I return."

Before my father had even passed out the door of my hospital room, I was tightly holding my portable urinal and praying for some help. For the next several minutes, I dreamed of wet waterfalls of cascading water, I envisioned the sound of a flushing toilet, as I tried to will myself to pee. Huge beads of sweat formed on my forehead, and I'm not sure if I wasn't trying so hard that perhaps I even began sweating blood from my pores.

At long, long, long last, I felt the slightest drip, then I heard drip, drip, and finally a weak and pathetic stream of urine dribbled from out of my painfully engorged bladder. To put it bluntly, I peed and I peed and I peed some more. I could feel the hot liquid inside my plastic urinal as it pressed up against my thighs. Suddenly, I came to the realization that my quart-sized urinal was reaching the overflow mark. Keeping one hand on the urinal, I reached for my nurse call button with the other and rapidly pressed the emergency button over and over.

It soon became evident that help would not arrive in time, and I faced the dire choice of stopping my flow that I'd worked so hard to start and possibly resulting in another catheterization opportunity with my father or to continue on with total disregard for the mess it would create. The choice was easy as I made the decision to go on. My urinal first reached peak capacity and then started spilling over onto my clothing and bedding. Just as I finished wetting myself, I let out a huge sigh of relief and satisfaction overcame me just as the nurse scampered into my room. It didn't take her long to surmise what had happened.

I smiled at her and said, "I'm sixteen years old, and it sure feels good to wet my bed."

As promised, a short while later my father came marching into my room all serious and preparing to do his job. I'll never forget the disappointed expression on his face when he found out that I would not need his special services anymore. One can only imagine the humorous comments that have resulted over time from the events of that night in the hospital.

The next few weeks and months were not easy by any stretch of the imagination, but being a young, growing, teenage boy, my recovery progressed quite well. A youth at that age has an almost miraculous ability to heal fractured bones and damaged tissues. Since I was a strong, healthy farm boy, my physical therapy sessions for the weeks to come were very manageable in fact. In all, I spent about ten days recovering at the hospital and within a few short months albeit except for some very large surgical scars as permanent reminders on my left leg, I recovered back to 100 percent.

Though I would have many more surgeries in the years to come, following my first surgery, I was left with the comforting thought that both my father as well as my heavenly Father had both stood guard over me through it all.

TRACTOR TROUBLE—17 YEARS

CHAPTER EIGHT

The Lord your God will bless you in all your harvest and in all the work of your hands and your joy will be complete.
—DEUTERONOMY 16:15

Over the course of the previous year, I'd worked diligently to recover from my severe leg injuries obtained from our misaligned bridge episode. The doctor and my physical therapists were more than satisfied with my recovery, although the doctor warned me that as I aged I'd surely face future painful consequences from my injuries. I must admit, though, when a doctor informs a seventeen year of boy about his propensity for arthritis in one's damaged joints far into the future, it didn't result in much immediate impact.

The doctor confidently proclaimed, "Scott, you'll start suffering from arthritis and ankle joint pain well before old age sets in on the other portions of your body."

With that statement passing in through one of my ears and quickly exiting out of the other ear, I thought to myself, *What difference will that make since I won't likely live long enough to get old anyway?*

The day was overcast with more than a slight chill in the air for a typically late fall day in September. This was the time of the year when all the farmers in the area with livestock went about procuring and storing their corn silage for their animal's winter feed requirements. The fall season in Minnesota brings about an awareness that the frigid snows of winter will soon be coming just around the corner. On some of those dreary, cold and damp fall days, it would feel like one could never adapt to the onset of another winter gathering up force.

Several processes were required each year in order to procure enough feed for the cattle to survive the rigors of a Minnesota winter. Each springtime as the snows melted and the earth warmed, we would till our farm fields. Once the weeds were eliminated and the soil readied, we went about planting the corn seeds with our corn planter. As the seeds would germinate and the little corn plants would emerge, we crossed our fingers and pray to the heavens for timely rains to further their growth along. Over the next months, a few more passes would then be required to cultivate and provide crop protection applications for nutrient-stealing weeds or perhaps from plant-damaging insect infestations.

My father would always take me along for a walk into our corn fields exactly on the Fourth of July Independence Holiday to measure the growth of our corn.

Without fail, he always reiterated, "Scott, if the corn plants are at least knee-high by July 4, then we've done everything proper thus far and most surely a high-yielding crop will be forthcoming."

Every year, I made the assumption that my father and I were pretty good corn farmers because I never remember a year when the corn wasn't well above our knees by the date historically established to monitor our success.

During the hot, steaming days of summer, as the well-cared-for corn plants shot upward toward the sky, my father would jokingly proclaim, "The crop is doing so well that if you listen carefully, you can actually hear the corn growing when you stand out in the field."

As summer marched on, first the tall corn plants would begin making small ears while at the same time growing tassels at the top of each plant. In time, and under the right conditions, the corn field would pollinate; and as though magical, the barren and tiny ears would soon populate and swell with ever-growing and ripening kernels of corn. By fall each year, as the days shortened in length, the greenery of the lush corn fields would morph into an ever-browning field of drying maturing corn plants.

By this point on the calendar, each and every September, my father and I would have serviced and readied all of our silage harvesting equipment in preparation for our upcoming harvesting tasks. It took a massive amount of equipment for this harvesting process each year.

One of our first tasks was to connect our silage blower to one of our powerful tractors, then connect the blower to the large pipe running up the side of the tall cement silo. The next task involved my assistance to help my father hook another tractor up to the silage chopper machine, which in turn was hitched to a large silage chopper box used for blowing the chopped corn silage, once in operation, out in the field. Lastly, my father helped me hook up a third tractor to another empty silage chopper box so that I could bring it out to the field to switch with him every time that he'd filled up his silage chopper box.

With all the equipment readied and waiting, we took some final moisture tests of the corn plants to ensure that our silage was at the desired 65 percent moisture level. Seeing that it was, my father's voice would always rise a couple of octaves with excitement as he would announce, "All right, Scott, we've got cattle feed to harvest, so do your job like always."

My father and I would each mount our own respective powerful model 4020 John Deere diesel tractors and depart our farmyard in anticipation. The first field we always harvested each fall was also the one that was the farthest away. Being four miles away and driving tractors with a top highway gear of twenty miles per hour meant I had little time to waste in my assigned tasks to cover the distance.

The routine was always the same. My father would guide his big tractor with chopper and with wagon in tow up, and then down the rows of corn. From a distance away, one could hear the loud howling of the chopper as it ate ton after ton of corn plants. In one continuous motion, it chopped the plants into edible pieces for our cattle, and then blew the forage into the chopper box being pulled behind.

My job was just as important as I was expected to unhook the empty wagon from behind my tractor, and then unhook the full load of corn silage from behind my father. My father would then help me hook up to the full load, at which time I would in turn help my father hook up to the empty chopper box. Once completed, we would both speed off on our respective tractors whereby my father would begin filling another load, and I would scurry out of the field, drive as fast as possible the four mile span to our farm, unload the silage chopper box into the waiting silo blower, then scamper back once more with an empty box. If I wasted no time and nothing broke down, it was possible to keep my father waiting only briefly for my arrival.

Our multiple, large, cement-stave corn silage silos used for storing a one-year supply of cattle feed were sixty feet tall with an inside diameter of twenty feet. It took literally hundreds of tons of corn silage to fill a storage unit with such capacity. Each fall, my father and I would start the process of filling our silos with an excess of energy, but load after load, day after day would eventually take a toll on us as we fought exhaustion. We usually worked nonstop for seven to ten days in a row to harvest feed for our livestock.

It was critical to harvest the silage as quickly as possible because as each day passed by, the moisture levels kept dropping, thus lowering the palatability for our cattle. By the end, when our mission was completed each year, we had little left for energy reserves, but we were always left with the gratifying notion that there was once again enough feed in storage for another year.

The main reason that farming consistently ranks as the number one most dangerous occupation in the country is based on several factors. Farmers often must work long, hard, strenuous hours. Many times they are trying to outrun an impending weather storm front or beat the daylight clock just as the sun is setting below the horizon, or perhaps they are trying to rush their field work knowing that they are tardy for completing their livestock chores. While all of that is transpiring, a farmer tries to operate dangerous large equipment and machinery. As if all of the aforementioned conditions aren't enough to create a deadly hazard, then matters can complicate even further when there are dangerous equipment failures. No wonder the occupation of farming is steeped in the folklore of countless injury, dismemberment, or death.

We were about halfway through the process of filling our silos that fall. There was little doubt that my father and I, along with our equipment, were reaching our breaking points with fatigue. Neither farmers nor their machinery can run indefinitely before something gives way.

My father and I had just made another quick switch of our silage chopper boxes at the end of the field. As I pulled out of the field with my tractor and chopper box filled with several tons of cargo, I glanced back at my father to ensure he was back at his routine of cutting his swath of silage for our next go-round.

If only I'd had an intuition that perhaps I was looking at my father for the last time!

Once I'd maneuvered my ten-thousand-pound tractor, which was pulling another fifteen-thousand-pound load of corn silage out of the field and onto the road, I pressed down on the tractor clutch with the left leg I'd injured only the year before, and then shifted the tractor transmission effortlessly into the fastest road gear. After I'd eased the clutch pedal back, the massive equipment surged forward ever faster as I throttled the engine speed up to the maximum rate. I did not take my responsibilities lightly, fully realizing that it was me and only me that would be guiding my twenty-five-thousand pounds of equipment and payload along the four-mile course back to our farmyard.

I remember glancing quickly at the combination tachometer and speedometer gauge on the dash of the tractor and made a mental note that I was up to the twenty-mile-per-hour road speed. To put the speed issue in perspective, most people can identify with customary road speeds of perhaps fifty or sixty miles per hour while traveling in a car. A speed of twenty miles per hour then may seem rather insignificant.

One must realize, however, that a car is lightweight, is much smaller, and is aerodynamically built to cruise at somewhat higher speeds. In fact, cars have been designed to handle speed quite easily. Tractors on the other hand are heavy, larger, and built powerfully to pull massive loads at a much slower speed of travel. Normally, a tractor under working conditions in a field will only travel at a speed of three or four miles per hour. Understandably then, flying down a well-traveled black-top highway at twenty miles per hour can feel like a breathtaking pace even for a seventeen-year-old boy who thrives on danger.

I was just settling back into the tractor seat and focusing on the road ahead when in an instant the tractor nearly flipped upside down while traveling at full speed! WHY?

During the countless trips back and forth to the field, the large bolts holding the massive right rear wheel onto the tractor had been working their way loose. Ever so slowly, the eight-hundred-pound wheel worked its way off the rear axle of the tractor. Unfortunately, it was moving so little with each round-trip to the field and back; neither my father nor I noticed that anything impending was about to occur. At that instant while traveling at the top tractor speed, the rear wheel suddenly separated itself from the tractor axle and went careening forward down the road before turning into the road ditch.

The centrifugal force of that immense eight-hundred-pound wheel traveling at twenty miles per hour made it a deadly force to be reckoned with. With little effort, the wheel blasted down the ditch and up the other side. At the top of the ditch was a well-built tightly constructed five barbed-wire fence. One might have thought that if such a fence was capable of restraining the most aggressive and massive beef bulls, then surely it would bring the rampant tractor wheel to a halt. Unbelievably, the wheel smashed through the impressive fence as though a hot knife slicing through soft butter.

The wheel finally lost its momentum and tumbled to a resting spot several hundred yards out into the field. One could only imagine the dreadful consequences had the runaway wheel hit a car or hit a pedestrian.

Needless to say, while the wheel spun out of control away from the tractor, I was in a life-threatening predicament of my own. One must first understand that a tractor sits very high in the air and engineered to have a center of gravity to be spread out over the top of a very large wheel base underneath the tractor. In a heartbeat, my massive, high-speed tractor became much like an unstable three-legged stool as it began tipping over with frightening force. My white knuckles gripped the tractor steering wheel in sheer fear as I realized that the tractor I was operating had none of the safety features of more modern tractors. I did not have the benefits of a safety crash roll bar or even a simple seat belt to confine me from falling beneath the tipping tractor.

I panicked as the speeding tractor's right side axle dropped with a crash onto the black-top highway. It plummeted with so much force that the still rapidly revolving axle drilled a twelve-inch hole deep into the highway surface. I held my breath as the tractor bucked and twisted while the intact left rear wheel of the out-of-control tractor suddenly lurched high off the ground. Although there had been nearly enough tipping force exerted to completely flip the massive tractor over and into the ditch, somehow, or something stopped the tractor in midair. It seemed as though time came to a standstill as I envisioned what it would feel like to finally die. All at once, just as quickly as the tractor had started to flip, everything came crashing back down to the road with a back-jarring thud. I wasted little time in taking the tractor out of gear and shutting the engine off.

I simply sat there and shook in fright, and then I stumbled off the deadly twisted tractor and fell onto the roadway beneath my feet. It had only taken a few seconds, yet I'd been merely an instant away from dying a most dreadful death. This statistic is one that can be confirmed over and over again whenever one hears about the several tractor rollover deaths that occur to the farming community each year in our country.

I was much shaken, but after a few moments, a car passed by and stopped. They offered to provide me a ride back to where my father was still chopping silage. After thanking them for the assistance, I waited as my father brought his tractor to the end of the field where I stood.

In a moment, he jumped off the tractor shouting, "My god, Scott, what happened to you? You're white as a ghost. Are you ill?"

After explaining every detail to my perplexed father, he next unhooked his tractor from the chopping equipment, and we spent the remainder of that day putting my tractor back into operation once more. We most definitely checked the tractor wheel bolt tightness for each and every tractor on our farm following my harrowing experience.

That night as I switched off my bedroom light and fell into bed, I relived the scary moments while staring into the face of death. I can attest it is a very unsettling experience and even worse if one has to face death on numerous occasions.

Before falling into slumber, I tightly folded my hands and whispered my grateful prayer to the Lord, giving thanks for shielding me from what should have resulted in certain demise.

For the record and so there is no misunderstanding, I'll repeat it again, "Thank you, dear Lord."

MOTORCYCLE MISFORTUNE—20 YEARS

CHAPTER NINE

Then everyone who calls on the name of the Lord shall be saved.
—ACTS 2:21

Motorcycling has been one of my greater passions throughout life, which just so happens to also be a primary cause for five of my closest encounters with death. In all, during my lifetime, I've actually dealt with the aftermath of five significant motorcycling accidents, but it was the fourth wreck, which I'll cover in a later chapter that left me at the very brink of death while suffering from the most severe injuries I'd ever incurred. In the following story, though, I'll review my initial motorcycling collision that began it all.

Growing up and living in the countryside with our home alongside a dusty rural gravel road made our travels into town a rather bumpy and dirty affair. Our rickety older model cars or our farm pickup trucks would rumble and groan each time we scampered off to town for something. While I was growing up, I had a strong fascination for motorcycles. Invariably, once our unsavory vehicles would make their way along our rural roads and onto the more modern highways, we would oftentimes witness the carefree expression of a passing motorcyclist racing by us.

From an early age, I was awestruck by how agile and snappy these motorbikes were. They almost appeared to my young impressionable eyes as though they were big, two-wheeled mosquitoes capable of darting in and out of traffic with reckless abandon and ease. To my way of thinking, the motorcycles were certainly a more remarkable form of transportation than were our lumbering farm vehicles that we occasionally ventured into town with. My ears would perk up each time a passing biker would roll the grip of their hand throttle, and I'd be spellbound by the instant acceleration of the machine and hear the thunder coming from the tailpipes.

No matter how thrilled I became each time a motorcycle passed by, my father would in turn get evermore angry toward the bikers. My father would always go into a rant by shouting, "Those damned crazy idiots have no idea that they are all going to end up dead or in a hospital if they keep riding those death machines."

I questioned my father's commentary only once and knew better than to ever bring the topic up again when I'd asked, "Gee, Dad, what is the big deal? Motorcycles are so fast and so cool."

Without taking a breath, my father gave me one of his most profound arguments. With my father's secondary job working the nighttime shift for the Mayo Clinic, he was always on call with the emergency room. Whenever there was a vehicular accident of any kind, he and a certain group of other medical specialists would be summoned in a hurry to perform their specific duties. Throughout our childhoods, my father never failed to remind my siblings and me just how many heartrending motorcycling accident victims he'd been required to work on over the years. My father would unleash a tirade on us kids sitting in our car whenever he'd spot a motorcycles zipping along the highway.

He would point out how the biker was speeding along only inches from the roadway without the benefit of a metal re-enforced frame or even the advantage of an enclosed car body to surround the operator with some life-saving safety features. Next he would explain that without any seat belts or air bags, a motorcyclist was simply a death statistic waiting to happen. He could never understand what drove them to live so close to the edge of sensibility.

My father's so-called words of wisdom left a pretty strong impact on my younger siblings, but his words fell on my deaf ears. The more my father complained about how senseless and dangerous he felt motorcycle riding was, the more I fantasized about the sheer joy of nearly floating through the air while traveling at high speeds suspended only inches above the racing roadway beneath. My father would really get rattled whenever he'd see a helmetless motorcyclist pass by our vehicle. That sight alone would turn my father into a "fire-breathing" dragon. He would shake his head from side to side in disbelief and sigh loudly as he questioned why such fools would not only risk their lives on such "death machines," but then do so without even wearing a precautionary safety helmet.

It became all too obvious to everyone in our family that our father was becoming more and more deeply troubled as time passed along from his personal witness to all the catastrophic motorcycling injuries he faced on a regular basis inside the emergency rooms of the hospital. I'm sure there is only so much mutilation, pain, and human suffering that any one person can absorb before it takes a stressful toll. Our father felt that if he preached his message hard enough, long enough, and often enough, he could steer his children away from dangers that motorcycling could possibly inflict upon them.

My father actually had a pretty good success ratio inflicting his motorcycling beliefs on his children, however, one of his five children seemed incoherent to such words of wisdom. Which one of his five offspring would one guess? Well, if you guessed me, then yes, I desired a motorcycle with everything within my being. Anything that could go fast enough to take one's breath away was enough exhilaration to spur my desires.

Whenever I could, I'd read motorcycling magazines in our high school library. I became a "closet motorbike" admirer, and during my teen years, I became a human encyclopedia of motorcycle knowledge and trivia facts. No one could stump me when it came to motorcycle facts and figures. With ease, I could spell out exactly which motorcycle model would have which size engine with what top-end speed it could achieve and, furthermore, sell for exactly what price tag, etc.

I became the envy of my friends and everyone (except for my father) knew that it would only be matter of time, and I would one day become a true biker. There was only one slight problem.

My father has always been a strong-willed and strict disciplinarian parent. Within our household, his will and direction always became a fact which could not be challenged.

My father was certainly very astute in realizing his inability to take away my obsession of one day owning and operating a motorcycle, but he made it CRYSTAL CLEAR to me on many an occasion by saying, "Scott, no child of mine will ever own or operate a motorcycle while living under my roof and while under my care." My father would always rattle on further by stating, "Someday you will grow up, you will become an adult, and then you will have my blessings to do whatever you desire, but until that day arrives, you must respect my demands at this time of your life."

The message was clear, and my respect for obeying my father's wishes was never in question. For his reasons and because of the demons he struggled with, I never let on just how much of a student of motorcycling I'd become by my late teen years. By the time I'd reached the age of seventeen, though, I already knew exactly when and how I would enter into the world of motorcycle ownership. I'd laid out a specific plan for which I knew all the details ranging from which brand of motorbike, to how much horsepower would sit beneath my legs, to exactly how fast my cycle would travel once I finally acquired it.

I'm sure that my parents were all too aware that their rebellious son would one day move on into the fast and the furious world of motorcycling, but they never stopped hoping that I would one day come to my senses on the matter. Out of the total respect which I've always held with both of my parents, I kept the subject of my passion for cycling hidden to myself for years.

In time, I reached the age of eighteen, graduated from high school, and moved out of my parent's household and on to college. Having reached young adulthood at last and having recently moved into my college apartment, I immediately purchased a used midsized motorcycle. In no time at all, I'd passed my written motorcycle exam, then passed my motorcycle driving test, and suddenly, I was legally able to ride the machine of my dreams.

Although my father was not happy when he found out that I finally owned a motorcycle, he was somewhat comforted because I chose to wear a safety helmet while operating the motorbike. I noted a twisted smirk arise from the corner of his mouth when he shared, "At least you'll have some hope of surviving an accident if you wear your 'brain bucket' over your head."

It is difficult to describe my initial experience with my motorcycle. I remember shaking with delight as I mounted the sleek and racy machine. With a quick turn of the key, I brought the roar of its throaty engine to life for the first time. With a downward click of the foot gearshift, I engaged the transmission, and with the release of the left hand clutch, my motorcycle and I sped off for the very first time. I'd liken it to one's first kiss or perhaps one's first love. It was simply an unforgettable experience which I've treasured always and whose memory never fades.

For my entire life, I've been drawn to anything that makes my heart race and takes my breath away. As I raced along the highways on that virgin motorcycle ride, I experienced an unbelievable joy as the bike and I became as one. We leaned together while twisting quickly and easily through curves in the roads with a feeling such as I'd never experienced before. With merely a slight twist of my right throttle grip, the two-wheeled machine ratcheted up its speed in an instant.

Riding a motorcycle for the first time left me with an insatiable desire to never want to give up such a feeling of pure, unadulterated freedom and joy. How something so wonderful could create so much distain from my father was beyond me.

It was summertime, and I'd just moved my meager belongings away from my beloved room inside my parent's home and which I'd shared with my brother, Jerry, for so many years, then relocated everything to my apartment about one hundred miles away in the metropolitan mega of Minneapolis. I had been in such a hurry to reach adulthood and to acquire a motorcycle of my own. I moved away that summer without so much as looking back and instantly began working a summer job in my effort to earn some college tuition funds. When fall arrived that year, I began my classes at the University of Minnesota after surviving a few months of big-city dwelling.

Each and every day I rode my motorcycle to and from my temporary job. I was in so much ecstasy riding it, that rain or shine, cold or warm, I rode, then rode it some more. It didn't take long to figure out the benefits of motorcycle ownership for a young college student. For starters, the motorbike only sipped gasoline by achieving well over fifty miles per gallon, which really helped me with low-cost travels. With its maneuverability, I could move in and out of the congested big-city traffic with an ease such as I'd never experienced before. Finally, with such a petite size, I was always capable of parking my cycle anywhere and everywhere, which could not so easily have been accomplished with larger cars and pickup trucks.

I'd become quite accustomed to the advantages of motorcycle ownership as summer evolved into fall, and I began my first college courses. Most of the other college students' rode buses to and from college each day. A few students had a vehicle of some sort to drive, but it was a rare few of us that in fact possessed a motorcycle to maneuver about campus and travel the city.

Living away from our farm and suddenly dwelling within the big city while attending college was not an easy adjustment for me at first. I was all too aware of the sheer numbers of people all around. How different it was living within the city where one could hear sounds and voices emanating from every direction inside of one's apartment versus the quiet solitude inside of our farm house. The mass of vehicles and hurried pace of the city made for a difficult transition for me.

Without doubt, upon moving to the city, I became somewhat suspicious and mistrusting of my belongings. So much so that each evening as I parked my motorcycle at my apartment, I would secure it with a large chain and padlock it to one of the large metal security light poles in the parking lot of the apartment complex where I lived. At night, I could always sleep better, knowing that I had removed my ignition keys, then locked the front forks of my motorbike, then chained and locked it securely before walking away.

This methodology of protecting my new motorcycle worked wonderfully for the first couple of months. One morning, however, I arose early for my summertime job, showered and dressed, then headed out into the parking lot to ready my motorbike for my hasty departure. Suddenly, I stopped in my tracks as I looked into the empty parking space where my cycle had been safely secured. Only the severed large chain remained and where it was still wrapped around the large security light pole, which I'd mistakenly believed could protect my bike.

In a matter of moments, I called the area law enforcement department to report that my much-adored motorcycle had been stolen. I angrily waited until the two Minneapolis policemen knocked at my door and stepped into my apartment. After providing a detailed statement for their police report and divulging everything I could in regard to my motorcycle, they stood up preparing to leave. As I walked them to the door, I asked how long they felt it might take before my precious motorcycle would be found, the thief who stole it arrested and incarcerated, and then my bike returned to me.

The policemen burst out into laughter, when they announced, "Son, you must have grown up somewhere in the sticks because your motorcycle has probably already been parted out overnight and is being sold for motorcycle parts as we speak!"

I felt my face flush with anger as I responded back by saying, "Well, there must be some chance of getting my machine back, isn't there?"

Again, I drew a chuckle from the cops as they responded, "Look, it would be best for you to simply turn this theft over to your insurance company, have them provide you with a payoff for the stolen motorcycle, then go out and buy yourself another one if you are so inclined."

With that, they marched out of my apartment and departed. I never heard from them or the police department regarding the matter of my stolen motorcycle ever again.

I sat down in disbelief at how violated I felt. How could some worthless criminal take what I'd fantasized about for so long, what I'd worked so hard for and that I'd enjoyed so heartily without even the slightest care or concern for me? *Welcome to the real world, farm boy*, I thought to myself.

I grew up a lot that day as I realized that all of God's children do not travel the same path in life, but rather, good versus evil can be a prevailing theme. I was so young and so ignorant about what could transpire outside the confines of a simple and honest life on the farm.

Not to be defeated, though, I went ahead and made that call to my insurance company and before long I was shopping for another motorcycle. It seemed surreal that I'd only acquired my first motorcycle a short while ago, and now in less than ninety days, I was about to purchase my second motorbike. As is so often the case, after my insurance deductible was subtracted and then they calculated how much my stolen motorcycle had depreciated in value while under my ownership, I was paid only a portion of what I'd invested in order to purchase that first bike.

Remember that at this time, I had moved away from my home destined to pay my way through college as well as own and operate a motorcycle. My parents did not approve of either choice but had granted me the freedom to make my own decisions as a young adult. Since asking my father for some financial help to either pay for my college costs or worse yet to help me purchase another motorcycle was OUT OF THE QUESTION, I went forth with my plan.

The insurance company settlement for my stolen motorcycle was a payment of about two-thirds of my original investment.

Having no additional funding at the time, I walked into a Minneapolis motorcycle business and said, "My midsized motorcycle has recently been stolen, and I only have enough money to cover the cost of one about two-thirds the size of my previous one."

After looking over several model designs and choices, I soon drove away on a new, yet smaller on-road-off-road motorcycle. Although I had to sacrifice some size, some power, and some speed with my new downsized bike, I had gained a more nimble, dual purpose motorbike. Not only could I legally travel along the roads and highways, albeit at much less speed potential, but I now had a machine with high-traction tires and a tough suspension allowing me at any time to veer off the traveled highway and travel into the rough hills and trails to become one with nature during my riding experience.

Immediately after obtaining my new motorcycle, I vowed to never allow it to be stolen as had been the situation with my first bike. Beginning the first night of ownership, I parked the new motorcycle in a new location. Rather than parking it in the parking lot as before, I started parking my motorbike immediately next to the large bedroom window of my apartment. As always, before leaving my motorcycle for the evening, I would remove the ignition key and lock the front forks of the motorbike. Rather than lock and chain the bike to an immovable object, however, instead I connected a hidden wire, which I tied to the rear wheel of the motorcycle, then ran the wire through my bedroom window, and which was lastly attached to a bell inside of my bedroom. Then for the next four years of my college education, each night I slept peacefully throughout the night with a loaded automatic .45 caliber handgun beneath my bed. I never worried again, and I had no doubt about how I would protect myself and my property from criminals if and when the need arose from a ringing bell inside my bedroom.

Graciously, the Lord never tested my resolve in this matter, and thankfully neither my motorcycle nor I were ever violated again.

Before long, I had become one with my new machine and fell in love with the new feats I could complete with it. No longer was I restricted to traveling down a mundane highway. I now controlled a two-wheeler with the athletic ability to go nearly anywhere in the wilderness that a deer or perhaps even a horse could venture, only do it with more speed and excitement. With every chance I had, I would travel out to backwoods areas with my new motorcycle as I powered up hills, broke new trails, sped past ponds and rivers, and jumped high into the air with abandon. I had always loved the adrenaline rush from doing similar activities while rushing through the trees and hills with my horses, but the thrill from this new mechanized mode of trailblazing was unequaled in my mind.

In time, I became a skilled rider both on the road and off the road with my versatile new motorcycle. In no time, I developed a timing and a balance, which allowed me to maneuver my bike through the most challenging scenarios yet come away unscathed and intact. If my parents could only have known the antics I had become accustomed in the short while since I'd owned my two different motorcycles.

It was a sunny weekend Saturday in the early fall during my first year of college. Following a long week of studies and working every evening on my part-time job during the previous week, I was prepared to finally enjoy some "me time" and to unwind from the long week. I dressed, then went outside to ready my motorbike for a few hours of rough riding on the trails. First I put on my leather motorcycle jacket, secured my helmet onto my head, inserted my hands into my thick leather riding gloves, then fired up my cycle and drove away.

After giving my motorcycle and me an extreme workout for a few of hours, I guided my bike back toward my apartment complex to end the fun time for the day. The design of my apartment complex was such that on one side of the parking lot was several apartment buildings, including the apartment which I resided in. Positioned along the other side of the parking lot was an expansive athletic field where various college intramural sporting activities took place throughout the week.

Since I was returning from riding some wilderness trails with my motorcycle, I felt that I had one more exciting daredevil motorcycle jump left in me before calling it a day and parking my bike. I was about to attempt the same motorcycle jump that I'd completed several times previously, but because of the dangers, I knew that I had to be careful regarding certain factors.

I quickly surveyed the entire apartment complex and made a mental note that all was quiet, both all around the apartment buildings, as well the fact that there was no one in or around the black-topped parking lot itself. I was relieved that no people were to be seen, albeit many times there were young children playing on the sidewalks or possibly a car or two would be moving about the parking lot. Had that been the case and I would have detected any movement at all, I would have aborted my last motorcycle thrill of the day.

From the road then, I jumped my motorbike over the curb and without so much as a second notion, I gathered speed while crossing the barren athletic field. I was keenly aware of the logistics of making the motorcycle jump that I was about to attempt. From my previous jumping attempts from this same location, I knew from experience that it could be a somewhat tricky landing since the paved parking lot of the apartment complex was positioned a full eight feet lower than the surface level of the grassy athletic field. I also knew, though, that with just the correct amount of speed, my motorcycle would reach the edge of the athletic field and then the momentum would launch me several feet up into the air. When done correctly, my bike and I would sail effortlessly for up to one hundred feet or more before landing with a spine-numbing force onto the parking lot pavement.

In a flash, my motorbike had crossed the field as I made one last mental note of the lack of activity that day all around the apartment complex. Seeing nothing, I rolled the throttle of the dashing bike ever further to really attempt a high, long jump.

Over the edge we flew, higher than I'd ever attempted before, when suddenly my blood ran icy cold as a car hidden beside a large van, slowly backed out of a parking spot and directly into my path of decent. Although I'd never spotted a glimpse of her inside of her hidden car, I'd discovered later that she'd been sitting for a while inside of her car writing a letter to someone. At the most unlucky moment for me, she finished her task, started the engine of her car, and then proceeded to back out into my path of impending destruction.

My bike and I were already launched at high speed into midair with no chance to abort, to slow down, or to change direction when she backed out and into my path. I knew within an instant that I was about to come face-to-face with death even though I'd tried to do everything within my power to prevent something such as this unavoidable crash from occurring.

Flying through the air at about fifty miles per hour, my entire body flexed into a knot of muscles as the looming midair crash with the car unfolded before my terrified eyes. While still in midair and with a force beyond description, my motorcycle smashed broadside into the left, rear quarter panel of her car with such a blunt force that the rear bumper on her car flew cleanly off her vehicle. The motorcycle's smaller size and forward momentum was no match for the unyielding larger car. The motorbike literally went from a hurling speed of fifty miles per hour to an instantaneous dead stop as the front wheel exploded from the impact, and the strongly constructed steel front forks twisted like two pretzels made of soft bread dough.

Immediately upon impact, it is difficult to describe what thoughts were going through my mind. I was launched forward as though shot from a cannon up over the top of my motorcycle, up over the top of the car, and slingshot out into the paved parking lot a distance of nearly one hundred yards before sliding, scraping, and rolling to a complete stop.

I lay there in utter disbelief realizing that I'd just hit a car broadside at a shattering fifty mile per hour with my motorcycle, yet for some reason, I wasn't dead. By this time, the flustered woman had exited her car and had rushed to my side expecting to see me injured beyond description, or perhaps dead, or at the very least bleeding profusely.

Although I was severely stunned from the impact, she carefully aided me to my feet. She kept repeating over and over again, "I'm so sorry, I backed out from behind that van with the big blind spot on my left side, and I simply didn't see you! I pray you didn't break anything or have any internal injuries."

I slowly stood up and began accessing my overall bodily damage. The first item I removed was the safety helmet from my head. I was shocked to observe that at some point while I came crashing down onto the pavement, my head had struck so hard that the helmet received a large crack which ran down the entire helmet, yet somehow, I had sustained no head or neck injuries. Next I looked down at the pant legs of my denim jeans only to find that my left pant leg was torn all the way from my ankle up to my hip as a result from my losing battle with the parking lot surface. Oddly, I felt no pain as I cautiously walked around and somehow I hadn't fractured even a single bone through it all. My heavy leather motorcycle jacket had done its job magnificently because although deeply scarred and scraped, it had successfully prevented me from attaining even the slightest case of road rash.

I don't know if it was the woman whose car I'd smashed into or it was me who was more shocked at my noticeably absent injuries after such a traumatic collision.

She breathed a slow sigh of relief then loosened up a bit when she joked, "You must go to the right church because that crash would have killed anyone else for sure!"

I smiled weakly at her, but I didn't have the heart to inform her that I was becoming all too familiar with my perpetual encounters with death.

We exchanged contact information after which I helped her load her damaged rear car bumper into her car and then she departed. With more than a little effort, I hoisted my fractured and disabled motorcycle into the upright position, then pushed, dragged, and pulled it to its resting spot near my bedroom window.

After rising from bed the next morning, I was so thankful to have had the weekend off from working or attending college. It took everything in my power to rise up from bed. I staggered to my bathroom mirror and noted that much of my body was covered front and rear with swollen dark bruises. I nearly fainted as I pressed my fingers into the muscles of my arms, my neck, my chest, my back, and my legs. I was literally unable to find one muscle group on my entire body that wasn't aching from intense pain. It was at that moment that I realized what must have happened to my body just a few hours earlier.

Just prior to making impact with the car, my body and all of my muscles instinctively tightened in reflexive anticipation for the impact. Then the collision resulted in me being thrust off the motorcycle where I landed with a tremendous force upon the pavement. No wonder then why every muscle within my body went on to ache for days to come.

In time, my miraculously minor aches ceased. Before long and following the repair of my damaged motorcycle, I was once again riding my two-wheeler as though nothing had ever occurred. More than ever, I came to appreciate the absolute enjoyment of the feeling of the wind blowing upon my face again.

Some folks will never understand the reasons why others of us are drawn to ride motorcycles. I can sum it up with this cute anecdote: "Motorcycle riders are the only people on earth that fully understand why a dog always sticks its head out of the window of a speeding car with an expression of sheer delight upon their face!"

Looking back, I feel so blessed that the woman who backed into my path was uninjured. Certainly, I realize and accept that somehow I was protected by an angel once again.

The final unanswered question that one may ask, though, is how did my father ever respond regarding this incident where I could easily have died while on my motorcycle? Did my father quip I told you so?

The answer is that he never knew about any of what had happened, and ultimately, he will have to read about the incident just as you have done in this book for the very first time. I'm afraid that even though a few decades have elapsed since my first motorcycle accident, my father will hardly be able to contain himself about lecturing me. I can hear him now with all the intensity he can muster, "You crazy idiots that operate those death machines!"

AIRPLANE FLIGHT CASCADE—21 YEARS

CHAPTER TEN

I will praise the Lord at all times.
I will constantly speak his praises.
I will boast only in the Lord;
let all who are discouraged take heart.
Come, let us tell of the Lord's greatness;
let us exalt his name together.
I prayed to the Lord, and he answered me,
freeing me from all my fears.

—PSALM 34:1-4

Each and every day of my entire life, I've strived with everything in my being to garner the most that I can from whatever life has had to offer. Friends and family have always contested my obsessive attitude toward getting the most out of every last minute of the day, and for that matter, I've often been known to pull the most out of as many minutes of the night as well.

As adults, we oftentimes point a finger at someone with such absurd ambitions for maxing out every moment of time as someone perhaps not right in the head. Someone that commits too much effort into a job is often categorized as a "workaholic" by others. Whatever the name-calling or finger pointing directed my way, I've just kept on with my own course of action in life.

Throughout my life, I've been blessed or depending on how one perceived it, I've been cursed with the ability to function at peak levels with little to no sleep for long periods of time. For much of my life, I've commonly slept between two to four hours per night; and countless times over the years, I've simply skipped sleeping at all if the need was required.

It is a known fact that not all people require the same amount of slumber to function. The famous inventor Thomas Edison was well-known for seldom sleeping during any given night but instead would catch occasional short twenty minute cat naps to remain totally refreshed as he toiled around the clock. Within my own immediate family, my father worked a nighttime shift for twenty-five years while operating a large livestock and grain farm. During all of those years, my father seldom slept more than two hours during any twenty-four hour period. My youngest son, Travis, similar to his grandfather, Dave, and much like me is also capable of functioning very well with little to no sleep.

With my own minimal sleep requirements growing evermore defined by my college years, I was soon able to accomplish some almost inhuman feats. For instance, over my four-year postsecondary education, I worked a full-time forty-hour-per-week job while carrying a full-time sixteen- to twenty-credit classroom load. Along with that fulltime agenda, I also actively participated in ten different campus clubs and organizations as well as spent two grueling years as a member of the University of Minnesota Livestock Judging Team, which demanded extensive travel throughout the entire United States.

As if I wasn't drawing enough negative comments from my college friends and instructors, I really put forth an insane push during my final semester of college. With only a few short months of college left prior to obtaining my bachelor of science degree in animal science and a bachelor of science degree in agriculture education, I tried to put a final nail in my coffin.

During my last semester, my list of activities went something like this. I ramped up my college credit load to a massive twenty-four class credits, which is considered about twice the class load of many full-time students. I continued to work forty hours per week on my job. Each seemingly endless day began with me starting my job a 2:00 a.m. I would work until my first class started at 11:00 a.m. I would attend classes throughout the day and also took night classes in order to fit in all the class credit hours. Each night, following my last class, I would fall into my bed about 11:30 p.m., only to rise again a mere two hours later to repeat the process over once more.

Unbelievably, throughout this test of endurance, I was somehow able to secure all straight A grades, resulting in a 4.0 grade point average from what I termed the semester from hell. As though somehow possessed with a battery pack that never ran out of electrical charge, I filled any available spare time during my final days of college. I participated as an active member of the college rodeo team, the college livestock judging team, the college archery club, the college block and bridle club, the college agriculture education club, and the college intramural sports club; all while attempting to author my first book.

If one isn't almost exhausted contemplating such insane commitments, then it becomes obvious that I was capable of thriving on very little sleep. Oftentimes, I've heard the saying that one's college days are the best times of one's life. Perhaps that is true for some. For the record, I had several classmates who partied and played their way through their college education. Right or wrong, I never attended a single party or dance because I simply didn't have any available time to do so.

As mentioned earlier in this chapter, my friends, instructors, and family determined that I must have lost my mind during this period of my life. For me, it was a matter of simple arithmetic. I reasoned that there was so much yet to accomplish at college yet so little time to fit everything in.

The primary reason I demanded so much of myself in my final semester of college was that I decided to obtain a private pilot's license before departing college.

The University of Minnesota had a small fleet of single-propeller airplanes that they rented out to university students at a greatly reduced fee. Through my college courses, the university offered evening classroom flight instructions, which then went along with weekend flying instructions in one of their planes.

It took a lot of effort to learn the complicated processes of flying a plane. The classroom training taught our class how to prepare a flight route, how to check weather reports, how to file a flight plan, how to calculate fuel requirements, how to determine flight course based on speed and direction of winds aloft, how to react in an emergency, and so on. Physically exhausted though I was each night during my evening flight training classes, I realized that falling asleep in that class could spell disaster one day once I began actually flying airplanes on my own.

During my weekends, I would try to log as many hours of actual flying instruction as my instructor would allow. There was never a question in my mind that I would learn everything necessary for me to be an outstanding private pilot one day. True to my word and just before graduating from college, I passed both my written and flight aviation tests. It was one of my proudest moments the day that I joined the elite ranks of individuals capable of soaring high above the clouds with the freedom of a bird in flight.

In order to qualify for a private pilot's license, one must log many hours in a plane, not only with an instructor, but also perform several hours of solo flight activities. My private pilot license was for a VFR (visual flight rules) certification, meaning I was not instrument rated. A pilot with an instrument rating is qualified for instance to fly in the clouds or at night or even through the fog since they are trained and certified to fly their plane utilizing only their aviation instruments if necessary. Even though a VFR pilot also uses their flight instruments, they are not certified for instance to fly the plane or try to land the plane unless they are able to view the ground at all times.

After completing all of my flight classes, logging all of my flight time, and passing all of my aviation exams, I finally held my cherished pilot license before the ending of my college days.

The first phone call that I made once I became a pilot was to my father since he'd been closely monitoring my flying progress. The two of us had fantasized many times just how wonderful it would be once I could fly both of us around the country in a plane to attend some of the state fair cattle shows around the upper Midwest.

During my college years, my father would milk his dairy herd of cattle twice each day and perform the many other chores of his farm. During this same time period, my younger brother Jerry began exhibiting some of our purebred Hereford beef cattle at various state fairs around the country. Unfortunately, my father was seldom able to attend one of these cattle shows because there was no way for him to milk his cows in the morning, then drive several hundred miles and back again from a cattle show, and still make it back in time to milk his dairy cows by the evening milking shift. That was until I obtained my private pilot's license.

From my college apartment in Minneapolis, I held the phone to my ear and spoke, "Dad, I passed my aviation exams, and we can now fly together to the cattle shows. Shall I prepare a flight plan to fly us to the Wisconsin State Fair in Milwaukee for next weekend's beef cattle show that Jerry will be exhibiting our cattle at?"

My father had sudden reservations as he retorted, "Scott, I'm not so sure anymore. I wasn't ever really sure if you would pass all of your flying exams. You know that I've never been in an airplane before, and now I don't know if I am able to handle the thought of flying, especially in such a tiny plane. I think I might be more comfortable in a big jumbo jet."

I was taken back to say the least since my father and I had dialogued so often about just how great it would be when the day arrived for our first actual flight together. With some strong persuasion, I was able to finally convince my father that he would be perfectly safe on his maiden flight.

As I hung up the phone, I felt an ominous chill come over me, which I couldn't explain. For the moment, I shrugged it off, thinking perhaps even I was slightly skeptical about my father's comments.

My only main concern regarding my father was his propensity for motion sickness. He was never able to spend even a few moments out on the water and in a boat before nausea would overcome him, and he'd be leaning over the edge of the boat. Much the same, unless my father is always able to be the person physically driving a car or a pickup truck with the steering wheel in his hands, he suffers terribly from car sickness. Whenever someone else has been at the wheel, my father is soon vomiting beyond control. My greatest fear was that once my father and I became airborne the upcoming weekend, I wondered just how badly his motion sickness would become within the tiny confines of the cockpit.

Before long, the weekend arrived, and I made my way to the University of Minnesota airplane hangars at the airport. I had reserved one of the planes from dawn until dusk for the entire Saturday. I completed my required paperwork, made my plane rental prepayment, and filed my flight plan. In moments, I throttled up the airplane engine and sped down the runway. The little plane effortlessly lifted off as I banked southward toward the Rochester airport to pick up my anxiously awaiting father.

It took a mere forty-five minutes to fly nearly one hundred miles from Minneapolis to Rochester. I made my radio call to the airport tower and then landed the plane with ease. I coasted the plane up to the hangar area then shut down the engine. I went inside to find my father and then filed my flight plan with the proper officials. Before departing, I took a few minutes to recalculate my estimated aviation fuel needs, and everything demonstrated that I would have no need to refuel the plane until reaching the Milwaukee airport a short few hours later.

I made one last call for an updated flight weather report, which sent up a "red flag" as the report indicated some slight ground fog was developing along the Mississippi River border between Minnesota and

Wisconsin, but all else reflected that it would be a great morning for a VFR flight.

Once again, as with the week before, I sensed a strange and ominous chill run across me while my father observed me completing the preflight airplane inspection. Once completed, we both entered the cockpit and closed the door of the plane.

Once I fired up the engine, it didn't take me long to realize just how terrified my father actually was about flying. I glanced over at him and noticed the pale look on his face. Normally my father carries on an endless conversation, but he was barely able to dialogue with me.

I reached over, and while patting his knee with my hand, I stated, "Dad, I know that everything must seem a bit frightening, but I assure you, everything will be just fine and we will make it back home again. I promise."

I taxied the snappy little plane out onto the runway and then radioed my departure call in to the tower. Within moments, we were roaring up into the sunny, clear blue sky.

Before departing that morning, I'd spent some time explaining to my father that flying an airplane required my total and complete focus. I'd asked him to keep any conversation with me to a bare minimum so that I could fly us safely to our destination across the border. My father was keeping his commitment as he tightly clutched his air sickness bag and stared fearfully forward.

Within a few minutes, I trimmed the wing flaps of the plane as it climbed ever so steadily up to our designated elevation of six thousand feet. With my hands, I guided the yoke and tail rudder as I set my direction for a southeasterly course. It was 8:10 a.m., and I felt elated as I scoured the view all around us. There was nothing but a gorgeous, sunny blue sky above the plane and a vast array of rivers, fields, and tiny towns passing clearly and quickly beneath our wings.

About one hour into the flight, my father had settled into a look of quiet contentment. We were already about one third of our way to our destination. As we neared the great Mississippi River along the border, the beats of my heart sped up slightly as I viewed the ensuing ground fog that had been detailed during the Rochester airport weather report.

Just to be safe, I radioed the tower asking for an update of visual flight conditions for a Milwaukee flight course. The alarming response came back that an ever-increasing ground fog was encompassing the state of Wisconsin from the Mississippi River and eastward. I reminded the tower that I was only VFR certified and that I should abort my present flight plan and return immediately back to the Rochester airport. My pulse quickened evermore as the tower responded back with, "Negative, the Rochester airport has just been socked in with a dense fog cover as well so you will be unable to land at this time!" After a few more radio transmissions, the general consensus was that I needed to continue on with my flight plan in hopes that the ground fog would clear up soon. I most likely would fly out of it within a short period once the ambient air temperatures warmed the ground surface high enough to melt off the fog.

Trust me when I say, nothing is more frightening than flying an airplane with a VFR private pilot license knowing that one will have to fly blind even if only briefly. Following my final radio transmission, my father leaned over asking, "Is everything okay, Scott?" I nodded my head up and down as we overtook the dense layer of ground fog below us.

It was very surreal to me that we were suddenly maintaining our six thousand foot altitude on our southeasterly course as demonstrated by the instrument panel on such a glorious sunny day all around our plane, yet on the underbelly of the plane lay an evil, endless white floor of opaque fog without a glimpse of land in sight. My anxiety level increased as we surged ever further into the abyss. The danger level began climbing significantly with each nautical air mile we covered.

What happens once one loses visual contact while in flight is a rather complex and often harrowing experience to say the least. Although my instrument panel still showed that our course heading was correct, I no longer had any visual references beneath me to gauge my actual flight path. For instance, just after takeoff and after reaching flying altitude a course heading would be based on a set of specific prefactored wind conditions. If let's say for example that one might encounter an eighteen knot crosswind from the northeast. As the airplane covers distance, the pilot continually looks out the cockpit windows for landmarks for which to compare back to the cockpit flight maps. As an example, let's assume that with the original course headings based on the assumed wind speed and wind direction indicates that the plane should be flying directly over the city of La Crosse, Wisconsin. With visual sight, it may be determined though, that for some reason the plane is actually flying off course and too far to the south of the city. With the aid of visual detection, one can determine whether the wind speed or wind direction has changed and then make the proper flight course corrections.

A very tight knot began to form deep inside my belly as we flew deeper into our blind flight path. By this point, I'd flown for more than one hour without being able to see any visual landmarks. Although nervous, I remained somewhat calm by relying solely the directional backup of my VOR (VHF Omnidirectional Range navigation system) to cross-reference my location. With VOR, a pilot can simply, accurately, and without ambiguity navigate from point A to point B. The basic principle of operation of the VOR is very simple: the VOR facility transmits two signals at the same time. One signal is constant in all directions while the other is rotated about the station. The airborne equipment receives both signals, looks (electronically) at the difference between the two signals, and interprets the result as a radial from the station.

Based on my VOR instrument readings, I was still on the proper flight course even though I was now over two hours into my flight and still without visual sight of the ground below. For reasons which I'll never understand, suddenly the aircraft radio transmitter along with the VOR navigational systems ceased functioning in midair. My eyes glazed over as my worst fears were realized. We now had no means whatsoever of transmitting a Mayday signal, we could not make a one-hundred-and-eighty-degree turn to go back, and even worse, we no longer had any means of knowing our flight course. How could matters get any worse?

Based on the calculations of my flight plan, it became all too obvious that within the next thirty minutes, several catastrophic factors would result in the crash or destruction of our aircraft. The plane's dual fuel tank gauges were nearing the empty mark, so the idea of flying around in circles hoping for the ground fog to clear was not an option. Without a radio, there was no way to transmit our emergency, and there was no way to call an airport tower to request a radar fix on our plane.

My father sensed the eminent gravity of our situation, yet he kept calm and allowed me to do what I'd trained so many months for.

I looked my father in the eye and said, "Dad, we are in a bit of a fix here. We are close to running out of fuel, I can't see the ground to make an emergency landing, and our radio navigation system stopped working."

My father looked back at me with concern and replied, "I hope you don't have any more bad news."

I replied, "Well, only just that we have no other choice but to continue flying on our current course in hopes that it is still correct. Once we fly past the fogged-in eastern border of Wisconsin, I'm hoping that just as we fly over the edge of Lake Michigan, perhaps the temperature difference will allow us to make eye contact with the open body of water."

My father spoke with alarm saying, "And then what?"

I replied, "I'm going to have little choice other than turning the plane back around toward the land mass and crash-landing the plane in the water as close to the shoreline as possible." My father was stunned and remained quiet as he looked out the window of the fateful plane that was destined to become our tomb.

I began praying silently for God to please come to our aid. I kept glancing down at my watch noting that too much time had elapsed with still no breaks in the abundant ground fog covering the earth below our plane. Based on the flight plan that I'd filed, we should have been nearing Milwaukee assuming that we had somehow inexplicably stayed on course for the past three hours without visual references or without a working VOR navigational system to guide our path.

Perhaps I should have prayed sooner, or perhaps being so high in the sky my prayers were heard quicker. To my amazement, at nearly the same instant that I pleaded and prayed for my Lord's help, I suddenly spotted a small break in the fog cover below catching my first glimpse of land in nearly three hours. Even my father's hopes swelled as he caught a glimpse of a larger break in the fog cover on his side of the plane. In all of my life, I've never had a prayer answered so instantly or with more impact directly upon my well-being. It was as though the very breath of God suddenly dispersed the dense ground cover and opened our path toward safety.

Through the murky haziness I somehow spotted an airport runway from our high vantage point in the sky. I shouted to my father, "Dad, I have no idea what city we are over or what airport that is just below us, but I'm going to attempt an emergency landing right now before we run out of fuel, so hang on!" With that, I executed what is called a direct-approach landing rather than make the customary multidirectional landing approach.

My father and I both watched closely from every angle of our cockpit windows for signs of other nearby aircraft either landing or taking off. Without hesitation, I guided the plane straight down to the waiting runway. Miraculously, at the exact same instant that the wheels of the aircraft impacted the runway, the radio crackled with static and started to function properly once again.

I nearly fainted when the radio sprung to life emitting, "Niner, two, one, two, zero, one this is the Milwaukee Tower clearing you for immediate taxi towards the aircraft maintenance hangar. Do you copy?" My heart leaped for joy as I responded, "Roger that, tower. We thought we were doomed with our radio and navigational system inoperable, but today, we had the helping hand of God bring us to the right airport in just the nick of time. Thanks for your guidance, tower. Over and out."

After I'd taxied the plane to the hanger and shut down the engine, my father and I exited the cramped quarters of the cockpit. We steadied ourselves briefly while trying to stand on our ever-wobbly legs.

I looked at my father and said, "Sorry about your first flight being so terrifying."

My father responded with, "I'm very proud of how you handled the entire incident, Scott. You were as professional as any pilot could ever be, and you didn't crack even under such dire circumstances."

With instructions for the airplane mechanic to fix our defective radio and navigational system, my father and I made our way by taxi to the Wisconsin State Fairgrounds to meet up with my brother. Unbelievable after all that we'd just been through, we had been on course and on time to meet our objective.

Following a very successful cattle show, we headed back to the airport. The electronic problems had been corrected, and before long, we were airborne once more on our return flight. My father's second flight was without incident, and before long, he was met at the Rochester airport by my mother following our landing.

Later, as my father milked his cows for the evening milking, he was simply amazed that within one full day he'd been able to fly all that distance, watch the cattle show, and still perform all of his twice daily milking chores. He looked forward to many more opportunities to attend cattle shows that flying would allow.

The frightening duration of that flight left an indelible memory the likes of which I've never been able to clear from my memory. I can't emphasize enough how close to an aviation disaster we came on that tense day up in the sky. Seemingly, as a result of another miracle, I'd somehow averted my ninth close call with death.

What has always been vividly clear to me, though, is how near to me was God. Tested and tried though I was, while under his watchful and loving gaze, the plane stayed exactly on the proper course, even though we flew entirely blind. Through God's protection, the fog lifted just in time for the correct airport to surface below our searching eyes. Anyone with any flying experience would suggest that we somehow had an awful lot of luck on our side to survive such an ordeal that day.

Perhaps others may think that luck had something to do with it, but my spiritual faith and belief knows otherwise.

CAR WRECK CESSATION—23 YEARS

CHAPTER ELEVEN

This is the Spirit of truth, whom the world cannot receive,
  because it neither sees him nor knows him.
You know him, because he abides with you,
  and he will be in you.

—JOHN 14:17

In retrospect, after reading the first few chapters of this book thus far, it should have become obvious as to why my parent's hair grayed prematurely. Already by the youthful age of twenty-one, I'd previously survived my first series of nine separate life-threatening scenarios. Somehow, in the midst of angels, I made it through each painful or frightening encounter with death, yet somehow lived on. Going into my twenties, I had an epiphany when I realized that perhaps I could live through almost anything that came my way.

The previous chapter came to a close while I was still completing my final postsecondary studies attending the University of Minnesota. Over the four long, hard years it took to gain my college degree, I'd packed what felt like a lifetime of experiences into those few short years.

As mentioned earlier, I worked a full-time forty hour per week job while attending college on a full-time basis. For my entire college education, I had worked at the U of M Dairy Research Barn Facility. There was no better or higher paying job on the college campus that could have allowed several of my dairy farm-raised friends and me to earn precious dollars to offset our expensive college educations.

The job hiring process at the U. of M. dairy barn required each applicant to simply explain to the barn manager what one's own family dairy farm consisted of and then agree to never be late for work and accept not to ever miss a scheduled work shift. I couldn't believe it when I was offered the job as a senior milking technician. I was paid far more per hour than nearly all of the other university students in their various other part-time jobs, yet all I had to do was exactly what I'd been doing my entire lifetime while growing up and working on my parent's farm.

The university research dairy barn housed a herd of one hundred and twenty dairy cows of which countless feeding trials were conducted all throughout the year. The herd of cattle represented top-level dairying genetics and the cows had the ability to produce vast quantities of milk for human consumption.

The one detail that always bothered me regarding working at the university dairy barn was just how antiquated and outdated the facilities were. The dairy barn itself was built at the beginning of the 1900s. For this reason, there was little mechanization inside the facility. Imagine climbing a tall corn silage cement silo, which was sixty feet tall and with an eighteen foot diameter and then using pitchforks to throw enough forage down the chute to feed over one hundred hungry cows. Most modern-day farming operations simply switch on a motorized unloader.

It almost seemed unimaginable having to feed each dairy cow by hand using a scoop shovel and then having to use wheelbarrows along with shovels to scoop up the manure waste coming out of the back ends of those rather large bovines. Nearly every dairy in existence had automatic barn cleaners, which evacuated the manure waste from behind the cows. On top of this, our milking process involved using very outdated milk buckets to harvest the milk from each cow, and then we had to weigh the milk, and finally empty our pails of milk into waiting ten-gallon milk cans for transport to a refrigerating cooler. Modern-day dairies had evolved to utilizing long lengths of stainless steel pipelines to transport milk to the cooling tanks.

Needless to say, most of us students working at the university research barn were embarrassed whenever a tour of modern-day dairy farmers visited the barn because we were forevermore hearing comments such as, "Can you believe that all the research coming out of this college dairy operation is based on technology and equipment that hasn't been used in today's dairy industry for decades!" They would often continue on by saying, "As dairy farmers, every one of us has far more modern-day operations than this old relic." It was usually about then that most of us student laborers, out of pure shame, would make ourselves scarce.

All this being stated, the manual labor requirements to operate the university dairy barn allowed twenty-one of us students to earn a sizable portion of revenue, which we then used to pay our way through college. Ironically, a few years following my departure from college, the University of Minnesota built a new ultra-modern dairy research facility and dairy barn. The historic old barn, which I'd spent so many long hours working in, was eventually remodeled and converted into a series of university classrooms. From the day of the new dairy barn, though, it required only a minimal amount of student labor to function, which deprived many students from earning their extra income.

I personally owe a great deal to having been able to earn income at the dairy barn while attending college. As a person who requires little sleep, I asked for and was granted the early morning milking shifts which began at 2:00 a.m. At the campus dairy barn, the dairy cows needed to be milked twice every day of the year. The 2:00 a.m. shift that I requested was not the most popular milking shift for typical college students to say the least, even if they were hard-working farm-raised kids, so I gladly accepted every shift the manager would assign to me. As incentive to get enough students to milk the herd at such early hours seven days per week, those of us who took the graveyard shift were granted an extra one dollar per hour wage increase.

For four long years, I worked forty hours per week while attending a full-time college curriculum. During the short summer months while I took a break from my class schedule, I would log sixty-hour-work weeks to earn even more income toward my tuition expenses.

As I neared the end of my final college semester, it became almost like torture since I was physically and mentally burned out from the schedule I'd put myself through for so long. I was simply tired and fed up with everything ranging from attending classes, to working such long, hard hours at the university dairy barn. Frankly, by the end, I had developed a somewhat negative attitude, and I wanted nothing more than to be free of my bondage to the campus and to get on with my professional life after college.

With only a few months of campus life remaining, I aspired for no further aggravations in my life. That was until a fateful day that I worked an afternoon shift at the university dairy barn and smashed headfirst into a life-changing moment.

As mentioned previously in this chapter, there were over twenty farm boys working at the research dairy barn. During most of the working shifts, it took all the physical strength we could all muster just to perform the strenuous manual labor since the barn had very little automation.

About one time per year, however, the barn manager would ensure that each and every male student laborer under his supervision would come face-to-face with what became our greatest aggravation. At least annually, the sadistic barn manager would hire one female student employee. They were often a short, petite, frail-framed young lady that started their new dairy barn role with great enthusiasm only to discover quickly that they were no match for the physical requirements of such an outdated dairy facility.

Every time the barn manager would introduce the newest female employee, the majority of the male employees would simply roll their eyes and sigh loudly. Often they would comment later to each other about their disgust while wondering to themselves if the boss would ever learn from his past female hiring mistakes. For the record, I've always believed in gender equality. I also believe that in the example of the university dairy barn, females and males should have an equal opportunity to be employed and be paid equally for said work.

Where the lines blur, however, is with each passing year, at least one new female student would start working at the barn. Each was paid the same pay scale to do the same manual labor as all the male students. Problems always arose, though, because she would soon realize her physical shortcomings trying to work in a barn lacking automation. During any given female employee's short tenure on her new job, each of us male employees would have to do far more lifting, more shoveling, and do extra work because the female students were unable to complete many of their assigned tasks.

With less than three months of college left, I walked into the university dairy barn office one afternoon and stared directly into the eyes of a short, petite, blond female sitting on a chair next to the boss.

The hair on the back of my neck prickled immediately as the manger seemingly took great delight in proclaiming, "Well, Mr. Scott, I've just hired a Meeker County Dairy Princess, and this girl is going to show you a thing or two."

My face turned crimson with anger as I spun instantly around in my tracks, and while heading back out the door, I shouted, "Over my dead body she will!"

The door slammed behind me as I stomped down the barn corridor on my way to collect the afternoon silage feeding for the dairy cows. All too suddenly, I felt a slight tap on my shoulder as the new female employee had rushed out the door and down the hallway to catch up to me.

As I spun around to look at her, she questioned, "Did I do something wrong?"

Without the slightest hesitation, I retorted back, "You haven't yet, but I assure you that you will do something wrong!"

We strode into the inside of the silage room, which was attached to the two large upright concrete silos holding the corn silage supply of feed for the cow herd. Since the young lady who stood before me was new to the job and since she'd obviously deceived the barn boss into believing she could actually perform her job duties, I harshly explained the process. Intimidating as I tried to be, she listened intently and expressed little emotion. It was easy to imagine that she was looking at me while thinking to herself what a massive creep I was.

I drilled out my instructions to her as I explained that I would climb the long and harrowing ladder up into the bowels of the silo standing sixty feet up into the air. I continued to throw insults her way as I described how her job was to push the two very large wooden feed carts underneath the silage chute whereby the silage I would pitch down would then fill each cart.

She began looking at me with genuine disgust as I stated, "You will need to yell for me to stop throwing down silage once the first cart is full, and then if you are even strong enough, try to push the full cart out of the way, and then push the empty cart underneath the chute."

If looks could only kill! As I insulted her with nearly every sentence coming out of my mouth, she began to show some real fight behind her glassy stare.

Without further ado, I started climbing up the silo, only to feel her tug at the bottom of one of my pant legs.

I glanced down at her as she mentioned, "I'll climb up into the silo and throw down the silage."

I was so shocked that I nearly lost my grip on the ladder rungs.

Carefully climbing back down the treacherous silage chute, I stood within inches of her face and responded, "Oh, you think you are going

118 Scott D. Gottschalk

to climb all the way up that tall silo, then throw down enough silage for one hundred and twenty cows?"

She looked at me in silence as I lambasted her once more with, "You do realize that you must use a big pitchfork to throw the silage out through a small opening at the top of the silo, and we need to finish this small portion of our afternoon work sometime before next month?"

With mixed emotions, the new girl started climbing the silo, while softly speaking down in my direction, "I've thrown silage out of our silo back home on our dairy farm for most of my life, so this won't be anything different for me."

Her words silenced me in my tracks as I stared dumbfounded up the silage chute, watching her disappear from sight.

Even yet to this day, my most vivid memory from my first encounter with the new girl was just how wonderful her backside appeared to me as she climbed ever higher into the tall silo that afternoon. Even if I didn't like her much, she didn't look just too bad.

No sooner had she reached the top of the silo and entered into its large cavity, when the silage started plummeting down the chute and into the empty feed cart. My jaw dropped open as I witnessed the cart filling up faster than most any of the rawboned male employees I worked with were capable of. In mere moments, I shouted up for her to briefly cease, and once the second empty feed cart was switched into place, she began tossing silage down the chute once again on cue. With the second cart filled in near-record time, I shouted up for her to stop and come back down so we could begin feeding the cows their fresh feed.

As the new girl climbed back down the chute and then dropped to the ground from the final rung of the silo ladder, she stood once more before me. All at once I noticed something that up until that moment I'd never seen before from any girl that I'd crossed paths with. This very same new female barn employee was literally ringing wet with perspiration from all of her exertion to complete her assigned chore up in the silo.

The reason that a sweating female was such a foreign concept to me was directly tied to my upbringing while growing up on our own family farm. It was on our farm where my father, my brother, Jerry, and me worked and perspired all the time in an effort to complete our seemingly endless farm tasks. On the contrary, my mother, as well as my three sisters Julie, Sally, and Marcia seldom set foot outside of our home to aid with chores. The females in our family certainly all worked hard at their responsibilities, but the outside labor on our very traditional family farm was reserved for the males of our family.

One can only imagine my surprise then when before me stood a hardworking, gasping for breath, profusely sweating young lady. WOW, was I impressed!

Impressed though I was, there was still plenty of time during her first work shift that day to validate what a big mistake the boss had made by hiring her. I directed her to push her full silage feed cart alongside the cows and scoop out feed for each cow just as I also went about doing in another portion of the dairy barn.

Surprisingly, the cow feeding went just as well working with the new girl as it usually did when working with the guys. Try as I might, I couldn't seem to catch her doing anything wrong, and she was certainly carrying her own workload. Just after finishing up our feeding chores, the new girl and I began preparing the equipment to milk the cow herd that evening.

About that time each day, and just before going home for the day, the dairy barn manager would usually pop his head into the milking equipment room to check if everything is okay. Much to my dismay, I had nothing negative to report about the new girl, but there was still ample time to show her a thing or two!

We pushed our milking equipment carts out into the large U-shaped dairy barn where I dictated my orders once more to the quiet young blonde.

With all the intensity I could portray, I drilled, "I want you to go to the opposite side of the barn and then milk the sixty cows on that side while I'm milking the sixty cows on this side of the barn."

I went on to say, "You must milk each cow very carefully, then weigh and record her milk. It is very important that you don't cheat on your weights because the boss checks the individual milk weights compared with how much milk gets sold from this barn."

Then I got within a fraction of an inch from the new girl's face while gritting my teeth and said, "You make sure you don't take all night long to milk your portion of the barn because none of us guys appreciates milking more than our half of the cows simply because the other employee is lazy."

I continued badgering her by announcing, "If I have to milk too many of your cows, I'm going to ensure that you won't be drawing a paycheck from this dairy barn too long after today!"

The new girl gave me another one of what was becoming her patented "looks that could kill" glassy-eyed stare as we separated and went about milking the herd of cows.

For that singular milking, I set about to prove once and for all that the new girl did not belong with our elite crew of guys. During that milking session, I utilized every trick I'd ever learned from my four years of employment in that research dairy barn. On that evening milking, I was destined to show the new girl up once and for all. The sweat nearly lathered on me as I milked at a speed more rapid than ever before.

Due to the U-shape design of that barn, two employees milking cows on opposite sides of the barn were unable to view each other until near the end of milking the cows. I was over confident that I'd done all that I could do to get far enough ahead of the new girl that she would resign from her new job in shame once she watched me milk several of her cows. I could feel the adrenaline surging through me as I rounded the corner of my side of the barn and where the remaining twenty cows waited their turn to be milked.

My heart nearly stopped when I spotted the new girl standing up from beside one of the cows close to me. I demanded to know what she thought she was doing. I'm sure my face lost most of its color when she confessed that she had not only milked all of her sixty cows, but that she was nearly finished with milking an additional ten of my cows!

Since I knew that I was one of the fastest and most skilled workers at the dairy barn, it was easy to assume that she must have cheated or done something wrong to outdo my efforts with such ease. As soon as we had finished milking the cows and cleaning all the equipment, with a chip on my shoulder, I investigated her work further. I counted every cow that she milked and added up the milk weights from each cow she had handled.

The results did not favor me as I was aghast at the realization this new girl not only had milked more cows than me, but for whatever reasons, her cows had given more milk than any of the guys working at the barn could harvest.

As I turned out the lights to the university dairy barn and made my way back to my apartment, I struggled with how badly the new girl had shown me a thing or two that long afternoon and evening. While I'd done all the challenging and posturing, she had quietly gone about demonstrating how it was possible for a female to not only do the work, but then also to do it better than the guys.

Astrid was the new girl's name who I met for the first time that day in the research dairy barn. The Lord works in mysterious ways because as of the writing of this book, she went on to became the mother of my two sons. In addition, she has greatly blessed me as my wife, my partner, and my best friend now for well over thirty years of marriage. And oh, by the way, she still shows me a thing or two nearly every day.

*   *   *

Astrid and I were making preparations to get married in 1980 following the completion of her college education. We were ecstatic to begin our lives together as college educated, new young dairy farmers, but first things first.

After obtaining my college degree in 1979, I entered into a farming partnership on my parent's farm. Typical of the intensity I've always tried to glean out of life, I was juggling a lot of balls at that time. Each day began for me together with my father by milking our more than one hundred dairy cows starting at 4:30 a.m. Immediately following the morning milking, I would quickly shower and change clothes as I scurried off to a nearby high school to spend the entire day teaching vocational agriculture classes to my students. Once my teaching duties were completed for the day, I would once again be back on our farm milking the dairy cows at 5:30 p.m.

As if this didn't appear insane enough, at this time, I also had organized a country western entertainment band called the Wranglers. As a vocalist and a guitar player, I and our group would entertain at dances, nightclubs, and bars most nearly every weekend all throughout a tristate area. A typical weekend for me consisted of milking cows twice per day along with doing the daily farm chores, and then be off playing music in some smoke-filled dance hall from 9:00 p.m. until 1:00 a.m.

Our exhausted group of musicians would then disassemble all of our equipment, load the equipment into our vans, and then drive back to our homes. At one point during this period of my life, our group played for thirty consecutive weekends in row. After completing each evenings session, I would drive back home arriving just in the nick of time to milk cows during the 4:30 a.m. shift. "No rest for the weary" became my call to action in those days.

On a stormy weekend in January of 1980, Astrid drove her vintage Ford Pinto economy car down from her parent's farm in central

Minnesota to spend the weekend with my family and me. With only months remaining until our impending wedding date, we wanted to work on wedding invitations as well as make other marriage arrangements.

Astrid arrived at our home on that Saturday morning. We spent nearly the entire day working on our nuptial arrangements. With a lot of effort, we finished our processes for the day and then we decided to drive Astrid's small economy car into the city of Rochester and attend a local dance to let off a little steam. The weather reports were not good, however, since we were experiencing an uncommon winter freezing rain storm, which is a very rare occurrence for Minnesota in the month of January.

We listened to the local weather report, and with some uncertainties, we decided to attend the dance together anyway. The short eight-mile drive from our rural home outside of the village of Byron and into the larger city of Rochester was slow and cautious. Although the roads were slippery with the freezing rain, the local highway department trucks were out in force laying sand and salt down on the roadways to improve the traction.

Astrid and I had a marvelous time at the dance that evening as we enjoyed our much-deserved close time together gleefully dancing the night away. Sometime around midnight, we left the dance hall and held tightly to each other as we shuffled our way across the treacherously slick parking lot toward Astrid's little car.

After helping her into the passenger seat of the car, I cautiously made my way around the car trying to scrape away what appeared to be about an inch of thick frozen ice covering the entire car and all the windows. At last, I finished clearing the windows, and I lowered myself into the driver's seat. As I watched the lights of the city slowly diminish in our rearview mirror, we hunched nervously in our seats as I tried to keep the little car's wheels from spinning out of control.

We hadn't driven too far along the road leading out of the city when it became obvious to us that the highway department trucks had ceased putting sand and salt on the roadways. Evidently, the freezing ice on the roads had ultimately won the battle by covering over any sand that had previously been laid down on the road. Ahead of us was one long, steep incline in the road whereby any westward traveler needs to climb before reaching the village of Byron. I grabbed the steering wheel tightly with both hands as I indicated to Astrid just how little control I felt with the car.

Upward the car and we climbed slipping and sliding all over the road as we tried to reach the top of the grade. Just when the car neared the top of the climb, something tragic and horrifying occurred.

Somehow, the little car lost all the traction of its four wheels as it spun completely around in first one circle, then another circle. Next the spinning car slipped down over the edge of a treacherously steep ditch. As the car spun back toward the direction we had driven from, it suddenly plummeted twenty-five feet down through the thicket and smashed into a large electric power line pole on my driver's side of the car. In a moment, the speeding car came to an instant stop as my head crashed completely through the driver's side window. As I smashed through the window glass of the car door, my head missed impacting the large electric pole by a merely a fraction.

The impact of our car crash was so severe that both Astrid and I were rendered completely unconscious. For nearly twenty minutes, we were both knocked out cold. Finally, my mind started to somewhat register what had happened as I tried to clear my head. At that point, I had no idea what had happened, but I knew that we were somehow in trouble. I remember thinking why was it so black and why were we sitting in our car in the middle of a cold, stormy, winter night with the windows rolled down. With cobwebs clouding my mind, I reached over to Astrid while calling out her name but failed to get a response from her.

At long last, she stirred and let out a moan. She whispered softly begging me to roll up the car windows because she felt really cold. I surmised that she was in shock as I responded back that I had tried rolling up the windows, but they must somehow be frozen open because the window handles would turn, but for some odd reason, the windows would not close. I blindly felt around the inside of the pitch dark car until I discovered a flashlight.

The two of us looked on in terror at the scene illuminated by the flashlight beam. The first detail we noticed at once was that somehow the car had crashed into a large electric pole on the driver's side. Not only had the impact blown out the driver's side window, but all the front and rear windows on both sides of the car were blown out, thus discovering the reason why we couldn't close the open windows in the dark as we regained consciousness. Our next observation sent chills up our spine as we became aware of the massive amounts of blood oozing from our heads and faces from the countless chards of broken window glass that had punctured our skin. We both appeared to be some sort of scary monsters from a horror movie. We became aware of how difficult it was to move our feet and legs, and soon the flashlight beam revealed the reasons why.

The car had impacted with such a force into the huge unyielding pole that it actually broke the steel frame of the car as the vehicle wrapped itself tightly around the pole. The exterior of the destroyed car collapsed so severely that it resulted in the vehicles interior being squashed together much like an accordion musical instrument squeezes together. Somehow, the interior crushing stopped just short of severing or crushing both of our legs, yet our legs were so tightly compressed that we had to help each other pry the others legs free.

Knowing that I couldn't open the driver's side door with the large pole crushed into the door, Astrid and I tried with all our might to open her passenger door without success. At last we unbuckled our seat belts and carefully crawled out through the jagged broken passenger side car window.

It was nearly impossible, but somehow, we aided each other as we crawled on our tattered hands and knees up out of the frozen, icy ditch, which had nearly claimed our lives. At last we made it up onto the frozen ice-skating rink that was once a road. Since it was well past midnight, we couldn't see any farmyard lights in which to direct our path toward help and safety. Since this was in an era long before the use of portable cell phones, we had no choice other than try to walk in an effort to find help soon. With each passing minute, our risks increased from either perishing from possible injuries, from going into shock, or from freezing to death in the severe wintery weather conditions.

The road was so slippery that we were unable to walk up the steep incline we'd been traveling toward without falling down. Astrid and I held hands and held tightly to each other as we staggered our way down the treacherous road hoping to stumble upon a darkened farmyard. We traveled what felt like forever when at last we observed one distant illuminated lamp through the trees well off the darkened highway. We shuffled along ever so carefully as the pain within our bodies increased from the trauma of the accident. At last we were at the doorsteps of a stranger's house knocking on the door.

We knocked and waited, then knocked again. Before long we heard a response coming from behind the closed door shouting, "Who is out there at this time of night and what do you want?"

With what little strength I had left in me by this point, I responded, "My name is Scott and my fiancé and me just had a dreadful car accident up on the big hill on Old Highway 14. Our car is totally wrecked, and we need help."

With that, the door suddenly opened and within minutes a kindly retired farm couple was seeing to our needs and bringing us warm cups of tea to sip on.

Remarkable as it seems now, we had just come through a car collision that should have killed both of us, yet somehow we had escaped with only some minor cuts and bruises. The collapsed vehicle should have severed our legs, but somehow it stopped just short of doing so and without fracturing a single bone in our legs. As my head smashed through the car window, I should have collided with the immovable pole, killing me instantly or at the very least fracturing my neck, yet I inexplicably missed the pole by a fraction. In addition, we were driving a model of economy car with an infamous reputation of being an unsafe "tin can." Along with that distinction, our vehicle was also a model with several documented gas tank explosions resulting from impact collisions, yet on that night, no explosion resulted.

Miraculously, the only object that died on that night and was severely injured was in fact the car itself. Our human frailties were somehow spared even amongst the jagged and twisted metal fragments and broken glass.

The following day after the winter storm had passed, my father drove Astrid and me to the accident scene. There, we observed as a large tow truck operator working alongside a highway patrolman as he winched Astrid's battered car up out of its frozen tomb. Everyone gasped as the car split in half as it was dragged away from the lethal electric pole.

The words of the patrolman are still burned into Astrid's and my memories as we recall his words, "My God, you two must have had guardian angels crossing your path last night in that wintery storm. I've never witnessed anyone surviving such a crash so intense that it splits the vehicle in half and completely destroys the car."

We counted our blessings as my father drove us back to our home. He lovingly reached out and patted Astrid on the knee while saying to her, "You have no idea what you are in for by marrying Scott! This is only the beginning for you, and I sincerely hope you won't mind watching your hair turn white at a very early age."

DEATH WISH ON A MOTORCYCLE— 24 YEARS

CHAPTER TWELVE

O Lord my God, I take refuge in you; save and deliver me from all who pursue me.

—PSALM 7:1

Following our nearly catastrophic car crash only a few months earlier, and with the grace of God, Astrid and I were able to exchange our wedding vows in March of 1980, thus beginning our married lives together. My father's prophetic words warning Astrid of my propensity for risk and danger during the final months of our engagement still seemed to echo in our ears as we moved forward with our adult lives together.

By the time I reached the age of twenty-four, I was becoming almost accustomed to surviving near misses with my life, but this was an all too unfamiliar experience for my new bride to be sure. At times, it was as though I felt nearly invincible and beyond reproach when staring death in the face. As each day passed at this youthful time of my life, I became more emboldened to seek out risk and to challenge my very existence. It was during this year of my life where I entered a realm that few people would ever care to enter.

Growing up as a teenager of the outlandish 1970s, my view of the world in general was inadvertently modified and somewhat tainted. The '70s came blasting into my life just as much of the youth in America shifted their lifestyles toward longer hairstyles, bell-bottoms, loud rock music, and watching crazy television shows.

One television show that left an indelible mark on me was called *The Dukes of Hazzard*. Seldom would I miss an episode of watching Bo and Luke Duke outwit, outsmart, and outdrive Roscoe P. Coltrane who was the inept Hazzard County deputy sheriff always trying to catch the Duke cousins doing something wrong. Each week I watched in fascination as Bo and Luke Duke in their awesome orange GTO muscle car named the General Lee would outrun the law enforcement time and again. The radical vehicular stunts amazed me as countless scenes showed cars jumping over barriers or leaping across canyons, then speeding away only to leave the cops in the dust each and every time.

Watching *The Dukes of Hazzard* show each week began imprinting a dangerous thought in my mind at an impressionable young age. Although much of the antics on the television screen were obviously contrived and nothing other than television fantasy, it still somehow planted some precarious notions within my mind during each passing week. My mind was so imprinted that even years after *The Dukes of Hazzard* television series was no longer on television, I still aspired to one day be like the Dukes and leave the cops in the dust.

From the time I received my driver's license at sixteen years of age until my twenty-fourth birthday, I suffered numerous vehicular speeding infractions. In fact, I averaged between two and three speeding tickets per year during that short nine-year span of time. In all, I received twenty-five speeding and moving violations before I even reached my twenty-fifth year of life. Absurd as it may seem, I loved to drive fast and loved the feel of a powerful engine gathering speed as I guided various cars, pickup trucks, or motorcycles down the road at my command. Over time, it even became a light-hearted joke as I would reiterate to my friends about how I'd seen the interior car design of every model year of highway patrol car for the past nine years; all while sitting in a patrol car receiving yet another speeding ticket.

Living in Minnesota, the moving violations ruling was such that a driver was allowed up to three moving violations within any given calendar year. On the fourth moving violation, however, then one earned the privilege of standing before a traffic court judge who would decide whether or not to suspend the driving privileges of the guilty party. Twice during that nine-year period of my life, after earning my fourth speeding ticket within the same calendar year, I stood before a judge while he demanded to know why I should not have my driver's license temporarily suspended and until I could learn to obey the posted traffic speeds.

Although each court appearance was unsettling for me, and even though I was severely reprimanded by the court, somehow, I never once lost my driving privileges. In retrospect, perhaps I should have lost my driver's license for a period of time, which might then have stifled my desire for speed and danger while operating a vehicle. The traffic fines I encountered were a mounting problem. With each moving violation I was cited for, the fines increased proportionately. So the first violation may have been a fine of $70, then the second violation may have been a fine of $150, then the third violation may have been a fine of $325, and by the fourth violation, the fine and consequences of losing one's driving privileges were enough to make even someone such as myself sit up and take notice of the pain and discomfort it could inflict on one's lifestyle.

With each driving violation, my parents would unleash a torrent of angry challenges onto me asking why I was so incapable of controlling my excessive driving habits. They were extremely upset as they would endlessly remind me that I was such an insurance risk that it was becoming nearly impossible to find affordable auto insurance coverage for me. Although my mother and father never completely understood, the underlying reason for my compulsion for speed was that I simply loved to go fast, and I loved to feel the unbridled power at my beckoning touch. That feeling is one which I'll probably never fully diminish, but as I've matured over the years, I've learned to control my insatiable desire for speed. This in and of itself has been a forced behavioral change since I no longer desire to pay such lofty fines to the traffic court systems or pay such exorbitant auto insurance premiums.

It is easy to imagine then as one analyzes my mind-set and historical love of speed why by the age of twenty-four and newly married, why I was destined to get myself into some real trouble before my new wife, Astrid, could even react.

*   *   *

In a previous chapter, I mentioned my love of motorcycles and how much I've always enjoyed the sense of freedom they provide as one seemingly flies down the road through the open air. That being said, one of my first married-life transactions involved trading my relatively small and very slow college motorcycle off for something more fitting for my desires.

For years, I'd been reading every motorcycling magazine I could lay my hands on. I'd become somewhat of an expert on every variation and design the motorbiking world had to offer. It had not gone unnoticed to me that in the late 1970s, Yamaha had designed and manufactured the fastest street legal motorcycle available for purchase. I had the Yamaha XS1100 Special specs and test-drive reports all but memorized. That amazing machine boasted a lightning fast acceleration, and on the test track, it had logged speeds of 152 mph!

From the moment I read about that blazingly fast machine, I set my sights on owning one someday. In the back of my mind, one thought remained vividly clear. If I could somehow find a way to acquire such an unbelievably fast motorcycle, then I would never again have to deal with a speeding ticket from a law officer since there would be no way their cars could keep up. I foolishly believed that if the Duke boys on *The Dukes of Hazzard* could show up the cops, then one day so would I one day.

Much to my new wife's dismay, shortly following our wedding day, I traded off my Honda 250 and paid a few thousand dollars to boot as I took possession of the fastest stock motorcycle in America at the time. The sleek, racy two-wheeled machine would take my breath away as it effortlessly accelerated to outlandish speeds with a mere twist of my wrist on the throttle. Never before in my lifetime had I ridden a machine with such thrust and instant acceleration. From the moment I rode my new high-speed motorcycle away from the dealer, I believed I would never again be caught by a law officer desiring to cite me for a speeding violation.

It didn't take Astrid very long following our wedding to realize that she had married someone drawn to high-risk behavior unlike no one she'd ever witnessed before. On the day that I dialogued with her about my intentions to go skydiving, all she could do was stare blankly at me. Since I held a private pilot license, she had flown with me on a few occasions. As if that wasn't enough for her to absorb, she was now listening to me state matter-of-factly, "I've learned to fly an airplane, but now I want to learn to jump out of one!" In her way of reasoning, she couldn't figure out why any sensible person would even contemplate jumping out of a perfectly functioning airplane. For me, however, the palms of my hands got sweaty just from the sheer thoughts of such an exhilarating parachute jump from an airplane.

The stage was set, and my life was about to take an irreversible course that day many years ago. Astrid and I had made our first home together in central Minnesota, but the skydiving school I'd signed up for on that weekend was in southern Minnesota. I kissed my fearful wife good-bye and indicated to her that I'd see her safe and sound within a couple of days. With that, I threw a backpack on my shoulders with some extra clothes and some toiletries, put my full-face motorcycle helmet on, and then mounted my new motorcycle. My motorcycle was so new in fact that it had less than one hundred miles on the odometer, and I was carrying the license and registration application in my pocket since the actual license plate for the motorcycle had not yet arrived in the mail.

I could almost sense the taste of adrenaline in my mouth of what was to come as I left our driveway and sped off down the highway with the fading view of my new wife disappearing in my rearview mirror.

A few hours later, I'd arrived at my destination and was participating in the classroom instruction portion of the skydiving training. In our training, we learned about the physics involved in parachuting from an airplane. We were taught what to do if our main chute failed to open and how to properly deploy our reserve chute. We were trained how to jump from the plane, then we were instructed on the proper procedure for landing. In all, due to the dangers involved, we spent several hours of skydiving classroom instruction before we were then legally able to jump from an airplane and with our own parachute deployed. I must say the classroom portion became very monotonous and repetitive, however, I would admit that one doesn't want to discover that you don't know what to do in an emergency when you are free-falling through the sky at over 160 mph.

At long last, our skydiving classroom instruction came to an end. My six classmates and I were suited up and our parachutes were attached. Next, we hopped into a powerful airplane modified for skydiving jumps, and within moments, we were climbing to an altitude one mile above the earth. Once we reached our jumping altitude, our instructor asked for someone to be the first to jump from the plane and indicated that it was always the hardest to jump first but, whoever does so, seems to help the other novices gather courage to also make their jumps. I didn't hesitate even for a moment as I raised my hand to volunteer to perform the lead jump. Not surprisingly, no one else wanted to go first.

Since I'd flown an airplane several times, I'd seen the view of the earth many times from such a high altitude, but it is almost indescribable what a feeling it is to force one's legs to take a leap of faith from an airplane with the hopes the parachute will open without incident. My skydiving leap went flawlessly, and the rush of adrenaline provided a flush of excitement such as I'd never experienced before. I'll never forget my feelings of invincibility as I floated nearly one mile back safely to the ground.

To say that I was on a "high" following my successful leap from an airplane would have been a massive understatement. At that moment, I remember having the sensation that I was almost indestructible and was beyond being able to actually die. I literally felt as if I could walk through a wall of fire and go unscathed. With such disproportionate thoughts, one can only imagine the trouble I was about to face on my motorcycle journey back home.

I departed the skydiving airport parking lot on my motorcycle with thoughts of making it back home in record-breaking time since I had the fastest stock motorcycle in America between my legs. I was traveling on a stretch of highway that had a steady, steep incline up out of a river valley that climbed for several miles. I was riding my motorcycle at about the posted speed limit when my motorcycle and I quickly came upon a big truck struggling to maintain speed up the steep incline. Without even a moment's hesitation, I twisted the throttle on my motorcycle built purely for speed and dashed around the truck in an instant. Within that instant, I'd been traveling at about 55 mph and with only the slightest twist of my wrist, the motor bike shot up to over 90 mph as I raced past the truck.

Much to my dismay, just as I pulled back into my lane of traffic, a state highway patrol trooper came over the top of the hill toward me. Whatever my speed was at the moment that his radar detected me, I can assure you that it was well over the posted speed limit. As the trooper's car passed by, he hit his sirens and flashers. At that precise moment, I thought to myself, "If the Dukes can do it, so can I."

Just as I rounded the top of the hill that the state trooper had just come over, I cracked my throttle again. Due to the twists and curves in the road, I limited my speed to about 125 mph. I kept nervously glancing back in my rearview mirrors, and since I never saw a patrol car ensuing, after a couple of miles of travel I eased back off my throttle. I was feeling a strong sense of satisfaction that I'd made the correct decision to purchase a motorcycle that couldn't be caught by a police car.

I was settling back into my motorcycle seat and relaxing when I viewed a most frightening image in my rearview mirror. It was a very angry state highway patrol trooper pushing his 440 cubic inch, four-barreled carburetor, specially equipped police interceptor squad car for every mile per hour it could muster. Those police interceptors in the day were capable of achieving speeds of up to 135 mph.

I simply cannot describe my fright at seeing the oncoming police car and hearing his roaring engine appearing to prepare to hit me from the rear. By instinct, I twisted the throttle once again, but by this time, the road had straightened out and I gave the motorcycle all the throttle it could take. Since my motorcycle had no windshield for protection, I'll never forget the unbelievable force of the wind pushing back on my body as the speedometer leapt up to 135 mph, then continued climbing to 140 mph, then 145 mph, and finally hovered at 148 mph.

It was everything I could do to hold on to the racing machine. It almost felt as though I were doing pull-ups on the handlebars simply trying to hang on at such breakneck speeds. Slowly but surely, the 13 mph faster travel of speed allowed me to pull away from the ensuing state trooper.

For a brief moment, my mind drifted back to *The Dukes of Hazzard* television show as I thought to myself, I've finally made it a reality. The actual reality of the matter, however, is a fast motorcycle speeding at 148 mph may be able to outrun even the fastest "Police Interceptor" squad car traveling at 135 mph, but no matter how fast a motorcycle can travel, it can't outrun a police radio!

Traveling at a speed of 148 mph, I was shocked at how fast a mile would click over on my odometer and in moments our high speed chase had elapsed several miles. As I came to the outskirts of a rural town, I became suddenly aware of a mass of police cars converging on me from every direction. At that moment, I surmised that from a law enforcement officer's perspective, this is what may have been transmitted over their police radios.

"Trooper 243 is requesting emergency backup assistance. In high speed pursuit of an unlicensed red-colored motorcycle which may be stolen. Motorcycle driver is wearing a full-face helmet and is presently unidentifiable. Due to the suspicious nature of the chase, there is reason to believe the motorcycle operator may be transporting illegal contraband as well in the backpack being worn."

As I quickly came to the outskirts of the small town, my vision scanned an unbelievable scene. The police radios were certainly working overtime because I had one squad car immediately behind me coming from an easterly direction, I saw two more squad cars racing toward me from the west, I saw another squad car blazing in my direction coming from the north on different road, and lastly, I spotted the local town police squad car heading out of town toward me coming from the south. At that point with a total of five police cars chasing me, I suddenly felt hopelessness such as never before. My brain struggled with what to do next. One side of me said stop immediately and surrender before you die. The other side of me was driven by fear and spurred onward by adrenaline. I was convinced that trying to surrender only to plead sheer stupidity with the angry law officers might prove extremely risky at best. I literally feared for the beating I felt I might be in for if I tried to stop.

Without much time to weigh my choices, I decided it would be better to die trying to escape rather than be beaten by an army of angry cops. With that, I locked the brakes on my speeding motorcycle as I whisked up to the edges of the small town. I turned off the main highway and directed my machine into the heart of the rural town. There were several squad cars in hot pursuit with their sirens blaring and their lights flashing as I picked up speed on my way through the town. Luckily, there were no pedestrians in sight as I blasted through the small town. By the time I'd reached the other side of the town, my speedometer read in excess of 130 mph. With five police cars in chase, I literally leaped over the town's railroad tracks, and at 130 mph, the high speed jump through the air would have made the Duke boys proud. The trouble was, the Duke boys were merely Hollywood contrived fictitious characters, and I was in a real struggle for life.

As I sped away from the town heading south, I once again pushed the upper speed limits of my motorcycle. After only a couple of miles, I suddenly realized that there were now two additional law officer squad cars coming from the south and heading in my direction. Once again, I locked up the brakes of my large motorcycle and maneuvered the machine down a dangerous rural gravel road. Racing motorcycles such as mine were never built for rural gravel roads, but I had become desperate to find a path of escape.

I raced over a hill traveling at over 90 mph when suddenly I found myself trapped. What I'd thought was a rural gravel road was actually a long gravel driveway leading into a dairy farmer's yard. I'll never forget the look of terror on the eyes of the farmer and his wife as they were crossing their yard making their way to their barn to milk the cows.

They stopped dead in their tracks as I sped into their yard followed by two squad cars in pursuit. As I entered their farmyard, adrenaline must have given me superhuman strength as I spun my heavy motorcycle around as though it were a mere bicycle then raced on past the two police squad cars that had suddenly entrapped each other in the farmer's yard.

Out of the farmer's driveway, I raced once again as I made a mental note of the treacherous barbed wire fences near both edges of long gravel driveway. As I once again crested the top of the hill leading away from the farm, my speed was in excess of 90 mph. My next view was almost too much to comprehend. Only a mere one hundred yards ahead of me were two state trooper squad cars forming a V-shaped roadblock. There was only a three-foot section of space between the squad cars where both troopers stood facing me with their handguns drawn and aimed directly at me. At that instant, I believed that one way or another I was going to die. I instantly reasoned that I had three choices I could make, and I had to decide without even a split second to contemplate my options. Choice one would have been to lock up my brakes at 90 mph on a dangerous gravel driveway, only to crash since the motorcycle could never have made a stop in such a short distance. Choice two would have been to try to slow down as much as possible and at the last moment veer off and crash into the treacherously jagged barbed-wire fencing. Choice three and the option I opted for was to maintain my speed, and then hope I could make it through the small three-foot spacing between the squad car roadblock, praying the officers would not actually shoot me.

It all happened so fast that comprehending the next chain of events is unsettling to me. Once the troopers realized I was unable to stop my motorcycle in the short distance before encountering their squad cars, they jumped away from the opening they'd been posting in front of. The memory is seared into my mind as one of the troopers shouted, "Stop or I'll shoot." Since I was unable to physically stop my motorcycle, I surmised that I was indeed about to die and perhaps the time had come when my Lord felt enough was enough with this rampant human being. The trooper's .357 Magnum pistol made a deafening crack not once, but twice, as I dashed past the officer. Suddenly I started losing control of my motorcycle as my mind raced to decipher why was I doing this and had I simply gone mad. At first I wondered if I'd been shot, thinking that perhaps I was so amped up on raw adrenaline that possibly I couldn't even feel the bullet enter my body. My next thought was that perhaps one of my motorcycle tires had been shot out, which was why I was losing control.

As it all played out that day, neither had happened. I was somehow miraculously unscathed by two close shots from a deadly handgun. My tires were somehow miraculously intact. I had simply hit a patch of loose gravel and nearly dumped the motorcycle as a result.

As I came to the end of the driveway, the rest of the squad cars were pulled into the driveway along one side of the drive. My sense was that they had parked their squad cars fully expecting the fleeing motorcyclist to be apprehended by the first four squad cars committed to the farm driveway. I hit the road leading back into the small rural town going north, and in an instant, I was again at the top end of the speedometer reading. I made a quick glance back over my shoulder and couldn't believe my eyes. There was a total of seven law officer squad cars involved in chasing me down, but because of the nature of the narrow and restricted farm driveway, each and every one of them were blocking each other's exit. I gained valuable time in my escape as they methodically worked to turn themselves around.

As I entered the town for the second time, I brought my speed down considerably. The first time I passed through during the high speed chase, I hadn't spotted a single pedestrian. On my second pass back through the town, with all the commotion, with all the loud sirens, and with all the flashing lights, suddenly everyone in town had come out to see what was transpiring. The sidewalks on both sides of the street were literally lined with hundreds of citizens. I knew my battles with the police radio were still unfolding because up ahead the fire station had been summoned with a request to drive their longest fire truck out onto the main street of town in one last effort to stop or delay the criminal riding the rogue motorcycle.

I carefully slowed as I closed in on the huge fire truck blocking my escape. With everything that I'd encountered, at that point, I could see no reason to run over or hurt the countless pedestrians who were lining the street. I quickly surmised the situation realizing that I couldn't make it around the fire truck on the right side. I also realized that there was no way to maneuver my motorcycle underneath the large truck. It did seem plausible, however, to inch my way around the back of the massive fire truck since there was a small space between the truck and the fire station door opening. I remember several firemen peeking around that corner wondering what to do. As I aimed the motorcycle for the space behind the truck, all the firemen scattered, leaving me with an easy path of escape.

Just as I reached the outskirts of the town once again and directed the motorcycle toward my final path of escape, I glanced back toward the town one last time only to view the firemen fervently trying to remove the large fire truck from the main street that was then blocking the path of the seven law officer squad cars who were back in full pursuit.

The delays in the town afforded me safe passage out of the area, and when at last I reached home from that horrendous day, I had a lot to contemplate. On that day, I came to the conclusion that while it was possible to evade a ticket with a fast enough motorcycle along with some heightened riding skills, and with a whole lot of luck, it was apparent that it wasn't as easy as what my favorite television show had demonstrated. One would certainly think that a very strong lesson should have been learned that day as I nearly died trying to escape a simple speeding ticket. Did I learn my lesson? Well of course not!

With each passing week following my harrowing high-speed motorcycle chase, my confidence grew and my risk-taking behavior expanded. Sure, for the first couple of weeks following the incident, I laid low and took it easy regarding my driving tendencies. I knew, though, that there was little to fear regarding being discovered because since my motorcycle was so new at the time, it had not had a license plate and because I had been wearing a full-face helmet during the chase, I was fairly confident that there was simply no way of identifying me or the motorcycle.

As the summer progressed, I grew bolder. As I reflect back on that year long ago, I realize now that the best situation for me would have been to get caught. Had I been caught, I would have dealt with the consequences and hopefully corrected my misguided behavior. As it turned out, though, I continued to push the limits and felt more invincible with each passing week.

It was late summer during the very same year. I'd ridden my motorcycle from my home in central Minnesota down to help my father and brother exhibit some of their Hereford cattle at the Iowa State Fair. Following the cattle show, I departed for the long drive back home. I was traveling on the Interstate Highway near Minneapolis. Although the flow of traffic at the time was traveling at more than the posted speed limits, I felt compelled to travel at an even higher rate of speed. I was very pleased with the amount of time I was saving as I darted my ultra-fast motorcycle in and out of the flow of cars. I was pleased that was until I rounded a bend of the highway and viewed a state trooper using radar to check vehicles for speeding.

As I passed by the trooper, he instantly flashed his lights, triggered his siren, and began pursuit. I must say that only an idiot like me in my state of mind would have made the decision to engage in a second high-speed motorcycle chase within the same summer. As I'd mentioned, however, reflecting back, I believe the only way that I was going to cease my rampant behavior was to finally get caught or to die trying to escape.

My motorcycle was once again asked to perform at breakneck speeds as I dashed in and out of the flow of traffic, and at times, I would dash right between two cars or two semitrucks. Although I put some quick distance between the law officer and myself, he quickly found the fastest way to keep up with me was speeding along the outside shoulder of the highway. I decided that my best option of escape was to exit the Interstate Highway, so at the next exit, I sped onto the off-ramp and then quickly accelerated onto an adjoining highway.

Almost as though I were stuck in the same reoccurring nightmare, the police radios started encircling a noose ever tighter around my neck. As with my first chase a few months earlier, I had the speed and motorcycling driving skills to evade and outrun any immediate squad cars, but this time I couldn't seem to evade the incessant call of the police radios demanding more backup assistance for a high-speed chase.

I was keenly aware of at least four squad cars chasing me down through the traffic dense area when at last I locked my brakes and made a hard left turn down what appeared to be a back street. This decision was the beginning of my end. As I raced down the street in hopes of finding some opening in which to outmaneuver and ultimately escape the ensuing squad cars, I suddenly realized that I'd driven down a dead-end road leading to a community park and playground. It was déjà vu all over again as I re-enacted nearly the same scenario as I'd driven down the dead-end farmer's driveway only a few months earlier.

Envision me coming upon this hidden park at a high speed of travel followed by five squad cars in hot pursuit. Since it was a warm, lazy Saturday afternoon, the park was overflowing with parents and their young children.

All at once, a soccer ball came bouncing out onto the street followed by a young child chasing it down only about one hundred yards ahead of me. This was one of the most profound moments in my life as I made a split-second decision about what had to be done. The choice was actually very easy since I could've either continued on with my current high speed path only to run over an innocent child or choose to lock up my brakes, drop the motorcycle to the pavement, and pray for the best.

All these years later, I'm still haunted by the frozen look of fear on the child's face as I made eye contact with him. I did everything within my power to lock up the brakes on the motorcycle. My speed was too fast, however, and I lost control of the large motorbike. The motorcycle came crashing down onto its left side while crushing both my leg and ankle underneath. It seemed an eternity as the motorcycle continued to slide down the street in a shower of sparks toward the frozen little boy, only to come to a complete rest a few feet from the child.

In a flash, there were police cars and police officers everywhere. I pulled myself out from underneath my severely damaged motorcycle somewhat relieved to still be alive and very thankful that I'd averted a collision with the small child. People from the park were quickly gathering around as the first of several law officers equipped with their billy clubs made their way to me as I sat in a daze upon the street next to my damaged motorcycle.

What I'm about to explain next is not easy to describe and was an unfortunate circumstance for all who were involved on that fateful day. What happened next was the very thing I'd always feared the most if caught following a high-speed chase. The officers involved in my chase were obviously amped up on their own adrenaline as they carried out their high-speed pursuit. Law officers are often asked to risk their safety in pursuit of criminals. Once they have a fleeing suspect contained, it can be all too easy to lose control of the situation.

Although I was still groggy from the impact of the motorcycle accident, I was all too aware of the angry law officers running toward me with their billy clubs poised to strike. I raised my hands in a sign of surrender and to emphasize that I was unarmed, only to be hit squarely in the middle of the face by the first law officer's billy club. The impact broke my nose and shattered my eyeglasses. As another officer arrived, I raised my right hand in defense hoping to avoid being hit again in the face, but the small baseball batlike billy club connected with my right forefinger, giving me a compound fracture of my finger. A third officer then began smashing me on the back with his billy club. I took such a beating on my back that it caused my entire back to turn black and blue a few hours later.

The three law officers continued to express their excessive anger toward me in the form of a billy club beating and doing so in front of a large group of pedestrian witnesses when at last a ranking law officer finally arrived at the scene and demanded his patrolmen cease their actions. I was so thankful to have the beating stop as I lay in street in my own ever-growing pool of blood. The actual motorcycle crash had been painful, but it paled in comparison to the beating the law officers had administered.

Everything from here out is a blur to me, but I know that I was handcuffed with my hands behind my back, and then read my rights. Next, I was put into the backseat of a squad car in excruciating pain as I was forced to sit on my handcuffed hands, including sitting on my right forefinger with a bone protruding through the skin. I was then transported to the local jail. It was at the jail that I was fingerprinted and then allowed to clean my wounds and eventually give my statement. I was asked several times if I wanted to be attended to by a doctor, but I refused the offer. I ended up spending the night in jail before being released by paying a bond to await my court appearance.

I arrived in court about one week later a very scared and very pitiful young man. In my heart, I felt the Lord had finally found a means to break me of my bad habit. No matter the beating I'd taken at the hands of the out-of-control law officers, in my mind, I knew I'd been raised to take responsibility for my own actions, and I was prepared to do just that.

My wife, Astrid, drove me to the Hennepin County Courthouse that day and neither of us had any idea of what to expect. I signed in with the clerk of court, and then we waited for our court hearing. We waited for what seemed forever, and we worried about what the eventual outcome of my wayward activities would be.

At last I was called before the judge. He asked me where my representing attorney was. I proclaimed that I was in court to plead guilty and to take responsibility for my actions. The judge sat quietly as he read my case file and surmised the beating I'd been given during my arrest, which was fully documented within the file.

He leaned over his bench and said, "I would strongly suggest that you obtain a lawyer who can review your case and guide you towards the proper plea." He went on to state, "If you can't afford an attorney, then the court will appoint one on your behalf." Lastly, he commented, "This is a pretrial hearing, so I'm recommending that you obtain the services of an attorney and properly prepare for your upcoming court case."

The judge looked down at me with total disbelief as I responded, "Your Honor, I've never done anything illegal in my life, except that I've incurred a few speeding tickets. This time I made a big mistake that I'm not proud of, but I've been raised by parents who instilled in me to always own up to one's mistakes and pay the price." I went on to say, "I respectfully decline your suggestion to obtain an attorney. I would like to request that rather than appearing back in court at a later date, I would like to enter a guilty plea at this time and ask for your sentencing effective immediately."

One could hear a pin drop in that courtroom that day as the judge contemplated my request under such a unique set of circumstances.

At last he looked down at me and asked, "Why did you do it when your history demonstrates that you are a decent, law-abiding young man?"

I shared, "I've always been drawn to speed, and this time, I let it get the best of me. I would even have to admit that my fear of getting beat by law officers probably helped drive my illegal actions to flee."

The judge once again proclaimed, "In my opinion, I believe that the circumstances and harshness of your arrest, along with your clean record, warrants an attorney's representation on your behalf."

I responded with, "I appreciate your input, Judge, but I still plead guilty and request sentencing at this time."

With that, the judge stared me straight in the eye and went on a rant as he remarked, "Young man, as you stand before me, you are faced with a total of twelve misdemeanor counts, gross misdemeanor counts, and felony counts, the worst of which is a felony assault charge with a deadly weapon, namely using your motorcycle to potentially run down another person. In addition, you are faced with multiple violations of fleeing a police officer, resisting arrest, reckless driving, reckless endangerment, speeding in excess of 100 mph over the posted limit, failing to yield, failing to stop, crossing over the center line, passing in a none-passing zone, failing to signal, and illegally passing on the highway shoulder."

I stood before the judge as though a statue as he briefly stopped his rant and sized me up.

Suddenly, he proclaimed, "It is the court's belief that your history reflects a decent, law-abiding background, yet it is apparent you have a propensity for speed, which eventually led to a severe lack of judgment on your behalf."

With that, the judge imposed his sentence upon me, and I was forever changed as a result.

The judge spoke again by stating, "You have pleaded guilty to the charges before you. It is my decision to drop all of your charges, except for a gross misdemeanor charge of fleeing an officer of the law. As a result of your actions, I'm fining you fee of $1,000 payable today to the clerk of court. In addition, the court hereby sentences you to a one-year term in jail to be served immediately in the Hennepin County Workhouse."

I felt my knees go weak as the judge continued, "I'm electing to stay the final eleven months of your sentence, and you will earn your release upon good behavior after which time you've served thirty days of your sentence behind bars. Following your release from incarceration, you will meet with your parole officer to discuss your future direction."

I stood in stunned silence as the judge gathered his thoughts for one more proclamation.

As the judge pointed his gavel at me, he firmly stated, "Young man, I'm placing you on a lifetime probation, meaning if you ever so much as get the slightest moving violation while operating a motorcycle anytime during the rest of your life, the court reserves the right to incarcerate you to serve the remainder of your eleven-month sentence behind bars."

With that, he slammed his gavel and demanded the court bailiff to handcuff me and had me transported to the county jail.

As I was led from the courtroom in handcuffs, I looked back at my teary-eyed wife sitting alone in the courtroom and who was as unsure of what had just happened as I'd been.

*   *   *

That was a long time ago, but my life was and has been forever changed for the better as a result of that summer. I could go into great detail about what it feels like to spend day after day behind bars in a cell so small one can reach out and touch the walls. Or I could make comments about quality of jail food or how one keeps their mind functioning properly with nothing but bars to stare at day after day. I could even delve into how challenging it is mixing with a general population of convicts, many of whom have made a lifetime career in the criminal element. I could make an entire chapter out of just this fraction of my life, but I'm not going to.

What I am going to do is mention the good that came from my experience. During my thirty days of incarceration, I had a lot of time to think about what kind of a man, what kind of a husband, and what kind of a person I wanted to be. Although by some standards, a thirty-day sentence behind bars is nothing compared to some jail and prison terms, I assure you it was plenty long enough to impact a change on me.

What a glorious day it was when my loving wife, Astrid, arrived to take me back home. I would never have believed I could miss anyone as much as I'd come to miss her. On our emotional drive back home, I promised to gain control of my compulsion for speed. To show my commitment to avoid any future jail time, I immediately sold my beloved motorcycle. I reasoned that it would only take one lapse of judgment where the power and acceleration of the speedy motorcycle might cause me to lose control, and I'd then be destined to spend the remaining eleven months of my sentence behind bars. I was so motivated by the judge's threat that it was nearly twenty years later that I finally purchased another motorcycle and began passionately albeit cautiously riding again. For the record, however, in the nearly twenty years of riding motorcycle once again, I've never come close to getting a moving violation on it for obvious reasons.

It seems like a lifetime ago that I had a death wish on a motorcycle. In one fateful summer, I was consumed by the power and speed provided me by a dangerously fast motorcycle. That along with my risk-taking personality combined for not one, but two exposures to certain death. Was it possible for someone as me to be only twenty-four years of age and still somehow survive death twelve times?

A great deal of time has passed, and as a result, I've learned some important lessons in life as a result of that summer. Through all of those trials and tribulations, I came to realize two infallible facts in my life. One fact was that my wife unconditionally loved me and was willing to stand by me through even the worst possible scenario. The second fact was that God has never forsaken me even when I've made no sense at all.

MACHINERY CATASTROPHE—24 YEARS

CHAPTER THIRTEEN

For I want you to know, brothers and sisters,
that the gospel that was proclaimed by me is not
of human origin;
for I did not receive it from human source,
nor was I taught it, but I received it through a revelation
of Jesus Christ.

—GALATIANS 1:11-12

I can only envision how difficult I must have made life for my wife, Astrid, during our first year of marriage. Lord knows I pushed every button as I brought that first full year of marriage in with a bang as depicted by the events of the previous chapter. The good news was that a little personal time in jail really did help get my head screwed on straight and set my priorities clear. With time, it became evident that I was actually ready to perhaps settle down a bit as I neared my midtwenties. Astrid and I delved into our chosen career path of farming with our passionate desire to till the soil and milk a herd of dairy cows.

As depicted in an earlier chapter, I'd been engaged in farming on my family farm following graduation from college and teaching high school agriculture classes prior to getting married. Once Astrid had completed her college studies, we both entered into the holy state of matrimony together with the dreams and aspirations to raise a family in a farming environment just as we had both been fortunate enough to be raised.

There was never a question of doubt of what we wanted to do for our joint careers together. Nearly every time we were together during

143

our premarital engagement period, we dialogued endlessly about what terrific farmers we would one day become. Since we were both born and raised on dairy farms and since we met each other and fell in love as the result of a chance meeting in a dairy barn during our college days, then it only stood to reason that we should and would pursue a similar path in animal agriculture.

Just prior to our spring wedding, Astrid and I faced one of the toughest decisions we'd ever faced up until that point in our young lives. We knew we would become farmers following our impending wedding, but it was where we would farm that was contentious between us. The problem was that Astrid had promised her parents that she would one day return to her family farm to carry on her family's farming tradition. Since Astrid's parents were actually older than my grandparents at the time, it seemed like a well-thought-out estate plan to transfer ownership of her family farm over to her and her soon-to-be husband. Astrid's parents were forty-five years her senior, so she had taken over many of the farming duties even during her high school years. Once she enrolled in college, however, her parents were forced to sell their dairy herd of cows and rent out their farmland since they were incapable of operating their diversified farm on their own without their daughter on hand to help with the daily demands.

Astrid had sworn an oath to both her folks that once her college studies were completed, she would then return back home and bring the family farm back to all of its former glory. Well, that was a noble thought process shared by Astrid and her parents, that is, until I came into her life and "muddied the waters" so to speak.

As previously stated, I'd been financially divested in my own family farming operation for nearly two years prior to our marriage. No matter how Astrid and I tried to dissect our future farming situation, the conclusion always ended up that we had little choice other than to continue a farming partnership with my family. This very concept nearly broke Astrid's heart, however, since that decision literally meant the demise of her own multigenerational family farm. Astrid was not only her parent's only daughter, but she was their only child as well, and she was sadly the end of lineage and family name on her father's side of the family.

Astrid and I had finalized our decision to continue the partnership on my family farm. One day, however, we were summoned for an interesting meeting with Astrid's parents, Hilbert and Mildred Sammeli.

Neither Astrid nor I knew the purpose of the session with her folks, but we sensed the meeting would be serious and difficult to be sure. As the four of us sat around the kitchen table in the farmhouse on her family farm that day, her father began to speak in a quiet and calculating tone.

He asked, "Scott, how do you get along with your father when it comes to farming?"

I responded, "Well, pretty good I guess."

Hilbert then asked, "So, Scott, how much older is your father than you?"

"Nineteen years older," I replied.

Astrid and her mother Mildred sat quietly as Hilbert continued, "I know you are saying that you and your father get along pretty well, but I'm curious on how much decision-making authority he provides you since the two of you only share a nineteen-year age difference?"

With that, my carefully guarded emotions relented somewhat, as I shared, "Well, in all honesty, my father and I seem to argue and fight more often than ever before. In fact, I feel like I've got some great ideas on how we could modernize our farming practices, but ever since I've returned home from college, he stills responds to me as though I were only ten years old."

Hilbert retorted, "That doesn't surprise me, since I dealt with trying to farm with my parents once upon a time as well and I had the same frustrations." He continued on with, "Mildred and I would like to make a proposal to you and our daughter for your consideration. We would like you to consider selling out your partnership in your family farm and start farming on this family farm with our daughter."

My senses were on high alert as I replied, "Our decision is already made and we can't change our plans now." I went on to state, "Besides, I don't mean you any disrespect, but there is simply no comparison between your farm and my own family farm."

"How so?" replied Hilbert.

I retorted, "Our farm in southern Minnesota is blessed with the richest, most fertile soils in the state, and we don't have a single bothersome rock in any of our fields to try to farm around. Furthermore, my family farm has much newer and nicer farm buildings not to mention that our family has always prided ourselves with trying to have one of the prettiest farmsteads around."

Hilbert gathered his breath and said, "Sure, I must admit that our soils are sandy and rocky here in central Minnesota, and I'm aware that our farm buildings are older and more dilapidated than what you are used to. From that perspective, then I would agree that there can be no comparison between our family farm and your family farm."

Uncomfortable as the dialogue had become, I started to let my guard down since it appeared that Hilbert was on the defense, and I might survive the all-too-serious family meeting after all.

For what felt like hours of nerve-wracking silence, nothing more was uttered until Hilbert suddenly looked me in the eyes and stated, "I'll tell you what I'd offer if you and my daughter decide to try your hand at farming on this family farm, albeit older and more rundown."

Hilbert went on to mention that we could sell off my financial investment in my family farm and then reinvest the money into buying a herd of forty dairy cows. He shared that if we were willing to borrow enough money from a bank to purchase the machinery and tractors necessary to farm the land, then he and Mildred would establish a lease-to-own agreement with Astrid and I with such an "offer we couldn't refuse" so as to ensure that we could with relative ease, eventually acquire total ownership in the farm.

While everything Astrid's parents were proposing seemed sincere enough, I still couldn't envision the two of us trying to earn a living on their family farm. It simply was too much of a stretch of my imagination. I readied myself to respond with a profound response of no for the final time.

Hilbert sensing my impending negative response, leaned forward with his elbows on the kitchen table, looked me squarely in the eyes, and said, "Your father will always be only nineteen years older than you, and it makes me wonder how old you will have to become one day before you and my daughter will have the authority to farm your family farm as you see fit without interference from your parents."

The tone of Hilbert's voice deepened as he continued with, "Look at me, Scott, I'm an old man already in my upper sixties for age. If you and Astrid decide to farm our family farm, I promise you will never have me interfere in your decision-making processes and everything the two of you do will be entirely on your own farming merits. You will be able to take all the credit for your successes, but you will also be liable for all your mistakes as well."

Shortly after the life-changing meeting with Astrid's parents, we had a similar life-altering gathering with my parents. I shared with my folks that as difficult as the choice was to make, my wife and I felt it would be better for all if we were to sell off my share of the family farm partnership to my younger sister Marcia and her husband and then to start our life of farming on Astrid's family farm.

Although my parents would have preferred to keep their partnership with me intact, they graciously allowed for the partnership transfer so I could move on with my goal and dream of independently farming on my own. Within a few short weeks, Astrid and I were buying our own herd of dairy cattle and purchasing machinery to till the land. Each morning, we would rise before the sun to milk our cows and each morning we watched with delight and awe as the first rays of warm sunlight would reach our faces as we peeked out the open barn door of our dairy barn. With the passing weeks, we tilled our fields and planted our crops. Astrid and I worked very hard to clean up the old farm site, fix the dilapidated outbuildings, and put paint where no paint had been for decades. Within our first year of farming, there was a total metamorphosis of Astrid's family farm, which we now proudly called our family farm.

Through it all, Astrid's parents never strayed from their promise to steer clear of how we wanted to operate our farm. True to their words, it had become our farm, and it was always our decision on how to operate it as we saw fit.

*   *   *

Farming is literally the most dangerous occupation in America. Farmers often face injury or death as a result of enduring long, difficult hours on their farming operations, compiled by working on a daily basis with massive machinery and equipment. Throughout my lifetime, I've suffered many an injury and dealt with so many close calls with death as a result of some of the challenges that a farmer faces. This story describes one of those times as I was about to test death for an unlucky thirteenth time.

The first year of farming on my own had a new set of challenges since everything was a novel experience as I learned to farm on Astrid's family farm. Where I'd grown up the soil was rich and dark, but now I was faced with a steep learning curve of how to learn to produce marginal crops on light and sandy soils with an abundance of field rocks. One had to either pick up those rocks and haul them away or suffer the consequences of the broken machinery they imposed. The fields of my youth were flat and nearly perfectly square in shape and expansive, yet at this point, I was trying to learn to farm up one hilly field and down the next hilly field with each field being but a mere fraction of the size as well as being extremely oddly shaped compared to the fields that I'd grown up with.

There were days that I longed to be farming again on my own family farm as I fretted over the lack of rain and watched our crops withering in the thirsty sandy soil. It never failed to amaze me at how poorly our crops appeared to grow, yet the weeds somehow grew as though they were in the best of growing conditions.

During our first spring after our marriage, Astrid and I first tilled our fields and then we picked all the rocks that were larger in size than a common potato. Shortly thereafter, we planted our more than two hundred acres of fields into corn and soybeans. As any farmer knows, even before the cropping seeds can germinate and shoot skyward from the soil, the countless varieties of weeds have germinated, and they are working hard to choke out any emerging grain crops. For this reason, each planting season, farmers must purchase crop protection herbicides and crop spray their fields. These herbicides never totally rid a field of pesky weeds, but with them, the crops are at least provided a good chance for a successful yield.

The day before, I'd been into town to purchase my crop protection herbicides. I was left with "sticker shock" at how much cash outlay it took to farm. It seemed at every turn, I was adding to my ever-growing debt load in order to operate our farm. The sad fact was that I could invest literally tens of thousands of dollars into my cropping operation, yet if there wasn't enough rainfall, or if the fields were damaged in a hailstorm, then my wife and I would have nothing to feed our dairy cattle nor would we have any crops to sell in order to pay off the loans we had acquired to plant the crops. Those kinds of risks were and still are enough to keep one awake at night. It is obvious to see why it is easier to be a consumer and simply go to the grocery store to buy one's food, than it is to be a farmer trying to raise the food to feed our nation.

Following the morning milking chores, I busied myself preparing my tractor and four-hundred-gallon pull-behind crop sprayer for the weed spraying task ahead. I'd serviced my older-style tractor with its somewhat dangerous narrow tricycle-wheeled front end then proceeded to hook up the big crop sprayer to the rear hitch of the tractor. My next process was to place a hose into the four-hundred-gallon sprayer tank and fill it up with water. Lastly, I added just the correct weights of two different crop protection herbicides and then agitated the entire weed-lethal mixture.

With everything readied for my first attempt to spray weeds on our new farm, I hopped up onto the tractor's seat and waved at my new wife as I directed the tractor down the road toward the first field. I remember thinking on the way to the field, "With nearly two tons of crop spray in the big tank behind me, I wonder how this relatively small, antiquated tractor can handle the weight." My apprehensive thoughts were prophetic to say the very least for what lie ahead.

I maneuvered the tractor and sprayer into my first field of recently planted corn. Although I could not see any tiny emerging corn plants yet, I had little difficulty seeing the growing mass of weeds overtaking the hilly field that lay before me.

As luck would have it, this was not only the first field I chose to spray that spring for my initial attempt at crop spraying but that field was also our most treacherous and dangerously hilly field. As I engaged the tractors rear end power takeoff, the pump on the crop sprayer sprang to life as it began pumping the herbicide out through the nozzles of the long booms attached to the sprayer. Crop spraying can be very complicated since one needs to make exactly the correct mixture of herbicide, then one needs to have the correct nozzles to administer the proper spray pattern, and finally, one needs to operate the tractor and the sprayer at exactly the correct speed.

As if all of the above aren't enough to overload a farmer's brain while trying to safely farm, one also must navigate sometimes treacherous field conditions in order to ensure proper displacement of the herbicide. Even the slightest variation of any detail can result in a failure to curb the weeds.

Since I'd grown up on a farm with flat, relatively square fields, I'd learned to start on one side of a field and drive in a circular motion around and around the field until the entire field had been covered. Even though on my new farm the fields were very hilly and oddly shaped, I saw no reason why I shouldn't start on one side and drive in a circular motion until I'd crop sprayed the entire field just as I'd always done before. That was my intent anyway, but it proved to be an unwise decision.

I made my first pass along the bottom side of the hilly field with no problems whatsoever since that was the flattest portion of the field. I then rounded the far end and directed the narrow-wheeled tractor and very, very heavy crop sprayer up the steep side of the hilly field without giving much thought as to how top-heavy my nearly full load of liquid herbicide was. I reached the steepest portion of the field barely able to hang on to the steering wheel of the tractor as the tractor tilted dangerously toward the bottom of the steep hill. I felt a strange uneasiness about how sharply the tractor and sprayer were leaning.

I no sooner felt the intuition of impending danger when suddenly the several thousand pound sprayer full of liquid herbicide went past top-dead center and started ever so slowly tipping over while trying to roll down the hill. I almost began sweating blood because not only was the sprayer about to roll down the steep incline of the field, but it's bulk started to pull my old tractor over with it.

I only had an instant as I shouted, "Dear God, please don't let this tractor roll over on me," just as the rear tire of the tractor lurched upward.

By this time, I felt as though the scene was playing out in slow motion as the massive crop sprayer was about to roll down the steep hill and the tractor was being twisted over along with it. There was little doubt in my mind that I would not survive the tragic farming accident that was about to happen.

There was no time to react, and there was no possible way to leap off the rolling tractor. All I could do was hang on and watch with widened eyes, hoping that if I were about to die that it would be instantly without suffering too much pain.

Suddenly, as though the invisible hand of God had reached out, I heard the sound of ripping and twisting metal. I couldn't believe my eyes as I watched the crop sprayer hitch break in half, then felt the tractor instantaneously fall back down on all of its wheels once it was released from the lethal grip of the tipping sprayer. Without hesitation, I safely stopped the tractor and then held the sides of my face with both hands as I watched the nearly four hundred gallons of toxic herbicide go cascading down the steep hill of my field as the broken sprayer rolled over and over, time and again.

It took a few minutes for me to gather my senses after coming that close to near certain death. I thought about being over one mile away from our farmstead and imagined how long it might have taken Astrid to determine why I wasn't coming home had the result been different. My entire body started to shake as I came to the realization just how quickly life can be terminated, and suddenly, I understood just what a gift it can be when one's life is spared.

Eventually, I collected myself enough to drive my tractor away from the field and back to the farmstead. As I drove into the yard with only the broken sprayer hitch left intact and dragging along behind the tractor,

I was met in the driveway by Astrid and her father, Hilbert. I'm sure the color of my face was still as white as a ghost as they inquired about what had happened to the sprayer. I recanted the entire frightening account only to witness my wife take a step back as she realized just how close she'd actually been to becoming a young widow again.

As for Hilbert, he had a couple of remarks the likes of which I'll never forget.

He said, "Don't you flatlander farmers even have enough common sense to know that you need to have the crop sprayer at least half empty before you try to spray on a dangerous side hill so it isn't so top-heavy?"

I retaliated with, "What has common sense got to do with it? I've never sprayed on anything except a perfectly flat field before, so NO I DIDN'T KNOW you should only spray on a side hill with your sprayer half full!"

It hadn't taken me long to get overly sensitive as my body started trembling once again while coming down from the adrenaline shock I'd just been through. The fact was, however, Astrid's father had said it like it was, and even though I thought I was as smart as any farmer out there, the truth of the matter was I had just proven how much there was to learn yet. Hopefully with a little bit of luck and the helping hand of God, I would live long enough to eventually gain some of the vast knowledge that my father and Astrid's father had acquired during their lifetimes.

Later that day following my near miss with death, Astrid helped me drag the severely damaged crop sprayer back to the farmyard. It took me a couple of days of buying and replacing parts, along with welding the broken hitch and twisted metal, but without too much delay, I was back spraying my fields once again that spring. I can assure you, I was much wiser on how to tackle some of the hillier fields, though.

*   *   *

Each crop growing season thereafter and for over a decade, Astrid and I would scout our fields taking note of how well any particular year's crops might look. Each year, we also breathed a silent sigh of relief as we viewed the huge bare spot running down the abrupt hill side of our steepest field. Like a constant reminder, that spot was sterile and barren of any plant growth from either grain crop or weeds for over a decade. Each year, it posed an ominous and constant reminder of just how close I came never reaching my first wedding anniversary.

HARVESTING DOWNFALL—25 YEARS

CHAPTER FOURTEEN

I am the alpha and the omega, says the Lord God,
who is and who was and who is to come, the Almighty.
—REVELATION 1:8

It takes no great stretch of the imagination to appreciate the level of danger involved for those whose occupation is producing food for human consumption. Farmers and agriculturalists the world over are often faced with dangerous and death-defying circumstances. Whether working with large, obstinate animals or working with massive, dangerous equipment, injury and even death are constant reminders of that chosen profession.

The honeymoon was over so to speak. My wife Astrid and I had survived our first year and a half of marriage with all the ups and downs associated with being a young married couple setting a course for the future. We were young, we were strong, and we were in love, yet the endless days of toil and labor began taking a toll on us.

A typical day for us began well before sun up as we rose by 4:00 a.m. each morning to take care of our herd of milking dairy cows. Our first chores were to check for and care for any newborn baby calves, which may have been birthed during the nighttime hours. We then set about with a flurry of chores that included feeding the cattle, milking the cows, and finally spreading the manure from the dairy barn out onto the adjoining fields to aid with our crops plant growth with the all-important organic nutrients. All of these chores would take Astrid and me from 4:00 a.m. until 7:00 a.m. each morning, seven days per week, and 365 days per year. There is no such thing as a day off on a dairy farm, which is why dairy farmers are a rare breed of folks to be sure.

At precisely 7:00 a.m. each morning from Monday through Friday, I would then depart our farm to work at my full-time second occupation. Astrid was then always left by herself on the farm to toil with the additional farm chores and field work for the remainder of the day.

You see, not long after our wedding, Astrid and I were somewhat shocked and quite disappointed to discover that no lender would borrow us the funds necessary to begin our chosen life of farming. We were informed that either Astrid or I would probably need to take a full-time job working off the farm to help meet our living expense needs and to assist with making our loan payments. It simply didn't seem feasible to require a farmer to have an off-farm occupation to assist with one's farming occupation in order to obtain a farming loan, but those were our requirements to begin a farming career.

No matter, however, because in all we were turned down by fifteen different lenders all of which proclaimed that it was simply too risky to borrow such a large sum of money to a young newlywed couple trying to start farming during such difficult and turbulent times.

Never one to easily be deterred, and in order to acquire the desired farming loan, I began working as a dairy cattle nutritionist for the Land O'Lakes Feed Division. With a secondary career secured, we were then able to obtain our hefty farming loan and begin our chosen career paths.

For that reason, each day I would travel countless miles calling on and working with dairy farmers all throughout central Minnesota while helping them to reach a stronger financial position within their own farming operations through healthier and more productive cows.

Following a long and grueling day away at work, each late afternoon, I would then return back to our dairy farm, only to begin a long and tiring sequence of evening chores once more. Seldom did Astrid and I finish our nightly farming and milking chores prior to 10:00 p.m. each evening. It was only at that time of the evening when we could finally sit down at our supper table, give thanks to the Lord for our many blessings, and then engulf food for our hungry yet exhausted bodies. Every evening was then brought to a close by taking a quick bath and then we would both collapse into bed, nearly asleep even before our heads ever hit the pillows. Endless eighteen hour workdays take a toll on a new marriage and take a toll on ones overall productivity and safety to be sure.

Times were tough in agriculture during those years, and we struggled to make ends meet. Not only did we have large monthly loan payments to make, which absorbed nearly all of our monthly milk-selling reimbursements, but in addition, each fall after our crops were harvested and then sold, we were required to make one gigantic loan payment totaling tens of thousands of dollars. It was no wonder that at times such as those we felt either our backs would break or our very spirits would succumb to the rigors of our daily grind.

*   *   *

It was the fall of our second year of farming, and Astrid and I were deep into our fall harvesting of grain crops. A few weeks earlier, I'd combined all of the soybean fields with our antiquated Allis Chalmers Gleaner combine. This old relic was nothing like the modern-day combines of today. Our old combine would shudder and sputter its way slowly along the rows of crops in the fields trying its very best to ingest the fall's harvest bounty.

Although the soybean crop harvest posed no real problem, the corn harvest was another matter altogether.

Since most of our cropping land had been planted into corn that year, we knew that we had our work cut out for us to bring in our harvest before the temperatures turned bitter cold and the snows began falling. Farmers most generally have only short windows of time in which to bring in their harvests. If by chance winter sets in early, then the valuable crops must lay idle in the fields while engulfed in snow throughout the long, dreary winter. Unfortunately, harvesting in the spring is never desirable since major portions of the crop is often destroyed or damaged during the winter months, causing major financial losses for the beleaguered farmers.

Due to some untimely rainy weather that fall, we were delayed for a couple of weeks from beginning our normal corn harvest season. When at last the skies cleared and the fields dried, Astrid and I headed out to our corn fields to begin our delayed harvest. Combining fields of grain can be extra challenging for a dairy farmer since each day and each evening is interrupted by livestock chores and milking the cows. For that reason, most of the combining that I would accomplish would be during the middle portion of any given day, and then once again throughout the nighttime hours, going without sleep in order to bring in the harvest before the ever-imposing weather would stall our pursuit.

To harvest our corn crop, we needed between two and three weeks, along with a little bit of luck from machinery breakdowns.

To be certain, our luck that fall only lasted one day.

Astrid and I had worked throughout that first day to bring in our corn crop without hesitation. On that day, we had milked the cows in the morning, and then we had combined the corn fields throughout the remainder of the day. That evening, we stopped combining the corn fields long enough to milk our dairy cows for their evening milking. We rushed along with the milking chores, in hopes of getting quickly back out into the fields with the combine enabling us to harvest all throughout the long night.

With the evening chores completed, Astrid and I departed our dairy barn, only to observe a horrifying sight. There in the middle of our farmyard where I'd parked the combine, now stood a combine with flames of fire flickering up into the night sky and clouds of smoke belching from its underbelly.

In an instant, I'd garnered a fire extinguisher and was trying my best to smother the flames. Astrid ran for a water hose attached to a nearby water hydrant and together we doused the flames and smoke.

Tears welled up in our eyes as we sank to our knees and held tightly to each other. We knew that somewhere on the complicated inside of our combine, a bearing must have worn out during my final pass in the corn field that evening. It became painfully obvious to us that while we were milking our cows, the red-hot bearing must have ignited the dust and the chaff on the inside of the combine, creating the machine-destroying fire within. A combine fire is one of the worst machinery breakdowns one could endure since the heat from the fire destroys nearly every bearing and movable part on the inside of the combine. Combines are very difficult to work on because the main working parts are restricted tightly in the deep inside where it is nearly impossible for a person to gain access for repair work.

Astrid and I were distraught beyond belief because our choices were suddenly so limited. We felt absolutely helpless. Since it was peak harvesting season and all other available combines were in use, it stood to reason that there would be no way to even rent a combine from an equipment dealer in the area. We were also all too painfully aware of our stressed financial situation, knowing that we did not have the money to buy another used combine, and in fact, we didn't even have enough money to pay what would be an exorbitant shop repair bill to fix our damaged combine. To put more insult on us, the weather forecasters were predicting a heavy snowfall and the onset of an early winter coming within the next two to three weeks.

Just as we were about to admit defeat and realized that the setback from our combine fire might spell the end of our beloved farming career, Astrid's father, Hilbert, surfaced behind us. It took him only a moment to surmise the situation, and he laid out a plan of action.

Hilbert said, "You kids don't have the money to pay an equipment shop to repair this combine, and besides, by the time a repair shop finishes the job, the snows will be falling and your harvest will be ruined."

I responded back with, "What choices do we have? I don't know the first thing about repairing a combine, so without a repair shop fixing it, how will we get back into the fields?'

Hilbert stared at the combine as he said, "I'll make you a deal. Since I'm an old man and unable to do that kind of mechanical work anymore, I'll oversee you while you do it."

I stood up in a state of shock and faced Hilbert, saying, "You've got to be kidding me. There isn't any way even with your guidance and suggestions that I'm capable of totally repairing this destroyed combine."

Astrid's father simply commented, "You and my daughter get a good night's sleep tonight because tomorrow I'm going to park my butt in a lawn chair next to this burned-out piece of equipment, and you are going to restore it back to working order as quickly as possible!" With that, he slowly walked away, leaving me in a state of disbelief.

The following morning even before Astrid and I emerged from our dairy barn after milking the cows, as promised, Hilbert was sitting in his lawn chair next to the big blackened combine. I didn't think it possible, but without hesitation, we began the near-impossible task of bringing the combine back into operation.

Astrid's father had earned the reputation of being one of the best military mechanics while serving in the armed forces of World War II. It was said that there was no engine he couldn't repair nor was there any broken piece of equipment he couldn't fix.

Hilbert talked me through every microscopic detail of resurrecting the complex machine. He described which specific tools I would need to remove a stubborn pulley or disassemble various inflexible parts. Hilbert sat alongside the combine hour after hour trying to shade himself from the sun while I labored to repair the steel beast. Whenever we discovered a part that needed replacing, then Astrid or her mother Mildred would make a rapid trip to any number of towns to locate and purchase the replacement parts.

As though a miracle happening before my eyes, in only three days, I had disassembled, then replaced parts, then finally reassembled the intricate machine under the guidance of Hilbert who took great pride in his uncanny mechanical abilities but who also couldn't believe what an absolute mechanically unskilled idiot his son-in-law was regarding machinery repair.

When at last the final nuts and bolts were tightened with a wrench, I mounted the combine for a test run. I could almost hear a drumroll in my subconscious as I turned the key and started up the lifeless machine. I kept my fingers crossed as I directed the combine into a nearby field of corn and made a round through the dense corn stalks. The hopper filled with the golden kernels of grain, nearly bringing tears to my eyes.

As I left the field and pulled back into the farmyard, I watched as Astrid and her mother began gleefully clapping their hands together and dancing a little jig. As I made eye contact with Hilbert and thankfully gave a nod of my head in his direction, I spotted a joyful twinkle in his eyes.

With the support and knowledge of Astrid's parents, we were able to repair our fire-damaged combine in less than half the time and for a fraction of the cost had we been forced to bring it to an equipment repair shop.

I breathed a sigh of relief knowing that maybe, just maybe, we would be able to complete our harvest on time after all, and perhaps we just might remain financially solvent to farm yet another year.

In only four days following the combine fire, I once again directed the combine back into the fields. I held on to my hopes and offered my prayers that Astrid and I could bring in the entire remaining harvest. This would not be easy, however, because a harvest-season-ending snowstorm was predicted to arrive within one week's time.

Being an optimist, there was never a doubt in my mind that it could be accomplished. After all, we had always come out victorious over the most terrible of circumstances. Probably we would complete our harvest just in the nick of time and without further incidence. OR WOULD WE!

*   *   *

Knowing the insurmountable odds we faced, Astrid and I came up with a fail-safe plan to complete the corn harvest before the big storm hit. We agreed that I would ask permission of my employer to take the upcoming week as vacation days. Then Astrid and I determined that we would reduce any and all extra farming chores down to the barest essentials to allow for more time harvesting our fields. Lastly, I mentally prepared myself to combine around-the-clock, twenty-four hours per day, and go without sleep for as many days as required to complete our monumental task at hand.

Together Astrid and I surged forward with our plan. Each of our harvesting duties varied considerably.

Astrid's role in the entire process was to drive our big grain truck out to the field and wait while I combined the corn, and then filled the truck with corn from the combine. With each loaded truck, Astrid would drive the big truck back to the farmyard where she would then back the truck up to a corn-unloading auger, start the tractor which ran the unloading auger, and then ultimately unload the hundreds of bushels of corn into the enormous corn storage bins. In addition to all of this, Astrid also had to ensure that the grain drier and fuel source were working properly and make adjustments according to the moisture levels of the incoming grain.

My role in the process was to keep the combine guided up the endless rows of corn plants as it gathered the produce of which our next loan payment would derive and for which our cattle would have enough feed to consume for the upcoming year. Running a combine hour after hour, day after day can be rather tedious and monotonous, but it requires a lot of aptitude nonetheless. Throughout the day and night, the conditions of the cornstalks and the moisture levels of the grain require that the combine operator continually make equipment adjustments. In addition, one must keep a watchful eye out for large rocks that can be sucked into the combine, causing havoc to the machine and resulting in more unwanted repair bills and unproductive downtime.

Astrid and I were well into our insurmountable task that fall harvest season when I had another close call with certain death.

We had made it six days and nights of completing our farm chores and then combining without ever laying down in our bed once during that time frame. Astrid was exhausted, but she was able to somewhat keep going due to the fact that she could catch quick cat naps while waiting in the truck out in the fields for me to fill up the truck with grain.

I, on the other hand, continually kept maneuvering the combine through the endless rows of corn knowing that if it snowed, I would then receive more forced sleep that I desired. I smothered the ebbing thoughts of failure, knowing that to fail meant that our crop would rot in the fields, and we could possibly face financial bankruptcy.

Throughout my life, I've never slept more than two to four hours per night, so during this sleepless marathon, I surmised that over the course of six or seven days and nights without sleep wouldn't be all that difficult.

About midnight on my sixth night of continuous combining, Astrid pulled the emptied grain truck into our final field of corn. She breathed a heavy sigh of exhaustion knowing that if all went well, then before the sun set on the following day, the harvesting season would at long last thankfully be over. It was a good thing too because as she listened to the radio the weather reports were indicating a nearly 100 percent prediction that our part of the state of Minnesota was in the direct path of a severe snowstorm, which would likely bring everything to a permanent stop in its wake.

Astrid dozed off, and then awoke as I pulled the roaring combine alongside the grain truck to empty the first of three hoppers full of grain into the truck. She stuck her head out of the window, and just as always, she waved at me and I gave a half-hearted and sleepy wave back. Even in my tired and groggy state of exhaustion, I realized what a blessing she was in my life. Few on earth could equal her work ethic or match her selflessness. She was and continues to be a saint in my eyes and to many who have come to know her.

As the last of the kernels of corn transferred from the combine's auger into the truck, I pulled away to once again guide the combine through the dark and eerie rows of corn. I was so, so tired that I questioned if I even had enough left in me to finish the last big field and reach the virtual harvesting finish line.

Astrid nestled down a bit in the grain truck seat and rested her head against the rear window as her heavy eyelids so desperately sought out sleep. She was almost asleep when she caught sight of the combine lights out in the sinisterly dark field abruptly change course! She instantly sat upright as her senses became keenly aware of a problem. With that, she then bolted out the door of the truck.

Fright gripped her as she grasped what was happening before her eyes.

Inside the combine, my fatigued body and my mind had finally reached the threshold of no return. As close to the harvesting finish as I was, sleep would no longer be deprived. As I fell asleep at the combine steering wheel, the massive machine began to slowly veer off to the right. Astrid watched in panic as the combine began going diagonally across row after row of corn, running over the corn and destroying the remaining crop beneath.

She began running wildly toward the rogue combine as fast as her legs would carry her while yelling my name at the top of her lungs. She could only fear the worst that her husband had fallen asleep in the combine or, worse yet, perhaps he had somehow died of a heart attack or stroke while operating the huge machine.

Suddenly, Astrid stopped in her tracks only to realize that the combine was edging ever closer to the huge drainage ditch running alongside the field. This ditch was so steep and so deep that were the combine to go over the edge and fall into the ditch, it would spell certain disaster and most certain death.

Astrid realized that she could not run fast enough to catch the combine before it would fall over the edge. She also realized that no matter how hard she tried screaming, I was beyond hearing anything over the roar of the churning combine, and it was hopeless anyway because of the deep slumber that I'd fallen into.

With all hope nearly erased, my loving wife reached out to the only one she knew was always listening.

In the middle of the dark field, Astrid fell to her knees, folded her hands together, faced the stars up in the sky, and prayed out loud, "Heavenly Father, please, please protect Scott and please don't take him from me. I pray this with all my heart and soul dear God."

Astrid's prayers had no more than left her lips, and the rampant combine was only a few feet from the edge of the ditch when suddenly one of the wheels lurched over a large rock on the edge of the field. The combine bounced so hard that I found myself suddenly awake and acutely aware of how close to certain death I was. I slammed my left foot down on the clutch while slamming my right foot down on the brake as the combine came to a teetering rest just hanging out over the edge of the treacherous ditch.

For a few moments, I sat motionless while my body began to shake all over. After a few moments, I carefully shifted the machine into reverse and backed away from the ditch. As the combine once again faced back in the proper direction, I determined that I'd better make haste back to the grain truck to alert Astrid as to what had just happened.

Imagine the shock on my face as I turned the combine toward the truck which was located way on the far side of the field, only to have the lights from the combine suddenly outline the shape of Astrid running up to the combine. I shut the machine down and crawled down the big ladder of the combine and down onto the ground.

To this day, I will never forget the bear hug and the kiss I received from Astrid as she reached me. The tears ran down her cheeks as she wept while sharing what had happened with her, with God, and with me.

*   *   *

We finished our bountiful harvest that fall with no further problems. We were also able to make our loan payments and feed our livestock for yet another year.

The snowstorm hit the next day just as we were finishing up our final rows of corn. Although countless other farmers were unable to finish their harvests that fall due to the severe early winter, we somehow had assistance in many forms to safely finish our harvest.

I ask, do you believe that our Lord can intervene and change an outcome? Did God place that large rock in the path of my combine that so miraculously jarred me awake?

Astrid and I certainly believe in divine intervention following my fourteenth escape from the grips of death.

EQUIPMENT CATACLYSM—26 YEARS

CHAPTER FIFTEEN

O Lord my God, I cried out to you, and you restored me to health.
You brought me up, O Lord from the dead;
you restored my life as I was going to the grave.
—PSALM 30:2-3

In the very same field in which I almost lost my life while combining corn just months earlier, I nearly lost my life once again for the fifteenth time in a freakish equipment accident.

*　　*　　*

The harsh Minnesota winter was especially vicious following the close of the previous harvesting season. Mountains of snow accumulated, which then combined with the brutal northern winds. There were literally hard drifts of deep snow in every direction as far as the eye could see.

One good detail about living in Minnesota, though, is the sturdy inhabitants can often benefit or some would argue suffer from four completely different seasons of the year. Minnesota summer can be as hot and humid as any sweltering place on the continent. Thankfully, during the fall season, temperatures moderate down to a more enjoyable range as the leaves on the trees turn into an array of all colors in the rainbow. Minnesota winter can be flat out miserable with snowstorms and plummeting temperatures that can dip well into the subzero ranges for days or even weeks on end. Springtime, however, is one of my favorite seasons, watching the snow melt and viewing the earth renew itself with luscious shades of greenery. It is during the spring season where every form of animal life and plant life is born anew with resounding vigor.

During the previous fall, I had no more than finished harvesting the final field of corn while narrowly escaping yet another close call with death when we were suddenly walloped with an early winter snowstorm. Sometimes an early snowfall can melt away, allowing the fall season to traipse along a bit further, but it was not to be that year. Winter came in early and came in with a vengeance as we all settled in for the drudgery of another Minnesota winter.

Since there had been no opportunity to fall-till the soils of our farm land due to the early onset of winter, I now busied myself working the ground to prepare for another springtime planting season. With the extra heavy winter snows, spring field work was already delayed as I waited ever so impatiently for the snows to melt and the soils to dry.

Over time, I was finally able to till all of our farm land that spring. The next process during the spring planting season was for Astrid and me to wage our annual war against the rocks in our fields. I could never understand how it was possible to glean every rock in sight from a field, yet a mere one year later, the same field would be covered with pesky rocks once more. It was as though the rocks grew from fertile baby rock seeds, which then matured every spring planting season of the year only to torment us.

Once all the fields were cleared of the equipment-damaging rocks, and just before planting the new corn crop, nitrogen fertilizer needed to be applied annually to the fields. One of the most common forms of nitrogen for farm use and the same form which I used on our land each spring was called anhydrous ammonia. Anhydrous ammonia can masquerade as a common place fertilizer, yet it is one of the most dangerous and lethal compounds available.

As mentioned earlier, farming ranks as one of the most dangerous occupations in America. I'll explain in detail how working with a fertilizer such as anhydrous ammonia can contribute to those dangers and yielded yet another close call with death for me.

Anhydrous ammonia is one of the most common farm-use fertilizers and is officially classified as a hazardous substance. Most accidents with anhydrous ammonia are due to uncontrolled releases. Few problems occur, however, when the ammonia is being handled and applied as intended. Anhydrous ammonia, though, has the potential to be one of the most dangerous chemicals used in agriculture today. It is used and stored under high pressure, which requires specially designed and well-maintained equipment. Those who work with anhydrous ammonia must be trained to follow exact procedures in handling it.

Ammonia is a chemical compound used as fertilizer because it is rich in nitrogen. Its chemical formula is NH_3, which means that it consists of one atom of nitrogen and three atoms of hydrogen per molecule. Anhydrous means the ammonia in this form is without water. Anhydrous ammonia is a clear, colorless gas at standard temperature and has a very characteristic, harsh, pungent odor. The odor is the strongest safety feature of the product. At only fifty parts per million, one sniff tells what is in the air. Normally, the odor alone will drive a person away from an area of a leak. A concentration of two thousand parts per million causes skin blisters and burns within seconds as well as serious lung damage, and a concentration of five thousand parts per million will disable a person so that escape is impossible and suffocation results.

The reason human exposure to anhydrous ammonia can be so deadly is because it contains no water. Anhydrous ammonia therefore has a very strong affinity for water, and instantly can flood the human lungs as it seeks out the water in the tissues. When anhydrous ammonia contacts water, it forms ammonium hydroxide. Living tissue is dehydrated quickly and the cells destroyed on contact. Anhydrous ammonia attacks any moist part of the body: eyes, ears, nose, throat, bronchia, lungs, and any moist skin. Any tissue containing moisture is chemically burned when exposed to this deadly compound.

There are several types of exposure that result in dangerous injuries or death.

Anhydrous ammonia causes freezing and chemical burn wherever skin and clothing are moist. The subzero temperature of escaping anhydrous ammonia freezes clothing to the body. The caustic nature of anhydrous ammonia causes skin and tissue burns similar to burns from heat or fire.

Eyes are continually bathed in moisture, and anhydrous ammonia will seek this moisture. The burns will result in damage to the eyes, such as cataracts, glaucoma, and possibly some permanent vision loss.

The entire respiratory system is very moist, so anhydrous ammonia will be attracted naturally to that part of the body. When a concentrated level of anhydrous ammonia is inhaled, it will burn the respiratory system quickly. The victim may be unable to breath, and the respiratory system may become paralyzed.

*   *   *

I was filled with excitement to begin my third springtime planting season. Although Astrid and I had faced our challenges during our young career in agriculture, and we did so during such difficult economic times; for the most part, we had established ourselves to be successful farmers. Little did I envision that I was about to face death for a third time in just three short years of farming.

Now that the fields were tilled and the rocks picked, I was preparing for the next task at hand. I'd already driven the pickup truck to the coop agronomy department to bring home the anhydrous ammonia application equipment. The agreement was that if one purchased the fertilizer from the coop, then free use of the fertilizer equipment was included in the package. I picked up a nitrogen applicator that was to attach to my tractor and which would knife the anhydrous ammonia deep into the soil. I also picked up a one thousand gallon tank of pressurized liquid anhydrous ammonia to be applied on my fields.

The agronomy department employees reviewed the entire safety precautions checklist with me as they handed me a set of eye goggles and a pair of thick rubber gloves to be used while hooking up the equipment to my tractor once back on the farm. They prophetically advised that I be extremely careful to avoid any accidents since several farmers were injured or killed each year working with anhydrous ammonia fertilizer.

With everything ready to go, at last I pulled my tractor and fertilizer equipment into the field to began knifing the anhydrous ammonia into the soil. Every once in a while, the slight breeze would send the faintest hint of ammonia odor toward me while I operated the tractor. It amazed me just how little ammonia smell it took to make my eyes water and slightly burn the inside of my nose.

After making a couple of passes down both sides of the field, I decided to direct the tractor and equipment toward one of the low spots in the field. I feared that the ground was too wet and sticky for the heavy tractor and equipment to pass entirely through, but it was necessary to test the outside edge anyway, just in case I would be able to apply the fertilizer in that portion of the field. As I neared the spongy ground, I increased the throttle of the tractor in hopes that a faster ground speed would allow me to pass over the wetter soil without bogging down the tractor.

It happened so quickly that I was barely able to react. I'd kept a watchful eye on my right front tractor tire, knowing that if that wheel started sinking into the wet soil, then the heavier rear wheels of the tractor would surely mire down in the mucky ground. Just as the front wheel of the tractor started to sink, I jerked the tractor steering wheel hard to the left in hopes of pulling out of the quicksandlike spot. The tractor tried to pull out, but in a flash both front wheels, and then both back wheels of the tractor were churning down deeper and deeper into the mud.

One trick that many a tractor operator has learned over the years is once the wheels on a tractor start spinning in the mud, it is best to immediately stop the tractor before the heavy machine digs and sinks ever deeper.

Seeing my predicament, I immediately stopped the tractor and shut of the anhydrous ammonia applicator valve. Next, I raised the applicator out of the ground and crawled down out of the tractor to survey my situation. I slowly walked around the low ground that my tractor and equipment were stuck in. As I surmised my problem, I realized that since I was over two miles away from our farm, and since I had no phone or two-way radio of which to call back to Astrid for help, then I had to try my own means to get my tractor unstuck.

After much consideration, I determined that I could pull the hitch pin that connected the large, heavy anhydrous ammonia tank from the applicator, which was attached to the back of the tractor. I deducted that with the large tank disconnected; perhaps then the tractor could maneuver itself out of the wet soil. If my idea worked, I would then be able to back up a safe distance from the wet ground and hook up a heavy tow chain that I carried on the tractor in order to pull the tank out to drier soil.

Great idea, except I forgot one VERY IMPORTANT DETAIL.

I pulled the hitch pin and released the anhydrous ammonia tank from the tractor. In my haste to rectify my situation, I somehow forgot to disconnect the large hose that feeds the dangerous anhydrous ammonia to the applicator on the tractor.

I mounted the tractor, gave the engine the entire throttle, and then guided the tractor out of the sticky mess that had entombed it. There was only one little problem. As the tractor and I pulled away from the nearly full tank of anhydrous ammonia, the connecting hose severed in half and started spewing deadly anhydrous ammonia gas in every direction.

Once I was clear of the wet ground, I stopped the tractor and looked back on a horrifying sight. The broken hose acted as though a large fire truck hose under full pressure as it flopped quickly from side to side while bouncing uncontrollably up and down.

My first thought at that moment was that it would be extremely hazardous to release an entire tank of anhydrous ammonia into the air since there were people living near the field. I simply could not endanger those innocent people. My second thought determined that the concept of releasing several hundreds of dollars of fertilizer into the air would not sit well at all with my struggling bank account.

Throwing all caution into the wind, I catapulted off my tractor, held my breath, and then ran straight for the erupting anhydrous ammonia tank in an attempt to stop a further disaster from happening.

Although I tried to avoid direct contact with the escaping gas as I ran to the tank, the flopping hose sprayed directly across the entire front of my shirt and pants, which instantly froze my clothing to my skin and scalded my chest and legs with a massive chemical burn. Knowing I had little time to waste, I jumped up on the front wheels of the large anhydrous ammonia tank and shut off the valve feeding the hose.

I began to feel very light-headed and ill as I knew my overall health and well-being were in jeopardy. Still holding my breath, I ran as far away from the crippled anhydrous ammonia tank as possible, and finally, I collapsed onto the farm ground beneath me. Try as I might, I could not inhale a single breath of life-sustaining air because the anhydrous ammonia had migrated into my lungs, seeking out the moisture. My entire respiratory tract was literally paralyzed as I was overcome by a fear like none other I'd ever experienced.

I've often contemplated on what form of death might cause the worst human suffering, and in my mind, I've always envisioned that perhaps death by drowning or death by suffocation might rank quite highly as some of the worst ways in which to die.

There were no witnesses to my life and death struggle that day. Once again I was ironically in a battle for my very life. Only God was present to determine my fate.

Imagine yourself in my precarious situation. As I neared death and my consciousness faded, I believed that the Lord was finally calling me. At last my duties of this world had come to a conclusion. I lay upon the dark dirt of my field in indescribable pain from the chemical burns to the entire front of my body, along with a searing, excruciating pain in my eyes, nose, ears, and throat. Little did it matter though because I'd gone too long without a breath of air and soon it would all be over.

I don't know how long I lay unconscious in the dirt or perhaps I'd even died for all I know. What I do know is that slowly and surely, I regained consciousness and opened my stinging eyes. I could hear my tractor still running some distance away. Most importantly, I was breathing freely on my own, albeit every breath felt as though I were breathing pure fire.

After nearly thirty minutes, I regained enough strength to weakly crawl back onto my tractor, then I guided it toward home.

The balance of that day was spent in a hospital tending to my chemical burns. For many weeks following this tragic incident, I had the nastiest, massive purple burn mark running up the entire front of my body.

*   *   *

That spring, I applied the balance of the anhydrous ammonia fertilizer on my fields without further incident. Soon thereafter, the crops were planted and eventually harvested as another year in the cycle of life came and went.

I had no residual effects of my dangerously close call that day. I had no permanent lung damage; I had no permanent damage to my eyes, and my only reminder was a permanent scar across my body as a result of the chemical burn I encountered.

I ask now that you go back to the scripture verse at the beginning of this chapter. Would you agree that our Lord will decide when our time to join him has arrived?

BUFFALO LUNACY—28 YEARS

CHAPTER SIXTEEN

So I say to you, ask and it will be given you;
search and you will find; knock and the door will be opened for you.
For everyone who asks receives, and everyone who searches
finds, and everyone who knocks, the door will be opened.
—LUKE 11:9-10

As described in an earlier chapter, I was drawn to horses by an early age much because of their speed, agility, and endurance. A thrill seeker such as me has no problem finding ways to increase ones' adrenaline levels while mounted on the back of such a magnificent equine athlete.

From my teenage years through early adulthood, I was fascinated by the several horses, which I owned and shared companionship with. Each horse became a new friend, and each had their own unique personalities along with demonstrating various levels of athleticism.

During my youth, our family enjoyed watching a popular western television show called *Gunsmoke.* I especially enjoyed our family evenings together watching the show as the cowboys would do some amazing activities with their horses. I was particularly fascinated with one of the characters on the program and his very different mount, however. Festus played the character of a deputy sheriff who just happened to ride a mule named Ruth. Week after week as our family was entertained by the antics and story plot on the *Gunsmoke* show, I became enamored with the uniqueness of the one and only mule on that television show.

Before long, I was doing research on mules at my high school library. I discovered that a mule is a sterile hybrid cross between a male donkey and a female horse. Since the mule offspring of such an odd genetic mating is a hybrid, it gets most of the best genetic traits and qualities from each of its incongruously different parents. For example, a donkey is one of the more intelligent animals on the planet who is also blessed with unbelievable endurance and sure-footedness. As a result, a mule then inherits most of those desirable traits from the donkey. Just as significantly, a horse is gifted with a sleek, fast, and powerful athleticism, which the mule offspring inherits as well. Although odd looking with its longer ears, a mule is really a most desirable equine that truly is superior in many ways to each of its vastly different parents, which are a donkey and a horse.

One evening, following our traditional family night of entertainment while watching *Gunsmoke* on the television, I proclaimed, "I've studied up on everything there is to know about mules, just like what Festus rides, and I've decided I'm going to mate my horse Dixie to a large donkey and try to raise myself a horse-sized riding mule."

By this time of my life, my family was seldom shocked or surprised in the least by anything that I dreamed up or which I desired to do, so my father simply replied, "Where do you think you're going to find a large donkey to mate with Dixie?"

I responded with, "Someone in my horse saddle club gave me the name of a man who has a large breeding donkey, so I'm going to contact him and make myself a baby mule!"

That was just exactly what I did, and the following spring, Dixie gave birth to the cutest, long-eared little mule foal anyone had ever seen. I had such an enjoyable experience with mules that I went on to breed, raise, train, and sell mules for much of my entire lifetime. Over the course of more than forty years, I've enjoyed working with dozens and dozens of mules. Those many mules came in all sizes, shapes, color combinations, and they came with a variety of talents and abilities just as their horse mothers and donkey fathers had held. My mules ranged in size from diminutive miniature mules standing a mere twenty-eight inches tall and weighing only a couple hundred pounds, all the way up to hefty draft-horse sized mules standing nearly six feet tall at the top of their shoulders and weighing nearly one ton each.

The mules I raised and enjoyed were used for an array of functions. The miniature mule's job description was basically to just be cute and act adorable. Although it was possible to train them to pull small carts and wagons around, I chose not to exercise that option with the smallest of my long-eared friends. I raised a handful of pony-sized mules, which were ridden by my own children and other smaller kids. In addition, I took great pride in the many exceptionally well-trained horse-sized mules, which I raised throughout the years. Each and every one of this particular-sized mule was trained to not only ride with a saddle extremely well, but each was also trained to drive on a single or multiple hitch cart or wagon. Lastly, over the years, I raised many teams of matching draft-sized mules, and when in harness, they were capable of pulling horse-drawn farm machinery or sleighs and wagons.

The following story that I will outline involved one of my favorite riding mules whose name was Skunk. Although her name was not very becoming, Skunk held the record for having my most overall affection in comparison to all of my other horses and mules during my lifetime. Ironically, I did not raise Skunk from a baby, nor did I train her, but she made an indelible mark on my life nonetheless.

*   *   *

Astrid demanded, "Now, Scott, we've discussed this matter countless times, and we can't afford to have as many mules gobbling up our expensive hay and feed as what you seem to think we need to have. You promise me, that you will sell Duke and Duchess at the Waverly Iowa Horse and Mule Auction, and YOU WILL NOT purchase any additional mules while you are at the sale. We need to downsize, and you know it."

I replied, "Yes dear," as I waved, then departed down the driveway with a pair of my matching draft mules loaded into the truck and trailer.

Since Astrid and I were engaged in our agriculture career, the mules were a fun sideline hobby, but we definitely needed to sell some of them occasionally to at least breakeven with the cost of their feed and care. The difficult part of raising and training my beloved mules was that whenever our numbers of mules approached ten mules, we faced the decision of determining which mule or mules needed to be sold. Our mule pens had limited space, and the cost of feeding too many mules posed a financial difficulty for us, so every now and again, we would thin our herd by selling one to four mules at a time.

After a lot of thoughtful consideration, I'd decided that selling Duke and Duchess at one of the largest equine auctions in the nation was the best way to secure a top price for them. There would be no doubt about their ability to command a high price since they were a full brother and sister pair, exactly matched in color and body conformation. Their desirable large draft-size, combined with their exceptional riding and driving abilities surely would excite any potential buyers at the auction.

I pulled into the parking lot of the massive Waverly Horse and Mule Auction several hours later following my long, tiresome drive. Without haste, I unloaded my pair of mules and housed them in their stall at the auction barn. For the next few days prior to the actual sale day, I paraded Duke and Duchess all around the sale grounds while demonstrating their uncanny riding and driving talents to any potential buyers. I had little doubt that before the end of the sale, my pair of draft mules would command the high-selling mule sale price and quite possibly set a new all-time record high sale price. That was until . . .

A big truck and trailer with Oklahoma license plates pulled into the auction sale parking lot with a full load of critters stomping around inside the trailer. I'd been walking through the parking lot when they arrived. It didn't take me long to notice through the side openings on the big trailer that the contents held an entire load of long-eared mules. I stopped and waited as a gristly old cowboy stopped his truck and trailer and began unloading a total of seven mules from the backend of the trailer. Each of the first six mules he tied alongside his trailer were awfully plain, incredibly common brown-colored mules none of which impressed me in the slightest. The seventh and final mule he unloaded was another matter altogether.

As the last mule jumped down from the trailer, I felt the tingle and sensation of "love at first sight." Standing before me was simply the most loudly colored and most athletically built mule that I'd ever witnessed before. She was a flashy-colored pattern as the result of inheriting her appaloosa mother's markings. This long, tall mule looked as though she had been bred and designed for speed. From a distance, she almost looked like a massive jackrabbit not only because of her large ears, but mostly because of her powerfully muscled rear quarters, which made her look as though she could go from a standstill to full speed in a flash.

All the countless onlookers and I gazed in amazement at perhaps the best mule any of us had ever seen before. Later that day, the cowboy saddled up his breathtaking mule and demonstrated to an ever-growing crowd what athletic feats she was capable of. In my years of experience, I'd only seen the most athletic of horses be able to quick start, twirl spin, and then skid stop the way the old cowboy was maneuvering his mule.

Anyone with mule experience will attest that while a mule gains many of the best traits from each of its parents, seldom can a mule match a horse for those kinds of ultra athletic traits. Amazingly, though, before me was more an exception than the rule in terms of mule qualities.

I walked up to the leather-faced old cowboy as he sat in the saddle of his mule and said, "What is the story on this mule, and why are you selling her?"

He looked down at me from high up in the saddle and responded, "Her name is Skunk, and I trained her to be my professional calf-roping mule. She is six years old, and for the past three years, she and I have won a lot of money at professional rodeo roping events all over the country. My dilemma is that I'm now in my sixties age wise, and I'm just getting too old to keep up with the rigors of doing rodeo, so I'm selling this mule and my other six pack mules that I brought along. I'm ready to retire and hang up my boots and spurs."

In my excitement, I remarked, "I'm thinking of buying Skunk with the proceeds from the sale of the two draft mules that I'm selling, so I'd like to ride her and give her a try."

Without a moment's hesitation and with little expression, the cowboy responded, "Up until this point in time, I'm the only man Skunk has ever worked for. I appreciate your notion, but this mule has got a hair trigger and only the most experienced rider will be able to handle her, so the answer is no. If you buy her, then you can ride her."

As the old cowboy turned away to scan the crowd gathered around him and his mule, I forcefully tugged at his denim jeans. He looked back in my direction as I said, "Let me rephrase my previous statement. I'm going to sell two mules in the sale, then I intend on buying this mule. However, I will not buy any mule unless I test ride it first!"

The cowboy replied, "Well, since you put it that way, then let's give it a go," as he stepped down from his saddle stirrup. He commanded, "I don't know how well you ride, and it would be a sure bet that you've never ridden anything with this much power and speed, so be very, very careful. Also, be careful about squeezing your knees or poking her with your heels since she has been trained to explode out of a rodeo chute while running down a speeding calf in the least amount of time possible."

My confidence waned slightly as he held Skunk by her bridle, and I pulled myself up onto the big western saddle. My eyes widened as I settled onto the mule and felt her entire body and muscles begin quivering.

The cowboy shouted to the crowd to make a path, then he looked back at me and said, "I hope you are ready for this," as he released his grip of Skunk's head.

For a brief moment, Skunk just stared directly ahead as she waited for my command. At first I clicked my tongue hoping to ease her forward, but this was not a verbal signal she was accustomed to. My next move was to grab onto the saddle horn with all my strength, and I ever-so-gently squeezed my knees together. I squeezed with so little pressure that I'm sure a butterflies wings provide more force. None the matter, though, because Skunk instantly lurched forward in the fastest burst of speed I'd ever encountered on a mule or a horse for that matter. Even though I'd grasped tightly to the saddle horn, Skunk's instant forward propulsion nearly threw me off the back of the saddle seat. With all the spectators around, I was ever so happy that I was able to hold my position difficult though it was.

After covering more ground faster than I'd ever been able on an equine of any specie, I pulled back onto the reins, only to nearly be thrown forward off the saddle as Skunk brought both of her rear legs underneath her belly and came to a skidding stop amongst a choking cloud of dust. My face flushed and beads of sweat started dripping from my forehead as I imagined myself straddling a flying fighter jet plane and wondering how that could possibly be any different than riding this mule. In every direction around me, the spectators began clapping with excitement at the impressive show Skunk had exhibited. Little did any of them know that I was in dire need of changing my underwear!

The following day countless horses and mules were auctioned off during the sale. With nearly all of the mules sold, my two draft mules, Duke and Duchess, held on to the precarious distinction of top-selling mule. That was an honor they held until Skunk "The Wonder Mule" entered the auction ring.

It only took a few bids from the crowd before the bid for Skunk was above the record price the mules that I sold had commanded. As the old cowboy and Skunk demonstrated uncanny maneuvers in the ring, the bids were coming in fast and furious. What was the outcome one might ask? Well, I was a bit nervous if you must know because as I loaded Skunk into my own empty truck and trailer, I wondered what Astrid's reaction would be. I was still in sticker shock since it had not only taken all the money I received from the sale of my two draft mules, but I had needed to ante up an additional one thousand dollars to buy just one record-selling mule! I somewhat consoled myself, though, as I realized that I now owned one of the most amazing and highest priced mules ever to be sold at public auction. The fact that waiting at home was my wife who I'd made a promise to not purchase any additional mules did not escape my thoughts either.

The long, tiresome trip back home from the sale did nothing to help me resolve what approach I would need to take with Astrid. She was one of the most patient and loving individuals around, but I knew that this time, my actions would result in an angry and probably warranted outburst from her.

Astrid stepped outside the door of our house and waved just as I pulled the truck and trailer into our yard. I could see Astrid's look of joy on her face change over to a look of disgust as she heard Skunk bang the inside of what was supposed to be an empty trailer. I met Astrid alongside the trailer as she got up on her tiptoes to peer inside the almost empty trailer. For hours I'd prepared myself for the lashing I would receive from my spouse and for which a lashing that I most definitely deserved, but surprisingly, she simply shook her head from side to side and merely walked away.

As I breathed an internal sigh of relief thinking how easy that had been, Astrid suddenly did an about-face and shouted, "I hope that stupid mule that you were not suppose to buy is a female mule because you are going to be sleeping alongside her in the barn for the next month!!!"

Ouch! Although Astrid did not enforce her directive to me to sleep in the mule barn, I did suffer through a few days of silent treatment from my wife as she punished me for my compulsive mule addiction.

In time, Astrid mellowed as Skunk and I went on to become a unified team. Over my lifetime, I've had the privilege of owning and working with hundreds of animals, but never before and never since has there ever been an animal that left such a mark on me as did this one amazing mule. For more than a decade, she safely and sure-footedly guided me through some of the harshest and most dangerous mountain terrain on earth. For many years, this steadfast mule pulled carts and wagons, and even pulled farm machinery if I asked her to do so.

I loved that mule as none other I'd ever experienced, but there was one area that I failed her miserably. Skunk had been bred and trained to be a professional roping mule. Soon after bringing her home, I gathered up a roping lasso and guided Skunk out into our beef cattle pasture to try my hand at roping some beef calves. As soon as Skunk saw the rope and felt its course texture rubbing alongside her neck, she pranced in nervous anticipation. She was an unbelievable athlete, and she had a strong craving to do her preferred and highly trained skill.

I singled out one of our calves, started twirling the loop of the rope above my head, and squeezed Skunk's ribcage with my knees as we exploded forward at breakneck speed. Skunk had little trouble bearing down on the running calf aided by her blazing speed. For a brief moment, I thought to myself, *With an amazing roping animal like Skunk, no wonder rodeo cowboys make it look so easy.*

When I was within range of the racing calf, I released my grasp on the rope and watched it sail aimlessly past the calf and fall hopelessly onto the ground below. I was unaware that a trained roping horse or mule is then trained to immediately come to a skidding stop, which then assuming the calf has been roped, will tighten the rope, and ultimately bring the calf to a halt so that the cowboy can quickly dismount and tie up the legs of the calf. Imagine my surprise as I watched the rope fall nowhere near the calf, then I almost face-planted myself onto Skunk's head as she came to an instant skidding stop. I'll never forget what happened next.

As I gathered myself and settled back onto my saddle, Skunk turned her head around in my direction and gave me one of the dirtiest looks I've ever received. If she could have spoken, her words would have been, "You idiot, I do all the work to chase down that calf, and you can't even do your part of the job and get the rope on the calf!" I assure you, there was no need for any spoken words, however, because I felt low enough to crawl under a snake's belly at my incompetence.

Although I tried a few more times that same day to rope a calf, and I tried on some other occasions as well, I simply was never able to master the art of throwing a rope from a speeding animal and get that rope to secure a loop around a calf. Throughout the years, Skunk and I became inseparable partners, but she never let me forget what a pathetic calf roper I was compared to the old cowboy and her original owner.

*   *   *

With as many activities as my beloved mule Skunk and I did together, it was only a matter of time before we would simultaneously face a close call with death.

Astrid and I were thrilled and excited to have been invited by some of our horse- and mule-riding friends to join them on their annual trail ride at Custer State Park in the Black Hills of South Dakota. We were able to find someone to handle our chores and thus we then left for a much-needed short vacation to enjoy time with our mules and our friends. We caravanned with the several other trucks and trailers, and at long last following the ten-hour drive out to the Black Hills, we arrived at our primitive horse-and-mule camp. Primitive camping consists of a rustic campground embedded into the forest area of Custer Park. Although there are outhouse-type bathrooms and water hydrants to draw water from, there are no other modernized facilities such as showers or places in which to sleep. There are horse and mule corrals in which to place one's animals during the evening hours, however, since the area has abundant wildlife such as bears, mountain lions, and buffalo free-roaming the area and looking to attack any unsuspecting horse or mule.

At sunrise the next morning, our camp was alive with excitement and activity. Some of the members of our group were busy cooking up a hearty camp breakfast of pancakes, eggs, and bacon on an open fire. Others in our group were actively feeding, brushing, and saddling our mounts for the upcoming all-day ride through the rugged terrain of the park. As we all gathered to engulf perhaps one of the tastiest breakfasts ever cooked, the seasoned veterans of the group laid out the plans for the ride that day.

We were instructed to recheck all the metal shoes on the horses and mules since the rough and rocky terrain would cause a bare-hoofed animal to go lame within only a few miles of riding. Next, we were instructed to pack along our noontime lunches, which along with our canteens of water, would provide our midday nourishment. Lastly, before departing, our group was instructed about the dangerous nature of the many wild animals that we might encounter throughout our ride. Although Custer State Park has a large variety of wildlife, the general consensus was that nothing was to be feared and to be respected more than the American bison herd or which are more commonly called buffalo.

I wasn't sure that encountering a buffalo on a horse or mule was quite as big a deal as the veterans were making it out to be, but I listened intently anyway. They shared that there was a herd of over three hundred buffalo in Custer Park, and because of their sheer size and speed, along with their infamously sour attitudes, it was deemed that the only sensible thing to do was avoid them at all opportunities.

As we all broke camp and mounted our animals, I remember thinking again, *Seems like overreacting to me. Just how tough could a buffalo be since the Native American Indians used to hunt them with their meager horses?*

Within mere moments of departing our campsite, we were suddenly in the midst of the most beautiful, secluded, and rough terrain that either Astrid or I had ever witnessed. Along we rode in single file with a breathtaking view of places that only a wild animal would encounter or a sure-footed horse or mule could bring you. We climbed trails and ventured into hidden canyons that no one on foot would be capable of trekking. At times it seemed we would see a different form of wildlife around each bend of the trail. Along the way, we spotted eagles, vultures, mountain goats, wolves, coyotes, elk, deer, big-horn sheep, and wild burros to name only a few. For some reason, we did not encounter any of the massive buffalo herd for much of that day, until . . .

Out in the distance, we could make out the dark images of a herd of buffalo. We stopped riding our horses and mules as we listened to the distant grunts and groans coming from the massive and wooly beasts. As we watched from a distance, one of the veteran trail riders began his buffalo instructions once again. He cautioned that there was no other animal in the entire park more dangerous to people or horses and mules than a buffalo. He warned that they may look slow and unassuming, but they were known to charge without mercy even if unprovoked. Lastly, he proclaimed that we should always avoid one of the so-called lone bachelor bulls as they were as dangerous as a keg of dynamite. Evidently, these are the oldest and largest buffalo herd bulls, which are eventually defeated in a battle for herd supremacy. Whenever a younger and stronger buffalo bull defeats the older bulls in battle, they are banished from the herd to live out their remaining days in exile with an intense hate for every living thing on earth. They have an especially rampant hate for humans with their horses and mules.

All of these scary buffalo tales seemed overly melodramatic from my way of thinking. I reasoned that this was no different than telling a scary ghost story around a campfire at night in hopes of frightening everyone out of a good night's slumber. It became evident to me that the other riders in our group including Astrid were scared senseless about the big, bad, bull buffalos. Skunk and I on the other hand had silently devised alternative ideas for a possible buffalo encounter.

Our riding group traveled along for nearly another mile of steeply rugged terrain when suddenly we broke out into a large, flat, open meadow. Still riding our mounts in single file, everyone spotted him at about the same moment. A few hundred yards away and laying well out in the meadow all by himself rested a huge lone bull buffalo. Everyone stopped their riding instantaneously and scouted for means of escape should the need arise. The burley buffalo nonchalantly peered in our group's direction then plopped lazily over onto his side with his legs up in the air and started rolling in the dry dirt he was laying upon.

Unable to contain myself for another minute, I nudged Skunk with my heels as her and I sped off at a full-speed run toward the unsuspecting rogue buffalo. Astrid screamed after me, "Scott, for God's sake, what do you think you are doing?"

As the space between us quickly widened, I shouted back, "I'm going to show our riding group how the Native American Indians used to chase buffalo" as I sped directly for the lone bull buffalo.

Unbeknown to me or Astrid, one of the members of our group had grabbed their video camera and decided to capture a film of my virtual buffalo trampling death.

As Skunk and I ran at breakneck speed for the buffalo, my thoughts were that I held the element of surprise on our side. I believed that even if a buffalo had thoughts of charging a mule and rider, surely this one would only scamper away with his tail between his legs if I could quickly sneak up and surprise him. What a bad plan and what an even worse idea to be sure.

Skunk and I were about to nearly run over the top of the buffalo when he rolled back to his knees and made eye contact with us. I let out a bloodcurdling scream that should have scared any buffalo completely out of their hide. This buffalo, however, had other ideas in his ornery mind. With the fastest, most effortless, fluid motion I've ever encountered, the nearly one ton-sized behemoth rose to his feet and charged without leniency.

I can assure you that neither my mule, nor I saw that coming, but I can attest I suddenly realized that my mule and I were in the throes of a deadly situation. It is a documented fact that a charging buffalo, no matter how large, can actually outrun even the fastest racehorse during a short burst. Perhaps it might have been better for me to have known that important fact before, rather than after, I tried to kill my mule and me in a buffalo-induced suicide.

Skunk unwittingly saved my life that day, even as I felt the very heated breath of death grunting and groaning and charging directly behind me in an all-out rush for survival.

With reactions that perhaps only the most highly athletic mule could have sustained, Skunk detected the enraged bull buffalo's charge, and then came to a skidding stop, whirled in her tracks, and exploded in the opposite direction in a literal sprint for our lives. Everything happened so quickly, it is simply amazing we survived one of my greatest bouts with stupidity. When one considers the laws of physics in what was happening, only a little divine intervention could have brought about a positive outcome on that memorable day.

Imagine the force of momentum on my body as Skunk stopped instantly as she sensed the buffalo's impending charge. With the sudden stop, I was nearly thrown over the top of my mule and quite possibly thrust onto the angry buffalo to do his damage. Somehow, I was able to grab enough leather and saddle to pull myself back onto my saddle. Before I could even adjust my positioning, suddenly, Skunk whirled, nearly tossing me off to the side of my saddle. Still not fully mounted back in place on my saddle, Skunk then literally propelled forward for her very life as I nearly fell off the saddle this time in a backward fashion.

As my back and shoulders fell back onto the backside of my mule, I could see, hear, and smell the rage of the bull buffalo as he quickly closed the gap between himself and Skunk. With all my strength, I pulled myself upright and back onto the saddle while we tried to race away from the demented buffalo as fast as Skunk's legs could hurl. With one more glance back, I came to the terrifying realization that he was catching us and in fact he was lowering the sharpened horns on his massive head in order to rip a gouge out of the backside of Skunk's hind legs.

It all happened so fast that I simply had no time for even a quick prayer, albeit, Astrid was busy praying on our behalf as she looked on in fright.

Just as the enraged buffalo was about to trample Skunk and I, the most unbelievable event transpired. When I ride mules, I always wear a felt cowboy hat that has a leather tie string that I snug up underneath my chin to keep my cowboy hat from blowing off in the wind or keep from falling off whenever my mule starts running. Throughout all my years of riding horses and mules, I've never once had my cowboy hat come off because of the way I secure it to my head. For reasons that defy explanation, on that day at that moment my cowboy hat somehow flew off my head and planted directly in the face of the infuriated charging buffalo.

How did it come off my head? Why did it come off my head? I can't explain, but since I did survive and was able to retell the story, what I distinctly remember most was that somehow the sight and smell of my cowboy hat brought the buffalo to an instant halt while Skunk and I made our final and hasty escape.

From a safe distance away, I slowed my panting mule and then turned to face the now distant buffalo. I wasn't sure whether I should laugh or cry as I observed the incensed buffalo first gore my cowboy hat with his horns, followed by stomping my cowboy hat into the ground with all four of his mighty hooves, and finally he squatted over my expensive $75 felt cowboy hat and urinated on it! At last he calmly walked away, convinced he had taught us a lesson that we would never forget. And we never did forget the lessons we learned on that fateful day.

As I made my way back to our shocked riding group, I can attest that I've never felt so sheepish and foolish. Everyone proclaimed that no one with any sense at all would have done such a foolhardy thing. I was nearly in shock following my close call, and with my face as white as a ghost, I expressed that it hadn't gone down the way I'd expected it to go.

At the end of that wonderful but trying day, our riding group made it back once again to our primitive camp where we settled around the campfire for the evening. It was then that the video camera was brought out which had captured the entire buffalo lunacy event in color. Our group gasped as we viewed my buffalo encounter first at normal speed and then viewed it again and again in painfully slow motion. No one in our group could believe just how close my mule and I had come to certain death, yet we somehow escaped.

Was I simply lucky that day, or was the hand of God at play protecting me once again?

RUNAWAY CARRIAGE ADVERSITY— 29 YEARS

CHAPTER SEVENTEEN

So if you have been raised with Christ, seek the things that are
above, where Christ is, seated at the right hand of God.
Set your minds on things that are above, not on things that are
on earth, for you have died, and your life is hidden with
Christ in God.
When Christ who is your life is revealed, then you also will
be revealed with him in glory.
—COLOSSIANS 3:1-4

All throughout my life, I've outwardly demonstrated one of my main objectives to live life to the fullest by having as vast a mixture of interests and hobbies as possible. It has always been my blueprint to attack any new interest with a vengeance, with a passion, and with what could probably be deemed excessively compulsive behavior by many.

As the years have gone by, I've heavily pursued my interests in rodeo competition, piloting airplanes, riding motorcycles, mountain climbing, white-water rafting as well as horse and mule activities nearly bordering on excess. In nearly all cases, when the adrenaline rush subsides and the excitement level wanes, I historically move on to other interests. More traditionally minded folks will often pursue far fewer and less risky hobbies and interests while usually investing much of their entire lifetimes on the pursuit of only a select few hobbies or interests.

The previous chapter outlined how engaged I'd become with raising, training, and working with mules. For several years, my wife, Astrid, along with our two sons, Trevor and Travis, and I invested as much of our available free time as possible doing any mule-related activity that we could find to participate in. We shared a lot of memory-making quality family time over those years by literally investing days or even weeks doing anything and everything a family could possibly do with their mule stock.

We proudly and successfully exhibited our mules at many state and national shows. I took great pride in entering my large spans of draft mules in various antique equine-drawn plowing and field-work competitions held throughout the upper Midwest. The mules posed an exceptional benefit whenever I utilized their sure-footedness, agility, and strength for riding and packing heavy loads into the mountain wildernesses of Wyoming and Montana for big game hunting. Over the years, our family entered countless parades as our mules pulled beautiful carriages and wagons for all of the spectators to enjoy. In addition, for several years, I provided a special newlywed mule-driven carriage service. A just-married couple could be romantically swept away from their church wedding with our fanciest harnessed mules, which I then hitched to one of our fanciest carriages—all decked out with Just Married signs. My family and I also utilized our riding mules time and again to enjoy experiencing some of the most rugged and beautiful national parks and mountainous regions of our country.

One of the most enjoyable family experiences that we shared together over the years was working with our mules and utilizing them to participate in various wagon train reenactments. I'll devote the next full chapter to just how one such wagon train eventually led to a near-fatal accident for my entire family and me.

*   *   *

It isn't difficult to imagine the many joys and experiences that can be provided when human beings share their lives with the likes of horses or mules. Seldom does one have enough appreciation, however, for just how big, just how fast, just how strong, or just how dangerous interactions with any equine specie can be if something goes tragically wrong.

In the previous chapter, I elaborated at length about what a tremendous mule Skunk was. Over the many years that I enjoyed her companionship, I became accustomed to saying that I didn't think there was anything she was incapable of doing if asked. In time, I asked more from Skunk than I'd ever asked from any other animal.

Some of the uncanny feats she performed were the kinds of things mule and horse legends are created from. I can't reiterate enough just how much I loved that animal. There was never anything that I asked of her no matter how physically difficult or how mentally trying whereby she would not try her best to accommodate my desires. Sure, I knew when I purchased her that she was exceptionally fast and agile for a mule. I was also well aware that the old Oklahoma cowboy that I'd bought her from had trained her to instantly obey all commands. This fact was emphasized to me on the day that I bought Skunk at a large national mule and horse sale.

When her former cowboy master placed her attached lead rope into my waiting hand that day, with misty eyes, he reflected, "Son, this outstanding mule has done everything that I've ever asked her to do. My guess is that in time, if you develop enough trust and respect for each other, she will do everything that you'll ever ask her to do as well."

He hesitated for a long pause while looking away, and then finished his lesson by saying, "My only caution to you is this. Don't ever ask Skunk to do something that you know she can't do because I promise you that she'll try doing it with everything within her being. She'll do this for you because she will trust your judgment and instincts. Listen now and listen well, son, if she is ever unable to do something that you demand of her, you likely will then have succeeded in ruining one of the best mules on the planet!" With that, he walked away without another word.

As I led my new mule toward the trailer that day for our homeward journey, I contemplated the old cowboy's reflections.

Over the next months and years, just as her previous owner had predicted, under my guidance, Skunk went on to perform feats that few had ever witnessed mules or horses accomplish before. During one national trail ride in some rugged mountains of Tennessee, a group of riders chose to attempt to ride their horses up a nearly straight and treacherous incline. One horse and rider after another attempted and then subsequently failed to overcome the steep incline. A couple of horses and their riders even tumbled down the impassible and dangerous incline, causing some injury.

From my distant vantage point, I surmised that perhaps Skunk and I had the determination, the strength, and the sure-footedness to navigate the extreme barrier before us. I nudged my mule forward with my heels, and she started her nearly vertical upward accent. Upward we climbed as perhaps only an indigenous mountain goat could. As we neared the top,

I clung to the saddle with all my might, sensing the loose sand and gravel beneath Skunk's hooves letting go, and suddenly, it appeared that we would fall backward in yet another failed attempt. At that point, I'll never forget the sensation from the seat of my saddle as Skunk remarkably dropped down to her knees in an attempt to alter her angle of accent, and then she surged upward with her powerful hind legs. She literally crawled as she strained to pull us up the last several yards of the perilous hill, and then leaped over the top edge. I thought my chest would burst with pride as the entire group of national trail riders exploded with applause and cheers of amazement.

On countless occasions, with me on her back, Skunk would cross the deepest rivers, climb the steepest trails, or allow me to guide her through some of the most impassible terrain imaginable and never did she balk or fail in any of her attempts. As others within our riding groups would witness such spectacular feats, Skunk eventually was christened with her nickname, The Wonder Mule.

The only difficulty with teaming up with an animal such as Skunk was that it became ever more difficult to discern exactly what her outer limits of capability were. One can only imagine with my own risk-taking behavior and adrenaline addiction what outlandish stuff Skunk and I were forever attempting. Since her uncanny abilities seemed to always result in perfection, I oftentimes guided her to many precarious close calls.

*   *   *

Astrid was not very happy with me when I announced that I wanted to single-hitch Skunk up to our antique carriage that day rather than harness one of our draft mule teams up to our big hitch wagon.

On that particular Saturday, we had been invited to join several of our mule and horse friends for a leisurely day of driving our carriages and wagons through the countryside. We were all to gather in the yard of one of our friends who lived about six miles from our home. About once per month, we would come together to enjoy each other's fellowship, followed by a picnic lunch together, and then drive our mule and horse hitches for a lazy drive on a sunny afternoon.

The reason for Astrid's concern was that even though I had recently trained Skunk to obey hitching commands while under harness, my cautious wife simply felt that Skunk was still too novice for our planned activities on that day.

Astrid pleaded, "Scott, I'm not comfortable with our sons Trevor, who is only three years old, and Travis, who is only one year old, riding with us in a carriage pulled by Skunk. She is simply too fast and too volatile in my opinion."

I was used to my wife's reservations regarding chancy encounters, so I responded, "Astrid, Skunk has never failed me yet, and so why are you so worried?"

Astrid argued back by stating, "I don't like or trust that mule even on a good day. She reminds me of an explosion waiting to ignite, and I'm not comfortable with my little boys and me riding all day in a carriage pulled by her. What if she gets scared, and we have a runaway accident?

My fateful response was, "What can possibly happen? Now stop being so apprehensive whenever you are around Skunk because she senses that you have no time for her and that in itself may cause some problems."

With that exchange of words, the matter was put to rest as I instructed Astrid to prepare our little sons for the ride while I went about harnessing and hitching Skunk to our beautiful, antique, single-seated carriage. With everything set, I guided Skunk and the carriage up to our house where Astrid loaded our picnic basket along with the boys and placed herself into the carriage. Down the road we went at a brisk, but pleasant trot.

What a magnificent day it was as we clip-clopped along the back country road on our way to our destination nearly six miles away. The cloudless sky was gorgeous blue, and we basked in the warmth of the sun on our faces as we traveled along in a form of transportation commonly used decades earlier. Riding in the carriage was nothing new for Trevor and Travis since they made countless treks by carriage and wagon and had each done so since they were each a mere six months of age. Astrid relaxed as she made a mental note that perhaps I'd been correct in my assumption that Skunk was trained well enough by this point to drive the carriage. Perhaps it was likely that nothing bad would happen on such a magnificent day.

I had just commented to Astrid and our youngsters about how blessed we were to be able to enjoy such a relaxing mode of historical travel by mule and carriage. I commented, "Isn't it amazing to be able to hear the birds singing in the trees as we pass by?"

All seemed so well with the world, when suddenly, Skunk's right front hoof came down on a discarded aluminum pop can that I had not seen laying in middle of the roadway. My family and I first heard the crunch of the can, and then each of our heads was jilted backward as we felt the instant forward surge of our carriage. The unexpected loud crunch of the can so badly spooked Skunk that she suddenly thrust forward in sheer fright. In a flash, Astrid and I knew matters were dire to say the least for our young family.

Under usual circumstances, I would most always hitch our big, slow, methodical, and plodding draft mules up to our carriages or wagons. A draft animal by nature of the beast is genetically built for power and strength to pull heavy loads while maintaining a quiet demeanor. Skunk on the other hand was a totally opposite animal being built for speed and quick reflexes. She was tall, athletic, and an extremely fast riding mule whose breeding was aimed at activities requiring anything but reservation and calmness.

As Skunk and the carriage gathered speed, in terror, Astrid clutched our young sons with all her might. I twisted the harness lines used to guide Skunk tightly around my hands while pulling back with all my strength on the bit in her mouth with the false hope of bringing her to a safe stop. We knew we were in deep trouble when my actions only resulted in Skunk momentarily rearing up into the air, then running on even faster with us in tow.

Suddenly and without warning, in her wide-eyed fright, Skunk made a quick lunge and changed direction, hoping to gain access to an open field sitting adjacent to the road that we were traveling. Unable to control her any longer, I watched in horror as she made the harrowing right-hand turn. Down into the ditch went the runaway mule and cascading carriage as I now feared for the life of my two young sons and their mother.

The speeding turn into the road ditch was far too much action for the old carriage to endure, and within an instant, our entire world was suddenly turned upside down. Over went the carriage with a gut-wrenching and splintering crash, which sent even further shock waves through Skunk in her wild attempt to escape her current circumstance. Somehow Astrid was able to keep our two little boys within her grasp as our overturned carriage was being mercilessly dragged through the ditch and up onto the open field.

What happened next has no real worldly explanation, but without a doubt, we should have all been critically injured or at the very least one or more of my family and I could have been killed as a result of our ghastly runaway.

For reasons that Astrid and I have never been able to explain, the harness and the wooden hitch of the carriage broke free from Skunk. The tattered carriage, which was being dragged on its side, came to a skidding rest as we watched an ever-frightened mule race off into the distant field. Although our family of four was disheveled and lying all atop each other, we were somehow miraculously unscathed through it all. It took a few minutes to quiet down our wailing young sons, but Astrid and I looked squarely into one another's eyes, realizing how blessed we were to have survived such a wreck and such a close call with our youngsters.

*   *   *

We never made it to our final destination that day. The balance of the day was spent trying to put everything back to normal. We were eventually able to find Skunk as she wandered the open fields waiting to be located and brought home. We loaded up the pieces of our shattered carriage and torn harness, so everything could eventually be mended. Astrid, Trevor, and Travis came through their runaway carriage ordeal with no injuries and no aftereffects. Incredibly, our entire family accepted the risks, and before long, we were all once again driving our mules on carriages and wagons once more.

What became of Skunk in the aftermath of that day one might ask? Well, it is common knowledge for those who work with and train mules that if a mule experiences something bad, then one must rectify and correct the behavior as quickly as possible. Failure to do so will leave the mule with the mind-set that whatever bad has happened becomes the norm for them. For example, if a mule bucks you off the saddle, one must immediately get back on the mule and ride again or one risks never being able to safely ride that same animal ever again. Similarly, I faced the consequences of a runaway with Skunk, so driving her under harness ever again was at risk to be sure.

Within one hour of our death-defying carriage crash, I had Skunk hitched once again to my heaviest wagon. The only exception this time, however, was that she was hitched in tandem alongside my largest and most trusted draft mule. My methodology was simple physics since I knew that if Skunk attempted to run away in fear again, and she did so repeatedly, I was comforted knowing that she would be unable to drag the other big draft mule weighing nearly twice as much as her, complimented by her inability to run away with the massive wagon in which the pair was harnessed to.

After investing a few hours of continuous driving, Skunk eventually relented and became ever more content while pulling the load.

I learned a valuable lesson that day because never again would I chance driving Skunk by herself in a single harness while being hitched to a lightweight carriage. She pulled her weight many times in the years that followed, but only while harnessed within multiple animal hitches to prevent any future blowups on her behalf.

*　　*　　*

On the very same evening of our mule-driving wreck and just before falling asleep that night, I praised and thanked my ever-lasting creator for sparing the lives of my family and me. Before sleep overtook me, I momentarily lamented about how my prayer was becoming all too familiar based on the way I chose to live my life.

RUNAWAY WAGON UPHEAVAL—30 YEARS

CHAPTER EIGHTEEN

You are my glory, the one who lifts up my head.
—PSALM 3:13

This chapter involves a final tale regarding how our involvement with mules and horses put my family and me within harm's ways on two unusual and extremely frightening occasions. Amazing as it may appear, by the time I'd reached only the age of thirty, my life had been jeopardized on eighteen separate occasions. Was it even possible for any one person to survive even one, much less two sets of "nine lives" confrontations facing death and still live to tell about it? Believe it or not, many more were still to come.

*   *   *

For twelve years running, my wife, Astrid, our sons, Trevor and Travis, and I participated in a very special annual fund-raising event called the Camp Courage Wagon Train. During a two-decade era, this noble cause helped raise more than one million dollars in donations, which were then used to enable disabled children to attend Camp Courage. Camp Courage is located near Annandale, Minnesota, and it hosts special-needs camps each year for children with a variety of disabilities. The special camp offers and allows children who have similar challenges such as hearing impairments or visual impairments or possibly youth with physical disabilities to participate in a youth camp, just as all other children have the opportunity to attend camp from time to time.

The dilemma, however, is that it can be financially challenging for the parents of a disabled child to send their child to Camp Courage. The cost of attendance can be prohibitive in part because of expense associated with the requirements of the camp maintaining a one special-needs counselor for every two camper ratio, which makes sense considering the special needs of the kids attending Camp Courage.

The basic premise of the Camp Courage Wagon Train was that the volunteers participating in the wagon train, not only donated up to ten days of their time and resources for the event each summer, but in addition, the wagon train participants also worked throughout the year collecting monetary donations for the Camp Courage kids. A common method of donation was to secure a certain financial pledge on a per mile basis for the distance one intended to travel on the wagon train. On a typical year, the Camp Courage Wagon Train would cover a two-hundred-mile-long route, and then finish the event by passing through the gates of Camp Courage. Once the wagon train arrived at Camp Courage, the group would then turn over the substantial donations to be used for the disabled children's camperships.

The first time that Astrid and I joined the Camp Courage Wagon Train, we used one of our horses to pull an antique single-seat wooden-wheeled buggy on the assigned wagon train route. As novices that year, we were wide-eyed in amazement at the unselfish sacrifices that so many volunteers made on behalf of a group of less fortunate children. In our first year, we did not travel with the group for more than a couple of days and our fund-raising efforts were weak at best.

We learned enough from our first year on the wagon train to return for a second year with a renewed vigor. As we joined the group for a second time the following year as two-year veterans, we were far keener to our surroundings, knowing exactly what to expect. Trevor, our two-year-old son, joined Astrid and I that year; and we used our horse once again to pull our newly acquired antique two-seated wooden-wheeled carriage for the entire two-hundred-mile route. No longer would our expanding family be able to travel such long distances confined within a single-seat carriage, so we'd upgraded to a roomier two-seat version. That year our passion fires were ignited as we realized how inspiring it could be by participating in such a noble fund-raising cause. We not only donated a full ten days of our time to participate, but we had worked extra hard that year to secure nearly one thousand dollars in pledges from friends and family members.

It is hard to describe the feelings one encounters during the long ten days of traveling by wagon train. With modern-day travelers speeding by in cars at somewhere between fifty and seventy miles per hour, one can barely imagine what it actually feels like then to travel a distance of two hundred miles at a snail's pace of only three miles per hour as the horses and mules of the wagon train clip-clopped slowly down shoulder side of the highway.

Each day began for the weary wagon trainers at 4:00 a.m. After a long, tiresome, twelve to fourteen hour day of riding or driving one's horses and mules on average for twenty or more miles, the wagons at last make it to camp. Once in camp, the group would then circle up the wagons in historical fashion each night. Many evenings were often spent sitting around a roaring campfire while listening to "old timers" sharing stories from the past. Many of those stories revolved around days long ago in which the storytellers had used horses and mules for farming or as their means of transportation. For those of us who were modern-day wagon trainers, it was fascinating to hear the wisdom shared from those elders who had actually earned their livelihoods during an era where real horsepower was used to build and feed our great nation.

One of my most vivid memories from that year was recalling how hot and miserable the conditions were each and every day. Hardly a day passed by when Astrid and I, and countless other wagon trainers dared to complain about our wretched plight. As the sun beat down on our weary horses and mules, many of us mumbled silently under our breath promising ourselves that surely we would not participate in anything so torturous again in the future. Astrid and I had secretly vowed to each other that we would not join the wagon train for a third year since there were more enjoyable ways to spend one's family vacation time together.

Somehow each difficult day drudged on by, but we found the fortitude to endure the entire two-hundred-mile journey over the course of those ten long days. We were hitching our horse to the carriage for the last time that morning as we prepared to break camp and travel with the wagon train through the gates of Camp Courage. Although it was our first visit to Camp Courage, we had only the thoughts of departing as quickly as possible on our minds. I simply couldn't wait for the last leg of the journey to come to an end so my family and I could depart for good from such a sadistic form of family vacation. That was at least until . . .

As I guided our horse and carriage for the first time through the gates of Camp Courage, we were met by hundreds of smiling, waving, and clapping children. What left an indelible mark on our hearts, however, was that some of those kids were confined to wheelchairs, while others were blind, and an entire group of children were deaf. Moments later as I stepped down from my horse-drawn carriage, a little disabled girl permanently on crutches and with steel braces on her frail legs hobbled over to my family and me. With big tears of joy in her eyes, she thanked us personally for helping raise enough donations enabling her to attend Camp Courage.

On that day and at that moment, Astrid and I emotionally broke down in tears. It had suddenly dawned on us that for the past several days, we had felt pathetically sorry for ourselves while we had constantly complained about how difficult the wagon train had been. We had complained about being tired, about being hungry, about being thirsty, and about being hot. In our own self-pity, we had vowed to never again participate because we thought it too difficult to endure.

As I was hugged by the emotional and thankful little girl, I became acutely aware of my own selfishness and felt shame. Before me was a little girl whose everyday struggles made anything in my life pale by comparison. That day I was humbled as we witnessed more than one hundred children with extreme disabilities show their appreciation for our wagon train efforts on their behalf. Astrid and I were overcome with emotion as we shared our special moment of elation and appreciation with a physically challenged little girl.

From that moment on, we promised to commit to more wagon trains in order to send even more children such as her to benefit from the Camp Courage experience.

*　　*　　*

After much consideration, I volunteered to be the wagon master for our family's third Camp Courage Wagon Train the following year. Let it be said that I threw myself into the task with everything within my power. At least once per week for nearly the entire year leading up to that wagon train, I met with countless community civic organizations all along the future wagon train route. I vowed to help create the largest modern-day wagon train to ever journey through our portion of America. As I met with the various groups from the towns and cities along the upcoming wagon train route, I would describe our cause at length and then request their assistance.

As I met with the assorted groups that year, I predicted that our upcoming Camp Courage Wagon Train would double in size from any previous year and indicated that we would have at least thirty covered wagons and carriages as well as an additional one hundred saddle riders. I shared that our traveling caravan of up to three hundred people would necessitate their help and sponsorship to ensure success. I asked for and received everything from portable toilets to vast quantities of water for the animals, to fields large enough for our group to stop, to meals to feed our masses. I even requested their assistance in planning for nighttime community fund-raising dances in which the proceeds could be donated to the wagon train fund-raiser.

For the record, when the Camp Courage Wagon Train assembled that year, our group consisted of not thirty, but rather, sixty covered wagons and carriages, and not one hundred, but rather five hundred saddle riders, and our entire group numbered not three hundred, but rather one thousand participants in all. The wagon train was so expansive that we spanned an unbelievable distance of nearly two miles in length as we journeyed down the side of the highways along our route. That year we pulled off a miraculous achievement that was never again equaled in size or scope for a modern-day wagon train.

Our wagon train became front-page headline news in nearly every newspaper, and it was covered by nearly every television station within the state of Minnesota. When we turned in our fund-raising donations that year at Camp Courage, we had garnered more than ten times the money for disabled children than the wagon train had ever risen previously.

With such a victorious success story, what could possibly have gone wrong?

*   *   *

Immediately following my decision to volunteer as wagon master for the upcoming Camp Courage Wagon Train, I decided to sell my one remaining horse, opting to drive an all-mule hitch the following year. Astrid and I dialogued how impressive it would be if the wagon master's lead wagon could be as authentic and historically correct as possible. We surmised that throughout the course of the upcoming year, we would acquire four large matching draft mules along with an authentic covered wagon. No one had ever attempted to drive a four-up hitch of horses or mules on the two-hundred mile wagon train, so we promised each other to be the first to do so.

Shortly after conceiving the idea of driving a four-mule hitch in the wagon train, I weighed in on the notion with Irv Lamb who was one of the wagon train elders and who had journeyed on every Camp Courage Wagon Train previously held. Irv was well into his seventies, and he had farmed with horses and mules for much of his lifetime.

When I asked, "Irv, do you think I could drive a hitch of four big mules on a wagon for the entire two hundred mile wagon train?"

Irv scratched his long white beard thoughtfully and then replied, "It could be done, but it won't be the easiest task you'll ever attempt. You see, Scott, those four big mules are so strong that they won't even realize that your covered wagon is behind them as you pull it down the highway. They will simply never tire, and in fact, for most of the two hundred miles, the wagon will be simply pulled by their mouths through the leather lines that you'll be guiding them with your hands and arms, rather than through the normal means of their harness pulling the wagon along. I don't know if your hands and arms can endure such a test of endurance for so many days. I'm even more concerned that you intend on having Astrid and your two little boys in the back of your wagon. What happens if those big mules get scared and runaway on you and your family?"

Looking directly into Irv's eyes, I shared, "I understand your concern and reasons for caution, but I'm committed to making it happen."

The first span of matching draft mules that I acquired were a brother and sister pair by the name of Duke and Duchess, which were mentioned in an earlier chapter. The next span of draft mules that I purchased were two matched sisters named Dolly and Dandy. Over the course of many months, I harnessed and hitched my four large mules to the covered wagon as I prepared for the task at hand.

At long last the first day of the Camp Courage Wagon Train finally arrived. Our volunteer wagon train preacher shared a prayer and a blessing with the group early that morning, and then I maneuvered my lead covered wagon and four draft mules onward toward our final destination, which was a long ten long days and two hundred miles down the trail.

One of the safety measures that we implemented on our wagon train was one in which we spaced the most experienced of saddle riders mounted on the fastest, most trusted horses all throughout the length of the wagon train. Our group knew from several past experiences that by putting so many horses and mules together with that many people was a runaway incident just waiting to happen. Since it was nearly impossible to deter all runaway incidences, we at least desired to have saddle riders in place and prepared to chase down a frightened runaway rider's animal or catch a runaway team on a wagon with a minimum of danger or injury.

Little did I know on the second day of the wagon train that year how important those saddle-out riders would become for my family and I.

Prior to departing on the second morning, I'd been interviewed by a television reporter along with his camera crew representing one of the Minneapolis-based television stations. Following the interview, he then indicated that they planned on setting up their cameras a few miles down the road to capture the traveling wagon train on film for the evening news broadcasts.

Although I had agreed to their request, I informed the camera crew on a few details to ensure the safety of our wagon train participants. I discussed the fact that under no circumstances were they to set up anywhere near the road that we would be traveling on, especially since my four large draft mules were pulling the lead wagon. I directed them to set up their cameras out in one of the fields, well away from the road that we would be traveling, so as to not spook any of my mules or any other animal on the wagon train for that matter.

I explained that mules with their larger ears and inborn perception of danger are extrasensitive to the high-pitched whirring sound emitted from a television camera. I further explained that inside of our covered wagon, my wife was caring for our six-month-old baby son Travis along with our three-year-old son Trevor. The camera crew agreed that with their expensive camera zoom lenses, they could easily obtain the shots they required from a distance well away from the traveling wagon train.

As the camera crew departed, I prayed that my words of caution would not go unheeded, only to then jeopardize the safety of my entire family.

The wagon train proceeded onward that morning without problems for the first couple of miles. I continued my vigilance of watching for the exact location of the waiting camera crew, but for some reason, I was unable to spot their whereabouts.

As our route took us leisurely alongside a farmer's soybean field off to our right, the road began to curve abruptly. As I guided my four big mules and wagon out of the curve, I was suddenly shocked by what lay ahead. The cameraman from the television crew was lying flat on his stomach and directly in the middle of the road with his large camera filming the oncoming wagon train.

I knew instantly that my family and I were in trouble as I shouted, "Get off the road this instant before you cause a runaway! I instructed you earlier to get out in the field so you wouldn't scare any of the horses or mules, so why on earth are you in the middle of the road?"

I had no sooner finished my sentence when the rogue cameraman leapt to his feet with his big camera in tow. By this point, there was far too little distance between him and my mules. My worst fears were realized when all four mules bolted to the right in fear of the cameraman and his strange equipment.

It happened so quickly that I could barely respond. First, my nearly three tons of powerful mules exploded in a burst of speed as they dove off the road in fright. Instantly, they then pulled my family and me and our covered wagon first down into the steep ditch then up out of the steep bank of the ditch and out into the field in a full-out running gallop. How the old wagon did not split in half I'll never understand, but within mere seconds, our runaway wagon was bursting along at full speed across the field. The mules with their thundering hooves were headed directly for the rapidly approaching steep bank of a large river directly in our path, and I could do little to deter them!

Try as I might, my strength was no match for the runaway mules. I pulled and pulled on the leather lines attached to the bits in their mouths to no avail. I couldn't alter their direction either left or right, and there seemed little hope of pulling them to a stop in time. My senses were on overload as I envisioned the death of my family and me as the steep river bank came ever closer. I could hear Astrid screaming in fear for the safety of our little boys as she sensed that within moments our demise was imperative.

All the while our mules were breaking away at full speed across the field; there were three of the fastest horses on our wagon train trying to chase our wagon down before we catapulted over the edge of the steep river bank.

A fearful moment that was forever captured in time by a lone photographer occurred next. One of the persons on the wagon train snapped several eerie photos that showed Astrid reaching out of the back of our runaway wagon attempting to hand our tiny six-month-old baby son Travis to one of the speeding saddle riders. The photos forevermore captured just how grave our situation had become as our little baby dangled by one arm out of the back of a runaway wagon as an attempt was made to safely transfer him to the speeding rider just prior to an impending crash.

Yet to this day, I believe that God changed the outcome a moment before that dangerous handoff of our baby son.

Astrid screamed, "I'm handing the baby out the back of the wagon and to the saddle rider before we all die!"

The very thought of such a tragic outcome with my wife and children and perhaps a little help from our Lord resulted in a sudden level of strength that I gained which defied all explanation. With only a few yards remaining before certain death or injury, I wrapped the multiple leather driving lines around my lower arms, then I placed my feet upon the metal-reinforced wooden front end of the wagon and pulled back with all my might while shouting at the top of my lungs, "Woo, woo, woo!"

Just when I thought the sheer strength of those four big mules would literally rip my arms out from their sockets and just as the front end of the wagon broke out with a loud snap, the mules and wagon came to a skidding stop. It was as though the hand of God had suddenly placed an invisible barrier in front of the wide-eyed mules. For a few moments, all I could hear was the heavy panting of my now statuelike mules, and I could detect the quiet whimpering coming from my young family all disheveled in the back of the wagon. As my own heart pounded in my eardrums, I looked in amazement at just how close we were to the dangerous embankment of the river.

Once we had all taken a few moments to gather ourselves, I then carefully guided the mule hitch and covered wagon back out to the roadway and to a "hero's welcome" from our waiting wagon train friends.

Later that same day during a scheduled wagon train stop, the television crew members sheepishly approached me with their most sincere apologies. I dare say, though, I did not have too many kind words for them since their dangerous and irresponsible acts nearly cost my family our lives.

*   *   *

For twelve wonderful fulfilling years, my family and I participated passionately in the Camp Courage Wagon Train. By the time our sons,

Travis and Trevor, were ten and twelve years old, they had been through a wealth of pioneering experiences that few youngsters in the modern era could ever imagine.

One humorous proclamation was directed toward me from Trevor and Travis one day when they jointly commented, "Dad, can't we please do a normal vacation one of these summers? All of our friends at school get to travel around America visiting cool places like the Grand Canyon and Disney World, but all we ever get to do is look at the boring view of the rear ends of our mules from inside a covered wagon!"

From their heartfelt commentary, I vowed to provide my family with some traditional vacationing opportunities in the near future when at last we had fulfilled our commitments to the wagon train and to the disabled children that benefited as a result.

A given fact is that if one spends enough time working with horses and mules, the moment will occur when something dangerous and unavoidable will happen. All the caution on earth cannot prevent one from eventually getting kicked or from getting bucked off a saddle or from experiencing a wreck while hitched to a carriage or wagon.

*   *   *

Trevor at age four and Travis at age two were two young boys already seasoned as wagon train veterans far beyond their years. Each had experienced runaway carriages and wagons, but still they enjoyed our multitude of family mule activities nonetheless. For the wagon train route that year, I decided to pull our covered wagon with my two newest draft mules.

I'd raised Crystal and Reba from tiny foals into one of the largest pair of draft mules in the entire country. Each mule stood nearly six feet tall at the shoulders, and they each tipped the scales at over eighteen hundred pounds. In all the years in which I'd previously raised and trained mules, Crystal and Reba were my shining pride and joy. They were gentle giants that were mirror images of each other, and their massive size gave them equal stature comparable with even the largest of draft horses. I knew that few other horses or mules on the wagon train could match their strength or challenge their magnificence. Never before had I presented a pair that was as highly trained as these two.

*   *   *

The Camp Courage Wagon Train was nearly halfway along its two hundred mile course on the fateful day that my family and I were once again thrust into harm's way. Up until that day on that year's wagon train, our group of hearty modern-day pioneers had suffered few if any challenges. Everything was going so well that in camp each night, there was talk around the campfire that perhaps this would be the year of our safest wagon train ever.

On the very next day, however, everything was to change in an instant.

I was driving our covered wagon pulled by Crystal and Reba at a leisurely pace and in line with the other covered wagons along a busy highway. We were in the seventh wagon spot from the front, and everything was going along almost too perfectly. The wagon train traffic safety riders were controlling vehicle traffic on the highway in the same manner we had all become accustomed to.

The traffic routine was such that only one lane of vehicular traffic at a time was ever allowed to slowly pass by the moving wagon train while the other lane of vehicles would be held up waiting to take their turn to drive slowly past the wagon train. Under no circumstances were any moving vehicles ever allowed to stop or take photos as they passed the wagon train since doing so could spook the animals, causing a runaway. The act of stopping a vehicle in the middle of traffic could even cause a multiple vehicle accident.

The trouble-free morning had elapsed into the lazy midafternoon. The warm sun made our eyelids heavy as I guided my mules and wagon on our westward route. I drove the team of mules while sitting on the right side of the covered wagon's wooden spring seat alongside Trevor whose eyelids were getting heavier and heavier. I chuckled to myself as I watched my little boy's head bob up and down as he would fall in and out of sleep to the gentle swaying motion of the slowly moving covered wagon. I glanced back over my shoulder to view the back of the covered wagon, which brought a slight smile to my lips at the sight of Astrid fast asleep in a chair as she clutched Travis who was also deep in slumber. I marveled at the notion of how similar this scene must have been compared to the mode of travel long ago as weary pioneers blazed the trails to the frontier. It was a moment of pure joy and contentment, and I wondered how anything at all could upset such a serene moment with my beloved family.

The traffic safety riders had just released the oncoming flow of single-lane traffic to pass slowly by the rolling wagon train. The first few cars passed by as normal and without incident. Suddenly, a woman driving a black pickup truck with two young children in it slammed on her brakes only a few yards in front of my team of mules. My senses became keenly astute as I kept my eyes on not only my large team of mules but on the improperly stopped pickup truck as well. Without warning, the woman equipped with a camera and her kids threw open their vehicle doors, jumped out onto the highway, and then started running toward my mules and covered wagon.

Unfortunately, at that moment, the wagon train was traveling along the right shoulder of the busy highway at a spot where the road ditch was extremely steep and treacherous. I was aware of the steepness of the ditch, but it hadn't posed any threat from my perspective—yet! That was until the woman and her kids ran directly at my two big mules. The mules quickly sidestepped to their right, momentarily catching me off guard, but in doing so, both right side wooden wheels of our covered wagon fell over the edge of the highway shoulder, causing the top-heavy covered wagon to severely lean downward.

I reacted instantly by pulling Crystal and Reba back to their left, trying to bring them back onto the flat roadway, but before I could correct their path of travel, the wagon starting tipping evermore downward toward the direction of the ominous ditch. I yelled for Astrid to wake up and pleaded with her to do her best to protect little Travis as I frantically proclaimed that our big covered wagon was going to roll over with us in it and while still dangerously attached to the mules.

It was as though everything went into slow motion as we felt the wagon slowly tip past top center, then creak and fall ever so slowly down into the ditch. As soon as the wagon came crashing down into the ditch, everything then sped up into fast-forward motion. I likened what happened next to what it would feel like to have our wagon harnessed to two kegs of dynamite about to explode. My family and I don't have a lot of recall of the events that transpired next, but the details were later recanted to us.

Both Crystal and Reba had instinctively turned to avoid the woman and her children running directly toward them. Until the wagon crashed down, I was still in complete control of both mules. Everything changed after the crash, however, because the giant pair of mules suddenly bolted forward and down further into the ditch in sheer fright. Their strength was so immense that they pulled the already crashed wagon forward and then flipped it end over end, resulting in the wagon crashing over the top of my family and me. The mules' runaway force was so extreme that they severed the front half of the wagon running gear, thus pulling the wagon completely in half, and then they went running away through the treacherous ditch, pulling only the severed front axle and wagon wheels behind them. They ran until they both became completely entangled in their harness, ultimately collapsing on top of each other in the adjoining cattails of a swamp several hundred yards away.

My family and I were another matter altogether as wagon train members converged on the wreckage of our once beautiful covered wagon. Astrid and Travis were the first to be pulled out of the wreckage. They were both dazed, but somehow unscathed. The true miracle lies with the fact that we were carrying a one hundred pound horse-shoeing anvil in the back of that wagon. Somehow by the grace of God, the wagon tumbled end over end, throwing that deadly anvil all about which could easily have killed Astrid or Travis, but somehow, they were pulled from the carnage without so much as a scratch or bruise upon their bodies.

Trevor and I miraculously survived the heavy wagon being flipped end over end on top of us while we were sitting on the seat, yet we were somehow pulled from the wreckage without physical damage whatsoever.

As we were aided back up to the flat surface of the roadway, we were aghast at the destruction before us. Our once beautiful covered wagon lay fractured in countless splintered pieces spread out over a great distance. Further away, we could see our disabled team of mules lying helplessly upon their sides in the mucky swamp.

Although my family and I felt fortunate to have survived such a vivid crash, our outlook was dim at best. We realized that we had no other option other than to somehow gather our broken wagon, load our mules, and depart for home with our "tails between our legs." Our spirits were shattered and our hearts were broken at the idea, but we were at least thankful to have survived what should have been a certain death.

My first task following the visual survey of my family's health and well-being was to free Crystal and Reba from their entangled harness. Once done, they both stood up and willingly allowed me to load them into a wagon train volunteer's waiting truck and trailer. Our family, along with our mules, was transported forward to the distant town where the wagon train planned to make camp for that evening. We dejectedly waved at all of the members of the wagon train as we passed them by, realizing just how low our spirits were.

Once we had arrived at camp, and as I was unloading the mules and tying them up to my own trailer, I contemplated how to bring our broken and battered covered wagon back into camp. I asked the volunteer that had brought our family and the mules back to camp if he would be so kind as to bring me back to the site of the crashed wagon. I left Astrid in camp to care for our sons and mules as I ventured back out to the wreckage site. I didn't have a plan, but I prayed for one to develop since nighttime was soon upon us.

As we pulled up to the spot of our demise, I noticed a trucker with his semitruck and an empty flatbed trailer standing alongside the ditch observing the shattered mess lying in the ditch. It was as though he'd been summoned from above. He then inquired about what had happened. I shared our story in vivid detail, and I nearly fell into shock when he said, "Well, let's get this broken wagon loaded on my flatbed truck. The least I can do is haul it to your wagon train campsite for the night."

I was nearly dumbfounded by his compassion and his desire to help out when only moments earlier, I'd felt only despair and hopelessness. Between the three of us, we picked up and loaded every scattered and broken piece of wagon onto the big truck. By the time we had arrived back at the campsite, the wagon train had also arrived.

As we began unloading the broken wagon pieces and placing them next to my own truck and trailer, it didn't take long before dozens of folks were helping with the task. Once his rig was clear, I sincerely thanked the trucker with all my heart and watched as he steered his truck back onto the highway.

As I turned back around, I was suddenly facing a large group of wagon train participants as well as a growing number of local town's people that had gathered around my broken and battered wagon. One particular local walked up to me and said, "The news of your wreck has been communicated to most of the towns' folks. We would like to know what your plan is, young man."

I looked him squarely in the eye and shared, "Somehow, I've got to figure out how to load all of these broken wagon pieces along with my mules into my trailer and go home. My family and I are obviously finished for this year's wagon train."

The elderly gentleman calmly stated, "Well, some of us local folks have another idea for you to consider."

"What might that be?" I asked.

The man went on to explain that he and several other towns' folks hearing about our plight had gathered to come to our aid. He indicated that he and six other men standing in the crowd at that moment were actually local carpenters and woodworkers by trade. He went on to explain that, with my permission, they would each take a various broken section of my wagon back to their woodworking shops, then work throughout the night to ready my wagon for travel the next day.

I stood there in disbelief and amazement that these strangers whom I'd never met before would be willing to sacrifice so unselfishly in an attempt to allow my family and me to continue on with our just cause of fund-raising for disabled children.

That night as the minutes and hours elapsed, one by one, the local carpenters and woodworkers returned with their finished projects. Little by little, our physically destroyed covered wagon began taking shape once more. As the hour neared 2:00 a.m., the immediate area around my wagon was alive with activity. Countless volunteers worked as the drone of a gasoline-powered generator powered the carpenter's tools and illuminated the flood lamps. Like a big puzzle being put together, our group reassembled the wagon back to near perfection.

With the help of the many volunteers, we readied the wagon for travel once more as we latched the canvas back onto the repaired wagon. Tears cascaded down the cheeks of my face when a resounding applause erupted from the weary group just as I placed the final item in its spot on the wagon. Emotions from the group ran rampant as I placed the large American flag back onto the wagon, which I proudly displayed on each and every wagon train.

Try as I might at the close of that long day and night, not a single volunteer would take reimbursement from me for their portion of rebuilding our wagon. Some of the carpenters had utilized some very expensive oak lumber and various other parts, not to mention the cost of their labor, yet no one would allow me to reward them with anything other than my most sincere verbal thanks and an embracing hug of appreciation.

The following morning, the wagon was ready for travel once more, but what of Crystal and Reba? What about my family and me? What about the reactions of the other wagon train participants that had witnessed our horrendous wreck?

It was decided to gather the group for a special wagon train meeting before departing that morning to discuss everyone's thoughts and ideas. The question was posed as to whether or not our mules and wagon should be allowed join in once more, even though the wagon was intact once again. Most of the elder teamsters agreed that with such a gruesome wreck occurring the previous day, our mules would pose a daunting task by trying to hitch and drive them in the aftermath. I shared that I wasn't sure if I had the fortitude and composure to risk driving them so soon after our runaway and crash. The more I'd thought about it, the more I felt it better to simply load up and go back home.

One of the most respected elderly mule skinner teamsters in our group named Ace stepped forward, sauntered up to me, grabbed me by the shoulders, and then said, "Scott, you've raised and trained one of the finest pair of draft mules in the nation without doubt. Obviously, you and your family are scared about what will happen if you hitch them up to that wagon today. I need you to hear and take heed to what I'm about to say, though. If you decline to hitch those critters today and decide to go back home instead, you will doom those two fine young mules."

I responded back with, "Doom them? That is crazy, what are you talking about?"

He moved ever closer to me and in a hushed voice said, "If you don't harness and hitch those young, powerful mules back onto that wagon this morning, then they will forevermore be a runaway risk beyond control. If you leave this wagon train today and go home with your mules, and their last memory is running away and wrecking that wagon, then you had better plan on selling them to a glue factory because you'll never be able to trust them or drive them again!"

I stared at him in disbelief, but several other elders surrounded the two of us and confirmed his directive. After some brief discussion with Astrid, I shared with the group that we would in fact hitch the mules that morning, but only if certain precautions were implemented to minimize the risk. I asked some fellow wagon train volunteers to let Astrid and our two little boys ride safely in their covered wagons for the next couple of days. I then asked for one of the strongest men in our group to ride alongside me for the next couple of days hoping that between our combined strength, he and I would be in a better position to control my mules if they bolted once more. Lastly, I requested that several of our most skilled saddle outriders position themselves alongside and in front of my team of mules prepared to overpower my team in the event of another runaway.

Once we had communicated everything to the entire wagon train group, the time finally arrived to make it all happen. I hitched Crystal and Reba up to our covered wagon, and we apprehensively rolled once again with the wagon train. For the next several hours that day, it was a nightmare trying to drive the skittish mules. Prior to the wreck, nothing had ever bothered them, but now every sound, every approaching mailbox, any approaching vehicle, or any walking pedestrian would instantly result in their attempt to bolt and run. They must have believed that the boogeyman was out to get them. Luckily, with all of our safety precautions intact, the young mules soon overcame their fears and realized that they were unable to break away no matter how hard they tried.

This story had a happy ending because by the second day, both mules were back to their passive, gentle demeanors. By the third day, Astrid and our two youngsters were back riding in the wagon with me. We safely finished the entire wagon train route that year and happily went on to complete many more with our team of mules and covered wagon.

*   *   *

After many years, my family and I moved on to other hobbies and interests, and we no longer participated in wagon trains. Something that will forevermore be embedded in our hearts, though, was what we witnessed that night long ago.

For my family and me to have a personally experienced such compassion and help from strangers has forever strengthened our faith and our belief in mankind. What a testament it was to observe people sacrificing for others while asking nothing for themselves in return.

It was and will always be one of the greatest gifts and lessons we could ever experience as a family. Our young sons benefited from a life lesson in ways that no classroom could ever teach.

HITLER DEATH CAMP COLLISION—
37 YEARS

CHAPTER NINETEEN

*Therefore, since we are receiving a kingdom that cannot be
shaken, let us give thanks, by which we offer God an acceptable
worship with reverence and awe.*
—HEBREWS 12:28

I selected the above scripture reading from the book of Hebrews, feeling that it so aligned with the resiliency of the Jewish people who were annihilated in the German concentration camps or so-called death camps during World War II. This is my firsthand observation from visiting one of those death camps and what led up to my own close encounter with death once again.

*   *   *

In 1992, I was contacted by the Land O'Lakes, Inc. International Division. The initial phone conversation changed the course of my life forever.

Through the telephone receiver I heard, "Hello, Scott, my name is Collette. Did you know that your employer Land O'Lakes, Inc. has an international division, which utilizes worldwide grant funding to provide agricultural consulting assignments all over the world?"

I responded by saying, "No, I did not know that, but I'm extremely curious as to why you are contacting me regarding that matter."

Collette replied, "Well, that is a fair question. I'm sure you are well aware of the demise of the former Soviet Union and their fall from communism a few short years ago. As one of the Land O'Lakes, Inc. International Division employees, I'm trying to locate an employee within our ranks with the expertise to develop a dairy production and management training course and then do an assignment abroad to refine the course materials. Since the country of Poland was the first to pull away from the ex-Soviet Union, we've been granted funding to provide consulting to help them improve their struggling dairy industry."

"Okay, but why exactly have you contacted me?" I asked again.

She stated, "Well, we've done a company-wide employee search seeking anyone who may have been a high school agriculture instructor or perhaps anyone who may have been an actual dairy farmer or possibly anyone who may have been a dairy consultant. The reason we are contacting you first is that of all the employees, you were the only employee to trigger all three of those experience-based benchmarks."

We continued on with our dialogue for some time as I was eventually asked to agree to develop an international dairy production and management training course, which would then ultimately be translated and taught in impoverished nations and third world countries across the globe and over the next several years.

It was scary to say the least when I accepted such a huge responsibility, but I became convinced that it was the right thing to do. Earlier, I questioned as to why bother with this kind of work. The response to my challenge had been that there were several ex-communistic nations struggling with their new democracies and freedoms. They were struggling so badly in fact that there was a real danger of their failure, only to fall back into a socialistic or dictatorship form of government once again. I accepted my international assignment knowing that the rewards, which I would gain over the years would be immeasurable.

For several months that year, I worked diligently while putting together a large binder of course materials. My biggest frustrations came from trying to research just exactly how dairying was done behind the secretive Iron Curtain of the former USSR. Try as I might, I was unable to locate any document or any person within the American dairy industry who could give me information to develop my course materials.

Eventually, I surmised that the dairy farming methods of Poland would probably have never have kept pace with the dairy industry technologies of America, so I built my course materials with the assumption that I would be instructing Polish dairy farmers that were likely ten years behind American technologies. I didn't discover the truth that their dairy industry was all of twenty-five years lagging behind until I'd arrived in Poland that November to deliver my three-week international dairy training course.

For the next few pages, I'll describe my first international consulting experience in detail so one can sense the experience vicariously through my eyes.

*   *   *

As I sat alone waiting to fly out of the Sioux Falls, South Dakota airport, my thoughts drifted toward my wife, Astrid, and our two young sons. Travis was only eight years old while Trevor was merely ten years old. The final moments we spent together as a family that day were guarded and tense at best knowing that I would be totally out of contact with them for nearly a one-month period of time. To heighten the anxiety, none of us had any idea of what I would encounter during my absence to such a strange land or whether my life would be at risk. This was to be our first experience as a family unit whereby Astrid was left entirely alone to care for our family and home as I prepared to travel halfway across the earth to help others who were struggling in their agriculture production. Little did I know that for the next four weeks, I'd be unable to communicate at all with my family or anyone else back in America.

My flight departed Sioux Falls at about 11:00 a.m. for the beginning of an eighteen-hour trip to my final destination. Due to the overall length of the flight, I flew business class for the first time in my life. The flight transfers took me from Sioux Falls, South Dakota, to Minneapolis, Minnesota, then on to Frankfurt, Germany, and finally on to Warsaw, Poland.

As I looked all around the business class cabin of the airplane, I noticed gentlemen wearing costly business suits while I was casually dressed in my flannel shirt, jeans, and boots. It didn't take me long to determine that I seemed a little out of everyone else's class. Earlier while boarding the plane, and then while attempting to locate my seat, one gentleman actually inquired if I was in the right section of the plane. Ouch, I felt that insult!

My assigned airplane seat appeared to be a roomy and comfy recliner chair. Much different than anything I'd previously experienced while flying in an airplane. Before long, the time arrived for our first of several in-flight meals. I was slightly taken back at the exceptional level of service given. First, one of the flight attendants provided a small tablecloth, and then followed suit by delivering a wet, scented hand towel to wash one's hands. Next, a hors d'oeuvre plate was placed in front of me yielding caviar, smoked salmon, and other unidentifiable treats placed upon mini pieces of bread. Shortly thereafter, I was instructed to order my meal from a menu with entries on it such as veal cabernet, saffron halibut, or citron duck. Those menu choices were not something that my upbringing was accustomed too, but I chose veal since I at least knew what that was.

The flight arrived in Frankfurt, Germany, at 11:30 p.m. by the time clock back home, but because of the seven-hour time zone difference, it was actually 6:30 a.m. in German time. I was more than ready for the night of sleep, which I'd just missed, so it wasn't too difficult understanding the effects of jet lag. As we departed for Warsaw, Poland, on the last leg of the journey, I looked out my window at the bright sunlit sky amazed at how small the world really becomes through air travel.

The plane touched down at 5:00 a.m. by the clock back home, but the clocks in the Poland airport reflected that it was actually noontime by their time standards. The total elapsed time from start to finish was eighteen hours, but my body and mind felt as though the trip had elapsed for several days.

I became keenly aware that I was no longer in the United States since everyone all around me was dressed differently and no one spoke anything except the Polish language. I could no longer read any of the signs throughout the airport. I was able to finally discover a bathroom. It didn't take too long to gain experience firsthand as to why I was briefed back home to bring along my own toilet paper and tissue paper. I can best describe my first exposure to eastern European toilet paper as a toilet paper that doesn't gently fold as I was accustomed to, but rather it harshly bends instead. I would also say that European toilet paper performs its necessary function by unsympathetically scraping one's most sensitive areas rather than softly and soothingly wiping. I came away from that experience thinking that woodworkers back in the USA likely used sandpaper with less abrasive qualities.

At last I was met at the airport by my first Polish contact. Her name was Aleksandra Orlik, but she preferred to be called Ola for short. Before long, she dropped me off at a hotel where I exchanged five hundred American dollars for 7.5 million Polish dollars. I was relieved that I'd brought along my calculator because dealing with a currency with so many zeros would pose a challenge to be sure in the days to come.

At the time, Warsaw, Poland, had a dirty, grungy look to everything as a result of utilizing coal for heating purposes. The air was fowl with thick, sooty smoke, which left tears in one's eyes. The city obviously demonstrated a strong Russian influence. All the cars being driven were extremely small, and everyone drove as though they were crazed. The entire city was overcrowded as cars parked in every available space, including parking directly upon the sidewalks meant for pedestrian travel. Even the mere act of simply walking was tremendously hazardous with so many lunatic drivers. I learned that car theft was rampant in Poland where ten thousand cars per year were stolen just in the city of Warsaw alone! I was left in shock by all the people populating Poland. I discovered that at the time there were forty million people living in the country of Poland, which was nearly the same land mass as my own state of Minnesota where we had only four million inhabitants.

As my first day in Poland drew to a close, I took note that the sky was already darkening by 3:30 p.m., so it was important to adjust to their much shorter days than I was accustomed too.

Having only slept for a total of three hours over the course of a three-day air-traveling period of time, I finally enjoyed my first complete evening of slumber. I fell asleep on that first night at 6:00 p.m., but unmercifully, I was totally awake again by 2:00 a.m. The time zone difference was simply too much to regulate as my body's sleep mechanisms rebelled against the change.

By 7:00 a.m. after lying awake for several hours, I went off to the hotel's breakfast buffet. I grabbed a plate, and with reckless abandon, I took small portions of most everything on display. The only food that I completely recognized was what looked to be runny scrambled eggs that must have been laid by a one hundred-year-old chicken. When I'd had my fill of the strange cuisine, I asked a waitress who spoke only the slightest English if she could explain what some of the foods were that I'd ingested. The ones that stood out in my mind were items such as stuffed cod slices, raw eel, jellied bull tongue, and many more which I chose to forget. I thanked her for her help and as my lower intestinal tract started rumbling and grumbling, I retreated back to my hotel room for a bathroom stop.

After spending a short period of time in Warsaw, Poland, making preparations for my upcoming dairy consulting training session, the time had at last arrived to depart for the isolated interior of the country. I was picked up in the morning by a young man named Roman Kazmierski who was to drive me to the Rzeszow region of Poland. As we traveled by car, I was amazed by the cultural diversity of "the old" versus "the new" along our pathway of travel. On one side of the road one would witness a small tractor plowing in a field, while on the other side of the same road one could see another farmer tilling his fields with horses. There were also countless vehicles driving on the roadways while hundreds of pedestrians walked along the road simply because they were too impoverished to have any other means of transportation. All along the route, farmers could be seen herding their cattle down the side of the roadways.

Before long, our travels brought us to the city of Lublin, Poland. It was on the outskirts of this small city where I experienced one of the most ghastly sights and felt the most shocking experience of my entire lifetime.

Roman, my young driver, indicated to me that Lublin was the infamous home of the second largest World War II Nazi German prisoner of war concentration camp that had existed. In time, these camps came to be referred to as "Hitler Death Camps." The camp in Lublin as had many other camps been established during the Nazi German occupation of Poland.

The mere mention of its name Majdanek (My-da-nek), sometimes referred to as Barrack #44, still to this day sends a haunting chill down my spine as a result of what I witnessed. It is something that I will never forget as long as I'm alive.

What makes the following portions of this story so profound is that as I engaged in my assignment in 1992, I was literally one of the earliest Americans to enter into Poland following the collapse of the former Soviet Union. Poland at the time was trying desperately to rebound from so many years under the failed communistic rule. The towns and their peoples were extremely poor from so many years of abuse. Few people if any had even the faintest notion of what the rest of the world's inhabitants encountered since most worldly communications had been withheld from the people. Therefore, when I asked Roman if we could stop by the "death camp" for a look around, he reacted rather strangely in response.

Roman stated, "Scott, the Polish people are very embarrassed and ashamed by what happened in these German concentration camps such as Auschwitz and Majdanek during the World War. Majdanek was unusual in that it was located so close to this major city and not hidden away at a remote rural location as most other camps were. This 'death camp' is notable as one of the best preserved concentration camps of the Holocaust. Since it was close to the Soviet border, there had been too little time for the Nazis to destroy the evidence as with most other camps. Since this camp was literally stationed within sight of Lublin, the local people then and now tried to act as though this never happened. Today the camp has been established as memorial museum to honor those that died, but please understand that this is not a tourist attraction and few if any people ever visit this awful place that represents such a horrific reign of terror to mankind."

I quickly responded by saying, "I understand what you are saying, but I've always been intrigued with history and historical events, so you must understand that there is simply no way that I'm going to allow us to drive us past this concentration camp without first letting me explore its interior."

Roman was tight-lipped and far from willing but still he guided our small car down a much less traveled roadway before finally bringing the vehicle to a stop in front of the ominous gates of Majdanek. As I left the confines of the car, I walked up to the somber-looking front gate, and then I entered a realm as no other before. It was beyond belief what I would soon discover. The camp was almost literally intact just as though it had been evacuated only yesterday rather than actually being evacuated decades earlier by the German soldiers.

The Majdanek "death camp" was in existence from 1941 until 1944 when it was captured nearly intact by the advancing Soviet Red Army. The massive footprint of the death camp covered seven hundred acres. As I surveyed the sight all about me, I envisioned somehow suddenly being transported back in time, back to the year 1944.

From my every vantage point, there were guard watch towers and double rows of what had been electrified barbed wired. The camp had been designed to house up to fifty thousand inmates at any given time. In all, over five hundred thousand inmates from fifty-four countries including from the USA passed through this terrible place. The German SS established these kinds of camps for the sole purpose of mass genocide and total extermination! In the largest one-day execution at Majdanek on November 3, 1943, 18,400 inmates were massacred. In all, over eighty thousand inmates most of which were Jews lost their lives at the Majdanek death camp.

The incoming prisoners were stripped of all their clothing and given only rags to wear even in severe cold weather. They were crammed into three high bunks with eight hundred people crammed inside dozens of barracks that were designed to only handle two hundred and fifty people per barrack. The inmates were issued only a thin blanket at night and were given less than one thousand calories per day to eat with no essential vitamins, protein, or energy to consume within the watery mixture they were fed. They were then given harsh work duties until they literally collapsed.

The tortures were beyond comprehension. Prisoners were beaten to death, drowned in pools, hung, dissected, used for games for attack dogs, crucified, shot, gassed, or given injections of poison straight into their hearts. In the first two years, the dead were buried in massive hand-dug trenches by the very people condemned to die in them, but after running out of places to bury the dead, a five-stall crematorium was built that incinerated one thousand murdered people per day. Imagine the terrifying statistic that in order to perform such a mass incineration, it meant that one human was cremated every eight minutes, twenty-four hours per day!

I simply cannot describe my feelings as I walked throughout the heinous camp. My jaw nearly dropped when I walked up to the still intact crematorium, opened one of the doors, and was shocked when I discovered human skeletal pieces inside. Next to the crematorium, it was all too horrifying to look at the mountain of cremation ashes and view the bones and skull fragments of the men, women, and children who'd been so terrorized. It was beyond my wildest comprehension as I walked into the actual gas chambers where so many had met their earthly fates. In an adjoining room, I stared in disbelief at the still-present canisters of cyanide poison used in the actual exterminations of so many innocents. My heart was heavy as I walked through the actual buildings before me. I witnessed massive heaps of the doomed prisoner's hair, which had been sheared off their heads for use in German factories. I also viewed piles of human teeth extracted for the gold and viewed buildings with thousands of pairs of shoes collected from the dead to be used in German leather factories.

With a quivering lump deep within my throat such as none I'd ever experienced, I paused briefly before making my exit. It was at that moment that I had the most eerie feeling as I could literally sense the presence of thousands and thousands of screaming and tormented souls. With a furrowed brow, I lowered my head and silently prayed that mankind would never again be allowed such an inhumane act of horror to transpire.

As I passed out through the front gates once again, I further contemplated what had been the most sobering two hours of my life. After witnessing such carnage firsthand, it continues to anger me each and every time there is mention from an ignorant individual or perhaps some radical group that believe that the Holocaust never actually happened. It most certainly did happen and let us never forget!

*   *   *

Following the traumatic experience of the death camp, Roman and I at last made our way on to the destination of my consulting training assignment located in the city of Iwonicz. It was there that I meet my interpreter whose name was Joanna Grzelak. Thankfully, Joanna spoke very good English as she interpreted my instructions to a classroom of twenty participants. Unfortunately, it didn't take me long to realize that my training course materials were far too modernized for the more primitive Polish farming environment. Therefore, from the onset of my teaching, I spent most of my evenings redoing and rewriting much of the instruction materials to be more applicable for the needs of my students.

The first week of classroom instruction went surprisingly well. I gave our class attendees a one-day break from class before starting again. On our day off, Joanna and I walked through the hilly, quaint village of Iwonicz. One of my goals had been to inspect one of the wells that I'd seen in nearly everyone's yard. During the early 1990s, Poland had countless hand-dug, turn-the-crank, and lower-the-bucket style water wells everywhere. We spotted an elderly lady leaving her yard, so we asked her permission to look more closely at her well. As I lowered the bucket and then brought up a pail of water, the woman explained that her well was dug sixty years ago by her uncle. It was about thirty feet deep, and she proclaimed that the water tasted very good.

As we prepared to depart, Joanna and the woman laughed when I explained that the only place in America where we see primitive wells is in certain Hollywood movies.

Joanna and I made our way through the many different shops, but I was grimly reminded of how bad it is in some parts of their country by how barren the shelves were compared to the overflowing shelves inside the stores back in America.

Joanna asked directly, "Can you only imagine how hard it is to survive in this country? The average income in Poland is less than $200 per person per month."

I try to imagine how people could survive with so little all while their inflation rates are so high, thus creating a very unstable economy.

Joanna further shook my thoughts when she stated, "The way things are presently in our country, socialism and communism was far better for the people because then even the poorest could afford a vacation and even they could afford to send their children to college."

I was awestruck to actually hear the people of a recently freed nation experience so much suffering and pain that they longed for their old, evil, and subduing system.

I challenged Joanna by asking, "How could the old political system be any good if your people were not free to excel or to have their own freedoms of choice?"

Joanna remarked, "Yes, that may be true, but it's difficult to believe in the freedoms that you Americans have come to expect when one doesn't have enough money to buy food or one can't get married to someone you may have loved for years simply because there is no money to begin a life together."

As I listened to her impassioned views, I became deathly quiet while pondering her words. With her words still echoing in my ears, it suddenly dawned on me that the date was November 26. I felt a twinge from being homesick as I realized far away on the other side of the planet, all my family had gathered on that very day for a huge Thanksgiving Day feast and celebration. It deeply saddened me that no one in Poland felt they had anything to be thankful for at all. From a humanitarian standpoint, I prayed that my training mission along with all other attempts to help these folks would prove successful and ultimately change the course of their lives for the positive.

Finally, my classroom instructions drew to a close. I hadn't had nearly enough time over the previous two weeks to cover everything I desired with my students. In my heart, though, I felt the group had been given enough building blocks to work with and improve their lot in life. I knew that if enough volunteers worked with enough Polish citizens in the near future, then hopefully communism would not ebb itself back into their impoverished lives.

With my classroom duties completed late that afternoon, I was met once more by Roman and Ola. Ola was driving a van to transport me back to Warsaw for my departure. Following my several long weeks of duties within the country of Poland, I was more than ready to get back to American soil. As the skies darkened and night fell, we eventually stopped by a wayside tavern for our evening meal.

The three of us sat ourselves at a table on the lower floor of the multilevel tavern. Just in front of us, and up on the second level of the tavern were some tough-looking young Polish folks playing a guitar, singing away, and drinking heavily. Ola surveyed the rough and tough looking environment within the tavern and mentioned that we should depart and find a more suitable establishment. Ola sensed that we were in the sort of tavern where trouble always seemed to develop.

Roman and I were amused by Ola's caution and requested that she calm down and enjoy the evening. We even joked that it might be okay to have a little action after surviving such a dull afternoon of traveling. Little did we realize how quickly everything would change on the scene.

It became all too obvious by the many empty vodka bottles that the rowdy group of ten in front of us were inanely intoxicated. Suddenly, a large elderly man walked up to the group and tried to pull the only woman in the cluster away by force. Imagine how difficult it is to understand what is transpiring when everything being shouted was in a foreign language. Ola tried her best to whisper some interpretation in my direction, but much went unexplained. The young woman being forcibly removed turned out to be that man's daughter. The man and his daughter started violently arguing when all at once one of the young men started fistfighting with the father. He pushed the father head over heels down the steps of the stairway.

Roman and I stared in disbelief as Ola kept trying to get up and leave, but we kept pulling her back down into her seat since we felt compelled to observe the scene develop before us. Shortly, the father stomped out of the tavern in heated anger, while his daughter continued to cry, scream, and carry on. Just when the emotions in the tavern started calming down a bit, and we were beginning to relax ever so slightly, the daughter's emotions ignited once again.

She began throwing empty and full bottles, glasses, jars, plates, and anything else she could lay her hands on. She literally threw at least fifty glass objects until the floor was covered with jagged glass as a result. As though in the scene of an old Hollywood western movie bar fight, I ducked just in time as one of her hurled glass bottles grazed the top of my head and shattered into the wall behind my back.

By this time, the alcohol-deranged group had escalated into an all-out brawl with each other and some of the other patrons of the tavern. I watched in disbelief as first a table and then chairs started being thrown about the tavern. I had always felt that barroom brawls only happened in the movies as more glass shattered all around me and jagged pieces landed on my clothing. A flying table landed and smashed to pieces only inches from me. At that precise moment, we bolted for the door, and then ran out into the safety of the nighttime air. I could sense the adrenaline pulsating throughout my veins.

Ola jabbed at me and said, "Are you crazy for sitting through all of that? Are you trying to get us all killed?" She continued to shout, "Drunks like that have no boundaries and have no sense at all!"

Little did any of us realize that at that moment, we were only partially through a night ominously filled with dangerously close calls.

As we drove away from the still-brawling tavern, I chuckled to myself at how bizarre the scene had been. Ola drove the van and Roman rode in the front with her, while I sat in the back seat of the van immersed in my thoughts. As I glanced at my watch, I knew it would be a long dark night of driving to get to our destination. I was also all too aware of the lack of safety seat belts for which to protect ourselves in the event of an accident.

A shocking statistic gleaned from USA state department data indicates that road accidents, not terrorism, plane crashes, infectious diseases, or crime are the number one killer of healthy Americans traveling abroad. During a recent seven-year period of data observation from January 1, 2003, through June 2010, about 1,820 Americans, almost a third of all Americans who died of nonnatural causes while abroad had been reported killed in road accidents in foreign countries.

Road deaths are the number one risk to American travelers because of a lethal cocktail of killer roads, unsafe vehicles, dangerous driving, and disoriented travelers that kills an estimated twenty-five thousand travelers to foreign countries each year. Worldwide, a staggering 1.3 million people die each year as a result of road fatalities. About half of the fatalities are occupants of motor vehicles with 90 percent of the world's road fatalities occurring in low- to middle-income countries.

With several miles behind us, a sudden odd premonition of impending danger came across my thoughts. I looked out the window of the van into the blackness of night and began wondering about how elevated the car accident death rates in Poland were. I pondered our situation as I realized we were cascading down a rainy, dark road. Polish roads at the time were extremely hazardous in the daytime, much less during nighttime driving because there was no highway lighting of any kind, and all the roads were devoid of any painted road markings of any sort. That combined with the fact that Polish vehicles had the poorest headlight visibility of any vehicles that I'd ever witnessed was of grave concern to me. My mind pondered the absence of seat belts inside of our vehicle and the dire consequences if an accident occurred.

The Polish roadways were extremely narrow with one blinding car's headlights after another coming at our van while driving though the pouring rain that night. To make the drive evermore dangerous, we had to navigate countless people many of whom were intoxicated walking along the road as well as maneuver around slow-moving trucks or tractors pulling unlit wagons, all while driving amongst curves and in hills.

In an instant, we were all staring into the face of death as we were hurled into our unavoidable accident. In a matter of mere seconds, we had been cautiously passing three slower moving trucks and cars when in a flash of fluid motion a man on foot near the oncoming side of the roadway bolted out into our path. I watched the scene develop before my eyes as I first felt Ola lock the brakes and then jerk the van hard into the lane of vehicles that we had been attempting to pass. I could hear screeching tires although unaware if it was from the van we were riding in or from the vehicles all around us trying to avoid a disaster. Next, the van began to hydroplane and spun out of control on the treacherous wet roadway. In an instant, we were spinning and careening down over the edge of the ditch. I sensed the rear tire beneath my seat explode, nearly causing the van to roll over onto its side in the process. Miraculously, the van somehow fell back onto all four wheels again, only to slide uncontrollably through the shallow muddy ditch and then smash frontward into an unyielding concrete electric pole positioned alongside the road.

As the van finally settled to rest, I looked at the suitcases and my training course materials strewn all over the inside of the van. I had been catapulted into the glass window of the van, but somehow, I only sustained a small cut above my eye and a badly bruised cheekbone.

Poor Ola with the steering wheel still tightly grasped in her hands was in a state of shock. Roman was not much better and appeared to also be going into shock as the color drained from his face. Oddly, I was not upset, scared, or frantic at that moment. Perhaps all of my previous experiences with dangerous encounters had yielded a calming benefit during that traumatic moment. With a sense of relief and calmness, I realized how lucky we had been to escape injury or even death. After surveying the damage to the van, I asked Ola to step out and hold a flashlight as I replaced the blown rear tire with the spare tire.

Neither Ola nor Roman desired to drive at that moment following our vehicle collision, so I volunteered to drive the remaining distance that night. With a little coaxing and some pushing, we were able to navigate out of the ditch and continue on with our journey into the night.

As we gathered speed once again, I quietly wondered why we hadn't hit the man who dangerously crossed into our path. I also considered the reasons why we had somehow evaded a head-on collision with the oncoming vehicles or for that matter why we had avoided a massive vehicle pileup that could have and probably should have ended our lives on that dark stretch of highway.

*   *   *

As the jet engines of my plane thrust upward exiting the skies over Poland, I thoughtfully peered out of my window at the nation below quickly fading from sight. I left that struggling country with my own set of torn emotions. After such a lengthy absence, I wanted to go home so badly, but beneath my departing plane there was so much unfinished work that needed to be accomplished. I was comforted, however, that hopefully my own small contribution, along with countless other combined efforts of assistance, would ultimately make a difference in the end.

In the years following, Poland went on to not only survive capitalism and democracy, but the nation and her people prospered with their newfound freedoms once the pathway was demonstrated.

I was so enthralled from the positive results of my initial international consulting assignment that, before long, I was compelled to serve again and again to help make the world a better place for all.

AFRICAN RIOT RUIN—40 YEARS

CHAPTER TWENTY

Can anyone ever separate us from Christ's love? Does it
mean he no longer loves us if we have trouble or calamity,
or are persecuted, or are hungry or cold or in danger
or threatened with death?
(Even the Scriptures say, "For your sake we are being killed
every day; we are being slaughtered like sheep.")
—ROMANS 8:35-36

In the previous chapter, I outlined in great detail the factors that brought me into the realm of international consulting. In 1992, I had tackled that initial assignment inside the country of Poland. In 1993, I then ventured out to complete an additional Eastern European international consulting assignment within the country of Estonia, which had been another former Soviet Union member that had abandoned socialism. By 1995, both my wife Astrid and I were asked to complete our first international team consulting effort in the country of Uganda on the continent of Africa.

In all, we completed, not one, but two separate consulting assignments in Uganda Africa both in 1995 and once again in 1997. On several occasions as a result of those two trips abroad, we were both put in harm's way while being faced with death all too frequently.

Astrid was extremely apprehensive when first asked if she would be willing to perform the duties of an international dairy consultant within such an impoverished third world country. She fully understood that her dairying skills, college education, and hands-on experience provided her a high level of expertise, but she was unconvinced at first that traveling across the world to such a dangerous location was acceptable for her to do. Furthermore, she languished over the challenges posed with the thought of both of us leaving our two young eleven- and thirteen-year-old sons behind while their parents embarked on a dangerous multiweek international assignment.

The main reason for which Astrid was asked to partake in the initial Africa assignments was because of the fact that within the country of Uganda, a majority of the dairy farmers are woman. Within many of the eastern African countries, it is believed that woman are the best caregivers of dairy cattle, and they stoutly believe that since woman themselves have mammary glands with the capability to lactate and nurse their children, then woman also have more intrinsic knowledge and understanding of lactating dairy cows. Putting it simply, the initial assignment in Africa demanded the credibility of a female American dairy expert capable of sharing knowledge with the woman dairy farmers of Uganda, Africa.

Astrid and I ultimately accepted our first joint consulting assignment together, fully knowing that the risks were greater and the dangers more ominous than anything we ever encountered previously in our lives.

For several weeks, we prepared our bodies and our minds for our assignment to the "dark continent" of Africa. In the years prior to our arrival, Uganda had been a country nearly destroyed by dictator leaderships and civil wars. The reign of terror from the two previous dictators had resulted in the slaughter of nearly a million innocent civilians. Over time, Uganda's economy went from one of Africa's wealthiest nations to becoming one of the ten poorest countries of the world. At the time of our assignment, the average Ugandan citizen's income was an impoverished $170 per year. Malnourishment was rampant, and the average life expectancy was only forty-three years of age. Within this poor country, the literacy rate was less than 50 percent. Uganda was also the epicenter of the world's AIDS outbreak. Unbelievably, on average, every household in Uganda had at least one member inflicted by AIDS with the alarming statistic of one out of every four people afflicted with the disease. By the time of our assignment, two-thirds of the world's population who had ever died from the AIDS disease had died in Africa.

Uganda is a country positioned directly on the equator, so its year-round temperate climate allows for a vast array of illnesses and diseases to abound. Factoring in the extreme poverty levels, the malnutrition levels, and the propensity for disease made Uganda an imposing consulting assignment for Astrid and me to take on.

In the weeks prior to our departure, we endured more mental and physical stress than most young married couples with young offspring should have to experience.

From a physical side, we had to submit to more immunizations and disease-prevention measures than we could have ever imagined. Africa has so many illnesses and tropical diseases that an extended stay in the rural sectors of such a country required up to thirteen various injections and preventative measures. These included malaria, yellow fever, hepatitis A, hepatitis B, typhoid fever, cholera, meningococcal disease, polio, and tetanus. Prior to our departure, there were times that we were required to receive up to four different shots at any one time. Often the result following such an assault on our immune systems were met with several days of feeling ill.

From a mental perspective, we not only invested a great deal of our time for course material preparation, but we had some distasteful personal matters to address as well. Obviously, a trip such as we were about to embark posed certain safety and health risks. Astrid and I were instructed to make preparations for the care and well-being of our two minor-aged children in the event that one or both of us died during our international assignment. As a result, we both endured the difficult process of updating our wills, selecting guardians for our children, and insuring that all our personal affairs were in order.

For example, Astrid and I met for several hours with our dear friends Jim and Helen Rokeh one evening. One cannot imagine how difficult our discussions were as we asked for and then received their unselfish agreement to become the guardian parents of our two sons in the event we would not return. With tears in our eyes, we dialogued at great detail with them about which colleges we would like our children to attend one day if we were not around to see them grow up. With great difficulty, we reviewed all of our personal files providing details of all of our financial matters, life insurance policies, and business affairs. How many parents could even attempt such a frightening course of action prior to departing for a dangerous third world country on the far side of the planet?

Not only was our session with Jim and Helen difficult, but imagine having a heartfelt conversation with one's two young sons as to why their mother and father were departing for nearly one month to try to assist impoverished people so far away. Envision if you will how difficult the dialogue was with anyone else with any relevance such as grandparents, friends, relatives, and teachers. For the record, our two sons, Trevor and Travis, faced our inevitable departure with perhaps the most maturity of all. They understood how passionate both of their parents were to accomplish the mission to help others less fortunate. Our family has always believed that the more one gives, the more one will receive back in reward.

On the night before our initial departure for Africa, Astrid, Trevor, Travis, and I sat in a circle on the floor of our living room, held tightly to each other's hands, and prayed together as a family for continued strength, for guidance in our tasks, for protection from danger, and for our sincere thankfulness for our countless blessings. Our family slept peacefully on that final night together, knowing that our God's protection would be our guide for the next few weeks.

The following day we departed the Brookings, South Dakota, airport, with transfers in Minneapolis, Minnesota; then London, England; then Nairobi, Kenya; and finally we landed in Entebbe, Uganda. Between layover stops and the nine-hour time zone difference, our total journey took forty-eight hours to complete with an exhausting twenty-one hours of actual in-flight time traveling.

What a temperature shock to our systems as we left the big jumbo jet and walked out into the stifling heat of Africa. On the cold February day back home, only two days earlier, we had boarded the plane with the outside temperature at a frigid 0 degrees Fahrenheit. Suddenly, we were baking in eighty degrees Fahrenheit heat while standing on the equator. Before long, we realized enduring such extreme heat was only the beginnings of our challenges. By nightfall, we were checking into our hotel room. We were initially surprised to find the room quite acceptable and even equipped with an air conditioner. Unfortunately, we soon discovered that the hotel shut off all the air conditioners in an effort to save on electricity expenses. To make matters even more unbearable, we were instructed not to open the unscreened windows in the room because of the danger of being bitten by malaria-infected mosquitoes. One can't imagine the difficulty trying to sleep in such conditions night after night as our room temperature climbed to the sweltering point. What an obstacle for two wintertime Minnesota residents.

For the next two weeks, Astrid and I taught in a classroom hosting forty mostly female students. Many of our students were young mothers between the ages of eighteen and thirty years of age. We were stunned at the time to learn that many of the young mothers within our classroom were single parents since the majority of their husbands had died from the AIDS disease. This became ever more alarming to Astrid and me when we returned back to Uganda in 1997 for a follow-up assignment. As we attempted to bring together our original forty students for a class reunion a mere eighteen months after our 1995 visit, we dreadfully discovered that nearly half of our class had recently died of AIDS and thus orphaning all of their young children!

During our classroom instruction, a few of our students could speak and understand English, but many could not. Our teaching instruction came about through the difficult process of translating through an interpreter whose name was Richard Bakojja. He would decipher every word that we spoke in English into their native Swahili language. Anytime one of our students asked a question, this slow process of communication was then reversed.

Over the course of our first consulting assignment in Uganda, we spent two weeks in classroom instruction, and we invested one additional week assigned for in-field instruction. It was during that week in the field that we visited many of the villages and dairy cow farms of our students. During those travels throughout the country of Uganda, we witnessed extreme poverty levels and detected human malnourishment such as none we'd ever experienced before.

During both of our two assignments to Africa, Astrid and I used extreme caution regarding most anything we ate or drank. For liquid intake, we each carried a couple of large empty plastic bottles. Since acquiring bottled water or safe drinking water was nearly impossible at the time, we would obtain drinking water through our own means. Most of the native Ugandans would obtain and then drink water directly from the nearest polluted river or lake. During our travels, we would ask to have the available water boiled in a pot prior to filling our bottles. I must say, it was never easy drinking this water since the water was usually murky-colored and held countless dead insects and floating debris. We had no choice, other than to drink it as we prayed that the boiling process had hopefully rendered the distasteful elixir safe for consumption.

Food intake was another difficult challenge altogether. During our two African assignments, we consumed a few native food items such as fish (often cooked with the head and body intact), goat meat, cassava, rice, native beans, soups, native potatoes, and fruits of all sorts. Our greatest dietary challenge arose from the never-ending consumption of the main

Ugandan staple food called matooke. Matooke is a mashed potatolike substance made from cooked green bananas no less. In Uganda, there are unlimited banana trees all throughout the nation, so the masses of malnourished people and children having little else to eat, ingest this high carbohydrate form of food for most every meal. It was commonplace to see people consume only a helping of matooke and nothing else. I can assure you from personal experience that three meals per day of this bland substance took a toll on my digestive system. Imagine eating only a helping of tasteless, unseasoned mashed potatoes for every meal, every day. Seldom would anything else be consumed. Without a balanced diet consisting of protein and other food nutrients, eventually, a continuous diet of matooke would lead to malnutrition and various health-related issues for the people.

During our field visits into the rural sectors of Uganda, we were surprised to learn just how primitive the cultures were. We visited native villages in outlying territories where their people had never seen a person with white-colored skin until our visit. We observed countless villages where the scantily clad inhabitants lived in mud huts with grass-thatched roofs.

One village visit comes to mind where Astrid and I came face-to-face with the stark cultural differences. As our vehicle came to a stop, the driver cautioned us that the people of this village had never been visited by a Caucasian person before. As Astrid and I stepped out of the vehicle, we were instantly surrounded by dozens of native Africans, many of which were reaching out to touch our pale skin. Poor Astrid was being groped by innumerable hands as they literally stroked her strangely blond hair and petted her fair-colored skin.

Our driver assured us that they meant no harm and that they were merely curious at the sight of our strange-colored skin and hair. As I surveyed my surroundings, I took note of several factors.

Astrid looked at the natives in wide-eyed apprehension as she stated, "I feel like I'm an animal in a petting zoo with all the children trying to touch and pet me."

My eyes scanned the gathering mass of natives before me as I curiously noted the lack of clothing, especially as related to the females of the village. The village chief worked his way toward us and began speaking authoritatively in his native tongue. Our driver translated that the chief welcomed us to his village and was honored to have such distinguished guests come for a visit.

As the dialogue was going back and forth, I noticed a strange sight very near to the center of the village. There was a larger hut with what appeared to be several dead natives laying all about the ground. It suddenly dawned on me that perhaps we were in a hostile village and that perhaps those poor collapsed souls had recently been murdered. Could we be next? I wondered in fear.

I raised my right arm and pointed toward the dire scene while questioning our driver. The chief reacted to my finger pointing by suddenly dragging me by my arm through the mass of villagers toward the fallen people before me.

In a panic, I looked back toward our driver and screeched, "What is happening? Are those people dead? What are they going to do to us?"

Just as Astrid and I were hurriedly escorted to the entrance of the central hut, our driver proclaimed, "Mr. Scott, the chief is honored by your visit and by your show of interest, so he wants to demonstrate to you how the village makes beer."

I looked at him in disbelief saying, "Beer! What are you talking about? Are you saying we are not in danger? I still want to know what happened to those comatose individuals lying crumbled upon the ground!"

Before our driver could elaborate further, the chief pulled Astrid and me into the hut where we observed a large, ominous black kettle. Just as my imagination was about to drift toward thoughts of being killed, then cooked, and then eaten by savage cannibals, our driver interpreted the scene before us.

He explained that once each week the villagers made a massive kettle of banana beer. Upon completion of the brew, then the entire tribe including men, women, and children consumed the alcoholic concoction until everyone was literally in an intoxicated stupor or had fallen into total unconsciousness. To our disbelief, he further explained that we were in the midst of a tribe of illiterate, uneducated natives with no occupations to keep the adults busy and no schools to attend to busy the children. This primitive village had no means whatsoever for any outside worldly communications by way of radios, televisions, or newspapers. Our driver explained that in their dismal existence, one of the few joyful things that every member of the tribe looked forward to was when the day arrived when each new batch of banana beer was available for community consumption.

I stared at the disgustingly smelly brew before me while thinking what a sad existence for these people if this was one of their only joys in life.

At last, I caught the chief's eye, and then I pointed to the toxic mixture and made a gesture asking him for permission to sample their tribal beer.

Our driver suddenly shouted, "No, Mr. Scott, you mustn't drink their beer!"

I spun around looking directly into his eyes and asked, "Why on earth not? I've always had the personal motto that one should brave most anything, and I want to try their beer."

Our driver responded, "No matter, it is now too late to refuse since the chief has already drawn a large vase of beer for you to drink. It would be disrespectful to refuse him now." He went on to explain, "Mr. Scott, since you requested to drink this beer, you must understand that it will taste very bad, and it is not made in the controlled fashion that someone from America would be familiar with. Please hear me clearly when I say, you must now drink the entire vase of beer as quickly as possible, and no matter how ghastly you believe that experience to be, you must react as though it is the best drink you have ever tasted."

I turned away from him chuckling to myself at his overreaction while thinking to myself, just how bad could the communal village beer be? With that, the chief placed the large vase of potent liquor into my hands, and I raised it toward my waiting lips.

Before the container of fluid even reached my lips, the stench infiltrated my sinus passages causing my eyes to water. Trying my best to hide my discomfort, I placed the vase to my lips and gulped aggressively. I will attest that at no time in my entire lifetime had I passed anything so putrid and appalling past my tongue and down into my throat. I experienced a gagging reflex like none other as in a panic I forced another large gulp down my throat. With every bit of courage left in my being, I forced the final volume of fluid down my throat and into my rebelling stomach. I had never ingested anything so revolting in my entire life, yet I somehow faced the chief and with a forced smile upon my lips as I shook my head up and down, while muttering, "Mmm-good."

The chief and the tribe let out a loud cheer of satisfaction. I nearly fainted as he removed the empty container from my grasp and prepared to dip it once more into the despicable mixture. Thankfully, our driver came to my rescue when he communicated that our time to visit had come to an end and that we had to immediately travel away to visit the next village on our agenda.

As we hurried toward the waiting vehicle on the edge of the village, my vision began to cloud and my stomach churned ever more. Once in the vehicle, it took every bit of strength I had to wave good-bye to the native tribe as we left their sight. I'll never forget how ill I felt as we bumped and bounced down the roughened dirt path for our escape.

Our driver looked at me with a devious twinkle in his eye and asked, "So, Mr. Scott, do you know how to make beer?"

In my weakened state, I eyeballed him and replied, "Sure, I know the science of how to make beer. First you take something such as barley grains or in that village's case they use bananas. Next some sorts of yeasts or enzymes are mixed in. Eventually, during the brewing process, sugars are converted into a form of alcohol, thus creating beer."

The driver responded, "Very good, Mr. Scott, but I want to explain to you why I tried to stop you from asking to drink their beer. As you said, to make beer, it takes some sorts of yeasts or enzymes for the creation of alcohol. Where would you suppose the primitive natives of that tribe secure the enzymes to make their beer?"

I suddenly made eye contact with him with a terrified look and remarked, "I have no idea since I don't imagine they buy yeast or enzymes from a grocery store."

The driver went on to explain that each week after the entire village had recovered from their drunken state, a new batch of banana beer was put into motion. He went on to describe how the massive kettle was filled with bananas and water from an unclean pond nearby. Lastly, he illustrated how every member of the village would then take turns spitting into the kettle to provide enough enzymes for the brewing process to begin.

With that announcement, I pleaded with him to instantly stop our vehicle in its tracks. I could endure no more as I fell out of the vehicle and vomited the evil contents of my stomach onto the barren ground.

In my weakened state, I crawled back inside as the driver said, "Don't say that I didn't try to warn you!"

Astrid could only shake her head silently back and forth in disbelief.

*   *   *

During our two African consulting assignments that transpired within an eighteen-month period of time, Astrid and I had experiences that were good and bad as well as at times either safe or dangerous.

Few people on this earth have been blessed with the experiences we've had exposure to, but such experiences come with a price. Each time we experienced Africa, we knew there were inherent dangers and risks. As a result of our African journeys, we had no fewer than six close calls with possible injury or certain death. By the grace of God, we survived each encounter with a renewed vigor and an impassioned will to continue.

These are the details of those six close calls while we were in Africa.

Number One: African Food Can Kill You

During the time of our African assignments, there were few modern conveniences to be found in the outlying locations. Most of the Uganda people lived in primitive mud-hut dwellings with no electricity, no available water source except from the river, no toilet facilities, and no cooking stoves. During our stays, most of our meals were prepared upon the bare ground and then cooked over open fires. With the way food was prepared, it was then commonplace to either end up crunching on sand, shells, bone chips, or some other unidentified foreign matter, so one had to be cautious not to break a tooth while eating. Every time we consumed food, we knew that it was only a matter of time before some form of stomach ailment was to set in, causing great discomfort.

During our initial assignment, for the first several days, our only food intake had been matooke. Astrid and I had quickly reached a saturation point in which we didn't feel like eating at all. We understood that eating any form of protein source such as meat was a rare commodity in Uganda, but we had ingested quite enough stewed, mashed bananas by that point. Richard, our interpreter, astonished us one day when he said that we would be traveling to the southern portions of the country that day and that he would provide us with a surprise for our evening meal.

As we traveled on that typically hot day down the dry dusty roads of rural Uganda, we came upon a roadside butcher stand. Astrid and I watched as Richard brought the vehicle to a stop, then hopped out, and purchased some goat meat from a carcass that had been hanging in a tree. We could only wonder how long the meat had been out in the baking sun while being invaded by flies and insects. Richard then placed the chunk of meat on the floor of the vehicle next to Astrid's feet as we sped away. He went on to explain that our surprise for that evening meal was going to be a goat meat barbeque. Compared to all the mashed bananas we'd been eating, we were sure that the goat meat would be a welcomed surprise even though there was no way to know how long that meat had hung in the hot sun or how long the dust from the road had washed across it or if the meat was unspoiled. For the remaining eight hours of travel that day, the chunk of foul-smelling meat rolled and bounced around on the floor of the hot, dirty vehicle waiting to become our evening meal.

As the day rolled into night fall, at last we stopped. Richard built a large fire after scavenging for firewood from a nearby thicket and then cooked the goat meat. In our hungered state, we ate every morsel with our dirty, bare hands, and it was an indescribable treat. In fact, at that moment, we had thought that we had died and gone to heaven, but alas, by sunrise the following morning, we simply felt that we had died and gone to hell!

We soon discovered that Ugandans are so used to eating and drinking high levels of bacteria and consuming spoiled foods that they are nearly immune to stomach ailments. As Americans, however, we were another story altogether. Astrid and I were thrown into a severe case of food poisoning that nearly brought our multiweek consulting assignment to an early ending. We both developed severe stomach cramping and uncontrollable diarrhea that persisted for six long days and nights. Did I mention that toilet facilities in Uganda were mostly a hole dug into the ground and where one simply squatted out in the open for all to see? For nearly an entire week, the two of us weakened from severe dehydration and failed health. Time and again, day after day, we were forced to bare everything as a result of our intestinal disruption. It was considered impolite to stare at someone squatting over one of these holes dug into the ground, but both Astrid and I drew countless stares from the natives because of their curiosity toward the color of our skin and our obvious digestive problems.

Since there was little medical care available at the time, we were readying ourselves to be medically evacuated from Uganda when at last our illness abated. For the remainder of our assignment, we were in a severely weakened state, but thankfully, we were able to continue on with our intended mission.

Number Two or Three or Four: African Wildlife Can Kill You

As a reward benefit for volunteering for certain international consulting assignments, at the end of the assignment, one may take some personal time at one's own personal expense to experience the wonders that nation may have to offer. During our two visits to Uganda, Africa, Astrid and I had the privilege to spend a few days on safari touring both the Mboro game reserve and the Queen Elizabeth game reserve.

We were delighted to be picked up by our safari guide in a four-wheel drive vehicle. Over the course of several days, we took in some excellent mountain range scenery and had some tremendous wild animal viewing. We had few disappointments in the spectacular beauty, the ruggedness, and the overall wildlife observations while in Africa. We couldn't believe the awesome numbers of animals we viewed. During our safari, we saw huge quantities of deer and antelope-type animals. Specifically, we saw impala, topi, waterbuck, bushbuck, oribi, and Kob. In addition, we spent hours viewing herds of elephants, zebra, and African buffalo. Along with all of these were a visual multitude of hippos, warthogs, baboons, monkeys, hyena, crocodiles, storks, pelicans, eagles, leopards, and lions.

As Astrid and I went to bed in our room at the safari lodge during our first night, I remember thinking how truly dangerous the wildlife in Africa could be. I thought back to the many road signs posted throughout the game reserve. Those signs threatened massive fines and/or jail sentences if anyone were caught venturing into the park at night and at no time were people on safari allowed to leave the confines of their vehicles. In truth, wildlife within the parks in Africa differs greatly from wildlife for example within Yellowstone National Park in America. The difference isn't very subtle either because in American Parks the wildlife is mostly humanized, thereby seldom creating problems with naive park visitors. In African parks, much of the wildlife considers humans to be nothing more than another part of their food chain, so danger surrounds one at all times.

As I closed my eyes to the nearby laughing sounds of a hyena and listened to the exotic grunts and groans from distant hippos and buffalo, my thoughts were of what a cherished gift to experience such a wild and untamed portion of the world.

About 3:00 a.m., I awoke with a start to some thunderous footsteps outside of the bedroom door of our safari lodge. I cautiously opened the door of our room and looked directly into the eyes of a six-thousand pound hippopotamus that had left the lake next to the lodge and was loudly grazing the grass next to our room, much as a cow would have done. After my initial stare down with the mammoth wild hippo, I carefully closed the door to our room and quickly woke Astrid from her slumber. I insisted that she gather her camera and then I directed that on the count of three, I would swing open the door, she would take a flash photo of our three-ton friend, and then I'd slam the door shut again.

As a result, we had obtained a once in a lifetime, close-up flash photo of a very startled-looking hippo. The following morning our safari guide severely scolded the both of us, though. For the record, hippos may look safe and friendly on television or in a zoo setting, but they are dangerous creatures in the wild with very bad attitudes. They have been known to charge and even physically tip a full-sized vehicle over in a fit of rage. Later after returning home from our trip, we read literature stating that hippos are perhaps the most dangerous creatures in all of Africa, so I guess we were lucky that our hippo was in a tranquil mood that night.

The next day we encountered yet another hair-raising experience while I was video filming a herd of about twenty elephants. After spotting the oncoming herd of elephants, our safari guide decided to shut off the vehicle. As the herd passed several yards behind the vehicle, I leaned more than half of my body outside my window trying to video some baby elephants that had stopped to roll and play in the dirt. All of a sudden, Astrid screamed and our startled guide hurriedly tried starting the vehicle. I spun my video camera around with my eye still looking through the viewfinder and while still hanging halfway out of the window. To my surprise, all I could see through the viewfinder of the camera was the massive gray space between the eyes of a huge, angry, charging elephant! I swear that I could feel its fiery breath as the charging beast stopped momentarily just a few feet from us, trumpeted with anger, and then spun around to rejoin the herd. After that horrifying experience, I was glad that I'd packed along some of my extra underwear for our safari since I was in need of a clean pair.

Another scary moment occurred later that same evening when we encountered a warthog while eating our supper at the outside café in our safari lodge. The outside café was totally surrounded by a steel safety fence to prohibit dangerous wild creatures from entering the compound and harming the guests. As Astrid and I ate our meal, we conversed about the strange-looking warthog inside the compound fence. I commented that the warthog must be a pet of some sort since he was allowed to roam around the inside the fence. Astrid disagreed and indicated that he was most surely a wild animal and that he had simply burrowed his way beneath the fence to gain access to the lush greenery of the protected compound enclosure.

Warthogs can get quite large, and I feel they may be one of the ugliest creatures on earth both in looks and in personality. Their face is large and square somewhat like a shovel, and they have extremely dangerous lower and upper tusks sticking out of their mouth. Following the completion of our evening meal, on our way back to our room, Astrid and I passed by this warthog who was calmly rooting up plants along the fence line. Astrid went as far around him as possible, but I stupidly chose a path much closer to him still convinced that he was somehow a pet of some sort. Thankfully I was wearing running shoes because I think I broke a one-hundred-yard dash record running away in fright when he snorted and then aggressively charged after me with lightening quickness and agility. Later, after my heart had stopped pumping so quickly, Astrid informed me that it was sheer luck that the warthog had stopped chasing me when he did because she said I'd definitely been losing the race with him as he closed in on my unprotected backside. Earlier during the start of our safari, I'd thought that I'd packed enough extra underwear, but by this point, I was no longer so sure of that fact!

Number Five: African Assassins Can Kill You

On our second African consulting assignment, we had a near miss with impending death that left an indelible mark on us forevermore. In 1997, Uganda was struggling with continuous civil unrest. In certain portions of the country, guerrilla warfare had become all too common. During the previous months of unrest, countless bandits and gun-toting snipers had robbed and murdered travelers along certain rural routes of travel. As a result of our consulting assignment, during this dangerous period of time, we were unfortunately required to have a driver transport us through one of the more dangerous routes to complete our required duties.

We departed the capital city of Kampala early one morning hoping to make it to our final destination before nightfall. Throughout the day, our driver maneuvered the vehicle around one road hazard after another. Following decades of civil war and unrest, Uganda's road system was pathetic at best. Each and every road was pockmarked with countless holes from bombing airstrikes or roads that were nearly impassible from years of lacking repairs of any sort. Our journey that day was destined to only cover about two hundred miles. In America, such a distance could be traveled by vehicle in a mere three or four hours, but road conditions in Uganda turned the trip into an exhausting ten- or twelve-hour journey in sweltering heat and choking dust.

As we progressed throughout the late afternoon, our driver became ever more concerned about our ability to make it to the village of our final destination where our evening hotel room reservations were waiting. As we drove down the nearly impassible road, he explained that we were in a very dangerous portion of Uganda and that recently many people had been robbed and killed in the nighttime hours while trying to navigate along this stretch of road. He asked our permission to stop in the next village and settle in for the night rather than risk driving farther as the sun began setting in the west.

We were so exhausted from the long day of travel; we happily agreed to stop as soon as possible even if it were but a few miles from what would have been our final destination for the day.

The following morning, we departed the small village just as the sun peeked out from the horizon. There was not a single movement within the village as we quietly disembarked. There was an eerie stillness to that morning, and it seemed odd that no one, except the three of us seemed to exist on that lonesome stretch of highway. Within only a few miles, we suddenly came upon a red bloody mess nearly covering the entire road before us. The driver slowed our vehicle, then stopped momentarily as we dialogued the strange scene in front of our vehicle.

Still aware of the dangers lurking, we opted to continue along our path with no further delays. I remember asking the driver where he thought all the blood had come from. He said he wasn't sure, but perhaps during the night, animal poachers had killed several animals, which had become an all too common occurrence throughout Uganda. I remember remarking that if it had been poachers, then why hadn't we discovered any animal parts near the carnage?

Within a couple hours of driving, we reached the town that we'd hoped to arrive at the previous evening. It was in that town that we were informed about the tragic news of what had happened on the bloody road we'd passed earlier. Sometime during the previous night, armed bandits at that spot in the road had stopped a bus carrying twenty-seven German tourists. Their bus driver had also been attempting to reach the next town. The bandits removed everyone from the bus, and then after robbing them of all their valuables, the assassins murdered the entire group in the middle of the highway with guns!

Thankfully, on that same night, we had chosen to conclude our travels rather prematurely rather than risk traveling on such an unsafe corridor. How easily it could have been us facing death that night.

Number Six: African Riot Can Kill You

During our two separate stays in Africa, we came to understand how extremely harsh and lawless it can be at times. During the times that we stayed in the Uganda capital city of Kampala, we would review an English version of their national newspaper. On a daily basis, the paper was filled with articles such as: "Two teenage boys attacked, killed, and eaten by crocodiles while fishing in the Nile," "Man sentenced to three years of prison for stealing a car battery," "Local village witch-doctor accused of poisoning seventeen people to death," "Man apprehended after beheading his wife with a machete," "Man jailed after killing his father, with frying pan showing evidence that he was eating the remains," "Thirty gangsters storm police station, killing all officers," "Two mutilated bodies found along the side of the roadway," "Man apprehended after stealing a child for sacrifice," and finally, "Three week old child dies while suckling from mother under a tree, when large fruit falls on baby's head."

We were all too aware that we were no longer within the civilized United States of America as we readied to depart from the capital of Kampala with our entire class of students for our first field trip. On that morning, we somehow crammed all of the members of our class into two large white vans. To fit, we all had to literally sit two and three deep on top of each other. Astrid and I felt the traveling sacrifice would be worth it to put some of our classroom theories into reality out in the field.

As we began driving through the ever-crowded streets of Kampala, we began noticing that for some odd reason, the streets were void of the countless white taxi vans that normally clogged all of the streets and roads. In their absence, we detected tens of thousands of angry pedestrians walking the streets looking for trouble.

Not until one day later were we informed about why we came so close to facing death that morning. The next day we were informed the day of our departure from the capital city, a mass-transit strike had been imposed and by which nearly every white taxi van driver had chosen to go on strike demanding more pay. We also discovered that because of the threat for excessive violence, the policemen of the city had not reported for work in fear of their own safety, thus leaving the city without any means to control violence.

Imagine then what a reality check we were faced with as our two vans drove up to an angry mob at the exit road leading out of the city. At first glance it was difficult to discern what was happening before us. Unfortunately, it became all too evident within moments. We stared in stark disbelief as we witnessed the mob of hostile rioters before us pulling the driver and passengers out of another white-colored van similar to what we were traveling in. With tire irons, metal pipes, and clubs, the bloodthirsty mob began brutally beating and killing the people before our very eyes.

Within moments, the angry mob encircled our own two white vans and proceeded to smash our windows while screaming obscenities. At that precise moment in time, I sensed death was closer than at any other moment in my life.

I held tightly onto my wife's quivering hand and whispered to her, "I'm so sorry that I brought the two of us into this horrible scene. I've always felt that I could protect you, and I've always believed that I could fix any problem. This time, I'm afraid we are doomed, and I can't do anything to stop it."

Astrid watched with tears streaming down her cheeks as the hostile rioters began reaching into the van. Sitting closest to the window, I resisted for all my might as too many hands and arms to count began pulling me through the fractured window of the van. I wasn't nearly as frightened of dying at that moment as I was saddened that my innocent wife would be sacrificed for no apparent cause, and I was helpless to change the outcome.

Just when none of us held any hope of surviving, Richard who was in the driver's seat leapt out of the van, lunged up onto the outside roof of the van, and then began screaming to the hysterical crowd at the top of his lungs. Though most of us were disheveled and struggling to free ourselves from the murderous rioters, we took note that the mob had suddenly stalled their attack. They looked up at and listened intently to the shrieking man on top of our van. Suddenly, Richard stopped shouting in his native Swahili language and placed himself back into the driver's seat of the van. I'll never forget the emotions I felt as I observed the angry mob part, allowing our two vans to depart the hostile city and travel onward to safety. As I looked out the rear window of our van, I detected that the rioting mob was once more beating and killing people in other white vans.

Inside our van, it took a few moments to gain our composure after such a close call with death. At last I asked Richard to elaborate on what had happened to draw such an attack. He explained that the rioters were killing and punishing any taxi and its passengers for not observing the mass-transit strike. Richard further commented that from the top of our van, he had demanded that the mob release us since we were not two white taxis as the crowd suspected but rather simply two white vans transporting some of their nation's top dairy leaders for training in the field. Richard indicated that he was very relieved to see the crowd depart after he'd challenged that if they harmed our group of students and their instructors, then the Uganda people would continue to suffer from poverty and malnutrition.

*   *   *

Astrid and I safely navigated through two dangerous yet exhilarating African assignments. Our memories of Africa are forever burned into our subconsciousness. As a result of our most pleasant experiences, we discovered the African people's amazing will to survive. We discovered how their faces lit up whenever they smiled, and we discovered how they willingly found ways to accept the lowly cards they'd been dealt in life yet somehow continued to strive to improve their troubled fate. We came away humbled by the experience from a continent so wild, so untamed, so beautiful, but also so impoverished.

As we reflected upon our African experiences, it became easy for us to compare our efforts in some ways to a form of missionary work. Astrid and I both felt that to save someone's soul first that someone must have a full stomach. Interestingly, on the initial day of our classroom instruction, we were asked by a student if we were there to provide them with money to buy cattle or equipment. Our answer was a resounding no. We went on to inform our students that the investment we were making was to help them help themselves.

We shared with them one of our favored parables from the Bible. "If you give a man a fish he then eats today, but becomes hungry again tomorrow. If you teach a man to fish, he will never again be hungry."

Astrid and I continue through our mission and journey through life trying to teach as many as possible to fish.

HIGHWAY TO HELL—41 YEARS

CHAPTER TWENTY-ONE

He is your God, the one who is worthy of your praise, the one
who has done mighty miracles that you yourself have seen.
—DEUTERONOMY 10:21

For most of my life span, I've been a high-mileage individual. By that phrase, I'm referring to the fact that I trek more road miles by various forms of vehicle travel than the average person. Most people will drive an average of ten thousand miles per year or less while I've logged closer to a one-hundred-thousand-mile-per-year average on an annual basis during much of my lifetime.

It would only stand to reason that the more miles one travels by motorcycle, by car, or by truck, then the greater the chances for problems to develop. It makes sense then that if one's annual mileage is ten times greater than the average person, then the road hazard and potential vehicular accident potential would also increase tenfold compared to the average individual.

Any high-mileage traveler will attest that in general they often acquire more traffic violations than most based on the odds of exposure. In addition, well-traveled people statistically have a higher incidence of mishaps involving vehicular accidents or vehicular impacts with various forms of animal life that happen upon the roadways.

With the massive miles that I've driven over the years, my list of animal-based collisions are numerous to say the least. In my lifetime while driving many kinds of vehicles, I've had the misfortune of colliding with a realm of wildlife including, but not limited to, pheasants, raccoons, foxes, skunks, and deer.

A collision with a smaller animal while tragic for its survival, oftentimes results in little if any damage to one's motor vehicle. In the worst-case scenario, a collision with a smaller creature will result in possibly a damaged front bumper or a damaged fender to one's car or truck but seldom is the driver at much risk for injury from such an impact. The previous statements hold true for the most part when operating a car or a truck, but hitting any creatures while operating a motorcycle can be catastrophic as I'll outline in a following chapter.

Colliding with a much larger animal such as a deer oftentimes results in more tragic results for the deer, for the vehicle, and for the driver of the vehicle. In my lifetime, I've had the misfortune of colliding with more than ten deer. In every case, I've hit deer that suddenly appeared from nowhere while they ran across the road in my direct path of travel. With so many deer collisions, I'm more than wary of the hazards they pose, yet there has been little I could do to avoid hitting them. Depending on one's speed of travel at impact, hitting a large deer weighing between one hundred and three hundred pounds can result in a terrible accident.

It is highly recommended that if a driver encounters a deer while driving on a road, then they should immediately engage the brakes but keep traveling in a straight line even if that means hitting the large deer as directly as possible. The reason for this well-documented recommendation is that most vehicular deaths involving deer on a roadway collision occur when the driver instinctively tries to oversteer the vehicle to avoid hitting the deer. This action oftentimes results in either crashing one's vehicle into an oncoming vehicle or perhaps crashing into the adjoining ditch resulting in a far more serious crash than simply hitting the deer with one's vehicle.

As a result of my many deer collisions, I've faced thousands of dollars of vehicle repairs over the years. My various deer-accident auto-body repair costs have ranged from anywhere from $1,000 to $5,000 per incident. With all the deer collisions that I've amassed over time, luckily, I only received minor injuries from one collision.

My friend Harry and I were traveling along a dark, winding highway one evening. I was driving my car while Harry sat next to me in the passenger seat. We were traveling at the posted 55 mph speed limit when suddenly a large deer catapulted from the heavily wooded ditch into our pathway. We impacted so quickly that I wasn't able to even engage my brakes. Before either of us could react, the car smashed squarely into the deer with a thunderous impact. In an instant, the force from the sizable deer caved in the front bumper of the car, dented the hood as it rolled up over the front of the car, and then nearly crashed through the front window. In fact, the deer's front and rear legs broke through two separate holes it punctured in the windshield, hitting Harry and me each in the chest with its hooves before being flung up over the top of the car roof, denting it, before finally bouncing off the trunk of the car causing a large ripple in the metal.

The car came to a skidding halt as Harry and I looked over each other with grave concern. I turned on the interior lights of the car and with great concern informed Harry that he must be severely injured since I observed countless trails of blood flowing freely down his face and along his hairline. Harry took one glance at me and shared the same description of my head and face. Upon further examination, we realized that not only were we both bleeding profusely from our faces, but blood was pouring from our arms and chests. Before long, we realized that when the deer had smashed through the front window of the car, hundreds of shards of glass had exploded into the front seat of the car and pierced our flesh. We both had countless slivers of jagged glass perforating our faces, arms, and chest, causing our excessive bleeding. Although our injuries looked bad, they were merely skin deep.

The result of that deer impact on that night was immense. For starters, the deer lost its life. My friend and I spent a couple of hours using tweezers to pick out the endless slivers of glass embedded into our skin and cease our bleeding. My car was so damaged that it needed to be towed to a repair shop. The overall repair cost was nearly half the overall value of the car since almost every portion of the car had somehow been damaged in the collision. The good news was that neither of us was severely injured as a result although I'll never forget what the highway patrolman that processed our accident report said that night.

He shared, "You men don't know how lucky you are that the hooves from that deer didn't injure or kill you both. I worked on one deer-car collision last year in which a deer's hooves came through the windshield just like yours, but during the struggle to break free from the windshield, the sharp jagged hooves of the deer cut the female driver's juggler vein, killing her almost instantly."

*   *   *

Seasoned high-mileage travelers understand that collisions with certain animals on the roads are unavoidable. Thus far, I've described the most common animal-related vehicular collisions that result from a vehicle striking a raccoon, a skunk, or perhaps a deer.

Far less common are occurrences of the largest animal impacts. When they do happen, oftentimes, the news media on the following day will report of the death of the driver and passengers inside the vehicle. The three most notable animal collisions that nearly always result in human death or dismemberment are when a vehicle collides at high speed with a moose, a cow, or a horse. Although impacts with these three massive animals seldom happen, when they do, the outcomes can be horrific.

The simple truth is that unless one is traveling through a lot of wilderness area, there is little opportunity to ever hit a 1,000-pound moose with a vehicle. Similarly, the chances of one ever encountering an escaped 1,100 pound cow or a 1,200 pound horse running freely across a highway would be miniscule at best. One can only imagine though how bad the carnage would be if one were to impact at a high speed with such an enormous creature.

In all my years, I've only heard about a handful of such vehicle impacts with one of these largest forms of animals and in each and every case, either the operator of the vehicle or the passengers were killed instantly as a result. In nearly all cases, the gruesome descriptions elaborated how the vehicle had plowed into the immense animal. The human deaths occur because generally as the front bumper of the vehicle hits the legs of one of these larger animals, it causes the animal to roll up over the hood of the vehicle and then subsequently to smash through the front window. It is not difficult to imagine how deadly an animal weighing in excess of 1,000 pounds crashing through the front window glass of a speeding vehicle could be. Such a wreck would nearly always result in death for the humans involved as well as for the animal.

Even with all the driving and traveling that I've done during my life, the chances of a life-threatening encounter with horse on the highway would be nearly unimaginable. Since I am who I am, and close calls with death shadow my every move, it should then come as no great surprise as to what I encountered one night on the "highway to hell."

*   *   *

It was late November, and I'd just completed a successful elk hunting trip in Montana with my two friends Greg and Warren.

One week earlier, I'd left my home in Minnesota and connected with Warren at Greg's home in South Dakota to make our final arrangements for our trip. Greg had been on several big-game hunts over the years and was equipped with all the essentials for a couple of elk-hunting novices like Warren and me. Over the years, Greg had been a big-game guide so he had everything necessary to stay for an entire week high up in the mountains of Montana seeking elk.

When we arrived at Greg's home, the only preparations left for our elk-hunting trip were simply to load our gear into his truck, then load Greg's three pack mules into the trailer that was attached to his truck. With all the mules and equipment loaded, we departed for our thousand-mile journey to the rugged Rocky Mountains of western Montana. I was amazed at all of the gear that Greg owned. He had a canvas sleeping tent that could be heated with a propane heater in frigid weather as well as a canvas cook tent and cook stove. In addition, he had equipment to either ride his mules or equipment to pack with the mules. It did not go unnoticed by me at how much financial investment my friend Greg had into his big-game hunting hobby as we traveled down the highway to begin our once-in-a-lifetime hunting excursion.

Greg started out driving, but he indicated to Warren and me that with such a long journey, we would all take turns driving the big truck and trailer switching places at every fuel stop along the way and back. When my turn came about to drive the fancy new truck and trailer, I took special note that the pickup truck was only a few months old and showed a mere twelve thousand miles on the odometer. I could only imagine how many thousands of dollars Greg had invested with all of his equipment, mules, truck, and trailer.

During the next week, I had the opportunity to see some of the most beautiful and rugged mountain terrain of my life. The three of us rode mules in high-elevation places that no man could venture and literally in places that only an elk or a mule could travel. By the end of our hunting trip, I was lucky enough to be the only one from our hunting party to bag an elk. We field-dressed the substantial bull elk then used the mules to pack the heavy quarters of meat down the mountain.

On our final day of intended hunting in the Montana mountains, we learned about a terrible early winter snowstorm that was heading toward our Midwestern homes. Due to the oncoming inclement weather, we opted to depart for home immediately that day in hopes of reaching our homes before the big snowstorm arrived.

Once everything was packed and loaded, we agreed that we would keep the truck and trailer on the road and only stop briefly for fuel stops and to revolve drivers. Greg started out driving, and a few hundred miles later, Warren took the helm of the truck. We had been on the road for many long hours when my turn to drive came up. By this time we had traveled all the way across the large state of Montana and were now traveling across South Dakota as the weather conditions continued to worsen.

Following a fuel stop at about midnight, I took over the driving duties while Greg fell asleep in the passenger seat next to me and Warren dozed off in the rear seat. I guided the big truck and loaded trailer down the desolated highway, praying that the harsh winter snowstorm would hold off until our arrival back home early the next morning. I became evermore alarmed, however, because the outside temperatures had fallen into the subzero range and the heavily falling snow was making it ever more difficult to see the dark stretch of highway before me.

It was 1:30 a.m. when I'd entered one of South Dakota's largest Native American Indian Reservations. The Cheyenne reservation covers an extensive territory with few towns or inhabitants within its boundaries.

With the plummeting temperatures and howling winds, the windows began icing up on the truck as it hurled down the lonesome and empty highway. I checked my cell phone for a signal, but it came as no surprise to me that there was none since we were traveling in such a desolated area. The more it snowed, the more the wind howled. I became evermore concerned with the snowdrifts starting to develop across the highway. The drifts ran across the entire width of the highway, and they were extremely dense. I was operating the truck and trailer at about fifty miles per hour with limited visibility as the truck pounded through one hard snowdrift after another. With each impact, the truck and trailer lurched and made a deep thudlike noise. I surmised that both Greg and Warren were thoroughly exhausted if all the noise and bouncing we were doing wasn't stirring them.

I began questioning how much longer we could continue on in such extreme driving conditions. My thoughts drifted to the dire consequences should we get stranded in such a barren area in such harsh weather conditions.

Suddenly I found myself squinting my weary eyes trying to figure out what kind of foreign objects were running across the road and almost appearing as though ghosts floating through the snowstorm. Without hesitation, I instantly forced my foot down hard on the brakes of the truck. At that point, everything transpired extremely quickly.

Since the highway was covered with snow and ice from the storm, the big truck and trailer started jackknifing and going sideways as soon as I hit the brakes. The only way to correct the dangerous path of the truck was to release the brakes, and just as I did so, I suddenly detected that directly in the path of our oncoming truck and trailer were a total of eight large horses running across the highway!

In terror, I shouted, "Greg and Warren, wake up now and hold on to something because we are going to crash into some horses!"

With every bit of vehicle-operating skill within my being, I used my instincts to maneuver toward the least destructive and least deadly pathway possible given the circumstances before me.

With only a mere moment to react toward our impending crash, I was all too aware of our limited chances of survival following a direct hit with one or more horses cascading directly in our path.

As the heavy truck and loaded trailer careened toward the horses crossing the highway at a full run, and just prior to hitting one of the horses, I instinctively jerked the truck steering wheel hard to the left attempting to avoid a full-frontal impact with the large beast. My theory worked because the truck suddenly veered left and sliced in between two of the galloping horses.

The results of that move to avoid a direct collision with a horse most likely saved all of our lives that night, yet we were still in for an intense crash nonetheless.

I missed a direct hit with the big black stallion that most surely could have killed the three of us, but I still crashed into the horse's back half. The truck collided so hard that the front bumper sliced open the horse's entire lower belly, killing him instantly. The mass from the large horse caused such an impact that the truck engine was pushed rearward by several inches, causing the motor to fail. The sheer weight of the horse damaged the entire front end and hood of the truck. As the horse was spun around following the impact, he came around hard and smashed into the right side of the truck cab, breaking out the truck windows and damaging the entire side of the truck.

Even though I'd been able to guide the truck and trailer between two of the eight speeding horses, the truck not only collided with the rear half of the black horse, but also collided with the front half of the appaloosa horse that had been following closely behind. The indirect impact with this horse cause more front-end damage to the truck as that horse was then spun completely around, causing it then to crash into the left side of the truck, resulting in even more damage to the truck.

Everything I've just described in detail took less than a few seconds to transpire, but the frightening memories that resulted have lasted a lifetime.

Following the multiple horse impact and by utilizing the dying truck's remaining forward momentum, I was able to with a great deal of effort maneuver the disabled truck and trailer onto the snowy shoulder of the bleak highway.

Somehow we had averted certain death from a collision with some rogue horses while traveling on a major state highway, but our troubles had only yet begun.

I was unable to restart the damaged truck's engine as smoke rolled out from under the crumpled hood. The vehicle's electrical systems were also disabled, so I reached for a flashlight to garner some light. Under the eerie glow of the flashlight, I took note of the ashen, pale facial color of both Greg and Warren who appeared to be in a state of shock as a result of our accident. I also became all too aware of what a dangerous situation we were in since several of our truck windows were shattered as the snow and wind blew with subzero gusts into the truck cab.

Our situation could hardly have been worse. Yes, we had avoided one brush with almost certain death, but we still had many more opportunities to lose our battle for survival.

Imagine then having just survived a frightening crash but then sitting in a disabled vehicle with broken windows with subzero temperatures in a snowstorm at 1:30 a.m. on a Native American reservation with no cell phone service and stranded in an area without any inhabitants for miles all while being marooned on a stretch of highway that would have no other travelers until the following day.

This became one of those profound moments in my life in which I chose to make lemonade out of lemons. I took control of an ever-worsening situation.

With some effort, I was able to open the door of the truck on my driver's side. I then hustled Greg and Warren out to the attached trailer where we determined that our three mules were more than a little upset from the thrashing they'd endured during the collision, but all were safe and uninjured. Next, we put on layers of our warmest hunting clothes, gloves, and boots. Finally, I hustled Greg and Warren back into the dormant truck and handed them one of our gas lanterns, instructing them to turn it on to provide both heat and light as I shared with them that my intentions were to seek out help.

I departed on foot back toward the direction we'd come from prior to our horse collision. It is a well-understood fact that one should stay with the stranded vehicle in severe weather conditions and opt for the aid of rescue parties. Although I was aware of the dangers of setting out by myself in the middle of a nighttime subzero snowstorm, I was driven by the vaguest memory of seeing a possible yard light from a dwelling perhaps a couple of miles back. With any luck, I felt that I could at least secure help and ensure our ultimate survival.

While trekking westward, and even though I was bundled up in my most protective mountain hunting clothing, I could barely endure the harsh blustery northwest gale-force winds. The below-zero wind chill became more than I could tolerate, so at last I was forced to turn around and walk backward. For what seemed like hours, I slowly took one step after another backward for over two miles before I spotted the dim outline of a distant yard light. With little haste, I altered my direction toward the welcomed beacon of hope.

At last I reached the front steps of what appeared to be nothing more than an abandoned shack with a large sheet of plywood covering the doorway. My spirits were shattered as I pounded on the sheet of plywood expecting nothing to come of all my noise making efforts. In desperation, I pounded once more on the plywood as I began to realize all hope was fading.

Just as I was about to depart without a secondary plan for survival, I heard a creaking sound behind the plywood barrier. I stepped back toward the door and realized that someone behind the door was pulling nails from the temporary plywood door with a claw hammer. I was about to whisper a thank-you prayer toward heaven when to my alarm a shotgun barrel came out through the small side opening and was ominously placed in the middle of my chest.

From inside the shack, the hidden man croaked, "Why are you bothering my brothers and me at this time of the night?"

In a panic, I responded, "My two friends and I hit two horses on the road a couple of miles from here. Our truck is wrecked and one of the horses is dead. Can you help us, or do you have a phone that I can use to call for help?"

With that, the loaded shotgun barrel drew away from my chest as I waited in anticipation for the remainder of the nails to be removed from the tattered sheet of plywood covering the door opening. Once the plywood was removed, I entered the small shack waiting for my eyes to adjust to the dimly lit room. The man placed his shotgun along the wall then began sealing the plywood back in place to keep the wintery weather outside.

My visual and nasal senses went on high alert observing the room before me. Lying on nearly every available space on the floor were ten heavily intoxicated Native American males clothed only in their underwear. Liquor bottles were strewn everywhere and the stench of the room nearly caused me to vomit. Obviously, this rowdy group had engaged in a long, hard Saturday night of drinking, and now I had the misfortune of standing in their midst with few alternative options.

I turned back to the man who had let me in, noticing that he also reeked from the strong smell of alcohol. He stood only in his underwear and coldly stared at me with contempt in his eyes.

Once again, I repeated our impossible circumstances and then asked for someone's help or inquired if I could at least use a phone to call the South Dakota state highway patrol to report our vehicle accident.

The man smugly laughed and proclaimed, "Don't you know that you are on the reservation? The South Dakota State Highway Patrol doesn't have any jurisdiction on our Indian lands."

I didn't think it could get any worse until he announced that it would be impossible for me to call anyway since they didn't have a phone in their dwelling. I began to get desperate realizing that I'd been gone for too long as I worried about the health and safety of Greg and Warren back at the truck.

"How do you seek help if you have an emergency?" I asked the man.

He indicated, "We have a two-way radio that goes to our tribal chief. He also has a telephone and he then calls the tribal police in Eagle Butte, South Dakota, to relay any emergencies. We could try to contact him, but it is doubtful that we will be able to stir him at 3:00 a.m. in the morning."

As the man and I walked toward the two-way radio, I whispered a silent prayer asking for something to start going in a positive direction after enduring such a horrible night.

With the radio microphone in his hand, the man called his chief over and over again. Again as before, I was losing any ray of hope when at last the voice of a very groggy-sounding man came across the radio speaker demanding to know why he'd been wakened at such a hostile hour of the night.

The man then thrust the microphone at me and instructed me to repeat my story to his tribal chief. Once I'd done as instructed, the man on the other end indicated that he would contact the tribal police. He instructed me to go back out into the wintery storm and hike back to the truck to await the arrival of the tribal police.

I sincerely thanked both the chief and the man in the dwelling and then trekked out once more into the blustery dark landscape. At last I arrived back at the truck to find both Greg and Warren huddled closely next to the gas lantern with their teeth chattering and their bodies shivering from prolonged exposure to the cold. Each of them perked up when I announced that help would soon be on the way.

"Soon be on the way" turned out to be a bit of an optimistic proclamation one might say since we were stranded within the grips of a snow blizzard and compounded by the fact that the tribal police were stationed more than fifty miles away.

Nearly two hours later and when we had reached all hopelessness, the headlights of the tribal police squad vehicle pulled up behind us. Before long, I was sitting in his vehicle providing my complete statement on what had happened several hours earlier. I was somewhat taken back when the policeman announced that the Native American who owned the horses, which we'd struck, had been in trouble with the law previously for a similar incident. The policeman shared that the horses' owner refused to keep his horses corralled, and only a few months earlier, the very same group of horses had run across the road in front of a car driven by a woman and her daughter. Tragically, both women were killed in the collision.

Nearly in a state of shock, I asked, "Why hasn't someone taken him to court and stopped his irresponsible behavior? Is he going to be allowed to continue to put travelers on the state highway in harm's way?"

The tribal officer laughed out loud and replied, "You are very naive because your people can try to take a Native American Indian to court, but you have no jurisdiction within our Indian lands. That being said, no one can stop his behavior."

I couldn't believe what I'd just heard. How insane was the fact that a rebel who refused to constrain his horses had already caused the death of two women and nearly caused the demise of my two friends and me on that fateful night.

The hour was nearing 5:00 a.m. on that early Sunday morning, and I'd finally finished the accident report with the tribal policeman. Next, he used his radio to call back to his police station and summoned two separate tow trucks to come out to our location. It was determined that we would need one tow truck to transport the disabled truck and another tow truck to transport the fully loaded trailer that was attached to the truck.

The policeman departed the scene of the accident proclaiming that he had done everything that he could do. We were instructed to continue our long, cold wait until the tow trucks arrived.

Finally at 7:00 a.m., the two tow trucks arrived and began hooking up to the truck and then to the trailer. We were never so relieved as each of us hopped into the warmth of the tow truck cab after enduring nearly six hours in the frigid elements during that endless night on that barren highway.

Greg instructed the two tow truck drivers to transport his truck and trailer the remaining distance back to his home that morning. The massive cost of the long-distance tow truck hauling as well as the expense to replace the "totaled" truck with only twelve thousand miles on the odometer was thankfully covered by Greg's insurance company. What a shame, however, that the insurance company had to cover the total expenses without even being able to get retribution from the owner of the horses who was actually responsible for our close encounter with death.

By the grace of God, I'd found the means to survive my twenty-first close call, but there could have been so many different outcomes for which this story could have ended.

RUN-OVER ANNIHILATION—43 YEARS

CHAPTER TWENTY-TWO

He commanded us to preach to the people and to testify that he
is the one ordained by God as judge of the living and the dead.
All the prophets testify about him that everyone who believes in
him receives forgiveness of sins through his name.
—ACTS 10:42-43

The catastrophic leg injuries that I encountered as the result of being run over by a heavy piece of machinery could easily have resulted in my death. Had the Lord not intervened, my saga of multiple survivals would have ceased at that moment in my life. At the very instant of my tragic accident, I physically felt the hand of God upon me and that experience has forever instilled in me the belief that God and guardian angels can and do protect us if only we open our hearts and our minds to the possibilities.

*   *   *

The excitement level for our two sons Trevor and Travis as well for Astrid and I were at an all-time peak. We were in the processes of putting the finishing touches on the property of our newly built home.

After spending ten years living and working in the southwestern Minnesota community of Minneota, a job transfer required that I move our family to central Minnesota. As a family, together we had selected a pristine location to build our home amongst the fertile farm fields, the ponds, and the lake surrounding our property. Not only did we orchestrate the construction of our new house, but as a family, we took great pride in designing our spacious, multifunctional steel machine-shed building on the very ground that only a couple of months earlier was part of a grain field of corn.

For several weeks, our family had lived only a couple of miles away with a family friend named Bertha while the final construction of our home took place. It was extremely convenient to be able to work most every day at the site of our new property and still have a bed to lay our heads by night.

Throughout the summer months, we worked diligently to complete our home-building tasks before the start of school for our sons. By the final week of August, we were able to move into our new home as Trevor and Travis readied themselves for their new educational system in Kimball, Minnesota.

The final major task left to complete that fall on our new property was to prepare the soil surrounding our home and then seed the more than five acres of ground into grass for our new lawn. Unlike small lawns and yards typical of urban dwellings that oftentimes install ready-made lawns with purchased rolls of sod grass, a rural homestead such as ours most often seeds a luscious large green lawn boasting acres of space.

On the final weekend before the start of school, our entire family of four worked endlessly in our effort to seed the five acres of grass. Our tasks and preparations were many to be sure. First, we had to level all the mounds of dirt left over from digging the basement to our new home. Next, we used our tractor to pull first a disk and then a drag across all of the bare ground, which tilled the soil, leveled the ground, and ultimately prepared the seed bed for planting. Our final duty prior to planting the grass seed was to walk every square inch of the large patch combing the ground for rocks or foreign debris that would possibly produce a lumpy lawn.

After two long, hard, backbreaking days of manual labor at last our family reached the moment when our barren plot could be seeded. Seeding a large lawn is preferable just prior to the fall months since the cooler, wetter weather helps germinate the fragile grass seeds while they in turn have less competition for nutrients from weeds during this season of the year.

Since Trevor, age sixteen, was the eldest son, I asked him to assist me with the grass-seed planting activities that afternoon. Our first activity was to hook our tractor up to the Brillion seeder, which is a specifically designed machine made for planting expensive grass seed in hefty quantities. After hooking the Brillion seeder up to the tractor, we then proceeded to use a large jack to hoist up each side of the seeder and remove the rubber tires. Once the two tires were removed, the Brillion seeder's ten foot wide massive steel roller-packer was properly positioned upon the ground. The one thousand pound steel roller-packer is what crushes any remaining clumps of dirt and then provides a hard, packed seed bed in which the tiny seeds of grass can then germinate and grow into a beautiful green landscape.

My final task prior to planting was to fill the grass-seed hopper of the Brillion seeder. Our large lawn had required the purchase of a vast quantity of grass seed with an exorbitant cost, so I didn't want to waste even the slightest amount.

At last, all the preparations were completed, and I jumped onto the seat of the tractor to begin planting. As I released the tractor's clutch and the equipment lurched forward, I turned back toward the seeder observing a dismal sight. Something was obviously wrong with the seed-rate adjustment indicator because rather than the appropriate small quantity of seed flowing from the machine, vast volumes of the expensive seed were cascading from the seed hopper.

I stopped the tractor and seeder instantly then walked back to determine the root cause of the problem. Trevor and I soon came to the realization that various-sized grass seeds would flow at different rates through the seeder, so the seed-rate adjustment indicator could only be used as a guideline.

Shaking my head with concern, I turned toward Trevor and said, "This seed costs a small fortune, and we are simply pouring it on the ground at far too great a rate. At the speed the seed is coming out, we will only have enough left to finish less than half of our ground."

Trevor shrugged his shoulders and asked, "What are we going to do then?"

I replied, "I want you to get on the tractor and drive slowly forward while I get in between the tractor and Brillion seeder. Since I can't set the proper seed rate by using the indicator, I'll have to walk backward between the tractor and seeder where I can try to adjust the seed rate by hand as you drive the tractor."

With those instructions to Trevor, I set into motion a nearly fatal chain of events that still haunt my dreams to this very day.

What a poor choice I made in my haste to try to save a few dollars of seed. Common sense dictates that one should never position oneself between a moving tractor and a dangerous piece of machinery. In my rush, I forgot the "golden rules" of safety.

As instructed, Trevor released the tractor's clutch and the ominous equipment surged forward. I was so intent on walking backward while physically adjusting down the flow rate of the grass seed with my hand that I simply forgot to heed the peril from the behemoth one thousand pound steel roller-packer thunderously crushing everything in its path below my gaze.

For a few moments, all was well and my satisfaction grew as I watched the seed rate finally reach acceptable levels. I knew that within only a few more awkward rearward steps, my mission would be complete and then I could take over the tractor driving responsibilities from Trevor.

All at once I sensed an anguishing bolt of pain that thrust upward through my lower left foot and leg. Although my instinctive reaction was to jerk my leg backward, I found myself unable to retract my leg even a fraction of an inch. I panicked as I instantly realized the immense one thousand pound roller-packer had first rolled over the toes of my left foot, and then continued to roll forward, crushing first my entire foot, then my ankle, and finally annihilating my leg.

I screeched in agony and pleaded with Trevor to stop the moving tractor as quickly as possible. As promptly as the incident had begun, Trevor brought the tractor to a halt. Even though he was a mere sixteen years of age, he exhibited machinery operating skills and decision-making abilities far beyond his age.

Thankfully, my scream combined with Trevor's quick reflexes brought the roller-packer to a halt after only a meager two feet of travel over the top of my foot and leg. It doesn't sound like that big of a concern as the crushing force of the machine came to a halt just below my left kneecap. To this day, I contemplate what would have become of my leg, my groin, my hips, and my vital organs had the machine not come to a halt as quickly as possible.

Imagine how quickly one can be severely injured during an accident such as mine involving a tractor and dangerous machinery. The bones and soft tissues of my leg were no match for the crushing force of the one-thousand-pound machine exerting immeasurable force per square inch. Within just a split second, my toes were entrapped, and then the machine rolled over the top of my foot, nearly destroying all of the tendons and ligaments in my foot. As the unbearable weight of the machine rolled further over my ankle, the ankle joint and ankle bones were smashed in several places. As the steel packer continued to roll over my left leg, my body was ruthlessly slammed backward at the same time, smashing my head and neck into the moving rear wheels of the tractor before my body fell helplessly beneath the curvature of the vast rear tractor tire. While the heavy roller-packer rolled over my lower left leg, I felt and heard the bones in my leg snap loudly twice as though my fractured leg were nothing more than a two-by-four piece of lumber snapping in half. The roller-packer was designed to crush and flatten everything in its path. By doing what it was meant to do, the large bone in my lower left leg was so badly compressed that the bone marrow inside my leg bone blew out through a dime-sized hole on the side of my leg.

Due to my unsafe choice earlier, I was now in a terrible predicament with a leg that would never be the same. From the idled tractor seat, Trevor saw my plight and pleaded for my direction. I knew that my choices were dim at best since suggesting that Trevor run back for the big jack and attempt to lift the heavy machine off me by himself was out of the question. I needed the machine moved instantly or risked losing my leg altogether.

In a state of searing pain and while lying face up on the ground beneath the damaging machine, I pleaded with my son to put the tractor into reverse gear and back the roller-packer off me. Trevor did as instructed, but no one could possible imagine the excruciating pain I felt as all one thousand pounds mashed my leg even further into the hardened ground beneath me.

In our heightened state of panic, neither Trevor nor I gave any consideration to the fact that I was pinned to the ground just beneath the curvature of the rear tractor wheel. I was simply too out of sorts to realize the danger I was in. Just as the massive wheel of the tractor was about to run over my head and upper torso, I felt my wife Astrid's hands pushing my shoulder forcefully away from the backing wheel, averting my certain death to be sure. At that point, the pain was so intense, I lost consciousness.

*   *   *

I regained consciousness moments later just as I felt myself being lifted up from the ground by Astrid on one side of me lifting underneath my left shoulder and Trevor on my opposite side lifting underneath my right shoulder. With their surging adrenaline, they began dragging my limp body toward our car as a wide-eyed fourteen-year-old Travis threw open the rear car door for my arrival. Although still in a hazy frame of mind, I was cognizant that the deadly machine no longer ensnared me, and even a bit surprised that I was somehow mercifully still alive.

Even though I was struggling with more pain than I could ever recall, I passively agreed with Astrid's decision to urgently drive me the twenty miles to the nearest hospital emergency room rather than wait for an ambulance to drive twice the distance first to our home and then back again.

Trevor was left alone on the property to take care of the destructive machinery as Astrid, along with Travis, departed with me in a flurry for the hospital. I've always contemplated how difficult those moments must have been for Trevor at his youthful age. He was never at fault for the outcome of that day, yet he was forced to live with the consequences of my unwise choices. Then to make it all the worse, he was left alone to battle his disturbed and tormented thoughts as he watched the rest of his family depart in frenzy.

My dear wife drove with the skill of a race car driver that afternoon. She maneuvered the car skillfully around every hairpin curve and twist in the road. She pushed the car's speed to the maximum. During the intense ride, I was doing all that I could do to remain conscious. The pain emanating from my destroyed left leg was beyond description as I shouted, "It doesn't hurt! It doesn't hurt!" over and over again in an attempt to make myself believe such a pretense. I was able to maintain that falsehood for approximately three quarters of the trip when at last I was overcome by the unbearable pain. I can still envision Travis's look of concern when at last I could endure the pain no longer as the tears began streaming down my face, and I began wailing in sheer agony at the top of my lungs.

At last we were at the hospital emergency room, and I was being hoisted onto a gurney. The emergency medical staff cut away my boots and pants and, then with grave concern, injected me with a merciful dose of pain-killing medication. I don't remember much detail after that, but the chief orthopedic surgeon was summoned while countless x-rays were taken of my gruesome injuries.

The room seemed to spin as I sensed many ghostlike individuals in white attire working ever so diligently all about me. I was being prepared for immediate leg surgery and already there were IVs, tubes, and an array of monitoring apparatus attached to various parts of my body.

As I faded in and out and just prior to the anesthesia rendering me unconscious, the surgeon who had recently arrived leaned over my face and introduced himself. He shared with me that my leg was most likely beyond repair with all the massive nerve, bone, circulatory, and soft tissue damage. He indicated that I needed to prepare my mind for the dismal fact that when I awoke, my leg would most likely be amputated.

Even though I was nearly unconscious at that moment from the effects of the anesthesia and relaxants, I reached out with my left hand, grabbing the surgeon by his white surgical gown and with all the anger I could muster, I said, "Don't you dare cut my leg off while I'm in surgery. Give me a chance to mend for God's sake. If I can't mend my shattered limb, then you can always remove my leg, but don't you dare cut it off now!"

With that final burst of contention, I collapsed, only to waken in the surgical recovery room a few hours later.

As a nurse began checking my heart rate and vital signs, I asked, "Do I still have both of my legs following the operation?"

I breathed an enormous sigh of relief when she replied, "The doctor said he's never seen anyone's leg so badly mangled and crushed, but he has attempted to put you back together much like a bionic man. You now have a twelve-inch titanium plate holding your fractured bones together with twelve stainless steel screws as well as a couple more screws helping to hold your shattered ankle bones back together."

The following day, my doctor shared the vivid descriptions of my extensive leg injuries and how he'd done all that he could in an attempt to save my leg. He remained very grim, however, as he reiterated that it was still highly likely that my leg would suffer from such poor circulation from all of my crushed blood vessels that he predicted amputation was still a likely possibility. The doctor continued to share his bleak analysis by proclaiming that I would never be the same again. He assured me that even if we averted amputation, my leg was so badly altered that I would never walk correctly again.

He showed me my x-rays, and I was stunned by all the strange looking metal that was now a part of my body makeup. The x-rays also demonstrated how my left foot and ankle were now permanently tilted at a ten degree angle as opposed to my good leg, so he assured me that if my leg could be saved, I would likely walk with a limp the remainder of my life. He also shared that it would take an immense amount of painful physical therapy to regain the use of my leg again, but even so, I would suffer continual pain throughout my existence. Just when I didn't think I could stand anymore bad news from the doctor, he finished up by informing me that I would also be doomed to suffer from painfully intense arthritis by the time I reached fifty years of age.

The doctor finally left my bedside, and frankly, I was quite happy to see him leave. I've always prided myself as an eternal optimist, so hearing the doctor share all the pessimistic notions of my future health did not bode well with me. As I'd done throughout my lifetime, I vowed to regain my strength, to work extra hard on my physical therapy, and to never let my severe injuries be a deterrent for continuing to gain the most out of life.

My mood was evermore improved when Astrid, Trevor, and Travis came by to visit me that same morning. As they walked through the doors to my hospital room, I was nearly overcome with emotions as I sensed my family's undying love, and I drew immeasurable strength from their love. Both boys were extremely curious to hear all the gory details, which I gladly shared with them.

With tears filling her eyes, Astrid drew near and gently hugged me, saying, "Scott, I was so scared yesterday because I thought we would lose you during that dreadful accident. Even though you still may lose your leg, at least you are alive."

As I hugged my loving wife in return, I commented, "You have no idea how thankful I am that you were able to reach me in time to push me safely out of the way of the tractor wheel as Trevor backed the machine off me. In all our haste, had you not gotten to me in time, the tractor wheel would have run over me and most certainly killed me."

Astrid pulled away from me with a disturbed and shocked look upon her face and replied, "What on earth are you talking about? Perhaps you are delusional from all the medications because I was nowhere near you yesterday when Trevor backed the machine off you. Don't you know that Travis and I were far out in the field picking up rocks when the accident happened? By the time I reached you, you were unconscious, and Trevor was already off the tractor trying to get you out from between the tractor and Brillion seeder."

I challenged her comments further by remarking, "I don't see how that is possible because just before the rear tractor wheel was going to back over my head, I distinctly remember feeling you pushing my shoulders and head out of harm's way. If you didn't do it and Travis didn't do it and Trevor was operating the tractor, then who pushed me out of the way?"

*   *   *

The answer to what or who saved my life on that fateful day many years ago can only be explained through an act of divine intervention. I was quite simply either physically pushed out of harm's way by a guardian angel or perhaps by the loving hand of the Lord my God.

*   *   *

Throughout my healing process following my severe injuries, I benefited from more pain tolerance and increased healing abilities than most by the grace of God as I drew strength through the power of prayer from all who loved me. Not only was I gifted with keeping my once-dilapidated leg, but I healed faster than my doctors or my physical therapists deemed humanly possible. Even though my x-rays can still document that my left ankle is tilted ten degrees from the correct angle of my undamaged ankle, I've never walked with a limp nor have I ever suffered from pain or arthritis as my doctor once predicted.

Today, my only reminders of that day where I evaded death once again surface only when I look at the gruesome surgical scars on my leg along with my almost comical inability to pass through airport security screeners because of all the metal encased within my body.

I continue to send prayers heavenward on a regular basis for my gratitude of still having two good legs, having a loving family, and the joys of a continued extension of my life upon this earth.

FALLING FROM ROOF HARDSHIP—
50 YEARS

CHAPTER TWENTY-THREE

"For I know the plans I have for you," says the Lord.
"They are plans for good and not for disaster,
to give you a future and a hope."
—JEREMIAH 29:11

By the time I'd reached my fiftieth birthday, I'd already stared into the face of death a remarkable twenty-two times. Throughout those numerous harrowing experiences, I'd subjected myself to more physical trauma and greater pain than most could ever fathom. Somehow, I've been blessed with the will, the strength, and the determination to continue enjoying the expression of my life no matter how extreme the odds or the setbacks incurred.

As previously stated, I was born into this world either blessed with or perhaps cursed with an extremely high-risk personality. The very thought of engaging in scary or dangerous activities has always drawn me much like a moth seeks out the illumination of a bright lamp. Most commonly, the average person avoids risk at all cost while my demeanor craves the thrill and excitement of danger.

*   *   *

From a young age, I discovered my love of heights. By the age of five, most of my young friends refused to follow me as I climbed higher into tall trees than they deemed safe. Unknown to my parents, by the age of nine, I was already comfortable climbing up the dangerous outside ladder of the towering sixty foot high corn silage silo on our farm simply for the pure exhilaration it brought me. I was enthralled with view from any lofty vantage point, and having no fear of heights whatsoever, I continued to look for thrill-seeking activities that brought me ever farther from ground level.

During my lifetime, I've scaled mountain peaks thousands of feet in elevation, bungee jumped from a one-hundred-and-fifty-foot-high crane, piloted airplanes, and plunged out of an airplane to skydive while falling thousands of feet back to earth. The simple thought of participating in such gravity-defying feats keeps most people's feet firmly planted on the ground, yet I've never experienced the faintest trepidation of extreme heights.

On the contrary, my polar-opposite wife, Astrid, has a massive dread of heights. She is so terrified of heights that she actually suffers from the dizzying effects of vertigo even when simply climbing up to the second or third step of a ladder, and she is virtually unable to ascend from ground level without suffering from extreme anxiety. My loving spouse has never understood my enjoyment from going ever higher. Rather than directly observe my high-elevation antics, she oftentimes closes her eyes and breaks into a cold sweat from anxiety.

Throughout our many years of marriage, Astrid and I always agreed that whenever a duty needed to be performed around our household demanding one's feet to leave the ground by more than a few inches, then I was the "designated climber."

On one frigid winter day in January, Astrid and I along with our two adult sons who were home for a visit sat in our house waiting out the aftermath of a severe Minnesota snowstorm that dumped ten inches of snow followed by high wind conditions. Those of us who have learned to endure harsh winters in the "north country" accept the fact that it serves little purpose to remove the snow from walks and drives until the winds die down and the snow stops piling into drifts.

As we waited for the blizzardlike conditions to subside, we entertained ourselves watching a movie on our television. Just as the movie neared the exciting climax, the television screen blacked out and was then replaced with a snowy haze much like the view of the wintery weather just outside our window panes.

At first indication, we thought perhaps our satellite dish attached to the roof of our home had been blown off its proper setting by the strong gusty winds. Although the outside weather conditions were still poor at best, Astrid, Travis, and I bundled up in our warmest winter coats and trudged outside to determine the problem with our television reception.

I led the way plowing a furrow with each step through the snow to the far side of our house. Looking up, we instantly realized why our television reception had faded since we could see a considerable drift of snow where the satellite dish was mounted. The heavy snows combined with the brisk northwestern winds had formed an immense snow barrier, blocking the satellite signal from reaching the satellite dish. It became evident that until someone in our family climbed up on the roof and removed the snow, the ability to watch any further television while waiting out the snowstorm would be out of the question.

With my height-loving reputation in our family, it is a given fact that I'm always the designated roof climber. With Travis's help, we carried our longest extension ladder through the deep snow and to the satellite dish side of the house. Astrid and Travis then observed as I climbed up the lengthy ladder armed with a snow shovel in hand to remove the troublesome snowdrift from just below the peak of our rooftop.

Although I found the aluminum extension ladder to be somewhat difficult to climb due to the icy wintery conditions, nonetheless, I was soon able to climb to the top and stepped boldly onto the steeply slanted roof. It was extremely difficult to breathe as the wind-whipped snow stung my face.

I looked at Astrid and Travis who were observing my actions from far down below me. I instructed them to remove the ladder from the side of the house and then step back out of the way so I could start shoveling the heavy snow from the roof without hitting them. When they had done as instructed, I began my task with little consideration to the danger of my situation. Oh sure, I was elevated high on top of a slippery, steeply slanted rooftop during a windy snowstorm and without a safety rope, but I didn't even consider such a scenario to be all that daunting.

I began tossing shovelful of snow after another off the roof as I slowly progressed toward the snow-encased satellite dish. It became ever more difficult to maintain my foot holds, however, because underneath the snow that I was removing was a thin layer of slippery ice clinging onto the roof. It became evident as I tossed the final shovelful of snow off the roof that I would have some difficulty navigating my way back off the treacherous rooftop.

The next sequence of events happened in the blink of an eye as I unwittingly confronted death once again.

With the snow finally removed, I flung the snow shovel off the roof so I could focus all of my attentions toward safely exiting the roof. As I cautiously inched my way back down the slippery slope of the roof, I shouted down to Astrid and Travis to replace the extension ladder back onto the side of the house. Just as the words had left my lips, both my feet slid out from underneath me, and I fell backward crashing down onto my back. I knew instantly that I was in peril as I began cascading down the steep slant of the roof, gaining momentum on the icy layer beneath me.

In extreme duress, I cried out to Astrid and Travis, "I'm going to fall off the roof, please CATCH ME!"

My words had barely escaped when I reached the highly elevated edge of the rooftop. I heard Astrid scream in fear as I shot off the roof and then plummeted downward toward my startled wife and son. I braced myself for the impending collision with the ground with thoughts of broken bones or possibly death flashing across my harried mind.

The trajectory of my fall nearly landed me on top of poor Travis, but he instinctively dove out of the way just as I came crashing down to earth in exactly the same spot in which he'd been standing. That pretty much destroyed any concept I might have had regarding my adult son hanging in there, standing his ground, and then attempting to break the fall of his middle-aged fifty-year-old father.

I hit the ground hard as my momentum slammed me feet first through the pile of snow that had been tossed from the roof. Thankfully, the snow partially broke my fall, but at impact, I felt a shot of pain go up through my entire body. Astrid and Travis rushed to me, knelt down by my side, and then helped me up my feet. In disbelief, I marveled at defying death by escaping such a fall. I inventoried the damage I'd done to my body, realizing that I was hurt, but not severely enough to warrant a trip to the hospital. As a result of the plunge, I'd sprained both my ankles, sprained one of my knees, and jarred my back.

Most of the following week was spent recovering with the aid of cold packs and heating pads, but those options were far more plausible than another visit to the hospital emergency room to refurbish another round of bone fractures.

*   *   *

Oftentimes, our family chuckles about the events of that day as we marvel about my propensity for "nine lives" experiences.

Today, my son Travis is a married adult and a father himself, but I still enjoy taking the liberty to tease him about his failure to break my fall from the rooftop on that wintery day.

I love to jest him by saying, "Travis, at the time you were a division one college wrestler with an absurd level of strength, speed, and athletic ability. Why then did you jump out of the way rather than break the fall of your frail father? I could have been killed you know."

Travis never fails to promptly respond with, "Don't always try to pin that one on me, Dad. Just because you're forever crazy enough to walk the fine line of danger, doesn't mean that I have to get injured trying to save you from your own stupidity. It seems to me that you've mastered the fine art of defying nature's natural culling processes for all organisms that make poor choices in life."

Ouch, if I didn't know just how much my son loves me, I'd almost take his banter seriously.

The truth of the matter remains that Travis reacted just as anyone would have since he was startled by my impending fall. No doubt the physics of the matter determining the blunt force impact from my fall onto Travis could have been an even worse calamity.

*   *   *

I ask that you go back and review the scripture verse that I chose for the beginning of this chapter to understand why I feel that all who believe in God will have great rewards in their lives from a truly loving and gracious Lord.

AFGHANISTAN DELUGE—51 YEARS

CHAPTER TWENTY-FOUR

I called upon the Lord in my distress and cried out to
my god for help.
From the heavens the Lord heard my voice;
my cry reached God's ears.

—PSALM 18:6

This story details how I willingly put myself in harm's way in order to help the people of an impoverished nation. This became one of my more dangerous international consulting assignments working on behalf of the Land O'Lakes International Division.

Beginning in year 2001, the American troops along with military allies from around the world entered Afghanistan to fight a long-drawn and brutal war against the evils of terrorism. Many lives were sacrificed fighting the Taliban and the al-Qaeda terrorist networks as the Afghanistan war continued on for more than a decade, only to become the longest-running war involving Americans in the history of the United States of America.

In 2006 near the midpoint of the war, I volunteered my services and then traveled to Afghanistan in an effort to establish a dairy-farming sector within that war-torn country. The objective of my consulting assignment was to establish a food-producing form of agriculture as opposed to the more prevalent form of illegal drug-cropping production, which was so common within Afghanistan at that time. I accepted the challenge of such a dangerous assignment, knowing that with even a modest success, many lives could ultimately be saved and countless malnourished children and adults would be nourished.

The various dairy-related assignments I've completed in my lifetime have without a doubt had a positive humanitarian impact as they've taken me all around the globe. I've had the privilege to work in such exotic places as Poland during 1992, followed shortly thereafter by Estonia during 1993, soon after the demise of the Soviet Union. My next assignments brought me twice to Uganda, Africa, during 1995 and 1997 shortly after the end of that nation's years of civil war, unrest, and genocides. Working in yet another portion of the world brought me twice to Siberia, Russia, in 2004 and 2005 to help reinvigorate their faltering dairy industry. During some extremely volatile times in the Middle East, I accepted consulting roles in Afghanistan in 2006 and then went on to complete a similar assignment in Lebanon in 2010.

Within the contents of the following pages, I'll describe in vivid detail my experiences while working in Afghanistan. The memories that formed in my mind delved in polar-opposite extremes. I not only dealt with some extremely harrowing situations, but was exposed to an abundance of positive outcomes as never before.

On a fresh, crisp, springlike day in April 2006, I departed the Minneapolis airport for what would be nearly a three-day journey to my destination. The trip intensified the effects of jetlag as the aircraft traveled through several time zone changes. After departing Minnesota, my first plane transfer was in Amsterdam, Holland, but the flight departure was delayed by nearly four hours in order to entirely check out the plane's electrical systems after it had just been struck by a midair lightening strike on its previous flight. Most of the passengers seemed upset with the delay, but I on the other hand sincerely hoped the airline mechanics were extremely content with their pay scales and labor contracts and that they would take all the time necessary to ensure the flight-worthiness of the aircraft. Next, I flew on to Dubai, which is a city near Saudi Arabia and then changed planes once more for my final destination of Kabul, Afghanistan, which is the capital city of that nation. Surprisingly, I arrived on time. My luggage, however, took a path of its own and arrived one day later, leaving me with only the first adversity of many more to come on the assignment.

During the several weeks prior to my international departure, I was e-mailed a weekly security update directly from Afghanistan. If the information in those security updates weren't enough to give one "cold feet" prior to an assignment such as this, then nothing could! On a weekly basis, I read about how many terrorist activities such as kidnappings, suicide bombings, car bombings, Taliban attacks, and military confrontations had occurred somewhere in Afghanistan during the past several days. Foreign internationals needed to be very cognizant of the risks that were posed while in the country of Afghanistan.

I also discovered that in the region of the country that my assignment was located, they were struggling with the dire consequences of hoof-and-mouth disease in their cattle as well as dealing with an Avian bird flu outbreak in their poultry. In fact, during my stay, several poultry flocks were destroyed in the area that I was in, which left the villagers very despondent and hostile. I was warned to observe the cooking practices of eggs or poultry I was to eat and to avoid contact with any live poultry. In addition, I received updates and warnings about everything from IED (improvised explosive devices) recognition, to being coached on the fact that there are millions of active land mine explosives buried all throughout Afghanistan. Unbelievably, every month, over one hundred humans were continuing to be killed or injured by land mine detonations. I was also provided information on how to act or react if kidnapped, or what to do if confronted with a robbery or an assault.

All of these scenarios, however, are the kinds of things that spur adrenaline junkies onward. I've often been asked by close friends and family why one would volunteer for this type of assignment knowing some of the dangers that are involved.

My response has always been, "Why do some climb mountains, skydive, bungee jump, ride rodeo bulls, ride motorcycles, or do consulting assignments in highly agitated countries?"

For some of us, life needs to be filled with high-level excitement, while for others, life takes on a slightly calmer demeanor. Obviously and thankfully, we are all different in how we choose to experience our time on this planet.

Some interesting facts about Afghanistan are that there are about twenty-five million of some of the very poorest people in the world living in this Middle Eastern country, which is bordered by Pakistan on one side and Iran on another side. At the time, Afghanistan held the rank of being the second poorest nation in the world, and the average life expectancy for its people was a mere forty years of age. Afghanistan's landmass is similar in size to the state of Texas, but in my opinion, its overall topography, all be it more extreme, is similar to the state of Colorado with the diversity of countless majestic snowcapped mountains, breathtaking river valleys, arid deserts, combined with everything from the harshest cold climates at high elevation, all the way to the searing 120-plus degree subtropical climates within the more arid regions.

The country of Afghanistan has been besieged by endless decades of invasions, fighting, and wars, leaving their social, economic, and political institutions in a state of disrepair. The Afghan populations have been some of the most exploited people on the planet. As a result of the endless years of warring invasions and battling, the Afghani people have evolved into some of the most feared and ferocious fighters on earth. Many can still remember the failed Soviet Union occupation during the 1980s, and most recently, the American troops and United Nations allies have fought to liberate the Afghan people from the tyranny of the Taliban and the negative effects of the al-Qaeda terrorist cells.

The negative aftermath of the Taliban control still permeates throughout all of Afghanistan. As an example, during the Taliban reign, females were literally positioned in their society as being seemingly nonexistent. Woman and girls nearly always had to enter into prearranged marriages. Oftentimes, by the age of fourteen or fifteen years of age or even younger at times, they are married to a much older man who often had multiple wives. It is hard to believe based on our cultural differences, but in that way of life, oftentimes neither the female nor male have ever seen each other until they are in fact married. In that culture, females were often doomed to be concealed within the confines of either their father's home or to be hidden within the confines of their husband's home with little or no interaction with society while being doomed to a harsh lifetime of toil, childbirth, and mistreatment. Afghan women have suffered some of the highest childbirthing mortality rates in the world, and in turn, Afghan childhood mortality rates are also some of the highest on earth.

Thankfully with the fall of the Taliban rule, some of that tradition slowly evolved into something more acceptable and humane, but even today, many females in Afghanistan are restricted from gaining an education or forbidden to receive medical care from male doctors since the former Taliban mandates forbid any female to be seen or touched by a man other than her father or her husband. Because of the lack of medical options, pregnant Afghan woman often literally starved themselves during their pregnancy in hopes of giving birth to an extremely small child. The children in turn if born alive were severely malnourished and often suffered from retardation or other birth defects. Today, even though for the most part the Taliban stronghold and control has been destroyed, a high majority of females within Afghanistan are still following these strict and harmful traditions.

Another example of how females were treated was when a female ventured out of her home; she was mandated to wear something called a burka. A burka literally and tragically transforms any female into a seemingly nonexistent human being. Imagine in a climate that can be stifling warm as in this Middle Eastern country and then seeing a woman wearing a burka, which entirely covers her from head to toe with several layers of flowing gownlike clothing. These females had only the slightest of semitransparent material near their eyes for peepholes for which to see out from. I was informed that one's vision was reduced to only about 20 percent from the view inside a burka.

While on my Afghanistan assignment, I found it eerily haunting to see what appeared to me to be humanless, ghostlike figures floating along a road. One literally could not make out one single human feature—no face, no hair, no arms, no torso, no body. Those females were not allowed to speak with another man or shake hands with a man, and they were totally ignored if as though they simply did not exist. It was hard for me to fathom that in our modern era those traditions were still being practiced. It was interesting for me to note the reactions of the Afghan farmers while showing them photos of my wife, Astrid, doing her work as the herd manager for a one thousand cow dairy.

While in Afghanistan, I met up with a friend of mine who I grew up with from Minnesota and who had been working there for nearly two years. He had become close to a neighboring Afghan family who were very traditional. Because of my friend's relationship with this family, he and I were invited into their home one evening for tea. This may not seem so special, but almost never would nonfamily men be invited into an Afghan home with all the females present and not wearing a burka or covering their faces with a veil. Had I not had this opportunity, I literally would not have known what Afghan adult females even looked like. Prior to entering their home, my friend coached me to only shake hands with the men and boys in the family, and under no circumstances was I to speak to, look at, or make contact with any of the females within their family.

Their simple home consisted of one large room entirely covered by beautiful and colorful Afghan rugs. Before entering the home, we removed our shoes, and then we sat on the floor around the edges of the room. Even though about fifteen family members were present, I was surprised to learn that not all their extended family was present. What a challenge it was for me to only look at or speak to the men and boys. I accidentally made eye contact with one of the women who were sitting in a corner of the room and she immediately dropped her eyes to the floor, leaving me feeling as though I had committed a mortal sin. I learned later from my friend that the room we were in served as a multipurpose living room, dining room, and bedroom for this very large family. I'm very thankful for having had the unique opportunity to be invited into the home of a very traditional Afghan family and to have seen what few outside men and even fewer Americans have ever witnessed.

Afghanistan at the time of my assignment was a nation considered to be in a very fragile state with its newly formed democratic government and constant in-country fraud, corruption, and violence. Continual resurgence of the Taliban and fighting amongst many of Afghanistan's various tribal factions was still occurring. The agriculture segments of that country were struggling under pressures to illegally grow poppy flowers whose seeds were in turn used for the production of opium and heroin drug production. The illegal agriculture resulted in good profits as opposed to the choice of struggling with poor profits from most forms of legal agricultural production.

Soon after my arrival into Kabul, Afghanistan, my senses immediately went on high alert. All around me were the sights and the sounds of a very impoverished third world country. The numbers of unemployed Afghans loitering around was staggering. I was shocked by the sheer number of amputees, who were victims of land mine explosions, who were lining the streets. The women, children, and men begging for money were a very depressing sight.

Soon after I arrived, I had a briefing session regarding my assignment, and we reviewed security and safety measures. Following that activity, I was provided some assistance at a local market to acquire some Afghan clothing to help me blend in since dressing blatantly American in the outer regions where I'd be traveling would have made me a target for a dangerous confrontation. At first my thoughts were that it would appear ridiculous to the Afghanis that I'd be working with if I tried to imitate their dress. I was assured by several Afghan people, however, that not only would my clothing choice be the safest, but that people would sincerely appreciate my gesture to display their native dress code. I was also pleasantly surprised when I learned that in their culture, "gray-bearded" men such as me were looked upon as being very wise and credible. At the time, I joked about wishing that my own kids back home would think the same thoughts.

As we walked amongst thousands of Afghanis in their market place, I felt the stares from being a stranger within their turf. I do want to explain that for the most part, the Afghani people liked Americans and sincerely appreciated the assistance we were providing them over the years. Americans, however, can also be prime targets for kidnappings or robbery because of the extreme poverty these people face. It didn't take me long to feel very uncomfortable with the countless stares being directed at my fair-colored skin and the American clothing I was wearing at that moment.

I exchanged some money on the street, which was the common practice since there were few banks in Afghanistan and because they were completely a cash society at the time. For that very reason, I was unable to utilize a credit card or even a form of travelers checks, but rather, I had to keep several thousand dollars in cash upon my body at all times. That was not a very comforting thought since I knew that everyone else in Afghanistan realized that any foreigner would usually be carrying a large amount of cash.

No sooner had I pulled out a few dollars to exchange on the street when I was besieged by an army of orphaned children and widowed women pleading with me for a handout. The sad detail was that if you handed out even the slightest amount of money, it only drew countless more with their hands tugging at your clothes and pleading with you for money. I can attest, they didn't give up easily either.

As a result of my Afghan clothing search in the market place, I was able to purchase a *pirhan-tumban* for about the equivalent of seven American dollars. Nearly all Afghani men wore a *pirhan-tumban*, which consisted of an oversized baggy pair of pants along with a long flowing knee-length shirt, which reminded me of a form of nightgown. This oversized, flowing outfit would then be worn with a long-cut vest, along with some form of headwear consisting of a type of scarf or perhaps a turban. I obtained both a scarf and a turban. Once I had clothed myself in traditional Afghan dress, combined with the full beard I wore on my face, I was awestruck by how I almost magically transformed when I viewed myself in a mirror. It didn't take me long to understand how practical and functional their clothing was for the environmental conditions of Afghanistan.

Within my first day in the capital city of Kabul, I began struggling with some respiratory issues. The entire city was almost always shrouded by a thick cloud of dust that literally could block out the sun. It didn't take me long to realize why everyone was wearing scarves or turbans over their heads and faces. I questioned the source of the massive dust cloud that left everyone coughing and struggling for breath. I was informed that part of the dust particle makeup came from the debris created by the destruction within a war zone combined with the simple stirring up of road dust from such a large mass of humanity on the move. As buildings were bombed and destroyed during war time, the minute dust particles were strewn in every direction.

Another shocking statistic that I discovered was that Kabul, Afghanistan, had over six million inhabitants at the time. That made the city infamous for being the largest city in the world without a formal sewer system. Imagine a city of so many people without any controlled form of sewage disposal. I was quite taken back when I was informed that an analysis of the Kabul dust resulted in 20 percent of the dust particle makeup being breathed was in fact made up of dried fecal dust particles. I can attest on how that will leave an aftertaste in one's mouth!

After my initial arrival and after spending only one day in Kabul, I was then driven the next day by 5:00 a.m. in a vehicle for a destination of Jalalabad to begin my consulting assignment. The original plans had called for a 6:00 a.m. departure time, but rumors had stirred regarding terrorist activity along the route, so for extra safety precautions, we chose to leave at the earlier time. Our hopes had been to depart early enough to not only avoid any heavy traffic along the poorly conditioned dirt and rock road, but we'd also hoped to avoid any possible kidnappers or robbers, which had been showing increased levels of activity along the beautiful but dangerous mountain road.

I can't even describe the severe road conditions as we traveled for over four hours on the roughest, nastiest, dustiest, pothole-filled road that I'd ever encountered. I doubt that anyone could make that passage without feeling some form of motion sickness. Along the way, I saw the most breathtaking scenery imaginable, yet along the entire route, I also spotted identified landmine fields and/or possible landmine fields. Along the route, we encountered people walking or traveling by donkey or camel while others traveled by car and truck. We saw countless shepherds with flocks of sheep and goats grazing on the mountain sides.

Four hours after our departure from Kabul, we had arrived in Jalalabad about 9:00 a.m. Bear in mind the fact that we had left one hour earlier than we had originally planned on that morning because at precisely 10:00 a.m. of that morning, Jalalabad was sent into mayhem when a car bombing killed five people on the only open road entering into Jalalabad. Had we kept our original travel plans, we would have been on the location of the roadside car bombing at nearly the same moment of the explosion!

Later on that same day, a missile was shot into a school only a short distance from the city, killing and injuring several children. The very next day, another bombing occurred on the new highway coming into Jalalabad, which had been under construction, only to wreak havoc once again. The reality of where I was and the potential danger sent shivers down my spine and heightened my sense of awareness. At least I had made it to the location of my consulting assignment, but I pondered the danger of three explosive blasts during my first twenty-four hours on location.

The basic premise of my assignment was that I was to be one of the first dairy-related consulting teams sent into Afghanistan to begin the process of establishing a commercial dairy industry. At the time, there was no real dairy industry to speak of in the country, other than individual families occasionally owning a cow for personal dairy needs. Sometimes if those families had small quantities of extra milk, it found its way to a local market to be sold as fresh milk out of an unsanitary bucket on the street. Those privately owned cows were extremely malnourished and usually produced almost nothing for milk yields. Many of the people of Afghanistan were also malnourished, so the mission of establishing a viable dairy industry was an extremely important humanitarian service both nutritionally and economically.

My actual assignment and scope of work was to rationalize the Nangarhar Cattle Farm as a commercial dairy cattle and production facility. That assignment was only a portion of a much larger total project scope of work directed at developing the domestic dairy industry to meet the needs of Afghan consumers. Besides meeting with and working through several government agencies, my primary focus was to mentor a Jalalabad private businessman who at the time owned an ice-manufacturing business and who intended to start a five-hundred-cow commercial dairy along with constructing a milk processing plant. The gentlemen's name was Haji Aziz, and he had no previous dairy production or agricultural background.

Haji Aziz had recently leased a semidemolished former government dairy farm built and operated by the Soviets during the USSR invasion from the 1980s. His farm lease included three hundred acres of irrigated cropping land. A major challenge was that the site of this dairy was located in a subtropical climate with up to +120 degree Fahrenheit seasonal daytime temperatures. Other challenges were to establish proper feedstuffs and balanced rations for a dairy herd when the most common cattle diet for Afghan cattle was merely a chopped straw diet. My main areas of emphasis were to assist with redesigning the dairy cattle facilities, assist in establishing appropriate animal health and husbandry procedures, balance proposed feeding rations, demonstrate proper milking procedures, and to train herdsman and other employees on evaluation techniques of high-producing dairy cattle.

The dairy housed one hundred and eighty head of Soviet-bred black-and-white dairy cattle and young stock. Never in all my life of working with cattle had I seen such malnourished and starving animals. Those standing carcasses were being fed an unpalatable, limited diet consisting of chopped straw and dried sorghum with a dry, sticklike consistency. No high energy grains or protein sources were being fed whatsoever. I witnessed the hand milking of this herd and was in total shock that the near-death cattle could milk at all, much less give their paltry one to four quarts of milk yield per day.

To put the laborer situation in perspective, the farm employed about forty male workers, consisting of several who milked the cows by hand, field workers, management, and security guards with very large AK-47 automatic machine guns. In fact, it took fifteen security guards simply to watch over the farm's three hundred acres of fields in an attempt to stop the poor peasants in the area from stealing their crops. It appeared to be somewhat futile as I witnessed countless people hiding down in the wheat fields as they stole the crop one small sack at a time, and I also watched as small herds of cattle, sheep, or goats grazed while crossing the fields. The laborers who milked the cows worked extremely hard as I spent several days with them observing their entire daily processes.

Milking began at 5:00 a.m., and it came as no shock that there was no mechanization of any form. All of the chores including the milking, to the feeding, to the manure removal, to the daily feed gathering while they carried the sacks on their backs in from the fields were all done by hand by those men during their long twelve- to fourteen-hour workdays. Their pay was a meager two dollars per day, and with that pay, their income was far greater than most of the population of Afghanistan.

After my first full day at the Afghan dairy site, I felt somewhat secure behind the walls protected by armed guards. The following day, however, I spent nearly the entire day walking through their cropping fields while completely out in the open. I made the decision to hire an armed security guard to keep an eye on matters. The cost of the guard was thirty-two dollars per day, which seemed like cheap insurance to me. My intent was to utilize the services of the guard occasionally during my assignment when I was faced with higher risk situations. Another dilemma arose, however, because having an armed guard nearby seemed to draw a lot of attention from folks wondering why someone was important enough to need protection. At times I wondered if faced with an attack or a kidnapping attempt, would it be better to have the fire power, or would it be better to be unarmed?

Early on in the assignment, I encountered difficulty with the translation. I struggled to understand my translator, so a second translator was brought in to assist. At that point I then basically had two translators that I couldn't understand barely a word they were saying to me, and they struggled with translating my agricultural dialogue into their Dari language as well. My next difficulty was discovering that they use the Persian calendar, so for instance, the year 2006 was in fact the year 1385 in their Persian calendar. This really made my work interesting as I tried to figure out the ages of all the animals on the farm. Then of course, my brain was in constant overdrive trying to convert everything from an unfamiliar metric system consisting of liters of milk and from kilograms of feed and from hectares of cropping fields and from centigrade temperatures. I watched in amazement as they wrote and read their language backward reading or writing from the right side of a page and going to the left side.

Each day during my assignment on the dairy, I had to take a deep breath and kept telling myself that the idea of that potentially large dairy becoming the start of an emerging commercial dairy industry within Afghanistan was not beyond hope, even though what I was witnessing was breaking my heart. I worked diligently evaluating the project and training the personnel during my every waking hour. At the close of my assignment, I felt a somewhat frustrated sense of accomplishment. I was confident though that some strong seeds were planted as a result of my work, but those poor seeds were in for a true test of survival to be sure.

During this assignment and based on my previous third world not-so-pleasant gastric experiences, I tried to exert extra caution with the food and water that I consumed. Each day I was transported to and from my lodging out to the dairy farm. I found the lodging and available food adequate where I stayed in the heavily guarded United Nations guest house. The walls were set up like a thick, high-walled fortress with barbed prison wire on all the top surfaces. To enter the UN compound, one had to go through a double entry gate guarded by several armed guards.

For meals, I ate breakfast and sometimes supper at the UN guest house prepared by their cooks. Breakfast usually consisted of scrambled eggs along with their traditional baked flat bread called naan. For supper each evening, a meal was prepared consisting of several exotic variations of mutton, beef, or chicken along with various combinations of soup, rice, vegetables, and red beans. For lunch each day while I was out on assignment, I packed along an MRE (meal ready to eat) rather than risk eating food out in the rural sector that could be hazardous to my health. For liquid, each day I drank bottled water when available, or I ensured that the water I would be drinking had been boiled.

While out in the public or while at the dairy farm location, I tried to only eat fruit with peelings on them, and I drank nothing but boiled tea. Even though I tried to be extra cautious, I still ended up consuming a meal out in the field. I sampled small amounts of the meal that had been prepared. In addition to that meal, on the same morning I had consumed some scrambled eggs that looked bad, smelled bad, and tasted bad. Did I eat them? OF COURSE I ATE THEM!! The outcomes from what I ingested that day was gastric suicide as I spent nearly the next twenty-four hours vomiting and spent nearly six days visiting the toilet on very regular intervals around the clock. I'd contracted food poisoning on one of my previous Uganda, Africa, assignments; and I was quite sure that I was suffering from my second bout with it. I can't describe the difficulty of trying to complete the final week of an assignment in such a weakened state and without basically being able to eat anything or get any sleep as one's head pounds endlessly as the effects of severe dehydration overtakes one's body. Unfortunately, medical options in the rural reaches of Afghanistan were limited at best.

The working week in Afghanistan seemed odd to me with Saturday being the first day of the week and going through Thursday. Then Friday was observed as a day of rest. On one of my Friday off days, I traveled with a couple of Afghani businessmen who requested my professional opinion. They were thinking of investing in a commercial dairy and asked that I travel with them to view two ex-Soviet dairies within only miles of the Pakistan border and on a route that was a high security risk.

The evening before our departure, some of the United Nations personnel shared with me that a large military offensive was about to be deployed near the area that we would be going the very next day. Evidently, one of the largest military coalition force gatherings since the 2001 American military involvement in Afghanistan was being deployed within the next couple of days to lead an offensive against the terrorist activities occurring in the bordering region. About two thousand five hundred military troops along with airplane bombers were being deployed.

The next day prior to traveling to this location, it was suggested that I not bring anything along that could identify me as an American. I was instructed to wear only Afghanistan clothing, and I was coached to leave my wallet, my money, my wristwatch, and my passport at the UN guest house. In the event we encountered a problem such as kidnappers, they would then have a more difficult time trying to figure out who I was and hopefully they'd be less likely to take me as a hostage.

Once we arrived at the abandoned dairy sites to inspect their capabilities, I was instructed to always walk on beaten-down paths and to follow a safe distance behind one of the Afghani people in the event of a landmine encounter. I took special heed of this suggestion as I witnessed a couple of young boys with amputated legs closely observing our activities. I breathed a sigh of relief when that day trip was over as it proved to be without incident and ultimately safe.

During my time in Jalalabad, I visited their university of more than three thousand students. I spent my time visiting with the department heads of the college of veterinarian medicine and the college of agriculture researching information about common cattle diseases, vaccination protocols, and reviewing various cropping options. Later, as I journeyed back to the inner city of Jalalabad, I stopped briefly at a market place to acquire a colorful handmade 50 percent silk and 50 percent wool Afghan rug. I paid a mere one hundred and thirty dollars for it, and I was later informed that in America, the same beautiful imported carpet would have cost well over one thousand dollars. Another item I acquired in Afghanistan was an authentic pottery churn used by local peasants to make butter.

When the field assignment stages of my work was completed in Jalalabad, I was instructed to fly back to Kabul in a special United Nations military plane rather than endure the dangerous long ride back through the mountains. Once again, I had an acute awareness of how dangerous this part of the world was as I was required to sign a disclaimer like none other I'd ever encountered prior to making a flight and even before they would administer my flight ticket.

The disclaimer read,

General Release From Liability in connection with travel by third parties on unproven aircraft in Afghanistan, I the undersigned, hereby recognize that my travel on the aircraft provided by the United Nations is solely for my own convenience and benefit and may take place in areas or under conditions of special risk. [Now there was an understatement!]

In consideration of being permitted to travel on such means of transport, I hereby acknowledge that:

A.) The flight is operated by the UN and is not offered as a commercial service for the general public.
B.) This flight is operated in an area of possibly hazardous conditions, including hostilities.
C.) The operating conditions of this flight do not meet national standards, which could pose special risks for the flight.
D.) United Nations shall not be responsible for any loss, injury, or death during such travel.

Well that got me real excited to make that flight all right!

The military security at the Jalalabad airfield was a sight to witness. I walked through countless earthen-filled bunkers and armed guard entry points. It was like a complicated maze trying to simply get to the airfield. As an American, I felt very proud talking with a few of our U.S. marines on duty. When I had finally made my way through all of the clearances, I was then escorted out to sit nearly on the airfield runway itself. Just moments prior to my departure, I was surprised to witness the arrival of a huge U.S. air force military cargo plane that nearly deafened me as it taxied to a spot just in front of me under a mass of U.S. military trucks and armament. The air force plane never slowed its engines down and then an army vehicle sped up to the rear entry cargo door of the plane, and I watched as they moved a wounded American soldier lying on a stretcher being quickly loaded. Then the air force cargo plane departed as quickly as it had arrived.

Just minutes later, the United Nations twin-prop plane arrived and performed what was termed a hot landing. The purpose of a hot landing is to keep the aircraft engines and propellers at nearly full speed. The roaring airplane then throws open a doorway, passengers are hustled into the plane, then the aircraft instantly begins takeoff procedures as the door of the airplane is quickly closed. I was informed that a hot landing was a necessity since several planes had been struck down by insurgent missiles over the previous weeks, and by implementing a hot landing, our chances improved for not being blown out of the sky. I was thankful that my prayers had been answered because our flight was safe and unhindered, albeit an adrenaline-spiking experience to be sure.

On my final evening in Kabul, Afghanistan, awaiting my departure the next day, I encountered more fireworks. About 2:00 a.m. in the morning, I was awakened by the blast from a nearby explosion. The entire hotel as well as the room I was sleeping in shook violently from the explosion. Plaster fell from the ceiling of my room as I got up from my slumber and looked out the window at what had happened. Peering out of my only window, I detected the aftermath of a large explosion with fire and smoke erupting from a building only a few hundred feet away.

As odd as it may seem, I crawled back into my bed and fell almost instantly back to sleep. Already, I'd been in Afghanistan long enough to become somewhat accustomed to the prevalent dangers around every bend. The following morning as I checked out of the hotel, I was informed that during the night the Taliban had bombed a nearby embassy, causing severe damage and resulting in human casualties. Somehow the news of that event had little effect on me. In only my short time in such a hostile environment, I'd become similar to the masses within Afghanistan simply thankful to live yet another day.

Later that morning, I departed by plane for the three-day marathon journey home. The long trip home allowed me plenty of time to reflect on my overall assignment. Obviously, an assignment of that kind wouldn't be for everyone. The rigors of the travel, the magnitude of the culture shock, and coupled with the insecurities of being in a high-risk environment can be a strong deterrent for many.

The real reasons I choose to do these types of assignments are because I feel such a strong sense of loyalty and passion for the worldwide dairy industry. My roots and history are deeply engrained in dairy food production. My grandparents, my parents, along with my wife and I have all lived our lives working within the dairy industry. I feel very privileged to be able to give something back to underprivileged peoples and nations because of my dairy industry experience and by providing some of my consulting services across the globe. I simply cannot explain the feelings one gets when one can personally make such a positive impact on so many unfortunate individuals in these poorest nations around the world.

Each time I return home from one of these challenging assignments, I'm ever more appreciative of our wonderful home that we call America. I'm also so very thankful and more appreciative of my family, of my friends, of my coworkers, and so thankful to be blessed with a career that I care so much about. I have been blessed by God to have seen and experienced things on foreign soils that a scant few will ever have an opportunity to witness. Most assuredly, I feel blessed to be able to make a small contribution toward helping farmers and fellow humans succeed in other parts of the world, which hopefully helps to make our planet a safer and better place for all of us in our journey through life.

*   *   *

It often comes as a shock to others when I describe the hostilities and dangers that I encountered while in Afghanistan. During the short duration of my international consulting assignment, I experienced a suicide car bombing, a bridge bombing on a newly constructed highway, a children's schoolhouse bombing, and an embassy bombing, all while walking and traveling in areas surrounded by landmines and various explosive devices. Upon my return to the United States, I discovered that each of the terrorist activities that I'd personally witnessed had garnered headline coverage on the *USA Today* newspaper and on the CNN television channel. Although my volunteer time in Afghanistan was literally spent within an active war zone, I had no military escorts or protection of any sort. I dressed in civilian clothing without a bulletproof vest or helmet and relied solely on protection from my Lord.

Nearly all of my selected international assignments have come with a calculated risk, which has led to some extremely serious discussions between my family and me.

For example, prior to departing for Afghanistan, my father and mother both asked, "Why on earth are you always volunteering for such dangerous assignments, Scott? Do you have a death wish? One of these days, we are expecting to be contacted about how you died in some strange and foreign territory far from your homeland."

Each time such a series of comments arises from my parents or my siblings or my wife and children, I respond with, "I believe that only God can determine my final fate. I refuse to acknowledge that I can somehow impact my own demise. Anyway, I can just as easily be injured or killed by a speeding truck while I'm crossing the road in front of my home to fetch the mail, so I place my trust in the Lord."

I believe those sentiments with all my heart. I sincerely feel that the more I generously give of myself through service to others, albeit dangerous at times, the longer my life will extend. My intent and life's goal will be to continue placing myself in harm's way if necessary, especially if the outcome benefits underprivileged souls who are simply trying to survive.

As a parting view, I would ask you to consider a haunting concept. What do you suppose were the astronomical odds of luck or perhaps God's blessing that you and I were conceived, then born, and have lived our lives in such a privileged nation called America? Have you ever considered that you or I could just have easily been born into this world to parents living in an impoverished, starving, war-torn third world nation?

GRIZZLY BEAR FIASCO—52 YEARS

CHAPTER TWENTY-FIVE

Then he said to him, "Get up and go on your way;
your faith has made you well"
—LUKE 17:19

We coined our guy foursome the Wild Hogs as we departed on the motorcycle expedition of a lifetime attempting to ride our motorcycles an astounding ten thousand miles round-trip over the course of eighteen days all the way from Minnesota to Alaska and then back again.

Maynard Moen, his cousin Jeff Moen, along with Maynard's brother-in-law Dennis Miller, and I had planned our extensive motorcycle journey for more than one year. Each of us had ridden together for a number of years, and we'd established a lofty goal of one day riding our motorcycles together within all fifty states within the USA along with motorcycling through every province of Canada. With our next cycling objective at hand, we'd studied several books whose subject matter was motorcycling in the wildernesses of northwestern Canada and Alaska, and we felt mentally and physically prepared for our trip in every way. Months earlier, we had mapped out an exacting route complete with motel reservations for each night's stop during our trip.

Our foursome group of extremely opinionated bikers was equally split regarding their preferred choice of motorcycle brand. Maynard and Dennis each proudly rode their large Honda Gold Wing touring motorcycles, while Jeff and I with equal pride each rode our large Harley-Davidson Ultra Classic touring motorcycles. The bantering and insults about whose brand of motorcycle was superior was ceaseless before, during, and following our Alaskan road trip. To hear our group throw insults at each other made casual observers wonder if we were actually friends at all, but our ultimate respect and appreciation for each other has never been in question.

At last we set out on our trip wondering if our machines would mechanically hold up for such an endurance test. Our established route demanded that we average well over five hundred miles per day for eighteen days in a row. Along the way, we knew that we would endure extreme weather conditions including everything from snow to rain and temperature ranges from a frigid thirty degrees up to a steamy ninety degrees Fahrenheit. Our road conditions were just as varied as we encountered everything from well-paved highways to dangerous rock roads to treacherous mud-covered stretches of road under construction.

As suggested by some of the books we'd studied about attempting such an excursion with motorcycles, each of us carried a spare gallon of fuel due to the lengthy distances between towns at times. Prior to setting out on our Alaskan motorcycle trip, each of us had our motorbikes serviced with new tires and engine tune-ups, but even so, Jeff and I each carried one spare motorcycle tire in the event that we might encounter tire troubles while deep within the wilderness territories.

Another sound suggestion from one of the books we reviewed indicated that when riding a motorcycle through wilderness areas populated by bears, one should never pack food or sweets of any kind either on the motorcycle or in one's clothing. The author cited a story of how he and a friend rode their motorcycles to Alaska. According to the story, his friend's Harley-Davidson motorcycle engine quit working many miles from civilization. Rather than leave his valuable motorcycle stranded along the highway and then ride tandem to the next town on the other bike, he opted rather to remain with his disabled motorcycle while his buddy drove off to seek help.

About two hours later, the buddy returned with a truck and was shocked by what he discovered. His friend's once beautiful motorcycle was strewn out along the highway laying in several fractured pieces, while he clung for dear life to a branch high up in a nearby tree. As the truck neared the carnage, he crawled down from his perch in the tree and explained what had transpired.

Shortly following the departure of his friend to seek out assistance, a large grizzly bear had lumbered toward the man and his motorcycle. In fear for his life, the man had climbed as high into a nearby tree as possible.

From his safe vantage point, he watched as the bear used his razor-sharp teeth and claws to shred his motorcycle into metal shrapnel seeking out the candy bars packed into the compartments of the motorbike. Even though the candy bars had been wrapped in their original packaging and although they were encased in sealed plastic sandwich bags, the grizzly bear's keen sense of smell and ravenous hunger drew it to the source. With little effort, the gargantuan bear ripped and tore the expensive motorcycle into irreparable pieces.

*   *   *

We began our ten-thousand-mile journey in a freezing rain with temperatures hovering near thirty degrees. Even so, our foursome was optimistic and raring to set out on our exploration adventure. The only items packed in any of our cycles consisted only of clothing and toiletry items. We had all mutually agreed that packing along any form of food or candy would be risky at best.

The miles flew by as we traveled scenic mile after mile through parts of the western United States, then parts of western Canada, and then we journeyed along the storied Alcan Highway through northwestern Canada in route to Alaska.

For the first several days, we traveled safely and trouble free. We were spellbound by the awesome and rugged beauty of the geography we covered. Never had any of us experienced such breathtaking views of mountains, glaciers, lakes, and valleys. We were mesmerized by the quantity of wildlife we encountered along the way. By the halfway mark along our route, we had already seen fifty bears along with countless elk, moose, deer, mountain goats, and mountain sheep to name a few. In fact, the wildlife encounters on our trip at times posed a road hazard as we had to be watchful to not hit some of the large animals as they often dwelled on or near the roadway.

Several thousand miles into our journey, it seemed that everything was all too perfect. Before long, I came to realize that my luck was about to run out as I was about to experience one of the most challenging forty-eight-hour periods in my entire life. And yes, another close encounter with the Grim Reaper awaited me.

We discovered that our group's good luck ran out as we were about to depart from one of the few isolated gas stations deep within the Yukon territory of Canada. Jeff's Harley-Davidson motorcycle barely started as we prepared to continue on our northerly course. With grave concern, Maynard, Dennis, and I walked over to try to determine the cause of Jeff's problems. After noting that his battery was losing charge on the voltage gauge, I instantly realized Jeff's motorcycle was probably in need of a new electronic stator and voltage regulator. Even though everything had gone so well over the course of the previous days of traveling, we knew the joyride was suddenly over.

We huddled together to determine our best course of action to take. It was obvious that Jeff's motorcycle battery was nearly drained, and since his electrical system was failing to charge his battery, we were all too aware that before long his battery would fail to produce the necessary spark to ignite the engine. We were concerned with how to get his cycle to a Harley-Davidson motorcycle repair shop. Luckily, I'd packed along a book showing all the available repair shops on the American continent. Much to our dismay, the closest shop was nearly seven hundred miles away in the direction that we were traveling. Unfortunately, our best option was to backtrack one hundred and fifty miles to a repair shop in a town that we'd traveled through only hours earlier.

I called the shop to alert them that Jeff and I would be traveling together back to their location, and I requested that they remain open until we arrived in an effort to get the repairs completed and put our trip back on course. We all agreed that it made absolutely no sense for all four bikers to ride an extra three hundred mile round-trip to get Jeff's motorcycle repaired. As a result, Maynard and Dennis departed with their Hondas on the original course while Jeff and I ventured back toward the direction we'd earlier traveled on our Harleys. We were never in doubt about implementing the buddy system while traveling in such extreme wilderness surroundings. If the books we had reviewed prior to our trip had taught us anything was that it was a good idea to travel with another biker at all times in the event that you or your machine has difficulties.

We waved good-bye to Maynard and Dennis, promising to meet up with them at our next motel stop many, many hours later.

Jeff and I had hoped that his motorcycle battery would provide enough spark to get us most or all of the way back to the distant repair shop. Unfortunately, his bike killed for a final time only a few miles down the path. We sat there uncertain on what to do next. I volunteered to allow Jeff to ride with me in tandem on my motorcycle to try to locate a truck for hauling his disabled bike. Jeff asked that I go alone to seek out assistance while he waited by the side of the road with his expensive Harley-Davidson motorcycle. I expressed my concerns about leaving him stranded all alone in a bear-riddled wilderness while I left to seek help. I cited the example once again of the story in the book we'd read where a grizzly bear had destroyed a motorcycle trying to get at a candy bar. It was to no avail as Jeff insisted that he would not leave his valuable motorcycle unattended alongside the road.

With that, I left in hopes of finding someone with a truck to transport Jeff's motorcycle to the repair shop before too much of the day had elapsed. As I once again traveled in a northerly direction putting on miles in the wrong direction, I prayed and hoped to find a solution to our dilemma. Several miles along my route, I came to a run-down pit stop along the side of the roadway. I inquired if there was anyone with a truck or a trailer that could transport my friend's motorcycle to a repair shop that was over one hundred miles away.

The man at the counter dialed a phone number and handed the receiver to me. Before long, I'd negotiated a hauling fee from the gentleman on the other end of the line. Within a half an hour, while riding my motorcycle, I led his ancient pickup truck in disrepair toward Jeff's position.

As we came upon the stranded motorcycle sitting alongside the road, Jeff was nowhere to be found, which left me with grave concern. I shouted out his name and then I whistled loudly wondering where he could be. All at once I spotted Jeff nearly a half a mile away as he came out from the thick timber forest on the opposite side of the road from where his motorcycle sat.

He looked ghostly white as I inquired, "What on earth are you doing way down there away from your bike?"

Jeff replied, "I was waiting alongside my motorcycle when all of a sudden a big black bear came out of the woods walking towards me. I knew I wouldn't be able to climb a tree, so I hiked down the road about a half mile and hid in the trees."

I started laughing almost uncontrollably as I stated, "Jeff, if that big bear would have wanted to get you, then your hiding in the woods would not have done you much good."

Poor Jeff was so distraught over his bear encounter, I couldn't help but throw a jab at him when I retorted, "You know, Jeff, I'm glad I'm riding with you on this trip and starting from this moment on, I'm taking off my heavy, thick leather biker boots and putting on my lightweight tennis shoes instead."

Jeff asked, "Why would you do something stupid like that?"

I could no longer keep a straight face as I broke out laughing and said, "If a big, mean, man-eating grizzly bear decides to attack us, I'm going to be able to run away."

With a questioning look on his face, Jeff said, "You can't outrun a charging grizzly bear because they can outrun a running horse for short distances!"

With a look of total seriousness, I remarked, "Jeff, I'm not going to try to outrun the grizzly bear. I only want to outrun you when he starts to chase us!"

I don't know if Jeff ever forgave me for those comments, but it sure gives me a chuckle when I think about it.

With all the drama behind us, we were at last able to load the crippled motorcycle on the rickety truck and transported it to the waiting repair shop. Although we arrived at closing time, the motorcycle mechanic remained on duty until Jeff's bike was completely road-worthy once again. Jeff paid the cost of his repairs, thanked them for their service, and we readied ourselves for our long journey to catch back up with Maynard and Dennis. The time was 6:30 p.m., and we had nearly four hundred miles to retrace before our extended day could close.

Just as we were about to leave the motorcycle repair shop, the mechanic remarked that the rear tire on my motorcycle looked low. Not giving it too much concern, I asked if I could borrow the air hose to fill my tire up to the proper level. Having done so, Jeff and I scurried off without any further ado.

It was well past midnight when Jeff and I arrived at the motel where Maynard and Dennis were impatiently awaiting our arrival. Tired though we were, our group of four Wild Hogs lay awake and laughed until we cried as we shared the stories of the trying day.

The following morning, we awoke refreshed, ate a hearty breakfast, and were ready to do battle with the wilderness once more. That is until I walked up to my motorcycle and noted that my rear time was entirely flat. With the help of my biker friends, we pushed my motorcycle over to an available air hose and filled the tire back to the proper inflation. Next, I rode my bike into a water puddle in the parking lot to determine where the leak in the tire was. It didn't take long to determine that sometime during the previous day's escapades in my efforts to help Jeff, I'd somehow run over a nail or some other sharp object which subsequently put a large, deep puncture in my nearly new rear tire. The air simply bubbled

SCOTT D. GOTTSCHALK

and gushed from the hole as we once again questioned what to do with another disabled motorcycle.

I might add that by this point in time, the two Honda motorcycle riders were chirping like jubilant birds about how it appeared that we would never complete our journey to Alaska since the Harley-Davidson motorcycles were always in need of some sort of repairs. All I can say is "ouch," but I've always noted that what goes around, sooner or later it comes around. Sure, the Hondas performed spectacularly during our lengthy journey on this trip, but the time came on other trips where the repair needs landed squarely on the opposite brand of motorcycle.

I scratched my head while looking at my leaky rear tire wondering what to do. I knew that replacing the rear tire on a Harley motorcycle requires some special tools and specific adjustments from a certified Harley-Davidson repair shop. Once again, I drew my book out to determine where the closest repair shop was along our chosen pathway. Much to my dismay, the closest shop was the one that had repaired Jeff's motorcycle just the day before. That shop was now four hundred miles in the wrong direction so an eight-hundred mile round-trip to replace my rear tire was out of the question. The only other choice was to try to find a way to limp my motorcycle on a bad rear tire nearly one thousand miles to the next certified repair shop.

Traveling such a long distance and through such wilderness conditions on a faulty rear motorcycle tire is an unsafe predicament to be sure, yet I had few acceptable options. I contemplated the idea of finding someone who could haul my motorcycle the excessive distance, but I determined that idea to be simply cost prohibitive, much less difficult to secure someone to make such a long haul anyway.

Risky though it was, I made the decision to overfill my rear tire at each and every fuel stop along the way, which worked out to be on intervals of about every two or three hours, and then ride on with our group, wasting no time as we tried to reach the next pit stop to reinflate my tire. A normal rear tire should be inflated to forty pounds of pressure, but over the course of the next two five hundred-mile days, I overinflated the tire to sixty-five pounds of tire pressure. The tire spewed out its air so rapidly that I learned to fill it up at the last moment before we departed from a fuel stop. Then as we traveled along the oftentimes poor road conditions, my rear tire pressure would fall ever lower with each passing mile. Many times in the final fifty miles, it would be rather difficult to operate the motorcycle with the rear tire so spongy and soft. Each time for each fill for the entire two days, my rear tire would fall from the sixty-five pounds of tire pressure down to only ten or fifteen pounds of pressure. I worried if my tire would even hold together until we reached the distant repair shop. With each passing mile, I feared a worst-case scenario of my tire blowing out and losing control of my motorcycle.

Thankfully, the tire held together all the way through the two-day ordeal and ultimately I reached to repair shop. Having called ahead a day earlier, I was the first repair job scheduled for that morning.

Maynard, Dennis, Jeff, and I were lying in the grass alongside the repair shop as we waited for my tire replacement. I felt terrible putting our entire group behind schedule since we were faced with a seven-hundred-mile journey awaiting our departure.

At last I remarked, "There is no reason for all of us to sit around here for an hour or two as we wait for my tire repair. I'd prefer that the three of you take off without me. You can take your time and even do some sightseeing along the way. As soon as my bike is finished, I'll take off, and since I'll be traveling by myself, I should be able to make up some lost time. My guess is that before the end of the day, I'll catch up to the three of you, and we can ride the rest of the way to our evening motel stop."

Maynard came back with, "No way, we already know what can happen when we leave someone in our group to fend for themselves in this wilderness country. Trust me and I speak for our entire group when I say that we don't mind waiting until everyone is ready to depart."

I retorted, "Guys, I appreciate your concerns, but I'd really rather you go on ahead without me. It will be fun to travel much faster by myself as I attempt to catch up to you. Anyway, I'm sure nothing is going to happen once my motorcycle tire gets replaced."

Famous last words, because YES something was going to happen!

My three buddies mounted their motorcycles and waved as they departed from the parking lot of the repair shop. Deep down inside, I was happy to see them go since I knew that they would enjoy their leisurely day of riding together without dealing with the stress of when my repair work would be completed or how late we would arrive at the motel. Truth be told, I was looking forward with anticipation at bringing up the rear all by myself as I attempted to catch up to our group.

Nearly two hours following the departure of my riding friends, my motorcycle was equipped with a new rear tire, and I was ready to journey forth. The sky was a beautiful shade of blue with only a few cotton ball-like clouds dotting the sunny sky. I savored each deep breath that filled my lungs and relished in the woodsy organic smells of the uncivilized wilderness area.

I was sixty miles away from the town where the repair shop had been located. As I twisted the throttle ever higher for more speed, a smile crossed my face as I thought about how lucky I was to be able to experience God's wonderful wilderness creation. For nearly one hour, I had not seen another vehicle or met another human being of any kind. My exuberance became uncontrollable as I began singing out loud while cascading down the highway at full speed. It dawned on me that at my current rate of speed, I would have little difficulty in catching up to the guys in my party. How wrong can one be?

All at once, my motorcycle engine backfired with a deafening bang as my motor stopped running altogether. I dare say I was very concerned since the past few days had been filled with one mechanical challenge after another for either Jeff or me. Without the engine operating, my bike and I silently coasted to a stop alongside the shoulder of the roadway. I had not seen a single vehicle for more than one hour nor had I traveled past any signs of human inhabitation. The dense virgin forest encroached upon the road on both sides for as far as the eye could view, which left me extremely nervous about my isolation.

When I tried to restart my motorcycle, I was astonished to realize that there was no electronics anywhere on my bike. All of my gauges were dead, I had no lights, and when I turned on the ignition switch, I was met with an absolute deafening silence. I carefully scoured every portion of the motorcycle looking for any reason for the electronic failure. Seeing none, I felt my heart rate elevate as I considered my scant options.

It was a long shot, but I turned on my cell phone only to discover that the screen flashed a No Service reading. Much earlier in our journey, our biker group had discovered that in the extreme wilderness areas cell phone coverage was nonexistent. Panic started creeping into my thoughts as I pondered what to do.

I was alone in an isolated grizzly bear infested area with a totally disabled motorcycle, with no cell phone coverage, and without any human encounters. My thoughts spiraled downward as I tried to determine what course to take. I knew that waiting idly along the side of the road was not a good option since roads such as the one I was stranded on seldom had motorists passing by. With the real risk posed from being hunted down by a grizzly bear I realized that I was not only a "sitting duck" if I stayed but also risked becoming a tasty grizzly morsel of food if I tried walking in either direction for help. The thought of walking seemed outlandish anyway since I knew the nearest town was sixty miles in the rear, and the nearest pit stop traveling forward was over seventy-five miles away.

In moments such as those, I find comfort and strength in prayer. Whatever the outcome, my experience reflects that God comes to my aid if only I will be humble enough to ask.

I sat upon my crippled motorcycle, folded my hands, bowed my head, and then prayed, "Heavenly Father, I try to direct most of my prayers towards thanking you for all of my many blessings. I've always felt it improper to pray too often for things that I'm in need of. Truth is, Lord, this time I'm in a bit of a fix, and I'm asking for your help and guidance to show me the way out of this dilemma."

Just as I closed my prayer by whispering, "Amen," my ears instantaneously picked up the faintest sound of a distant vehicle coming from my rear. I looked skyward and shouted, "Thank you, God!"

At first I couldn't understand why the distant truck was taking so long to approach me. From my vantage point, it appeared that the truck would drive a short distance and then stop while one or two men would walk to the back of the truck. It appeared that they might never reach me; so at last, I left my stranded motorcycle and started trekking back toward the remote truck. It suddenly dawned on me that they were some kind of road-repair crew patching potholes in the road. I picked up my walking pace when I began to fear that they might finish their road repair work on that distant stretch of road, and then suddenly might turn around and drive back to the town sixty miles away. I knew that I had to make contact with them before it was too late or face a far worse fate.

The men hopped in their truck for one last time and prepared to do a U-turn on the highway to depart in the opposite direction when they spotted me far out in the distance hurriedly rushing toward them while waving my arms high in the air. I let out a sigh of relief when I observed the truck stop in the middle of the U-turn and then drive in my direction.

The two Native American Indian men drove up alongside me and asked what I was doing. I shared my dilemma and indicated that I either needed to locate a landline phone to call someone for help or else I needed to find someone with a truck to haul my motorcycle back sixty miles once again to the same repair shop that I'd departed from a few hours earlier. I inquired if there was any way that they could haul my motorcycle in the back of their truck, but since it was nearly full of hot, smelly asphalt for road repairs, that choice was deemed out of the question.

Standing on the road and leaning into one of the truck's open windows I asked the two of them for any help which they could provide. They indicated that there were no landline phones anywhere in the region, and they stated the obvious when they reminded me that there was no cell phone service either. Next they indicated that there was a small Native American Indian encampment ten miles ahead, but they felt there would be little chance of anyone being present during that time of the day.

I pleaded with them to transport me to the encampment so that I could at least try to locate someone who could assist me. The two men were not too thrilled about the idea of making a twenty-mile round-trip journey in the wrong direction, but after offering to reward them with something for their services, I was soon squeezed between the two inside their rustic highway repair truck.

Before long, we entered the obscure encampment, and as the men had predicted, I knocked on door after door to no avail. It appeared the entire encampment was merely a ghost town. After knocking on ten different dwellings, I walked up to the final two feeling defeated and dejected. As I knocked on the door, I was surprised to hear the sound of a dog viciously barking. Next I heard an elderly man's voice shout at the dog to be still as I watched the door open ever so slightly.

The man peered through the crack in the door and asked, "Who are you and what do you want?"

I responded by saying, "I was traveling towards Alaska on my motorcycle, but about ten miles back everything stopped working. Would you happen to have access to a pickup truck or trailer, and if so, could I pay you to haul my bike and me back to the cycle repair shop seventy miles from here?"

The old Native American Indian proclaimed, "Yes, I have a pickup truck, and yes, I could haul you, and yes, it will cost you two hundred dollars cold cash!"

My prayers had been answered, or so I thought at the moment. I requested the services of the two road repairmen for a while longer to travel back to my stranded motorcycle and then assist with loading the heavy machine onto the pickup truck. They agreed, and in a short while, the four of us were attempting to load the eight-hundred-pound motorcycle onto the bed of the pickup truck.

The elderly gentlemen drove his truck down into the ditch and then positioned it so his open tailgate faced the shoulder of the road. We then placed a semi rotted two-by-six-inch board, spanning it across the shoulder of the road onto the tailgate of the pickup truck. We determined that the best way to guide the heavy motorcycle onto the narrow board and into the waiting pickup truck was for me to straddle the cycle and steer while the three men pushed from the rear.

That was a near fatal choice on my behalf because as I guided the motorcycle wheels across the creaking boards, it suddenly dawned on me that it would never support the nearly one thousand pounds of total weight amassed by the motorcycle and me. Before I could react and try to stop them, the three men pushed even harder on the bike. As I'd feared, the weight was too great and the near-rotten board splintered into pieces. Tragically, I was dislodged from the motorcycle and fell several feet to the ground just as the eight-hundred-pound machine crashed down on top of my rib cage with a thunderous impact.

My vision nearly dimmed as I struggled to remain conscious. For what seemed like forever, I made a futile effort to breathe since the impact not only knocked the wind out of me, but the brunt force also severely fractured three of my ribs. In addition, the falling motorcycle badly bruised my left hip and leg.

The startled men came instantly to my rescue by hoisting the heavy machine off my injured body. As I gasped for breath while lying dazed in the ditch, the three men somehow found a way to load the motorcycle and get it strapped down. I thanked and paid the two road repairmen, and then the elderly man and I made our trek back toward the repair shop.

The pain in my rib cage from that bumpy, harsh, one hour long ride goes beyond description. My ribs were so injured that I could move several of them around with my fingers. The pain was so intense that I was only able to endure short, shallow breaths.

Eventually we arrived back at the repair shop and unloaded the motorcycle. I sincerely thanked, then paid the man for his merciful help, and then watched as he drove away.

The mechanic who had replaced the rear tire of my motorcycle earlier in the day was quite shocked to see me back again and in such an injured condition besides. I explained exactly what had happened to the machine and to me. Before long, he proposed a theory to me on what he thought to be the electrical source of my predicament. He speculated that perhaps the thousands of miles that I'd logged on rough roads over the past several days had somehow loosened the electrical wires connected to my motorcycle battery. He showed me how the loose connection had started to create a burning electrical arc, which then in turn caused the main electrical circuit breaker for the motorcycle to fail, thus killing all of my electrical functions on the cycle.

The good news was that he discovered what he theorized was the problem and then fixed it. The bad news was that he couldn't positively verify for certain that he had in fact determined the root cause of the problem. He cautioned me that since the motorcycle was now started and running, that I should consider keeping it continuously running until I reached my final destination for the night. He suggested it might be a good idea to only shut off my engine once again when I had the security of being with my riding partners once more. I agreed with his recommendations, but I knew that it would be difficult at best to fill up my motorcycle fuel tank while leaving the machine running and vibrating.

It was time once more to try to head in the direction of my three motorcycling friends, only this time I was far less confident that I could reach them at all. The logistics didn't bode well for my travels of that day since Maynard, Dennis, and Jeff had all left the repair shop earlier in the day at 9:00 a.m. I'd left the shop for the first time about 11:00 a.m. following my tire replacement. Now because of all my difficulties, I was departing for a second time at 3:00 p.m., a full six hours behind my buddies. To make matters even worse, I was faced with a daunting seven-hundred-mile route through desolate wilderness traveling all by my lonesome self with broken ribs, a bruised hip and leg. As if it could be any worse, I had little confidence that my motorcycle would even keep functioning since the mechanic had instructed me to keep it running in the event the electrical problem had not actually been solved.

Before I left the safety of the repair shop and the town, I used their landline phone to call ahead to the motel that we were all suppose to be staying at on that night. I provided the desk clerk with all the details and then requested that she pass along the information to the rest of my biker group once they arrived. With that, I swallowed several aspirin to dull the pain coursing through my body and then I ventured back out into the wilderness again hoping to survive what had become a most grueling and excruciating motorcycle ride.

The miles on my motorcycle odometer started clicking by one after another. With my rib, leg, and hip injuries, my pain threshold was peaked higher than I could ever remember. Surely with the extent of my injuries an endurance ride on a motorcycle would not be what a doctor would have prescribed for me. Obviously, bed rest was not a viable option, but on a positive note, by enduring so much pain, I was able to keep from falling asleep from utter exhaustion throughout the seemingly endless hours and miles.

I literally held my breath as I approached the exact spot in the road sixty miles from the town and the repair shop. I gave a silent prayer of thanks as my motorcycle appeared to be contentedly rumbling along it's pathway past the troubled spot. Seventy-five miles farther, I pulled into my first fuel stop. As instructed, I left the motorcycle idling as I filled the vibrating machine's fuel tank with gasoline.

The fuel-stop attendant came outside and shouted, "Hey you, don't you know it is illegal to put gasoline in a tank with the engine running? You could cause an explosion or start a fire."

I responded back with, "Yes, I know, but I'm having electrical problems with my motorcycle, and I've got to keep it running or risk not being able to get it started again."

The disgruntled attendant threw his hand in the air, then spun around and went back inside. I ran inside as soon as I'd finished putting fuel into the motorbike, paid the man, then hurried along on my way once again.

I repeated this process over and over again while riding the several hundred miles through the wilderness. Late afternoon had long since become early evening, and eventually the clock was nearing the middle of the night. I made one final fuel stop about 11:00 p.m. I distinctly remember feeling three sensations. The first was how exhausted I'd become riding in total isolation for so many hours. The second was how much pain was coursing through my body as the endless hours of motorcycling was jarring every nerve within my injured body. Third, I realized that throughout the daytime and evening hours, I'd forgotten to consume any food. Tired, injured, and hungry wasn't a happy place to be in, but I knew if I could endure another two or three hours of riding, I would finally reach the final motel destination situated near the Alaskan and Canadian borders.

With my motorcycle still idling outside, I purchased a cold sandwich and a bag of M&M's candies. I was so hungry that I nearly inhaled the sandwich while walking back toward my motorcycle. I decided to pack my bag of candy into one of the compartments of my bike and intended to eat the candy later on down the road. This was a near fatal error in judgment because I knew better than to pack candy while traveling through grizzly territory.

I didn't think I would ever make it, but according to my calculations, I only had about fifty miles to go. I found it rather strange that since I was so far north, it wasn't all that dark considering it was nearly 1:00 a.m. in the morning. While speeding down the forlorn highway, I found it strangely comforting that *the land of the midnight sun* actually provided me a safer pathway of travel throughout the nighttime hours.

I lamented over the fact that I had been driving through that wilderness for over seven hours without seeing another vehicle on the road. I was so thankful, however, because even though I hadn't shut down my motorcycle engine for nearly ten hours straight, it was a fitting relief to know that it continued to bring me ever closer to my destination. I felt some euphoria with each passing mile knowing that within an hour, my endurance test would soon be over.

Perhaps the Lord had just one more test in mind for me, though.

Through the 1:00 a.m. twilight din of the sky, I detected a troublesome thunderstorm rolling across the mountain region that I was driving through. Up ahead, the vigorous storm clouds were spewing lightening, thunder, and I could see the trails of a heavy rain flowing from the ominous clouds. It suddenly dawned on me that my rain gear was packed away deep inside the compartments of my motorcycle. After such a harrowing day and night of travel, I couldn't envision being able to endure much more torture from a cold, soaking rain.

My first instincts were to simply ride through the downpour of rain though since I was a mere fifty miles from the end of my route. I determined that it would simply be better to get wet and then ride on rather than to take the time to stop and suit up in my painful condition. My initial decision was quickly altered as the pouring rain suddenly turned into marble-sized hail falling from the sky. In an instant, I stopped the motorcycle on the very center of the highway. The hail stones stung like bullets as I gingerly got off my motorcycle. By this time of the night, my broken ribs were screaming in agony, and I was incapable of moving too fast as a result of the pain.

As I prepared to locate my rain suit, I realized that I would need to shut off the engine of my motorcycle in order to first locate the rain gear, and then find a way to cautiously get into it with my severely injured ribs, hip, and leg. Had I not been in the middle of a hailstorm, I most likely would have reconsidered my choice, but with little time to contemplate, I shut down my motorcycle for the first time in more than ten hours.

The machine no sooner came to a silent rest when the hail ceased falling and the thunderous downpour slowed to a mild rain. I determined that since the motorcycle was shut down and since it was still raining, my best option would be to continue on with getting into the rain suit. I winced in pain as I raised my tender left leg and inserted it ever so slowly into the pant leg of the rain gear. With my leg half way into the rain suit, it suddenly dawned on me just how eerie and quiet everything around me appeared. I looked all about me suddenly sensing the hair on the back of my next starting to prickle. I sensed danger, but from what or from where?

I looked back down the highway from which I'd come and saw nothing out of the ordinary. Next I looked into both sides of the dense virgin timber nearly encroaching upon the highway. Still I saw nothing out of the ordinary, but why were my senses on high alert? Why was I sensing a strange sense of danger and paranoia?

As I glanced down the narrowing highway tunneled between the mountains and dense forest, I suddenly became keenly aware of my serious problem. My eyes strained and then focused on a gigantic grizzly bear that had emerged from the timber. The grizzly was about seventy-five yards from me, and it appeared that he was simply crossing the road up ahead of me. But, then he stopped, raised his nose high into the air and sniffed so loudly that I could hear him. As soon as I spotted the bear, I hadn't moved a muscle, but with his keen sense of smell, he suddenly turned directly toward me.

For what seemed like an eternity, the grizzly stared in my direction, and I stood motionless staring back with my left leg stuck inside the pant leg of my rain suit. The standoff between man and beast canvassed enough time that I was fraught with worry. It suddenly had dawned on me that the grizzly bear was trying to pick up not only my human scent, but he was most likely drawing on the sweet aroma of my hidden package of candies. My mind raced with thoughts of how to survive such an emerging crisis.

I devised two separate plans and readied myself to implement first one and then the other if my first plan failed. My first plan demanded that if the bear moved in my direction, then I would reach forward with my right hand to start my obstinate motorcycle hoping and praying that my failing electrical system would in fact fire the engine back to life.

My intent should the motorcycle fire was to then mount it as quickly as humanly possible considering my rib and leg injuries, then blast on out of the impending danger.

My secondary options were dismal at best under the circumstances of my motorcycle failing to fire. I knew I couldn't outrun the grizzly, and I was quite sure that I would be unable to climb into a nearby tree due the severity of my injuries. For those reasons, I devised the only plausible means of escape I could think of at the time. Should the motorcycle fail to fire, I intended to quickly reach for my M&M's candies, rip open the package, and then start dropping one candy at a time onto the ground while slowly walking backward. Even though my left leg was tangled inside the pant leg of my rain suit, I deducted that perhaps the bear would be so intent on slowly eating one piece of candy at a time that he would ignore my retreat. Well okay, I'll admit it now, this was not a very plausible scheme, but with a man-eating grizzly facing you, one's mind can only hope that the killer bear can be manipulated by his sweet-tooth craving.

As the bear stopped in the center of the road only yards from me, then sniffed the air, then turned to face me, I was simultaneously devising my two separate plans of escape. The total elapsed time was only seconds before the bear began walking toward me. My fear elevated, and my entire body was suddenly covered with in a cold, clammy sweat. I could taste the strange metallic sensation of fear inside my mouth as I reached for the starter of my motorcycle as the grizzly bear advanced.

Once again, I prayed, "Lord, please let this motorcycle start. This is not exactly the way I want to die."

In all of my life, I've never been so happy to hear a motor fire up as I was at the instant my Harley-Davidson engine sprang back life. I twisted the throttle allowing the ear-shattering exhaust pipes to fill the air with a most welcome roar. The oncoming grizzly bear was so startled that without haste he spun around and dove back into the dense timber.

I wasted little time in getting myself into the remainder of my rain suit and then I sped off down the dark trail toward my destination. As soon as I was up to speed, I cracked open my package of M&M's candies and relished in the fact that I was eating them rather than the grizzly eating either my candy or me.

*   *   *

By 1:30 a.m., I finally made it into the small town where the motel was located. I was met on the outside edge of the town by my worried riding partners: Maynard, Dennis, and Jeff along with two law officers. They had all feared the worst and had all gathered to form a search party. Their intent was to backtrack in hopes of locating me since I was late in my predicted arrival, and no one had received word of my whereabouts.

Everyone was mystified as I recanted my tale of mechanical troubles, injuries, and subsequent grizzly bear confrontation. It was only after telling of my encounter with the grizzly bear that the motel clerk shared some alarming information.

The clerk described another motorcyclist's encounter with a grizzly bear in nearly the same location as my confrontation only a couple of weeks earlier. We all listened in suspense as she told of how the biker had not turned up one evening. The following day, law officers were sent to search for him. About fifty miles back and in about the same area as my grizzly bear visit, they found the biker's motorcycle parked alongside the roadway. The officers shouted out his name without a response. Shortly thereafter, while walking along the road ditch next to the forest, the biker's helmet was discovered lying in the ditch. When the officer stooped to pick up the helmet, the man's severed head was discovered still inside the helmet!

Further investigation determined that a large grizzly had decapitated the man with a single powerful blow from one of its enormous paws and further blood-trail evidence proved that the grizzly bear dragged the body off into the timber. The body has never been recovered, and it was assumed that the grizzly devoured him.

We sat in stunned silence at hearing such a gruesome tale of another biker's demise in nearly the same location as where I'd encountered the mammoth grizzly bear.

I didn't sleep much at all that night even though I was thoroughly exhausted. Between the pain from my injuries and the haunting thoughts of what my grizzly encounter may have become, sleep escaped me.

The following day, I placed a call back home to inform Astrid of just how treacherous my previous day had been. She listened to every detail with grave silence. When I had finished, she asked me to hand the phone over to my friend Maynard. Although I thought it to be an odd request, I called Maynard over and indicated that my wife wanted to speak directly with him.

Maynard grasped the phone and said, "Hello, Astrid. What can I do for you?"

My dear, sweet wife who takes such pride in her quiet and calm demeanor without a moment's hesitation shouted into the phone, "Maynard Moen, if you ever let my husband out of your sight again on one of these biker guy trips to God-only-knows-where, I'm going to find you and tan your hide. From this point forward, I don't want you to let Scott out of your sight even if he goes into the bathroom. Is that understood?"

Maynard responded, "Yes, Astrid, I understand."

*   *   *

Over the eighteen days of our round-trip motorcycle journey to Alaska and back, we experienced countless wonders of our Lord's wilderness creation. We all survived the rigors of the trip and gained the experiences of a lifetime.

For whatever reasons, the Lord challenged me with several tests during a forty-eight-hour period. Through it all I suffered from injury, from pain, from defeat, and from unbridled fear. As the events of those trying hours unfolded, my faith in Christ was tested, and it was battered, yet my prayers were always answered leaving my faith to grow ever stronger.

MOTORCYCLE DEVASTATION—53 YEARS

CHAPTER TWENTY-SIX

For by grace you have been saved through faith,
and this is not your own doing;
it is the gift of God—not the result of works,
so that no one may boast.
For we are what he has made us,
created in Christ Jesus for good works,
which God prepared beforehand to be our way of life.
—EPHESIANS 2:8-10

It is with my deepest humility and faithful reverence to my God which led me to share this narrative. Without doubt, this specific story had such a personal life-changing impact that I was inspired to share an essence of the many saving graces throughout my lifetime within the pages of this book. As I illustrate the events that afflicted me in the next few pages, they have often been described by others as nothing short of miraculous. The saga of my near-death experience following such a catastrophic accident allowed me to bear witness to the wonders of the Lord and of his boundless mercy, grace, and love for his wounded and fallen children.

The subsequent account which I'll share ultimately answered an important question which I've always pondered. Why does the Lord allow my life to continue and does God have some unfulfilled mission for me yet to complete? During my lifetime, I've invested heavy deliberation trying to resolve what God's purpose for me really is. The following recount is a description of what brought me nearer to death than ever before and left me with the firm belief that writing *Nine Lives to Eternity* was one of God's intended plans for me.

I've been granted a God-given blessing enabling me to communicate through written words. Such words of faith have allowed me to fulfill a portion of what I believe is my mission to our Creator. This is my personal witness and testimony to the vast wonders of our Lord.

*   *   *

Motorcycling has been one of my greatest passions as formerly mentioned throughout this book. I can think of few activities in my lifetime that granted me such an exhilarating feeling of freedom. Anyone who has ever ridden a motorbike can attest to the thrill that can be derived by simply twisting the throttle and then surging forward with unbridled power and speed. The unobstructed view while riding a motorcycle is like none other.

For most of my adult life, I've owned and operated a motorcycle of one form or another. While there are countless high-quality motorcycle brands on the open market, my preference has been to own and ride the iconic American-made Harley-Davidson motorcycles. I've always loved throwing a leg over the seat and then settling down into the recesses of the machine, literally becoming one with it. Sometimes comparisons have been made that *one sits on* other brands of motorcycles, but *one sits in* a Harley. That being said, I've always been capable of riding immense distances on my Harley because it is arguably the most comfortable machine that I've ever driven.

I've constantly been able to log many more miles within any twenty-four-hour period of time on my motorcycle than in any other type of car or pickup truck that I've ever operated. For nearly a decade, I've annually logged between fifteen thousand and twenty-five thousand miles per year on a motorcycle. Those kinds of miles may seem implausible to some, but imagine if you will that I reside in the wintery state of Minnesota where the motorcycle riding season is oftentimes only three or four months in duration.

Other bikers that see my motorcycle during any given riding season will often ask whether or not I ever wash my bike. They are usually taken back by what twenty thousand miles of road grime and bug guts adhered to the motorcycle looks like. For the record, I only clean and wash my motorcycle one time each year always at the end of the riding season.

I'd much rather be riding than cleaning, and I've always chuckled how many motorcycle owners seemingly invest more time washing and polishing their machines than actually riding them. In today's modern fad-induced motorcycling cultures, there are countless owners that appear to haul their motorcycles around the country on a trailer more often than actually riding their machines.

Living in Minnesota, I'm often asked how I can log so many miles per year with such a challenging environment. I respond by saying warm clothes and good rain gear is worth their weight in gold. I also note that a fair-weather biker or a weekend warrior biker never logs too many miles. On the other hand, during our short Minnesota riding season, I try to ride my motorcycle every chance I can despite the inclement weather conditions. When I can, I try to ride my motorcycle for work-related activities as well as utilizing it for a couple of extensive motorcycling vacation trips each year.

The foursome biker riding buddies I described in the previous chapter would qualify as hard-core motorcycle enthusiasts by most definitions. Over the years, Maynard Moen, Jeff Moen, Dennis Miller, and I have canvassed America with our motorcycles. Those cherished friends would do most anything and everything for one another. Our Wild Hog group of guys have ridden motorcycles thousands and thousands of miles together covering all fifty states in the USA, all of the road-accessible provinces of Canada, and even ridden our motorized two-wheelers in Mexico. Each year we enjoy a lengthy motorcycle ride together that varies in distance from four thousand miles up to ten thousand miles. Our annual trip together is oftentimes in the beginning of the summer and results in only a fraction of the total miles each of us rides throughout any given biking season.

*   *   *

The annual trip we planned for the summer was intended to be divided into two separate portions. For this year's ride, Jeff was unable to participate so our foursome became a triad. The first portion of the route involved Maynard, Dennis, and I riding our motorcycles all throughout the eastern provinces of Canada as well as riding through the New England states in the northeastern sector of the USA. The second portion of our ride called for Maynard and Dennis to then continue together in tandem on their pathway toward their homes in Minnesota while I branched off to attempt a solo cross-country endurance ride.

During the first portion of our route, we had spectacular weather with only a few challenges. Partway through our journey, we did have to invest some time at a Honda repair shop to replace the flat rear tire on Dennis's motorcycle. I must add that I took immense glee in laying it on pretty thick with poor Dennis about what an irritation it caused that his Honda repairs were delaying our scheduled travels.

Maynard also had a harrowing near miss when he almost hit a deer. I was riding in the very rear of our group with Maynard just in front of me and Dennis leading our group. We were riding along at 10:00 a.m. in the morning and driving at the posted speed of sixty miles per hour when a deer bolted from the thick trees alongside the highway and rushed directly at Maynard's motorcycle. From my observation point, I was spellbound as the deer somehow timed its leap perfectly and literally jumped over the top of Maynard's windshield and then ran away unhindered. At the next pit stop, we dialogued what a close call Maynard had with the deer. If I remember correctly, Maynard indicated that he probably needed to change his underwear as a result of his deer encounter. We all agreed that a direct hit with the deer traveling at such a speed would have resulted in a tragic scene for sure. None of us were aware that it had provided a sinister premonition of things to come.

At last our wanton travels brought us to the state of Connecticut after we'd ridden together in excess of three thousand miles. The time had finally arrived to implement the second portion of our intended route. Maynard, Dennis, and I enjoyed one final evening meal together as we swapped tall tales and played jokes on each other. At last we prepared to check into our motel rooms. We gave each other good-bye hugs since Maynard and Dennis would be departing together on their separate destination and at a different time than my departure the following morning.

As I said my final good-bye to my dear friends on that evening, I had no idea that I might never see either of my biker brothers again.

I started my cross-country motorcycle endurance ride early the following morning. As a certified member of a long-distance motorcycle association, I'd already successfully completed several endurance rides over the years, so I knew my capabilities. Within the ranks of this association are over forty thousand motorcycle enthusiasts that enjoy the personal challenge of riding vast distances on their machines under quantifiable circumstances. Anyone who achieves their certification subsequently earns a bumper sticker that proudly displays they are the toughest bikers on the planet. Anyone of these endurance rides are not a race but, rather, is a ride that can only be sanctioned if safe, legal motorcycle practices are implemented.

The endurance ride certification that I sought called for riding one coastline of America to the opposite coastline. Furthermore, I customized my route to attempt to ride my motorcycle from ocean to ocean within forty-eight hours. It is no stretch of the imagination to understand why it is considered one of the most difficult of all the endurance ride certifications to attain. For this ride, a biker must secure two verifiable witnesses who document the time, the date, the address, and record the motorcycle odometer reading for both the start of the ride and then two additional witnesses must be secured to verify the completion of the ride.

The ride has always been considered an extreme ride because of the demands it places on both the rider and the machine. Since so few have ever successfully completed a certified coastline to coastline ride, I'd been dreaming of attempting the endeavor for years. Although one can choose several different routes, all of which have varied mileages, I chose the longest and most difficult course for my certification attempt.

Doing the extreme ride within the forty-eight-hour itinerary that I decided upon posed an extremely difficult option, but I've always subscribed to the philosophy of "No pain, then no gain." Some would say that the criteria which I established for my ride was pure insanity. The objectives that I set for my ride were to begin the time clock for the ride by pulling a symbolic sample of water from the Atlantic Ocean on the beaches of Connecticut. My chosen route was to then drive through the entire midsection of the nation on Interstate Highway 80 across the entire United States. My intent was to log the more than three thousand mile distance and then complete the ride by drawing a symbolic sample of water from the Pacific Ocean in California.

There was little room for error and for most the task appeared insurmountable. I relished in the challenge since I'm capable of functioning quite well on little if no sleep for days at a time. I'd done the calculations, and the sheer challenge of trying to average sixty-five miles per hour for forty-eight hours straight without a break really got my competitive juices flowing, but the concept put fear into all who knew what I intended to attempt. The key takeaway though is that participants in a ride such as this are not allowed to break the posted speed limits, and their ride is not certified if a citation is issued for breaking the law.

An important motto of the our elite group of long-distance motorcycle riders comes from the quote, "We should never go beyond our mental and physical limitations and that it is better to accept failure so we may live to ride another day."

Before starting this ride, my father had called me and shared, "Scott, you are one of the only people I know that takes delight in doing what any normal person on this planet would consider pure, unadulterated torture."

After getting the signatures from my two starting witnesses, I garnered my cherished sample of Atlantic Ocean seawater and then mounted my big Harley for the endurance ride of my lifetime. Mile after mile and hour after hour, I maneuvered my motorcycle westward through state after state. The endless series of road construction hurdles combined with heavy traffic near the large metropolitan areas kept me frustrated to be sure.

As my certification time clock ticked past the first twenty-four-hour benchmark, I'd logged in excess of fifteen hundred miles without a single incident. I was overjoyed to have ridden through the most densely populated portions of the nation while remaining slightly ahead of schedule. By the halfway point, I was so pumped to reach my target that I felt little if any fatigue even though I'd been operating the motorcycle nonstop for an entire twenty-four-hour time frame without stopping for a rest of any sort.

With each passing mile into the more sparsely populated regions of the western states, my spirits rose as I drew nearer to my goal. By that point, I was ever so slowly getting ahead of schedule since the posted interstate highway speed limits in most of those states was a blistering seventy-five miles per hour. With the miles on my odometer rapidly increasing, I had little doubt that I would become one of only a handful of intense long-distance motorcycle riders to attain the lofty goal of crossing the United States from ocean to ocean within forty-eight hours on a motorcycle.

At 9:00 p.m. on the second night of travel somewhere in the state of Wyoming, I made a call to my wife, Astrid, for the first time during the thirty-six hours that I'd been on the road. I said, "Hi, honey, I can't talk long since I've got to get back on the road. I wanted to let you know that I've logged over two thousand miles thus far, and I'm still on pace to reach my endurance distance target. I just have to drive all night for a second straight night and then I'll call you about 8:00 a.m. from the Golden Gate Bridge in San Francisco, California. Please give Trevor and Travis an update on my progress so they won't worry. I love you, and I'll call you in the morning when I've reached my target."

My wife, Astrid, stirred uneasily in a fitful slumber as the night came and then went. She rose with the morning dawn and impatiently waited for my 8:00 a.m. call. She watched with nervous anticipation as the hands on the clock first moved past the 8:00 a.m. mark and then moved past the 9:00 a.m. mark, and then past the 10:00 a.m. mark and still she waited for the promised call from her fanatical husband. Her intuition and instincts sensed that something was dreadfully wrong, but what? She knew that if I could have, I would have called by 8:00 a.m. no matter if I'd reached my target or not, so why wasn't I calling her?

* * *

I hung up the phone after talking with my wife evermore inspired to accomplish my long-distance motorcycling goal. As I roared out of the truck stop and onto the highway, I felt invincible knowing that I had less than one thousand miles left to reach my final mark. My thoughts drifted to how wonderful it would feel to take off my heavy motorcycle riding boots and socks and then let the warm California beach sand creep amongst my bare toes.

I was still making amazing time as I entered the state of Utah. At about 1:00 a.m., I stopped at a truck stop to fuel up near the Utah and Nevada borders. Throughout my cross-country journey, I'd been intermittently wearing my motorcycle helmet. Prior to my departure, I'd documented which states required motorcycle helmet usage and which ones had no helmet laws. I'm a strong advocate of freedom of choice rights when it comes to motorcycle helmets. I believe that under certain accident circumstances, a helmet may provide some protection, but I also feel that under certain accident circumstances a helmet may in fact cause critical neck injuries or possibly even contribute toward death. The bottom line is that I don't believe that all of our freedoms and rights should be legislated and mandated. Whether you are a motorcycle rider who wears a helmet or one who chooses to ride without a helmet, the simple fact is that most motorcycle crashes can be so horrific that a helmet can only provide minimal protection for saving the life of the biker.

Throughout my cross-country journey, I wore my helmet whenever it was mandated by state law and then I rode without a helmet while in any states that allowed the freedom of choice. Even the most ardent helmet-wearing motorcycle enthusiast would find it difficult to wear a heavy, hot helmet continuously for forty-eight straight hours. At 1:00 a.m., I strapped my helmet onto my head, knowing that I would shortly be entering into the helmet-mandated state of Nevada. In retrospect, I was glad that I chose that moment to wear my helmet.

For the next hour, I traveled in dark isolation at the posted speed limit of seventy-five miles per hour. As I crossed over the border into the desolate stretches of Nevada, I made a mental note of how few vehicles were traveling during that time of the night. The moon remained hidden, so everything around me was ominously black except for the shallow illumination of my headlight piercing into the night. I wondered to myself what the scenery might look like had it been daylight. Dark though it was, I could vaguely detect that I was traveling through a desert area of some kind because of all the large sagebrush thickets encroaching along the four-lane interstate highway.

I looked at the illuminated clock on the dash of my motorcycle and it read 2:00 a.m. I quickly did the calculations in my head and took satisfaction in the fact that I'd logged in excess of twenty-five hundred miles by operating my motorcycle nonstop for an amazing forty hours straight. I let out an immense sigh of satisfaction as I realized that I was still well within my targeted schedule. I was looking forward to covering the remaining five hundred miles within the allotted eight-hour time frame so I could finally bring a close to my endurance test.

The cruise control of my motorcycle was locked in at the posted seventy-five miles per hour. I was the only soul on the highway. Suddenly, my soul was in the grasp of the Lord.

The final memory I have from that night and one which changed my life forever focused upon the collision of my motorcycle with a substantial mule deer that had just darted into my path. I didn't even have time to say a prayer before the carnage began.

*　　*　　*

The Nevada State highway patrol accident report outlined the frightening facts. The large deer had appeared so suddenly in my pathway that I hadn't had time to hit the brakes on the motorcycle.

The cruise control on the obliterated bike was hauntingly still locked in at seventy-five miles per hour. The accident report indicated that the collision with the deer sent the motorcycle and I careening toward the right-hand shoulder and ditch of Interstate Highway 80 at a deadly high rate of speed. Based on the tire tracks lodged into the sand of the ditch, it appeared that I'd fought with the rampant machine trying to direct its course of travel back onto the highway. In my failed attempt to correct the doomed course of travel, the right-side foot peg of the motorcycle struck the thick wooden trunk of a large sagebrush plant. The momentum and mass of the motorcycle cleanly severed the thick bush near its base as though a hot knife slicing though butter. Consequently, the motorcycle flipped end over end a total of three times crashing to a battered stop one hundred and sixty feet out into the sagebrush dense desert. The accident report further described the measurements of each of the three separate and distinct divots left in the sand by the hurling motorcycle. With each horrific flip, the motorcycle left shattered wreckage strewn along the entire pathway of the accident.

It was 2:00 a.m. I was alone, I was unconscious, I was severely injured, I was nearly dead, and my fate lay with God. My fractured body lay alongside the annihilated motorcycle where I'd been catapulted far from the highway into the dark and eerie desert wasteland. No other vehicles had witnessed my accident, and no one traveling along the road would be able to detect my hidden plight. My body and my soul were truly in the hands of the Lord as my fragile fate was yet to be determined.

Four and a half hours later at 6:30 a.m., I was still undiscovered and still unconscious. How much longer could I possibly live with such extensive injuries while lying in such a hostile environment?

Out of nowhere, a stranger bent over my body and with his face only inches from mine shouted, "HEY, ARE YOU ALIVE!"

Perhaps I was already at heaven's gates, but suddenly, I was startled out the deepest recesses of unconsciousness as my eyes opened.

As my eyelids fluttered, the stranger responded with, "My God, you are alive. Can you move?"

At that moment, I had no concept of where I was nor did I have any recall of the collision that had occurred nearly five hours earlier. I found it extremely difficult to utter my words because I'd been lying unconscious for many hours with my mouth open. All throughout the night, mosquitoes by the hundreds crawled inside my mouth and throat inflicting their vampirelike damage.

I nearly choked as I spit out a dozen bloodsucking insects from inside my mouth. With my mind in a deep fog and while suffering from a swollen tongue and throat, I croaked, "Where am I?"

The stranger replied with a questioning look on his face, "You are lying in a desert in Nevada."

"Why?" I replied.

The man in disbelief said, "Heck, I don't know why you are in Nevada, but you've had a terrible motorcycle accident. Hundreds of other vehicles have been driving past this very location as we speak, but something compelled me to stop."

In my battered state, it was difficult for me to comprehend anything the stranger was sharing as I listened in silence.

The man continued by saying, "I was driving along with the flow of traffic at seventy-five miles per hour, I somehow detected a single-wheel track running off the interstate highway at an odd angle heading out into the desert. It seemed strange, so I stopped my vehicle on the shoulder of the highway and then backed up to the errant track in the sand. I can't explain it, but I was somehow compelled to follow the track. Before long, I spotted broken wreckage from your motorcycle scattered all the way out to this spot. To be honest, I can't imagine how you could have survived such a horrendous crash because there sure isn't much left of your motorcycle."

He asked me once more if I could get up. I was instantly all too aware of how badly I was injured as I made a failed attempt to roll onto my left side. My attempts to roll onto my right side and then to try to sit up were also met with dismal failure. The pain coursing throughout my entire body was beyond words as I became gravely concerned by my inability to move.

I dejectedly looked back into the stranger's eyes and said, "I don't know what is wrong with me, but I can't move or sit up. I don't think I'm paralyzed because I can move my feet and wiggle my toes, but the pain from trying to move is unbearable."

The man turned and quickly departed. As he left, he shouted back at me, "I'll get help . . ."

Before I heard the rest of his comment, I mercifully lapsed back into deep unconsciousness again.

Thump, thump, thump, thump, thump was the deafening sound emitted from the emergency medical air evacuation helicopter as it prepared to make an emergency landing on Nevada Interstate Highway

80. Unbeknown to me, state highway patrol officers had shut down the flow of traffic on the major highway thoroughfare, enabling the rescue helicopter and its emergency medical team to come to my aid.

I was unaware of how long I'd been unconscious as I drew ever closer to death, but the earsplitting reverberations of the spinning helicopter blades shocked me back into consciousness for a second time. The truth is that somewhere deep in the recesses of my mind, I could hear a strange and distant thunder as the helicopter prepared to land, but as I reopened my glazed eyes, I once again had no concept of where I was or why I was laying in such pain amongst the sagebrush on the floor of a desert.

Within moments from the time that I detected the booming sound of the helicopter, almost instantly there were four emergency medical technicians working in unison to stabilize me and attempt to save my life. I have the foggiest recall of one technician readying a stretcher to transport me. A second technician used a large scissors to first cut the strap on my helmet, and then carefully remove it. The technician made note of the excessive gouges and scratches on the helmet, realizing that for this accident, it had performed its duty admirably. Next, he used his shears to cut through the sleeves and the front side of my thick leather motorcycle riding jacket, and then he continued to cut through and remove all of my clothing, leaving me only in my underwear. A third technician worked feverishly to carefully place head and neck restraints on me in an attempt to prevent possible paralysis. The fourth technician inserted an IV needle deep into one of my veins and began administering some form of fluids and medication.

The last words I heard before everything went totally black again came from the technician just as he finished cutting through the front of my leather jacket. With grave concern, he said to the IV technician, "Oh boy, this guy has ripped his arm and left shoulder completely out of the shoulder socket, and his dislocated appendage is dangling across the top of his chest."

I don't know if the shock of those words sent my mind back into the abyss or perhaps the IV technician injected a sedative into my vein to ensure that I wouldn't have to deal with any more pain for a few hours.

7:00 a.m. The helicopter lifts off with a critically injured patient in route for the Elko Nevada Regional Medical Care Unit located twenty-five miles away and located east of the city of Reno. The hundreds of backed-up vehicles on the blocked interstate highway resume their travels once more wondering what poor soul required such an extreme medical air evacuation.

10:00 a.m. Astrid received a most terrifying call from the intensive care unit of the Elko hospital.

The nurse stated, "Hello, I'm calling from the ICU at our hospital in Elko, Nevada. Are you Scott Gottschalk's wife?"

With bated breath, Astrid replied, "Yes, I am, please don't tell me that my husband is dead!"

The nurse said, "I'm sorry to inform you that sometime during the middle of the night, your husband suffered a terrible motorcycle collision with a deer. Unfortunately, he wasn't discovered or air-evacuated from the scene of the accident for nearly five hours, so his medical condition is very unstable at the moment. He arrived by helicopter to our emergency care facility and currently he is having emergency surgery in the operating room. We have him currently listed in critical condition."

Astrid was so stunned that she could barely speak. She had wondered and waited for more than two hours for the promised call from her husband once he'd reached the shores of the Pacific Ocean, but rather, she bore the shattering news of her mate's demise.

Astrid asked, "Do you know what happened and what his injuries are?"

The nurse replied, "I'm sorry, but I don't know any of the details of the accident, however, I can tell you that he has been sedated since being airlifted to our facility. As soon as he arrived, we completed a CAT scan trying to determine if he had brain damage, then an MRI was performed on his badly damaged left shoulder injury, and finally, we completed nearly fifty x-rays of his body. Finding all of his fractures was almost as though looking for a needle in a haystack, but so far, we've determined that your spouse has fractured at least twelve or possibly thirteen bones including fracturing his back in three separate locations."

Astrid felt her knees weaken and the color drain from her face as the atrocious commentary registered in her mind. She remained in stunned silence as the nurse promised to contact her with more information as updated details became available.

11:00 a.m. My eyes slowly opened with my mind dulled from a deeper mental fog than I could ever remember. I was unaware that I was regaining consciousness following my major emergency surgery. The total elapsed time from the moment of impact at 2:00 a.m. until 11:00 a.m. was an astonishing duration of nine hours. Except for two brief moments of semiconsciousness at the accident scene, I'd been unconscious for an extremely long time. But I was alive!

As the haze began to clear from my mind, the doctor assigned to my case strolled into the surgical recovery room and leaned toward my face.

He spoke softly and said, "Mr. Gottschalk, I'm the doctor who has been working to save your life for the past several hours. I just want to mention that you are perhaps one of the most fortunate motorcycle accident victims anyone in this emergency medical facility has ever witnessed. I can assure you that we are never required to work on a biker who has crashed at seventy-five miles per hour because their limp bodies are always transported immediately to the morgue."

As I stared deeply into the caregiver's eyes, I whispered, "Thank you, Doc, for helping me." I then glanced upward toward the ceiling and silently prayed, "Lord, thank you once again for allowing me to escape the icy grip of death."

The doctor went on to describe my medical condition. He indicated that it was simply a miracle that I'd somehow survived so much physical trauma. The medial team had been amazed by the results of my CAT scan. They had expected to find massive brain damage including hemorrhaging and swelling of my brain, yet the results proved negative. In addition to running a CAT scan, more than fifty x-rays of my entire body were reviewed as they tried to determine the severity of my bone fractures. Lastly, the caregivers had completed an MRI on my shoulder.

The doctor continued his summary by telling me that I was presently in the surgical recovery room, following the first of my many subsequent surgical procedures. The surgery had involved putting my dislocated left shoulder and arm back into the proper alignment. I swallowed hard as he graphically continued to describe the internal havoc that I had invoked upon my body from the previous night of terror.

The list of my bone fractures was extensive. I had three broken vertebrae in my back. The right side of my rib cage was nearly collapsed. On impact, I'd fractured every one of the frontal ribs on that side of my body plus I broke three of those same ribs in a different place on the backside of my rib cage. My right-side collarbone was shattered in several places, plus my right shoulder was partially dislocated and had suffered torn cartilage. I also had fractured my left leg. Furthermore, I broke the finger joints of my left thumb and forefinger. Lastly, I broke one of the main molars of my teeth.

The doctor said that further x-rays would probably discover more fractures and injuries. He was especially concerned about three of my scores of injuries. The doctor shared that I would need several future surgeries. He went on to describe how badly the motorcycle accident had destroyed my left shoulder. During the impact, my left arm and shoulder socket had been dislodged. An extensive surgery would be required to not only rebuild my shoulder joint, but I'd severed all four of my rotator-cuff tendons and dislocated my bicep tendon, leaving my entire left arm virtually paralyzed. The doctor further explained that my multiple-fractured collarbone would likely require surgical plates and pins to mend it. Lastly, he described his frightening prognosis of the multiple fractures in my back. The doctor was quite positive that I would require back surgery to fuse my damaged vertebrae together.

As the doctor paused, I contemplated my future. I thought to myself that perhaps it would have been better to die out in the desert rather than suffer from so many life-altering injuries.

The doctor spoke once again, saying, "I know that your pain must be unbearable, but you should be happy to have survived. It is important though, that you prepare yourself for the consequences of life after your accident. I'm going to predict that you will eventually recover, but you need to prepare yourself to accept that your life will never be the same again. Following your many surgeries, you'll likely have limited spinal mobility, limited arm mobility, and you'll likely walk with a limp for the rest of your future. I know this is may be hard for you to handle right now, but you'll likely suffer from chronic pain and may require pain medications for the rest of your life."

The doctor left my side after mentioning that he would check back on me after I'd been relocated to my own hospital room. I silently thought to myself, I've heard pessimistic predictions from doctors in the past. Although I likened my doctor's description as proclaiming that my glass was half empty, I made up my mind that my glass was instead half full. Even so, one had to wonder if what I had done to myself would be worth the price I would have to pay.

Once the doctor had left my sight, I instantaneously began weighing my options. There were two distinct choices. I could succumb to the belief of only negative outcomes waiting in my future and then fall into a deeply depressed state of self-pity, or I could fight for everything within my power to recover. I chose the latter since I've always believed that one of my greatest strengths lies in my positive attitude and intensity to attain the goals I've established for myself.

It was settled then; I promised myself that I would overcome my difficulties and would eventually take delight in proving the fact that my medical prognosis was far too gloomy for someone such as me.

By the time that I was relocated to my own hospital room, my mind was fixed on how to beat the odds of such a crippling motorcycle accident that nearly cost me my life. Before long, the doctor was once more stationed alongside my hospital bed. The time had arrived for me to influence my own medical outcome.

As the doctor reviewed my medical charts, I began our dialogue by asking, "Doc, how long would you speculate that I'll have to remain in your hospital?"

The doctor looked up from the chart and responded, "Well, I'm going to predict that you will be here for at least three or four weeks. Your shoulder joint surgery that we just completed will be all that we can schedule for you this week. Next week, we will schedule the surgical procedure on your broken back and then in the remaining couple of weeks I predict we will complete your collarbone and leg surgeries."

With stone-cold seriousness, I said, "Doc, I don't mean you any disrespect, and I sincerely appreciate the life-saving tactics that you and your staff provided me. I'm telling you, that there is simply no way that I'm going to spend the next month lying in a Nevada hospital bed, which is one thousand five hundred miles away from my home back in Minnesota. I'll be honest with you when I say that I'm very concerned about breaking my back in three locations. I'm not concerned about any of my other extensive bone fractures, but I am perplexed about my back injuries."

The doctor stared at me in wonder and shared, "You should be extremely concerned about all of your injuries but particularly your spinal fractures."

I replied, "What I want to know, Doc, is what if I were to have my youngest son Travis drive throughout the day and night in order to arrive at this hospital room by tomorrow morning, will I risk paralysis if I get out of this bed and then travel back to Minnesota in my son's car?"

The doctor's face turned a shade of crimson. He was incensed as he retorted, "You must still be delirious. You don't seem to grasp the severity of your injuries. I can assure you that there will be no way that you will be physically able to get out of your hospital bed for at least one or two weeks. Even if you could, the only way to transport you back to a Minnesota hospital care unit would be by using a long-distance ambulatory carrier capable of meeting your medical needs during such an extensive trip."

I redirected my question again and asked, "You didn't answer my question about paralysis if I get out of this bed tomorrow."

The doctor was unable to mask his frustration with my perseverance.

He sternly commented, "All right, theoretically, if you could somehow miraculously get out of this bed tomorrow, it's not probable that you will paralyze yourself. As a result of your accident, you crushed three vertebrae in your spine, so you'll endure pain like you've never experienced, but since you fortunately did not severe your spinal cord, you will not likely suffer paralysis. What you can't seem to comprehend is that you viciously impacted your body with a blunt-force trauma similar to smashing yourself into a solid brick wall while traveling at a blistering speed of seventy-five miles per hour. You can dream all you desire, but I can assure you that by tomorrow morning when you think you want to leave our hospital, the front of your entire body will be bruised nearly the color of black all the way from your head down to your toes. You might think you'll have the fortitude to get up and leave our hospital, but it simply isn't going to be possible."

I responded with, "Doc, I'm not going to argue with you because if you can't make me stay, then I want you to give me a signed medical release so I can go home tomorrow."

The doctor stormed out of my room snapping back with, "Oh, I'll give you your medical release all right, but you'll discover tomorrow the reason why you won't be going anywhere. It will be unfortunate that your son will have to drive all this way, only to find out that you are bedridden!"

As the doctor left, my nurse sheepishly entered the room. I could tell that she wasn't use to a patient causing such a stir. Since both of my damaged arms were immobilized by arm slings and then strapped tightly to my chest, I asked the nurse for her help in making a phone call to my wife. The thoughtful nurse entered the phone number and then held the phone to my ear. After only one ring on the other end, my wife picked up the phone in a panic. I could hear her mixed sobs of happiness and relief as I shared all the details. At the conclusion of our conversation my loving wife prepared to implement the logistics for an escape from my Nevada hospital incarceration the next morning.

My son Travis and his wife RaeLynn unselfishly drove throughout the entire night allowing them to arrive at the Nevada hospital by 10:00 a.m. the day after my accident. The time was almost exactly twenty-four hours from when my doctor had stomped out of my room in anger. On my bedside stand lay the signed medical release from the disgruntled doctor, granting me permission to depart from their care facility, along with my signed statement agreeing to release the hospital and its staff from any further responsibility or liability due my personal decision for a premature departure from emergency medical care.

The joy I felt watching my son and his wife enter my hospital room was indescribable. Though severely injured, my spirits elevated the instant they arrived. I was somewhat taken back, however, because following closely behind Travis and RaeLynn were my entire medical team consisting of two doctors and four nurses. As all six of them lined up along the far wall of my room, it suddenly dawned on me that my caregiver audience was there to witness my failed attempt at leaving their hospital.

I caught Travis's eye and then motioned for him to step alongside the opposite side of my bed. He did as instructed and then I motioned that he place his ear next to my mouth.

With my son's ear close to my lips, I gently whispered, "Travis, I'm hurt real bad, but I need to get out of this hospital and go back home to Minnesota with you and RaeLynn. As you can see, the doctors and nurses don't believe I can do this, but I'm going to prove them wrong. This won't be easy since I have a broken back, broken ribs, a broken collarbone, a broken leg, and both my arms are immobilized, so I'll need you to help sit me up in this bed, Travis."

Travis straightened up and gave me a questioning look, and then he bent over placing his lips alongside my ear and whispered, "Dad, you are broken everywhere on your body. Where exactly am I supposed to grab you in order to help you up and out of this bed without damaging you further?"

Once more I motioned Travis to bring his ear toward my mouth as I whispered, "I want you to use your hand to grab the backside of my head. I'm going to count to three, and then I'm going to grit my teeth as you thrust me up into a sitting position. Whatever you do though, please don't let go of my head. I'm guessing the intense pain will probably cause me to pass out for a brief moment."

Such an absurd request to anyone other than a member of my family would have been considered sheer lunacy, but for Travis, it seemed a perfectly normal intention coming from me.

Travis readied himself, and at the count of three, I braced for the onslaught of pain. Just as I was propelled into the sitting position, the pain became so intense that the room began spinning, and I was blinded by a bright white light as I lost consciousness momentarily. As promised, Travis held tightly onto the back of my head as my body went limp. It took a few unsettled moments, but my vision cleared and the pain dulled. Travis gingerly helped me to the edge of the bed just as an absurd thought crossed my mind.

With all the force I could muster, I shouted in the direction of the medical staff saying, "I've got a dozen broken bones including and a broken leg. Would someone please be kind enough to get me a wheelchair, or would you prefer that my son drags me out of this hospital?"

I'd scored one small victory, but my long battle to recover was only beginning.

Travis and RaeLynn helped me into the wheelchair and then pushed me out of the hospital emergency room entrance. With great difficulty, my loved ones helped me out of the wheelchair and then lowered me down into the front seat of their compact Volkswagen car.

We were about to embark on a fifteen-hundred-mile journey that would require me to endure twenty-eight straight hours of nearly unbearable discomfort and pain, but at least I'd be home with my loved ones. Travis had no sooner maneuvered his little car away from the hospital when I shared some unsettling information with him. Just prior to leaving the hospital, one of my nurses had discussed some sensitive medical advice with me so I passed it on to my son.

I said, "Travis, one of my nurses mentioned that I would have to be very careful with my digestive system. She said it was concerning that I'd gone nearly forty-eight hours without food or drink and then went through a surgical process. She indicated to me that if I didn't find a way to avoid becoming constipated, I would suffer a great deal. Evidently, because I've broken so many bones in my upper torso, she felt that I'd be in too great a pain struggling with a difficult bowel movement."

Travis looked at me and said, "Wow, that was more information than I really needed right now."

I said, "I'm sorry, but she mentioned that I needed to instruct you to stop somewhere along our travels in order to buy me some industrial strength laxatives so I can avoid any problems. You don't have to stop and buy me some laxatives though until we need to stop for fuel somewhere down the road."

Suddenly another daunting thought crossed my mind as I turned toward Travis and said, "Oh no, I just thought of something. With my extensive arm injuries, I can't even move my arms or hands. I'm not too high on this idea, but when I'm afraid that whenever I do need to use the toilet, you are going to have to wipe my rear end, Travis!"

I'll never forget what happened next. We were cascading down the highway at the posted speed of seventy-five miles per hour when suddenly my son jerked the steering wheel of his car hard to right in an effort to take the final off-ramp exit before departing the city. I distinctly remember that instant as I cried out in pain by the car's erratic motion jarring my damaged body. In an apparent panic, Travis rapidly maneuvered the car into the parking lot of a large retail outlet store. With a stern look on his face and without speaking a word, he slammed on the brakes bringing the car to a stop near the entrance.

As my son bolted from the car, I shouted, "Travis, I told you that it wasn't necessary to buy my laxatives until the next fuel stop."

I looked toward RaeLynn and said, "Why is he acting so irrational?"

After only a short wait, Travis returned carrying a large box that he hoisted into the back end of his car. Without saying a word and with a deep frown on his forehead, he took control of his car and once again guided the car back onto the highway.

Finally, I said, "What on earth are you so upset about, and what is in the large box that you just purchased in that store? That doesn't look like a box of laxatives to me."

While sternly hunching over his steering wheel, my son replied, "I got your dumb laxatives, but I also bought a large case of rubber gloves because there is no way I'm going to wipe your butt with my bare hands!"

With all my substantial injuries and even though my broken ribs made the act of moving, breathing, coughing, sneezing, or laughing an unbearable experience, I still broke out in laughter.

With both tears of joy and tears of pain running down my cheeks, I said to Travis, "You've got to be kidding me. When you were a baby, I changed your diapers and wiped your backside over and over again. I would think that my son would at least be willing to return the favor to help his old man out in a time of need."

The frown never left Travis's brow as he commented, "Say anything that you want, but I'm still not going to touch your butt with my hands."

✳   ✳   ✳

It took twenty-eight hours of nonstop driving to bring me one thousand five hundred miles back to my home. By having my son transport me, the total cost was around two hundred dollars for fuel and food. Had I been transported by ambulance the same distance, the tally would have surpassed fifty thousand dollars.

Shortly after arriving back at my home, we received the first of countless medical bills, which invariably left my wife and me in a state of sticker shock. The first invoice we received was to pay for my emergency helicopter rescue. The costs allocated an astounding one thousand dollar per minute fee for each minute I was in was airborne inside the helicopter. From the moment that I was loaded onto the helicopter until it flew twenty-five miles to the emergency hospital until I was removed totaled a mere sixteen minutes. The resulting invoice identified that we were to pay sixteen thousand dollars!

For the next several months following my accident, I went through an array of five surgical procedures. In all, I required one CAT scan, three MRI scans, and in excess of one hundred and fifty x-rays. Following each surgery, I endured a daily regimen of new and evermore painful physical therapy that would have made even the toughest individual cringe in pain. The total medical expense for my care tallied more than one hundred and fifty thousand dollars. With each breath I continue to take, I'm in awe of the wonders of modern medicine's abilities to heal the wounded or save the dying, but medical miracles do not come without cost.

For months, I worked with several different teams of medical specialists. Those surgeons performed surgeries on each of my two shoulders, on my back, and on my leg. Each of four different doctors predicted that I would recover from my extensive injuries and continue to live a life with some semblance of normalcy. Each doctor, however, predicted that I would never ride a motorcycle ever again. The doctors based those predictions on sound medical knowledge since both of my shoulder joints were extremely damaged and the multiple fractures of my back would make future motorcycling impossible.

One day following the second of my three overall shoulder surgeries, I asked my doctor what it would take for me to ride a motorcycle again. He was taken aback by my request since most motorcycle crash victims are simply joyous to be alive and seldom ever attempt ride again.

I said, "Doc, riding a motorcycle is one of my most cherished life activities and you've got to tell me what it will take to ride again."

My doctor replied, "Scott, your left shoulder joint has been so badly destroyed that I'm going to predict you'll only ever regain 40 percent of your arm motion. You simply won't be able to raise your arms high enough to grasp the handlebars of a motorcycle. Regarding your broken back, you are destined for a lifetime of chronic back pain from your injuries, so riding a motorcycle is simply out of the question."

I retorted, "Doc, I'm going to ride again, so what will it require of me?"

The doctor spelled out a physical therapy regime that appeared impossible. He instructed me to meet with a professional therapist named Dan Ness who would help me understand my daunting task to fully recover.

The first time I met Dan, my assigned physical therapist, I was taken aback by his sheer size. Dan was a big man who had played college football years earlier.

His first words to me as he read my medical charts were "Interesting. Your charts indicate that you have a high pain tolerance. Is that true?"

I responded, "Well, throughout all of my recent injuries and following all of past and present surgeries, I've never taken any form of pain medication. I can also tell you that I've never used Novocain whenever a dentist has drilled my teeth, so yes, I do have a high pain tolerance."

Dan narrowed his eyes and smugly commented, "I've had tough guys like you give similar responses, but they are usually the first ones to cry like a baby when I start breaking down their scar tissue or forcing their frozen joints back into motion. Hop up on this table, and let's see just how much pain tolerance you can endure," he said with an evil smirk on his face.

As I lay down on the table, I retorted, "Knock yourself out because you are never going to get me to cry out, and I'm never going to beg you to stop inflicting your sadistic pain on me. I know what it will take to fully recover, and I intend on staying the course."

As Dan and I worked together over the course of many months, he and I became good friends with a high level of respect for each other. With each passing week, my recovery rate was far in excess of the vast majority of patients. Both Dan and my doctors were spellbound by my commitment and work ethic to recover. They were amazed that I was willing to rise each day at 4:00 a.m. and then put myself through two hours of painful physical therapy. I endured this each and every day for nine long months. During each session, I would twist and pull and lift and stretch every injured portion of my body. I had to do back physical therapy, I had to do left and right shoulder physical therapy, I had to do left leg physical therapy, and I had to do strength and mobility exercises until the sweat poured from my body and until the self-inflicted pain became almost unbearable to endure.

As I met with Dan and my doctors for one final time nine long months after my life-threatening accident, they said, "Scott, you have been one of the most amazing patients that we've ever encountered. Seldom have we had a patient with so much drive and determination to overcome their injuries. You have nearly fully recovered, and you somehow found a way to beat all the odds."

I sincerely thanked them for all of their contributions toward my recovery. I shook Dan's hand and then with a devious smile, I said, "You never could get me to cry out or beg you to stop, could you? I'm sure though that would have given you immense joy."

Before departing from my doctor's examination room, I asked, "Doc, am I now cleared to ride a motorcycle again since springtime has arrived and a new riding season is upon us?"

My doctor said, "I thought it impossible when we first started your medical care, but unbelievably, you have regained nearly all of your joint mobility and rebuilt all of your atrophied muscles. If you must, start riding that a motorcycle again, but try to stay in one piece, will you?"

*   *   *

On that very next spring following the year of my accident, I bought another Harley-Davidson motorcycle to replace the one that had been destroyed in the accident. During that riding season, I logged in excess of twenty-five thousand miles upon my new motorbike and then I took great pride by informing all of my "naysayer" doctors and friends. I'd done the impossible and was free to enjoy my life once more. At present,

I'm fully recovered with no lasting effects from my near-death experience. Miraculously, I have no back pain nor do I suffer from any other painful aftermath as a result of my injuries. Whenever anyone becomes aware of my story of victory, they are amazed that I lack any outward signs of injury or that I'm not wrought by chronic pain. The only physical indicators of my brush with death are the countless surgical scars that are riddled across my body. What a small price to pay for the wonders of modern medicine.

*   *   *

It may seem that my story had reached a conclusion. It appeared that I'd mostly benefited from nothing more than a man-made victory over death. But I've saved how the Lord's influence helped me conquer death until the very last of this account. Here is the rest of the chronicle as it played out.

A few weeks following my critical accident, I received an accident report in the mail from the Nevada State highway patrol. The report included photos of the accident scene and outlined in graphic detail just how close I'd come to the brink of death. The documentation showed each deep divot in the sand made by my motorcycle as it flipped end for end for distance of one hundred and sixty feet. The report detailed how during the initial frontward flip, the headlights of my motorcycle were subsequently discovered driven deep into the sand after being sheared off. During the tumultuous ride as I held on for my very life, the back end of the motorcycle forcefully smashed into my spine time and again. With each revolution, the lethal machine left a telltale mark across my back while fracturing my vertebrae in three locations. Nearly every detail of the accident was vividly described, yet nowhere could I locate the mention of the man who initially discovered me and in the end helped save my life.

Without haste, I made a phone call to the Nevada State highway patrol office. I asked for the name and a phone number of the man who'd found me so that I might contact him and properly thank him. I was informed that there was no record of anyone finding me.

I asked, "For the brief moment that I regained consciousness while lying out in that desert, a stranger came to my aid. Are you saying that no one was at the scene of the accident when emergency help arrived?"

The officer on the other end of the phone said, "No, there was no one other than the medical crew and patrol officers present at the scene of your accident. I would suggest that you contact the Nevada 911 emergency network to determine who called in your accident."

Without haste, I called the Nevada 911 and inquired, "My name is Scott Gottschalk and on June 30, 2009, I had a near-fatal motorcycle accident while traveling through Nevada. Sometime around 6:30 a.m. on that day, I was aroused from a state of unconsciousness by a stranger. My vision was unclear, so I can't identify much about the stranger, but I know someone came to my aid. I'm calling you so I can find out the name and phone number of that stranger, and then I can properly thank him for helping to save my life. Unfortunately, the official accident report doesn't include any information about the stranger, so it was suggested that I call you."

The response shocked me when the 911 operator said, "We can't provide you with that information because on that morning our 911 dispatch received an abrupt call lasting only a few seconds."

The 911 operator went on to say that the only recorded 911 messages on record say, "Critical motorcycle accident at I-80, mile marker 324, send help." With that, the caller immediately disconnected the phone.

The operator's tone firmed while saying, "That caller instantly hanging up was improper protocol. No one is supposed to hang up on a 911 emergency call until we release them, for the very reason that we want to identify the caller, get specifics of the emergency, and so on. All we can tell you is that, yes, someone left a brief message, but we have no documentation of who it was or how you could go about contacting them."

As I hung up the phone, I struggled with what I'd heard. How was it possible that a stranger had stopped along a busy highway, and then took the time to find me, awaken me, call in for emergency assistance, only to disappear without record? After all of that, one would think the stranger would have at least invested enough time to ensure my rescue. I've continually been at odds with this anomalous outcome. Why did the stranger appear, then disappear without a clue?

I've asked myself, "Perhaps he simply didn't want to get involved, except he was already involved by helping to save my life. Perhaps he was in fear of possible legal retribution from my possible paralysis after he asked me to attempt to move or get up from my prone position. Possibly the stranger was carrying something illegal in his vehicle, and he didn't want to be discovered. Perchance the stranger was simply late for work and left believing he had already done the work of a *good Samaritan*."

I have another theory that has forevermore instilled in me a belief in guardian angels. Hardly a day goes by since my tragic accident that I don't think about the moment the stranger startled me back from the brink of death. With each passing day, I more firmly believe that the stranger may not have been a real person at all.

Was the stranger even a man at all or was he an angel sent from God who startled me back into life by shouting, "Hey, are you alive?!"

With each passing year of my life, my faith continues to build. I've had far too many unexplainable circumstances to discount divine intervention. On that fateful day, I should never have survived, yet I did. I should never have fully recovered from my extensive injuries, but I have. I want to tell all who read these words that I've witnessed angels, and I've felt the loving hand of the Lord nudging me onward in life.

This is my witness and testimony. I believe in angels.

Do you believe?

PUSHING THE LIMITS—54 YEARS

CHAPTER TWENTY-SEVEN

And one called to another and said:
"Holy, holy, holy is the Lord of hosts;
The whole earth is full of his glory."
—ISAIAH 6:3

The previous chapter outlined my personal triumph over certain death. The will to survive had motivated my behavior to conquer permanent disablement and then continue living my life with intensity as never before. Through an astonishing dedication and commitment, and by never losing faith, I attained a full recovery enabling me to beat all the odds. During the course of my recuperation, I demonstrated to all the doubters that almost any physical limitation can be overcome through the power of positive thinking, a dedicated work ethic, and a belief in the power of prayer. Inexplicable miracles surface all the time.

*   *   *

As the new motorcycle riding season arrived exactly one year removed from the date of my near demise, I had made all the physical, the mental, and the mechanical preparations to ride a motorcycle once more. There was little doubt that I'd been given yet another chance to participate in the many experiences and pleasures that life can offer.

Prior to beginning a renewed motorcycle-riding season, I contemplated the numerous guardian angels that had mystically aided me during my times of trouble. In a somewhat humorous tribute to those angels, which I sincerely believe were sent to me by God, I bought and then permanently installed a tiny symbolic "guardian angel" bell underneath the frame of my motorcycle. Once in place, this bell continuously tolls while the motorcycle is in operation.

Motorcycle legend has it that a small bell attached to one's motorcycle, positioned close to the ground, catches the "evil road spirits." The little demons living on one's motorcycle cause all kinds of mechanical problems and life-threatening mayhem. The cavity of the bell attracts these evil spirits, but the constant ringing drives them insane, whereby they lose their grip, and then fall to the ground. In turn, their fall onto the roadway is a major cause of potholes developing in the road.

Okay, perhaps the legend is a bit far-fetched but, from my perspective, having one of those legendary "guardian angel" bells in place during any future motorcycle rides couldn't hurt.

*   *   *

My wife, Astrid, and I departed on our first motorcycle trip together since the events of my previous year's dreadful accident. The chosen route had a very special significance because we were traveling one thousand five hundred miles all the way back to the scene of my accident. I was drawn to return to the spot that nearly killed me so that I could put some closure on the matter.

After a few days ride while covering fifteen hundred miles, we slowed as we reached the infamous mile marker 324 on Nevada Interstate Highway 80. I brought the motorcycle to a halt, and we walked with trepidation toward the sandy shoulder of the highway. We both looked toward the ground in disbelief as we discovered that the deep tracks from my motorcycle accident were still embedded into the sand an entire year later. A chill went up my spine as we followed the trail leading out into the desert.

Along our trek, we detected the severed sage brush that had initiated my motorcycle and I to flip end for end for a distance of one hundred and sixty feet. It was spooky to be able to observe and sense the carnage that had occurred one year earlier.

I held Astrid's hand tightly within mine. Unable to contain her tears and her emotions, she cried, "Why weren't you taken from me? Looking at this rough terrain and seeing the path you took after hitting that deer with your motorcycle, I don't see how it would be possible for anyone to survive."

With my own outpour of emotions, I replied, "Only the Lord could have protected me that night, and I need to make my own private peace with him. Could you please walk back out to the highway and leave me alone for a moment?"

Once Astrid had turned and walked away, I dropped down to my knees in the exact spot where I nearly lost my life. I offered up a prayer of gratitude for my continued gift of life.

One year earlier, I had attempted to ride a motorcycle over three thousand miles by riding nonstop for forty-eight hours. The crash with a deer had stopped me in my tracks, nearly ending my life. With a sense of renewal, Astrid and I departed for the Pacific Ocean to complete the long-distance endurance motorcycle ride that had escaped me. I covered the remaining five hundred miles, and with great pride, I drew the sample of seawater that had eluded my previous year's endurance ride.

Due to factors beyond my control, I'd failed to complete my coastline to coastline ride within the allotted forty-eight hours. Although it took me nearly one year and a near-death experience, I had finally completed my objective.

During our motorcycle vacation, my wife and I canvassed much of the beautiful western states. We safely covered four thousand five hundred miles by the conclusion. My confidence grew as I made the final plans for another "extreme" long-distance motorcycle journey.

*   *   *

On that same summer from July 2 through July 11, I had a most unique and amazing opportunity to travel the highways and byways around our entire great nation. I choose to attempt what few motorcyclists have ever attempted.

As I've indicated previously, in my opinion, motorcycling has been and always will be the ultimate expression of personal freedom. As a biker, one is unrestricted albeit braving the elements, with nothing but an unhindered view from all directions. There is no comparison versus how restricted the view is from inside an automobile as opposed to the glorious sights to behold from the seat of a motorbike cruising down the road with the wind in your face. It has been said that motorcyclists are the only people on earth that fully appreciate why a dog sticks its head out the window of a vehicle while traveling at high speeds down the open road and then reflects an expression of pure joy upon its face.

As previously indicated, I'm a certified member of a long-distance motorcycle association which consists of forty thousand long-distance endurance motorcycle riders from across the nation. This group endorses the belief that they are the toughest bikers on the planet for obvious reasons. Over the years, I've certified several endurance rides. Not only are the rides challenging, but the exorbitant documentation required to get one's ride qualified is a massive task in itself.

These certified rides are not races but rather endorse long-distance endurance motorcycle riding. While the distances traveled by motorcycle for some of the rides seem an impossible task, I assure you that certain riders such as me simply enjoy the challenge of seeking out and achieving their long-distance riding goals. Such rides stress safe, legal riding; however, the miles and the hours can be excessively long to be sure. Each certified long-distance ride requires two witnesses at the start and two witnesses at the end of a specific ride to document odometer readings, time, date, location, etc. Along the way, each credit card fuel receipt becomes a combined time card, odometer recording document, fuel consumption monitor, and speed monitoring benchmark for distances traveled between fuel stops.

To become a qualified member of the association, a motorcyclist must successfully complete an initial one thousand mile ride in under twenty-four hours. All forty thousand association members have certified at least this specific ride, however, only a fraction of the overall membership ever chooses to do another ride or anything remotely more difficult than one thousand miles within twenty-four hours. If a novice motorcycle long-distance rider endures such a ride, then they are at liberty to select other rides in which to certify. The next-level rides also increase in difficulty and endurance. The first next-level ride is a one-thousand-five-hundred-mile ride which must be completed in less than thirty-six hours.

If desired to move on to even more challenging rides, one then enters into another world of difficulty categorized as *extreme* rides. The first extreme ride requires that a biker must ride at least one thousand five hundred miles in less than twenty-four hours. If one does the math, it then means that a motorcyclist must average well over sixty miles per hour for twenty-four hours straight while still fitting in fuel stops, bathroom breaks, and taking in some nourishment and fluids. Once one enters into the realm of extreme riding, extended sleep is not an option. This may seem dangerous, but some folks, me included, do very well on minimal sleep; however, the rules make it very clear that it is far better to stop and rest and simply not qualify your ride rather than to ride unsafe and tired and then perhaps die trying to earn a cheap certificate to hang on the wall.

Next-level ever more difficult rides requires starting in Canada, crossing through the border control, traveling over one thousand five hundred miles all the way through the USA, and then crossing into Mexico in under twenty-four hours. This is a ride that many attempt, but only a fraction are ever able to achieve because of the tight time restrictions required to achieve the goals of the ride and potential border-crossing delays.

Perhaps the most challenging endurance ride of all time is the coastline to coastline ride. This is the specific ride in which I hit a deer in Nevada, resulting in a horrific crash, which left me with twelve fractured bones including breaking my back in three places. Overall, this demanded a lot of surgeries and physical therapy for me to become whole again. The specifics of this ride are that a motorcycle enthusiast begins on the East Coast by collecting a water sample of the Atlantic Ocean. The custom route that I chose involved an attempt to travel over three thousand miles in less than forty-eight consecutive hours while averaging nearly seventy miles per hour in order to reach the West Coast and draw a final sample of water from the Pacific Ocean within the allotted time frame.

To date, only a handful of riders have ever accomplished such a ride, and I'd hoped to join their elite status. For the record, on this ride before my near-fatal deer collision, I was on schedule to reach my goal under the time limit. I had covered more than two thousand five hundred miles in forty straight hours of driving, all while averaging nearly seventy miles per hour when the crash put a fast ending to my ultimate riding objective.

With the descriptions of the previous rides, I will share that I'm probably considered a true hard-core distance motorcycle rider. To date, I've completed seventeen different one-thousand-mile rides within a twenty-four hour period of time. I've also completed seven different one-thousand-five-hundred-mile rides within a twenty-four hour period of time. In addition, I've successfully ridden a motorcycle from Canada to Mexico covering one thousand five hundred miles within a twenty-four-hour time frame. I've even unofficially completed a three thousand mile ride that would have been completed within a forty-eight hour period of time, however, this specific attempt took me one year to come back and finish it because of a deer collision with my motorcycle.

One of the most grueling of all the extreme rides is called the 10/10ths ride. This ride demands that the rider logs one thousand miles per twenty-four-hour day for ten consecutive days in a row. On July 2-11, 2010, I completed and certified that very, very difficult ride.

On day one, I obtained my two witnesses from a Harley-Davidson dealer at 1:00 p.m. on Friday, July 2, to begin the momentous task of attempting to drive more than ten thousand miles by motorcycle around the outside edge of the entire United States. I'd planned the route and trip for nearly three years. I had each evening's motel rooms reserved months prior to my departure. I even had appointments made weeks ahead with Harley-Davidson dealers in Texas, in Alabama, and in Florida to make quick stops during my route for any potential tire changes or service work.

The first challenge of the route occurred when I was forced against my will into an eight-hour delayed start as a result of a servicing lag performed by the Harley-Davidson dealership. They were unable to complete their service work on my bike in the promised time frame. Because it was impossible for me to rebook all ten nights of my motel rooms over the busy Fourth of July holiday, I was only going to get back on schedule by skipping my first night of sleep and then driving nonstop to my second motel stay. So in effect, day one rolled right into day two, which was like starting a massive endurance ride such as this with one foot in the grave so to speak. As a result of these circumstances, both my wife and I were uneasy because of previous year's catastrophic collision.

I traveled along my way on Interstate Highway 94 westbound through Minnesota, North Dakota, Montana, Idaho, Washington, and finally Oregon before stopping for the first time on my journey. For my combined first day and second day legs of the ride, I logged in excess of twenty-one hundred continuous miles in under thirty-six hours. The most difficult part of the first leg of my trip other than the protracted hours without sleep was that in the Rocky Mountains of western Montana at about 2:00 a.m. in the morning I had to deal with 34 degree temperatures, along with hail, and an ice-cold rainfall.

Knowing that I had a lot of miles through a very populated area of California to travel the next day, I only slept about two hours, and then departed about 2:00 a.m. For day three, I rode through Oregon, California, Nevada, and ended up in Arizona for the completion of my third consecutive one-thousand-mile day. I can't describe the beauty of nature that I witnessed while riding in solitude as each morning I saw dawn's early light peeking out from behind some beautiful mountain or rising up out of the ocean. The most difficult part of this leg of the trip was that the temperatures climbed to over 110 degrees near Death Valley, and then I traveled over eight hundred miles through the deserts of Nevada where the temperature stayed at 105 degrees for most of the day.

On day four, I traveled through Arizona, New Mexico, and ended up at my motel stay in Texas. Along this route of the southwestern USA, I endured lots more high heat traveling and due to the hurricane, which had recently made landfall near Texas, I was faced with countless hard-driving rains along this most southern USA route.

On day five, I traveled through Texas, Louisiana, Mississippi, Alabama, and ended up in Florida for my motel stay. Once again, the driving rains of the hurricane aftermath made for some extremely difficult motorcycling.

On day six, I traveled all the way down to the bottom of Florida, then back up the east coast riding through Georgia, South Carolina, and ending up in North Carolina for a motel stay. On this day, I had a near tragic accident, which could have ended it all had not my "guardian angel" once again been by my side. As I traveled north on Interstate Highway 95, the highway went up and over a huge suspension bridge in Savannah, Georgia. The flow of traffic was speeding along at over seventy miles per hour and all around me were semitrucks traveling at full speed. As I neared the top of the massive bridge, a huge gust of wind blasted from my left side, which resulted in literally throwing my motorcycle to the right and into the semitruck while traveling at seventy miles per hour. I can't describe my feelings as my motorcycle impacted into the rear dual wheels of the thundering semitrailer. A mere motorcycle is no match for a semitruck as the front faring of my cycle was smashed backward into my engine and my foot floorboard was driven over by the truck wheels, making it unusable. I impacted so hard with the truck that my sunglasses were knocked off my head. I used every ounce of adrenaline I could muster in order to keep my eight-hundred-pound motorcycle from falling beneath the semitruck wheels or worse yet crashing over only to be run over by the speeding traffic beside and behind me.

Somehow I righted the disabled motorcycle even at such a high speed. I daresay that someone with much less riding experience most probably would have met their fate on that day, but I feel very blessed to have safely navigated such a close call. Once I could exit from the dangerous bridge, I stopped my motorcycle along the busy interstate highway to survey the damage and make some fixes in order to keep me traveling down the road once more. By kicking and pounding with my legs, I was able to bend the twisted crash bar and cracked faring far enough away from the engine to once again make the machine operable. As I think back, I wonder what the passing vehicles thought as they watched what appeared to be an angry biker kicking his Harley repeatedly.

Next, I used all my strength to somehow bend and twist my right-side floorboard up into a position so that I could at least continue to ride the machine, but it remained so uneven that riding the next several thousand miles was anything but comfortable. I was shocked to see how much truck tire rubber marks were imbedded into the right side of my motorcycle. In the end, my motorcycle had earned some more character as it reflected the scars from doing battle with a semitruck. My motorcycle was scratched, was twisted, and was broken in a several places, but it kept going when the "chips were down." Upon returning home, I would discover that I had amassed over one thousand dollars in damage to my motorcycle.

What are the odds that I had somehow skirted death for an implausible twenty-seventh time? How could anyone surpass nine lives times three and still be alive to tell about it?

On day seven, I traveled through North Carolina, Virginia, Maryland, New Jersey, Rhode Island, Connecticut, Massachusetts, and ended up in New York for a motel stay. It was on this day that I nearly gave up on finishing my lofty goal of ten consecutive one-thousand-mile days. I cannot describe how difficult it was to travel in excess of one thousand miles per day, then attempt it again and again, day after day. It became evermore impossible with the population density, with the heavy flow of traffic, and with the never-ending road construction. Believe it or not, I hit Washington, D.C., during the morning rush hour where I was forced to endure five hours of stop-and-go traffic trying to simply get beyond our capital city. As luck would have it, I then hit afternoon rush hour traffic in New York City. At the time, the entire east coast was encased by a heat wave during this time period, so at 4:00 p.m. in 103 degree temperatures, I was gridlocked in traffic for over six hours. The heat coming off my air-cooled Harley engine while sitting endlessly in traffic nearly left me ill from heat exposure. At one point, I was forced to shut down the motorcycle engine, and even in the searing heat, I pushed the motorcycle nearly one mile simply using my legs since the traffic was moving only a few feet at any given time.

I had reached my lowest point during the entire journey. It began to dawn on me that my ten-thousand-mile motorcycle riding target was perhaps unattainable. I suddenly looked in my rearview mirror and noticed a so-called crotch rocket motorbiker come weaving in and out of traffic almost sounding and looking like a big mosquito as he navigated his way up through the endless view of seemingly stalled cars. At that point, I made a decision to follow suit. I wasn't sure if what the other biker was doing was exactly legal, but I could no longer risk inflicting permanent engine and transmission damage to my Harley.

A smile crossed my face as a comical thought came to me. If the car drivers compared his motions to be that of a mosquito darting in and out, then perhaps they envisioned me and my big Harley to appear as a big, huge hippopotamus! While I was able to navigate the path of the darting crotch rocket, I couldn't go nearly as fast as his nimble motorcycle could. I was shocked as he actually began watching out for me as he made sure that I could keep up with his lead.

Mile after mile, we worked our way up through the densely stalled mass of vehicles seemingly stalled upon the New York City highways. Suddenly my new biker friend quickly pulled his motorcycle back into a nearly stalled driving lane where I slid in next to him. It was then for the first time that we exchanged conversations, and he mentioned that he was quite impressed that a Harley rider would have anything to do with a crotch rocket rider. I smiled back at him and asked why we had pulled back into the lane of cars rather than darting in and out on the shoulders of the highway just as we'd been doing for miles. He stated that just around the corner up ahead would be a patrol car waiting to give someone a driving violation. Sure enough, we crawled slowly past a lurking squad car, only to scamper once again upon our journey when the law officer was out of our vision once again. At the time that young biker was my new best friend in the entire world as he assisted me to navigate through a nearly impossible scenario in New York City.

Somehow I endured the most physically demanding day of riding a motorcycle that I've ever encountered. That one-thousand-mile day began for me at 3:00 a.m. and ended a staggering twenty-three hours later at 2:00 a.m. I simply cannot describe how difficult doing something like that was with the temperatures in excess of 100 degrees and then trying to remain safe on one of the most congested series of highways in all of America.

In conditions such as those, it was impossible to take in enough fluids to remain hydrated, and I had little time to consume any real nutrients on any given day. For the most part, I survived my ten-day ride by eating protein and power bars throughout each day. The problem arose, however, when my electrolyte balance must have become very unstable by about day four of my endurance test. From that day forward, I suffered severe muscle cramping in the calves, thighs, and hamstring muscles of my legs each and every night. The overall pain was excruciating to say the least.

On day eight I traveled through New York, Pennsylvania, Ohio, Indiana, Illinois, and stayed at a motel in Iowa. The amount of tolls I had to pay to use the roads in the eastern half of the USA was staggering. The tolls just for my motorcycle on this trip tallied over seventy-five dollars. As if dealing with two severe rush hour traffic jams on the prior day in both Washington, D.C., and in New York City, within the same thirty-six-hour period wasn't bad enough, I also ran into the afternoon rush hour of Chicago nonetheless. Once again I was mired down in a sweltering heat wave as the traffic barely inched forward. For the record, I implemented some of my crotch rocket friend's maneuvers to reduce the agony somewhat. Later that night at about 1:30 a.m., I called my wife to let her know that I'd safely made it through another difficult and challenging day.

As I shared, I mockingly said, "I'm lying on my motel bed in the fetal position while sucking my thumb because of the stress. I've had to endure the three worst rush hour cities in the nation, and I encountered them all within a thirty-six-hour time frame."

We both got a little chuckle as a result of my plight.

On day nine, I traveled onward through Iowa, Nebraska, and Wyoming before stopping to spend my final night with my son Travis, his wife, RaeLynn, and my new granddaughter, Hiltina. On this ninth day of seemingly endless one-thousand-mile days, all I could think about was praying and hoping it would all be over soon. I had hit the wall so to speak with my energy tank nearing complete empty. By that point of my trip, it was difficult to determine what was keeping me going. I was physically depleted and mentally spent since the average day of operating my motorcycle was always somewhere between nineteen to twenty-three continuous hours. Each night, I would stagger into a hotel room between midnight to 2:00 a.m. At the end of each day, I would take a quick shower to remove an elongated days worth of road grime from my body. I would then sleep a mere two hours before heading back out onto the road again by 2:00 a.m. to 3:00 a.m.

On the tenth and final day, I departed once again at 2:00 a.m. traveling through Wyoming, Montana, back through Wyoming, South Dakota, and finally I arrived back at my home in the state of Minnesota. On that day, my spirits were uplifted knowing that with every mile I was drawing ever closer to my ending objective. Travel became easier as well because of the reduced volume of traffic within the midsections of our country. Such had not been the case while riding throughout the populated outside edges the previous nine days.

OVERALL SUMMARY OF TRIP

- Daily certified motorcycling mileage tally was

Day one:	1,053 miles
Day two:	1,043 miles
Day three:	1,049 miles
Day four:	1,025 miles
Day five:	1,049 miles
Day six:	1,011 miles
Day eight:	1,019 miles
Day nine:	1,076 miles
Day ten:	1,038 miles

- Grand Total: 10,382 miles
- Total States Ridden: 34
- It took 76 gas fills using 307 gallons of fuel for a cost of $917
- Average fuel efficiency was 33.8 mpg
- Logged 20 hours per day average (+200 hours in ten days)
- My Harley ran nearly nonstop for ten days and nights for over 10,000 miles without any mechanical difficulties. The engine required only two-thirds of a quart of oil for the entire trip. As a result of my extensive trip, I became more confident than ever that a Harley motorcycle can handle as many long-distance miles as any brand of motorcycle in the market.
- Averaged two hours per night sleep
- Total motel stops cost $346.
- Total food and beverage cost $200

- Total Toll Fees cost $76
- Grand Total Trip Cost: $1,538
- Overall Experience and Self-Satisfaction:
  PRICELESS!!

By successfully completing a long-distance endurance motorcycling trip of such magnitude, allowed me to fulfill one of my lifelong dreams. Few people could understand why anyone would even attempt something so challenging and painful. In my lifetime, I've struggled through some immense challenges but completing more than ten thousand miles within a ten-day time frame ranked as one of the three most difficult experiences that I've ever put myself through.

I would liken such an extreme motorcycle ride to be similar to someone's attempt to climb Mount Everest or someone's attempt to run a marathon. Each of us has a right to set our own goals. Why should anyone else judge another's goals as being unwise, unsafe, or unattainable? I believe that personal goals are important and the negative-induced thoughts of others shouldn't count for much in the overall scheme of things.

In all honesty, the tortuous act of completing such an extensive endurance ride was anything but fun. Still, I'll never forget the moments of pure exhilaration as I experienced the entire United States within a mere ten days. In my past, I've been fortunate enough to travel several times throughout all fifty states, and I've experienced nearly all of the tourist-trap activities. During each of those previous trips, I covered only a small portion of our great and wonderful nation. For this unique journey, however, I was able to breathe in the glorious magnitude, the grandeur and sheer beauty that our land beholds, all while canvassing its entirety within only ten days. The experience provided a perspective of our nation that I'd never captured before.

In the end, I'm only concerned with how I measure up to my own personal standards of living life to the fullest. I'm more than content to accept that I'm merely a common human who dreams big and thinks outside the box of normalcy. Through grit and self-determination, I've been able to accomplish some very uncommon feats that few on this planet could match. I guess if it were easy, then everyone would be capable of doing it.

ONE DAY CLOSER TO ETERNITY—
?? YEARS

CHAPTER TWENTY-EIGHT

*I focus on this one thing: Forgetting the past and looking
forward to what lies ahead, I press on to reach the end of the
race and receive the heavenly prize for which God, through
Christ Jesus, is calling us.*
—PHILIPPIANS 3:13-14

By the release date of this book, the good Lord has allowed me to somehow, someway survive up until and beyond the celebration of my fifty-fifth birthday. Trust me when I reiterate that my life hasn't been a painless journey while defeating death on a habitual basis.

Beginning as a mere infant at the age of nine months old and then continuing through fifty-five years, I've cheated death. During my life's journey, I've survived an unfathomable twenty-seven encounters with death. I've escaped death through seven different machinery and equipment mishaps. I've avoided horse or mule death challenges no fewer than five times. Although one of my life's greatest pleasures has always been motorcycling, I've paid a price by suffering through five singular accidents that should have terminated my life. Few in life could survive even one automobile crash, yet I've lived to describe three separate vehicular collisions. In addition, I escaped death from toxic fumes twice and twice averted death threats while working within dangerous third world countries. I've even fallen from a rooftop, nearly crashed in an airplane, and lived through a poisoning, yet by the grace of God, I've failed to become a fatality statistic.

I've often joked that for every day in which I don't read my own name within a newspaper obituary column that becomes a really good day for me. To survive so many brushes with death is difficult even for me to absorb. I've previously described myself as nothing more than a common man with uncommon dreams. My goal-driven ambitions have unfortunately brought me to the threshold of death numerous times. I've driven myself to limits that few would attempt. Early in life, I set a goal for myself to try and fit three lifetimes of experiences into my short time on this planet. As a youth, I never believed that I would survive beyond an age of forty years. Most certainly, my high-risk behaviors reduced my odds for a lengthy existence.

As my life unfolded, the numerous encounters with death became staggering. Between the ages of nine months up until nine years, I faced death three times. From the ages of ten years through my nineteenth birthday, death crossed my pathway four more times. During my tumultuous twenties from the ages of twenty years through twenty-nine years, I survived eight separate death encounters. Between the ages of thirty years through thirty-nine years, my chances of death slowed down to two. By the ages of forty years through forty-nine years, the Grim Reaper visited me on three separate occasions.

It came as an all too shocking revelation when I discovered that the pace of my death engagements was increasing as I reached midlife. From the ages of fifty years through fifty-five years, I'd amassed five singular close encounters with death. Perhaps that assertion should come as no surprise. Since reaching my fifties, I'd done little to slow down or reduce my zest for life and risk-taking determination. Few adults when faced with their own midlife crisis will attempt such outlandish feats as mountain climbing to the summit of Devils Tower in Wyoming or riding a motorcycle nonstop for ten thousand miles or consulting in the midst of a war within the country of Afghanistan.

I'm thankful for each and every day that I'm allowed the privilege of living. I try to give thanks and praise to my Lord every day for granting me the tenacity to overcome even the worst of survival odds. Through my strong faith and spirituality, and by never accepting defeat, I've been able to constantly repel the onset of death.

It is my sincerest hope that the pages of this true story will have provided some level of hope and inspiration for anyone suffering from some of the curveballs that life can throw.

As a young boy, I would lay awake in bed on many a night dreaming of the world that I would one day discover. Strangely, I somehow always believed that my life would come to a premature ending since my adrenaline-driven choices have often placed me in harm's way. Throughout my existence, I've never chosen a path of least resistance. In my lifetime, I've tended to trek down the pathway least-often traveled, believing that the rewards of such a journey would outdistance the challenges. And they have.

The challenges I've faced in my lifetime could be summed up in the well-known quote which states, "That which will not kill you shall make you stronger."

I'd like to share my own personal quote which says, "Have no fear, as death draws near."

Such a statement is not meant to be gruesome or sinister, but it simply acknowledges our human mortality. I strongly believe that the more one lets the Lord into their hearts, the easier one can accept the next step to eternity within God's heavenly paradise.

I would pose this question: if someone such as me has faced off with death twenty-seven times and still I have little fear of dying, why then should you?

As I draw my story to a close, I've come to really appreciate the blessings and the gifts in my life. Throughout life's journey, I've been surrounded by the love and support of my family. I never really believed that I would one day grow old with my loving wife, Astrid, but perhaps we shall. At the writing of this story, my youngest son, Travis, his wife, RaeLynn, and my lovely infant granddaughter, Hiltina, bring me such pride and joy. My eldest son, Trevor, his wife, Theresa, and their unborn baby epitomize how much there is to look forward to in life's journey.

With the break of each day's new dawn, I'm ever thankful to be one day closer to eternity as I dream of . . .

LaVergne, TN USA
16 February 2011
216873LV00004B/259/P